NEW PERSPECTIVES

Microsoft® Office 365™ & Excel 2016

INTRODUCTORY

June Jamrich Parsons
Dan Oja
Patrick Carey

Carol A. DesJardins
St. Clair County Community College

CENGAGE
Learning·

Australia • Brazil • Mexico • Singapore • United Kingdom • United States

New Perspectives Microsoft® Office 365™ &
Excel 2016, Introductory
June Jamrich Parsons, Dan Oja, Patrick Carey,
Carol A. DesJardins

SVP, GM Skills & Global Product Management:
    Dawn Gerrain

Product Director: Kathleen McMahon

Senior Product Team Manager: Lauren Murphy

Product Team Manager: Andrea Topping

Associate Product Managers: William Guiliani,
    Melissa Stehler

Senior Director, Development: Marah Bellegarde

Product Development Manager: Leigh Hefferon

Senior Content Developer: Kathy Finnegan

Developmental Editor: Robin M. Romer

Product Assistant: Erica Chapman

Marketing Director: Michele McTighe

Marketing Manager: Stephanie Albracht

Senior Production Director: Wendy Troeger

Production Director: Patty Stephan

Senior Content Project Manager: Jennifer Goguen
    McGrail

Designer: Diana Graham

Composition: GEX Publishing Services

Cover image(s): BMJ/Shutterstock.com

> For product information and technology assistance, contact us at
> **Cengage Learning Customer & Sales Support, 1-800-354-9706**
>
> For permission to use material from this text or product, submit all
> requests online at **www.cengage.com/permissions**.
> Further permissions questions can be e-mailed to
> **permissionrequest@cengage.com**

Mac users: If you're working through this product using a Mac, some of the steps may
vary. Additional information for Mac users is included with the Data Files for this
product.

Some of the product names and company names used in this book have been used for
identification purposes only and may be trademarks or registered trademarks of their
respective manufacturers and sellers.

Windows® is a registered trademark of Microsoft Corporation. © 2012 Microsoft.
Microsoft and the Office logo are either registered trademarks or trademarks of
Microsoft Corporation in the United States and/or other countries. Cengage Learning is
an independent entity from Microsoft Corporation and not affiliated with Microsoft in
any manner.

Disclaimer: Any fictional data related to persons or companies or URLs used throughout
this text is intended for instructional purposes only. At the time this text was published,
any such data was fictional and not belonging to any real persons or companies.

Disclaimer: The material in this text was written using Microsoft Office 365 ProPlus and
Microsoft Excel 2016 running on Microsoft Windows 10 Professional and was Quality
Assurance tested before the publication date. As Microsoft continually updates the
Microsoft Office suite and the Windows 10 operating system, your software experience may
vary slightly from what is presented in the printed text.

Library of Congress Control Number: 2016930367
ISBN: 978-1-305-88042-9

Cengage Learning
20 Channel Center Street
Boston, MA 02210
USA

Cengage Learning is a leading provider of customized learning solutions
with employees residing in nearly 40 different countries and sales in more
than 125 countries around the world. Find your local representative at
www.cengage.com.

Cengage Learning products are represented in Canada by
Nelson Education, Ltd.

To learn more about Cengage Learning, visit **www.cengage.com**

Purchase any of our products at your local college store or at our
preferred online store **www.cengagebrain.com**

Printed in the United States of America
Print Number: 04   Print Year: 2016

BRIEF CONTENTS

TABLE OF CONTENTS

Productivity Apps for School and Work

Corinne Hoisington

Lochlan keeps track of his class notes, football plays, and internship meetings with OneNote.

Zoe is using the annotation features of Microsoft Edge to take and save web notes for her research paper.

Nori is creating a Sway site to highlight this year's activities for the Student Government Association.

Hunter is adding interactive videos and screen recordings to his PowerPoint resume.

© Rawpixel/Shutterstock.com

Being computer literate no longer means mastery of only Word, Excel, PowerPoint, Outlook, and Access. To become technology power users, Hunter, Nori, Zoe, and Lochlan are exploring Microsoft OneNote, Sway, Mix, and Edge in Office 2016 and Windows 10.

In this Module

Learn to use productivity apps!
Links to companion **Sways**, featuring **videos** with hands-on instructions, are located on www.cengagebrain.com.

Introduction to OneNote 2016

notebook | section tab | To Do tag | screen clipping | note | template | Microsoft OneNote Mobile app | sync | drawing canvas | inked handwriting | Ink to Text

As you glance around any classroom, you invariably see paper notebooks and notepads on each desk. Because deciphering and sharing handwritten notes can be a challenge, Microsoft OneNote 2016 replaces physical notebooks, binders, and paper notes with a searchable, digital notebook. OneNote captures your ideas and schoolwork on any device so you can stay organized, share notes, and work with others on projects. Whether you are a student taking class notes as shown in **Figure 1** or an employee taking notes in company meetings, OneNote is the one place to keep notes for all of your projects.

Figure 1: OneNote 2016 notebook

Each **notebook** is divided into sections, also called **section tabs**, by subject or topic.

Use **To Do tags**, icons that help you keep track of your assignments and other tasks.

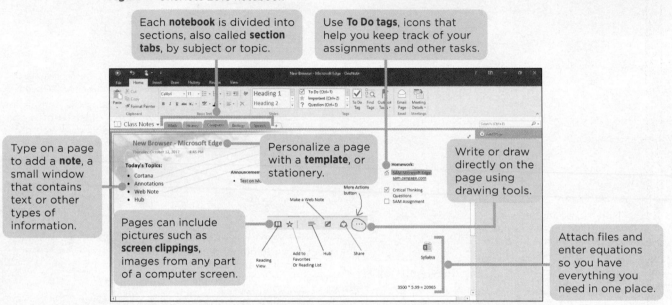

Type on a page to add a **note**, a small window that contains text or other types of information.

Personalize a page with a **template**, or stationery.

Write or draw directly on the page using drawing tools.

Pages can include pictures such as **screen clippings**, images from any part of a computer screen.

Attach files and enter equations so you have everything you need in one place.

Creating a OneNote Notebook

OneNote is divided into sections similar to those in a spiral-bound notebook. Each OneNote notebook contains sections, pages, and other notebooks. You can use One-Note for school, business, and personal projects. Store information for each type of project in different notebooks to keep your tasks separate, or use any other organization that suits you. OneNote is flexible enough to adapt to the way you want to work.

When you create a notebook, it contains a blank page with a plain white background by default, though you can use templates, or stationery, to apply designs in categories such as Academic, Business, Decorative, and Planners. Start typing or use the buttons on the Insert tab to insert notes, which are small resizable windows that can contain text, equations, tables, on-screen writing, images, audio and video recordings, to-do lists, file attachments, and file printouts. Add as many notes as you need to each page.

Syncing a Notebook to the Cloud

OneNote saves your notes every time you make a change in a notebook. To make sure you can access your notebooks with a laptop, tablet, or smartphone wherever you are, OneNote uses cloud-based storage, such as OneDrive or SharePoint. **Microsoft OneNote Mobile app**, a lightweight version of OneNote 2016 shown in **Figure 2**, is available for free in the Windows Store, Google Play for Android devices, and the AppStore for iOS devices.

If you have a Microsoft account, OneNote saves your notes on OneDrive automatically for all your mobile devices and computers, which is called **syncing**. For example, you can use OneNote to take notes on your laptop during class, and then open OneNote on your phone to study later. To use a notebook stored on your computer with your OneNote Mobile app, move the notebook to OneDrive. You can quickly share notebook content with other people using OneDrive.

Figure 2: Microsoft OneNote Mobile app

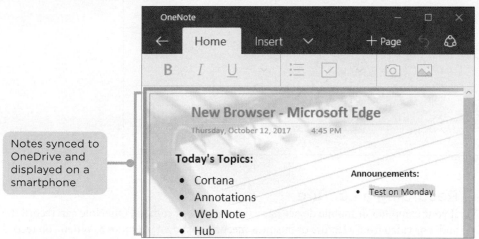

Notes synced to OneDrive and displayed on a smartphone

Taking Notes

Use OneNote pages to organize your notes by class and topic or lecture. Beyond simple typed notes, OneNote stores drawings, converts handwriting to searchable text and mathematical sketches to equations, and records audio and video.

OneNote includes drawing tools that let you sketch freehand drawings such as biological cell diagrams and financial supply-and-demand charts. As shown in **Figure 3**, the Draw tab on the ribbon provides these drawing tools along with shapes so you can insert diagrams and other illustrations to represent your ideas. When you draw on a page, OneNote creates a **drawing canvas**, which is a container for shapes and lines.

On the Job Now

OneNote is ideal for taking notes during meetings, whether you are recording minutes, documenting a discussion, sketching product diagrams, or listing follow-up items. Use a meeting template to add pages with content appropriate for meetings.

Figure 3: Tools on the Draw tab

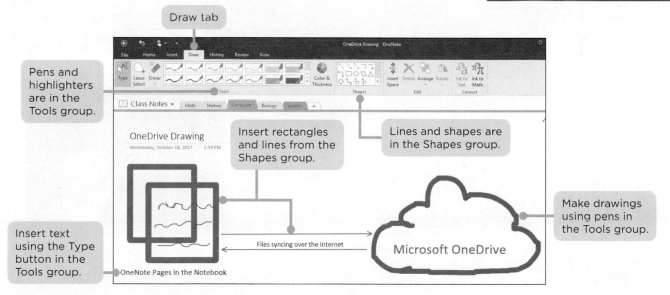

Draw tab

Pens and highlighters are in the Tools group.

Insert rectangles and lines from the Shapes group.

Lines and shapes are in the Shapes group.

Make drawings using pens in the Tools group.

Insert text using the Type button in the Tools group.

Converting Handwriting to Text

When you use a pen tool to write on a notebook page, the text you enter is called **inked handwriting**. OneNote can convert inked handwriting to typed text when you use the **Ink to Text** button in the Convert group on the Draw tab, as shown in **Figure 4**. After OneNote converts the handwriting to text, you can use the Search box to find terms in the converted text or any other note in your notebooks.

Figure 4: Converting handwriting to text

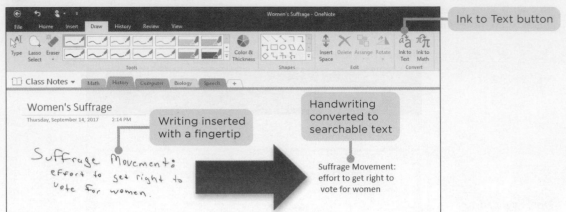

Ink to Text button

Women's Suffrage
Thursday, September 14, 2017   2:14 PM

Writing inserted with a fingertip

Handwriting converted to searchable text

Suffrage Movement: effort to get right to vote for women.

Suffrage Movement: effort to get right to vote for women

On the Job Now

Use OneNote as a place to brainstorm ongoing work projects. If a notebook contains sensitive material, you can password-protect some or all of the notebook so that only certain people can open it.

Recording a Lecture

If your computer or mobile device has a microphone or camera, OneNote can record the audio or video from a lecture or business meeting as shown in **Figure 5**. When you record a lecture (with your instructor's permission), you can follow along, take regular notes at your own pace, and review the video recording later. You can control the start, pause, and stop motions of the recording when you play back the recording of your notes.

Figure 5: Video inserted in a notebook

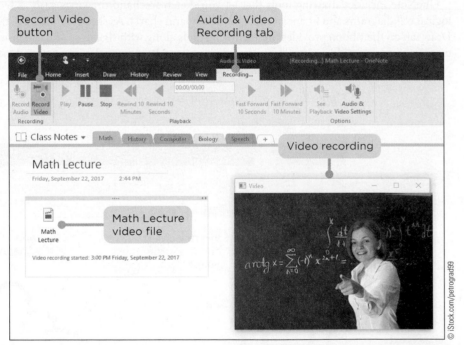

Record Video button

Audio & Video Recording tab

Video recording

Math Lecture
Friday, September 22, 2017   2:44 PM

Math Lecture video file

Video recording started: 3:00 PM Friday, September 22, 2017

© iStock.com/petrograd99

Try This Now

Learn to use OneNote!
Links to companion **Sways**, featuring **videos** with hands-on instructions, are located on www.cengagebrain.com.

1: Taking Notes for a Week

As a student, you can get organized by using OneNote to take detailed notes in your classes. Perform the following tasks:

a. Create a new OneNote notebook on your Microsoft OneDrive account (the default location for new notebooks). Name the notebook with your first name followed by "Notes," as in **Caleb Notes**.
b. Create four section tabs, each with a different class name.
c. Take detailed notes in those classes for one week. Be sure to include notes, drawings, and other types of content.
d. Sync your notes with your OneDrive. Submit your assignment in the format specified by your instructor.

2: Using OneNote to Organize a Research Paper

You have a research paper due on the topic of three habits of successful students. Use OneNote to organize your research. Perform the following tasks:

a. Create a new OneNote notebook on your Microsoft OneDrive account. Name the notebook **Success Research**.
b. Create three section tabs with the following names:

- **Take Detailed Notes**
- **Be Respectful in Class**
- **Come to Class Prepared**

c. On the web, research the topics and find three sources for each section. Copy a sentence from each source and paste the sentence into the appropriate section. When you paste the sentence, OneNote inserts it in a note with a link to the source.
d. Sync your notes with your OneDrive. Submit your assignment in the format specified by your instructor.

3: Planning Your Career

Note: This activity requires a webcam or built-in video camera on any type of device.

Consider an occupation that interests you. Using OneNote, examine the responsibilities, education requirements, potential salary, and employment outlook of a specific career. Perform the following tasks:

a. Create a new OneNote notebook on your Microsoft OneDrive account. Name the notebook with your first name followed by a career title, such as **Kara - App Developer**.
b. Create four section tabs with the names **Responsibilities, Education Requirements, Median Salary**, and **Employment Outlook**.
c. Research the responsibilities of your career path. Using OneNote, record a short video (approximately 30 seconds) of yourself explaining the responsibilities of your career path. Place the video in the Responsibilities section.
d. On the web, research the educational requirements for your career path and find two appropriate sources. Copy a paragraph from each source and paste them into the appropriate section. When you paste a paragraph, OneNote inserts it in a note with a link to the source.
e. Research the median salary for a single year for this career. Create a mathematical equation in the Median Salary section that multiplies the amount of the median salary times 20 years to calculate how much you will possibly earn.
f. For the Employment Outlook section, research the outlook for your career path. Take at least four notes about what you find when researching the topic.
g. Sync your notes with your OneDrive. Submit your assignment in the format specified by your instructor.

Introduction to Sway

Sway site | responsive design | Storyline | card | Creative Commons license | animation emphasis effects | Docs.com

Bottom Line

- Drag photos, videos, and files from your computer and content from Facebook and Twitter directly to your Sway presentation.
- Run Sway in a web browser or as an app on your smartphone, and save presentations as webpages.

Expressing your ideas in a presentation typically means creating PowerPoint slides or a Word document. Microsoft Sway gives you another way to engage an audience. Sway is a free Microsoft tool available at Sway.com or as an app in Office 365. Using Sway, you can combine text, images, videos, and social media in a website called a **Sway site** that you can share and display on any device. To get started, you create a digital story on a web-based canvas without borders, slides, cells, or page breaks. A Sway site organizes the text, images, and video into a **responsive design**, which means your content adapts perfectly to any screen size as shown in **Figure 6**. You store a Sway site in the cloud on OneDrive using a free Microsoft account.

Figure 6: Sway site with responsive design

You can display a Sway presentation in a web browser.

Sway uses responsive design to make sure pages fit perfectly on any device.

Learn to use Sway!

Links to companion **Sways**, featuring **videos** with hands-on instructions, are located on www.cengagebrain.com.

Creating a Sway Presentation

You can use Sway to build a digital flyer, a club newsletter, a vacation blog, an informational site, a digital art portfolio, or a new product rollout. After you select your topic and sign into Sway with your Microsoft account, a **Storyline** opens, providing tools and a work area for composing your digital story. See **Figure 7**. Each story can include text, images, and videos. You create a Sway by adding text and media content into a Storyline section, or **card**. To add pictures, videos, or documents, select a card in the left pane and then select the Insert Content button. The first card in a Sway presentation contains a title and background image.

Figure 7: Creating a Sway site

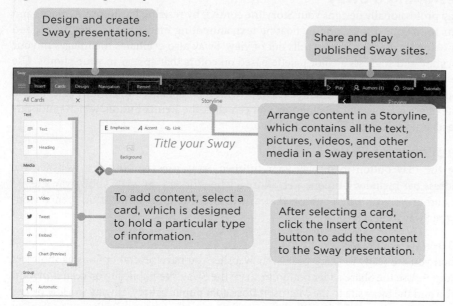

Design and create Sway presentations.

Share and play published Sway sites.

Arrange content in a Storyline, which contains all the text, pictures, videos, and other media in a Sway presentation.

To add content, select a card, which is designed to hold a particular type of information.

After selecting a card, click the Insert Content button to add the content to the Sway presentation.

Adding Content to Build a Story

As you work, Sway searches the Internet to help you find relevant images, videos, tweets, and other content from online sources such as Bing, YouTube, Twitter, and Facebook. You can drag content from the search results right into the Storyline. In addition, you can upload your own images and videos directly in the presentation. For example, if you are creating a Sway presentation about the market for commercial drones, Sway suggests content to incorporate into the presentation by displaying it in the left pane as search results. The search results include drone images tagged with a **Creative Commons license** at online sources as shown in **Figure 8**. A Creative Commons license is a public copyright license that allows the free distribution of an otherwise copyrighted work. In addition, you can specify the source of the media. For example, you can add your own Facebook or OneNote pictures and videos in Sway without leaving the app.

On the Job Now

If you have a Microsoft Word document containing an outline of your business content, drag the outline into Sway to create a card for each topic.

Figure 8: Images in Sway search results

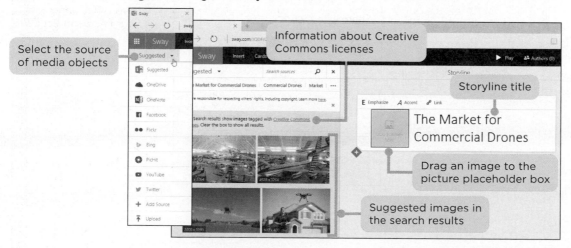

Select the source of media objects

Information about Creative Commons licenses

Storyline title

The Market for Commercial Drones

Drag an image to the picture placeholder box

Suggested images in the search results

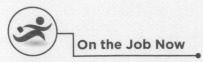

If your project team wants to collaborate on a Sway presentation, click the Authors button on the navigation bar to invite others to edit the presentation.

Designing a Sway

Sway professionally designs your Storyline content by resizing background images and fonts to fit your display, and by floating text, animating media, embedding video, and removing images as a page scrolls out of view. Sway also evaluates the images in your Storyline and suggests a color palette based on colors that appear in your photos. Use the Design button to display tools including color palettes, font choices, **animation emphasis effects**, and style templates to provide a personality for a Sway presentation. Instead of creating your own design, you can click the Remix button, which randomly selects unique designs for your Sway site.

Publishing a Sway

Use the Play button to display your finished Sway presentation as a website. The Address bar includes a unique web address where others can view your Sway site. As the author, you can edit a published Sway site by clicking the Edit button (pencil icon) on the Sway toolbar.

Sharing a Sway

When you are ready to share your Sway website, you have several options as shown in **Figure 9**. Use the Share slider button to share the Sway site publically or keep it private. If you add the Sway site to the Microsoft **Docs.com** public gallery, anyone worldwide can use Bing, Google, or other search engines to find, view, and share your Sway site. You can also share your Sway site using Facebook, Twitter, Google+, Yammer, and other social media sites. Link your presentation to any webpage or email the link to your audience. Sway can also generate a code for embedding the link within another webpage.

Figure 9: Sharing a Sway site

Share button

Drag the slider button to Just me to keep the Sway site private

Post the Sway site on Docs.com

Options differ depending on your Microsoft account

Send friends a link to the Sway site

Play	Authors (1)	Share

Share ◯ Just me

Share with the world

Docs.com - Your public gallery

Share with friends

https://sway.com/JQDFrUaxmg4lEbbk

More options

☑ Viewers can duplicate this Sway

Stop sharing

Try This Now

Learn to use Sway!
Links to companion **Sways**, featuring **videos** with hands-on instructions, are located on www.cengagebrain.com.

1: Creating a Sway Resume

Sway is a digital storytelling app. Create a Sway resume to share the skills, job experiences, and achievements you have that match the requirements of a future job interest. Perform the following tasks:

 a. Create a new presentation in Sway to use as a digital resume. Title the Sway Storyline with your full name and then select a background image.

 b. Create three separate sections titled **Academic Background, Work Experience**, and **Skills**, and insert text, a picture, and a paragraph or bulleted points in each section. Be sure to include your own picture.

 c. Add a fourth section that includes a video about your school that you find online.

 d. Customize the design of your presentation.

 e. Submit your assignment link in the format specified by your instructor.

2: Creating an Online Sway Newsletter

Newsletters are designed to capture the attention of their target audience. Using Sway, create a newsletter for a club, organization, or your favorite music group. Perform the following tasks:

 a. Create a new presentation in Sway to use as a digital newsletter for a club, organization, or your favorite music group. Provide a title for the Sway Storyline and select an appropriate background image.

 b. Select three separate sections with appropriate titles, such as Upcoming Events. In each section, insert text, a picture, and a paragraph or bulleted points.

 c. Add a fourth section that includes a video about your selected topic.

 d. Customize the design of your presentation.

 e. Submit your assignment link in the format specified by your instructor.

3: Creating and Sharing a Technology Presentation

To place a Sway presentation in the hands of your entire audience, you can share a link to the Sway presentation. Create a Sway presentation on a new technology and share it with your class. Perform the following tasks:

 a. Create a new presentation in Sway about a cutting-edge technology topic. Provide a title for the Sway Storyline and select a background image.

 b. Create four separate sections about your topic, and include text, a picture, and a paragraph in each section.

 c. Add a fifth section that includes a video about your topic.

 d. Customize the design of your presentation.

 e. Share the link to your Sway with your classmates and submit your assignment link in the format specified by your instructor.

Introduction to Office Mix

add-in | clip | slide recording | Slide Notes | screen recording | free-response quiz

To enliven business meetings and lectures, Microsoft adds a new dimension to presentations with a powerful toolset called Office Mix, a free add-in for PowerPoint. (An **add-in** is software that works with an installed app to extend its features.) Using Office Mix, you can record yourself on video, capture still and moving images on your desktop, and insert interactive elements such as quizzes and live webpages directly into PowerPoint slides. When you post the finished presentation to OneDrive, Office Mix provides a link you can share with friends and colleagues. Anyone with an Internet connection and a web browser can watch a published Office Mix presentation, such as the one in **Figure 10**, on a computer or mobile device.

Figure 10: Office Mix presentation

Adding Office Mix to PowerPoint

To get started, you create an Office Mix account at the website mix.office.com using an email address or a Facebook or Google account. Next, you download and install the Office Mix add-in (see **Figure 11**). Office Mix appears as a new tab named Mix on the PowerPoint ribbon in versions of Office 2013 and Office 2016 running on personal computers (PCs).

Figure 11: Getting started with Office Mix

Capturing Video Clips

A **clip** is a short segment of audio, such as music, or video. After finishing the content on a PowerPoint slide, you can use Office Mix to add a video clip to animate or illustrate the content. Office Mix creates video clips in two ways: by recording live action on a webcam and by capturing screen images and movements. If your computer has a webcam, you can record yourself and annotate the slide to create a **slide recording** as shown in **Figure 12**.

Figure 12: Making a slide recording

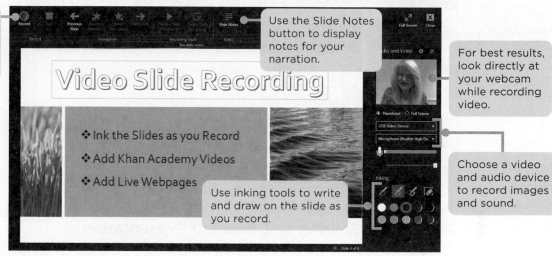

Record your voice; also record video if your computer has a camera.

Use the Slide Notes button to display notes for your narration.

For best results, look directly at your webcam while recording video.

Choose a video and audio device to record images and sound.

Use inking tools to write and draw on the slide as you record.

When you are making a slide recording, you can record your spoken narration at the same time. The **Slide Notes** feature works like a teleprompter to help you focus on your presentation content instead of memorizing your narration. Use the Inking tools to make annotations or add highlighting using different pen types and colors. After finishing a recording, edit the video in PowerPoint to trim the length or set playback options.

The second way to create a video is to capture on-screen images and actions with or without a voiceover. This method is ideal if you want to show how to use your favorite website or demonstrate an app such as OneNote. To share your screen with an audience, select the part of the screen you want to show in the video. Office Mix captures everything that happens in that area to create a **screen recording**, as shown in **Figure 13**. Office Mix inserts the screen recording as a video in the slide.

Figure 13: Making a screen recording

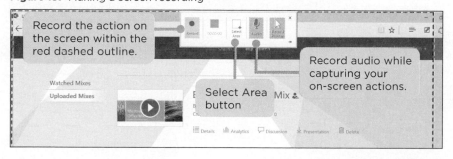

Record the action on the screen within the red dashed outline.

Record audio while capturing your on-screen actions.

Select Area button

Inserting Quizzes, Live Webpages, and Apps

To enhance and assess audience understanding, make your slides interactive by adding quizzes, live webpages, and apps. Quizzes give immediate feedback to the user as shown in **Figure 14**. Office Mix supports several quiz formats, including a **free-response quiz** similar to a short answer quiz, and true/false, multiple-choice, and multiple-response formats.

Figure 14: Creating an interactive quiz

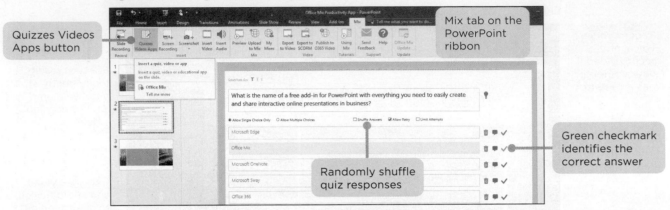

Quizzes Videos Apps button

Mix tab on the PowerPoint ribbon

Green checkmark identifies the correct answer

Randomly shuffle quiz responses

Sharing an Office Mix Presentation

When you complete your work with Office Mix, upload the presentation to your personal Office Mix dashboard as shown in **Figure 15**. Users of PCs, Macs, iOS devices, and Android devices can access and play Office Mix presentations. The Office Mix dashboard displays built-in analytics that include the quiz results and how much time viewers spent on each slide. You can play completed Office Mix presentations online or download them as movies.

Figure 15: Sharing an Office Mix presentation

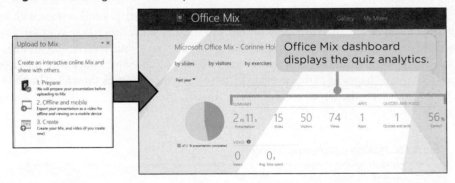

Office Mix dashboard displays the quiz analytics.

Try This Now

1: Creating an Office Mix Tutorial for OneNote

Note: This activity requires a microphone on your computer.

Office Mix makes it easy to record screens and their contents. Create PowerPoint slides with an Office Mix screen recording to show OneNote 2016 features. Perform the following tasks:

a. Create a PowerPoint presentation with the Ion Boardroom template. Create an opening slide with the title **My Favorite OneNote Features** and enter your name in the subtitle.

b. Create three additional slides, each titled with a new feature of OneNote. Open OneNote and use the Mix tab in PowerPoint to capture three separate screen recordings that teach your favorite features.

c. Add a fifth slide that quizzes the user with a multiple-choice question about OneNote and includes four responses. Be sure to insert a checkmark indicating the correct response.

d. Upload the completed presentation to your Office Mix dashboard and share the link with your instructor.

e. Submit your assignment link in the format specified by your instructor.

2: Teaching Augmented Reality with Office Mix

Note: This activity requires a webcam or built-in video camera on your computer.

A local elementary school has asked you to teach augmented reality to its students using Office Mix. Perform the following tasks:

a. Research augmented reality using your favorite online search tools.

b. Create a PowerPoint presentation with the Frame template. Create an opening slide with the title **Augmented Reality** and enter your name in the subtitle.

c. Create a slide with four bullets summarizing your research of augmented reality. Create a 20-second slide recording of yourself providing a quick overview of augmented reality.

d. Create another slide with a 30-second screen recording of a video about augmented reality from a site such as YouTube or another video-sharing site.

e. Add a final slide that quizzes the user with a true/false question about augmented reality. Be sure to insert a checkmark indicating the correct response.

f. Upload the completed presentation to your Office Mix dashboard and share the link with your instructor.

g. Submit your assignment link in the format specified by your instructor.

3: Marketing a Travel Destination with Office Mix

Note: This activity requires a webcam or built-in video camera on your computer.

To convince your audience to travel to a particular city, create a slide presentation marketing any city in the world using a slide recording, screen recording, and a quiz. Perform the following tasks:

a. Create a PowerPoint presentation with any template. Create an opening slide with the title of the city you are marketing as a travel destination and your name in the subtitle.

b. Create a slide with four bullets about the featured city. Create a 30-second slide recording of yourself explaining why this city is the perfect vacation destination.

c. Create another slide with a 20-second screen recording of a travel video about the city from a site such as YouTube or another video-sharing site.

d. Add a final slide that quizzes the user with a multiple-choice question about the featured city with five responses. Be sure to include a checkmark indicating the correct response.

e. Upload the completed presentation to your Office Mix dashboard and share your link with your instructor.

f. Submit your assignment link in the format specified by your instructor.

Learn to use Office Mix!
Links to companion **Sways**, featuring **videos** with hands-on instructions, are located on www.cengagebrain.com.

Introduction to Microsoft Edge

Reading view | Hub | Cortana | Web Note | Inking | sandbox

Bottom Line
- Microsoft Edge is the name of the new web browser built into Windows 10.
- Microsoft Edge allows you to search the web faster, take web notes, read webpages without distractions, and get instant assistance from Cortana.

Microsoft Edge is the default web browser developed for the Windows 10 operating system as a replacement for Internet Explorer. Unlike its predecessor, Edge lets you write on webpages, read webpages without advertisements and other distractions, and search for information using a virtual personal assistant. The Edge interface is clean and basic, as shown in **Figure 16**, meaning you can pay more attention to the webpage content.

Figure 16: Microsoft Edge tools

Forward button • New tab button • Web address in the Address bar • Add to favorites or reading list button • Reading view button • More button • Back button • Share Web Note button • Make a Web Note button • Refresh (F5) button • Hub (Favorites, reading list, history, and downloads) button

Learn to use Edge!
Links to companion **Sways**, featuring **videos** with hands-on instructions, are located on www.cengagebrain.com.

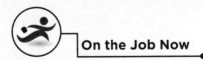

On the Job Now

Businesses started adopting Internet Explorer more than 20 years ago simply to view webpages. Today, Microsoft Edge has a different purpose: to promote interaction with the web and share its contents with colleagues.

Browsing the Web with Microsoft Edge

One of the fastest browsers available, Edge allows you to type search text directly in the Address bar. As you view the resulting webpage, you can switch to **Reading view**, which is available for most news and research sites, to eliminate distracting advertisements. For example, if you are catching up on technology news online, the webpage might be difficult to read due to a busy layout cluttered with ads. Switch to Reading view to refresh the page and remove the original page formatting, ads, and menu sidebars to read the article distraction-free.

Consider the **Hub** in Microsoft Edge as providing one-stop access to all the things you collect on the web, such as your favorite websites, reading list, surfing history, and downloaded files.

Locating Information with Cortana

Cortana, the Windows 10 virtual assistant, plays an important role in Microsoft Edge. After you turn on Cortana, it appears as an animated circle in the Address bar when you might need assistance, as shown in the restaurant website in **Figure 17**. When you click the Cortana icon, a pane slides in from the right of the browser window to display detailed information about the restaurant, including maps and reviews. Cortana can also assist you in defining words, finding the weather, suggesting coupons for shopping, updating stock market information, and calculating math.

Figure 17: Cortana providing restaurant information

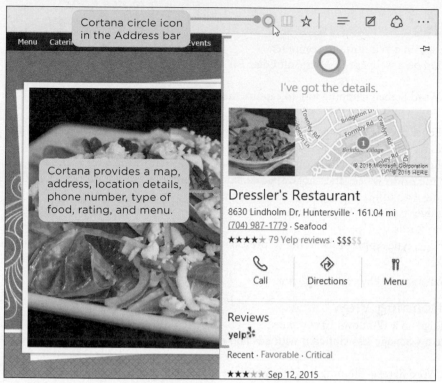

Cortana circle icon in the Address bar

Cortana provides a map, address, location details, phone number, type of food, rating, and menu.

I've got the details.

Dressler's Restaurant
8630 Lindholm Dr, Huntersville · 161.04 mi
(704) 987-1779 · Seafood
★★★★★ 79 Yelp reviews · $$$$$

Call   Directions   Menu

Reviews
yelp⁂

Recent · Favorable · Critical
★★★★★ Sep 12, 2015

Annotating Webpages

One of the most impressive Microsoft Edge features are the **Web Note** tools, which you use to write on a webpage or to highlight text. When you click the Make a Web Note button, an **Inking** toolbar appears, as shown in **Figure 18**, that provides writing and drawing tools. These tools include an eraser, a pen, and a highlighter with different colors. You can also insert a typed note and copy a screen image (called a screen clipping). You can draw with a pointing device, fingertip, or stylus using different pen colors. Whether you add notes to a recipe, annotate sources for a research paper, or select a product while shopping online, the Web Note tools can enhance your productivity. After you complete your notes, click the Save button to save the annotations to OneNote, your Favorites list, or your Reading list. You can share the inked page with others using the Share Web Note button.

On the Job Now

To enhance security, Microsoft Edge runs in a partial sandbox, an arrangement that prevents attackers from gaining control of your computer. Browsing within the **sandbox** protects computer resources and information from hackers.

Figure 18: Web Note tools in Microsoft Edge

Inking toolbar with Web Note tools for making annotations

Writing and drawing created with the Pen tool

Highlighted text

Save a copy of the webpage with annotations

Typed note

Try This Now

1: Using Cortana in Microsoft Edge

Note: This activity requires using Microsoft Edge on a Windows 10 computer.

Cortana can assist you in finding information on a webpage in Microsoft Edge. Perform the following tasks:

a. Create a Word document using the Word Screen Clipping tool to capture the following screenshots.

- Screenshot A—Using Microsoft Edge, open a webpage with a technology news article. Right-click a term in the article and ask Cortana to define it.
- Screenshot B—Using Microsoft Edge, open the website of a fancy restaurant in a city near you. Make sure the Cortana circle icon is displayed in the Address bar. (If it's not displayed, find a different restaurant website.) Click the Cortana circle icon to display a pane with information about the restaurant.
- Screenshot C—Using Microsoft Edge, type **10 USD to Euros** in the Address bar without pressing the Enter key. Cortana converts the U.S. dollars to Euros.
- Screenshot D—Using Microsoft Edge, type **Apple stock** in the Address bar without pressing the Enter key. Cortana displays the current stock quote.

b. Submit your assignment in the format specified by your instructor.

2: Viewing Online News with Reading View

Note: This activity requires using Microsoft Edge on a Windows 10 computer.

Reading view in Microsoft Edge can make a webpage less cluttered with ads and other distractions. Perform the following tasks:

a. Create a Word document using the Word Screen Clipping tool to capture the following screenshots.

- Screenshot A—Using Microsoft Edge, open the website **mashable.com**. Open a technology article. Click the Reading view button to display an ad-free page that uses only basic text formatting.
- Screenshot B—Using Microsoft Edge, open the website **bbc.com**. Open any news article. Click the Reading view button to display an ad-free page that uses only basic text formatting.
- Screenshot C—Make three types of annotations (Pen, Highlighter, and Add a typed note) on the BBC article page displayed in Reading view.

b. Submit your assignment in the format specified by your instructor.

3: Inking with Microsoft Edge

Note: This activity requires using Microsoft Edge on a Windows 10 computer.

Microsoft Edge provides many annotation options to record your ideas. Perform the following tasks:

a. Open the website **wolframalpha.com** in the Microsoft Edge browser. Wolfram Alpha is a well-respected academic search engine. Type **US$100 1965 dollars in 2015** in the Wolfram Alpha search text box and press the Enter key.

b. Click the Make a Web Note button to display the Web Note tools. Using the Pen tool, draw a circle around the result on the webpage. Save the page to OneNote.

c. In the Wolfram Alpha search text box, type the name of the city closest to where you live and press the Enter key. Using the Highlighter tool, highlight at least three interesting results. Add a note and then type a sentence about what you learned about this city. Save the page to OneNote. Share your OneNote notebook with your instructor.

d. Submit your assignment link in the format specified by your instructor.

EXCEL

OBJECTIVES

Session 1.1
- Open and close a workbook
- Navigate through a workbook and worksheet
- Select cells and ranges
- Plan and create a workbook
- Insert, rename, and move worksheets
- Enter text, dates, and numbers
- Undo and redo actions
- Resize columns and rows

Session 1.2
- Enter formulas and the SUM and COUNT functions
- Copy and paste formulas
- Move or copy cells and ranges
- Insert and delete rows, columns, and ranges
- Create patterned text with Flash Fill
- Add cell borders and change font size
- Change worksheet views
- Prepare a workbook for printing
- Save a workbook with a new filename

Getting Started with Excel

Creating a Customer Order Report

Case | *Game Card*

Peter Lewis is part owner of Game Card, a store in Missoula, Montana, that specializes in selling vintage board games. Peter needs to track sales data, generate financial reports, create contact lists for loyal customers, and analyze market trends. He can perform all of these tasks with **Microsoft Excel 2016**, (or just **Excel**), an application used to enter, analyze, and present quantitative data. He wants to create an efficient way of tracking the company inventory and managing customer sales. Peter asks you to use Excel to create a document in which he can enter customer purchases from the store.

STARTING DATA FILES

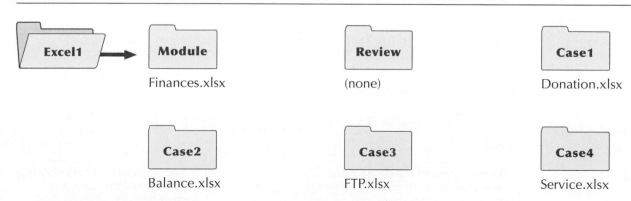

Excel1 → Module	Review	Case1
Finances.xlsx	(none)	Donation.xlsx

Case2	Case3	Case4
Balance.xlsx	FTP.xlsx	Service.xlsx

Session 1.1 Visual Overview:

The ribbon is organized into tabs. Each **tab** has commands related to particular activities or tasks.

Buttons for related commands are organized on a tab in **groups**.

Excel stores spreadsheets in files called **workbooks**. The name of the current workbook appears in the title bar.

The **ribbon** contains buttons that you click to execute commands to work with Excel.

The **Name box** displays the cell reference of the active cell. In this case, the active cell is cell H12.

The **formula bar** displays the value or formula entered into the active cell.

A group of cells in a rectangular block is called a **cell range** (or **range**). If the blocks are not connected, as shown here, it is a **nonadjacent range**.

The **row headings** are numbers along the left side of the workbook window that identify the different rows of the worksheet.

The **status bar** provides information about the workbook.

The sheet currently displayed in the workbook window is the **active sheet**. Its sheet tab is underlined, and the sheet name is green and bold.

Inactive sheets are not visible in the workbook window; their sheet tabs are not underlined and their sheet name is black.

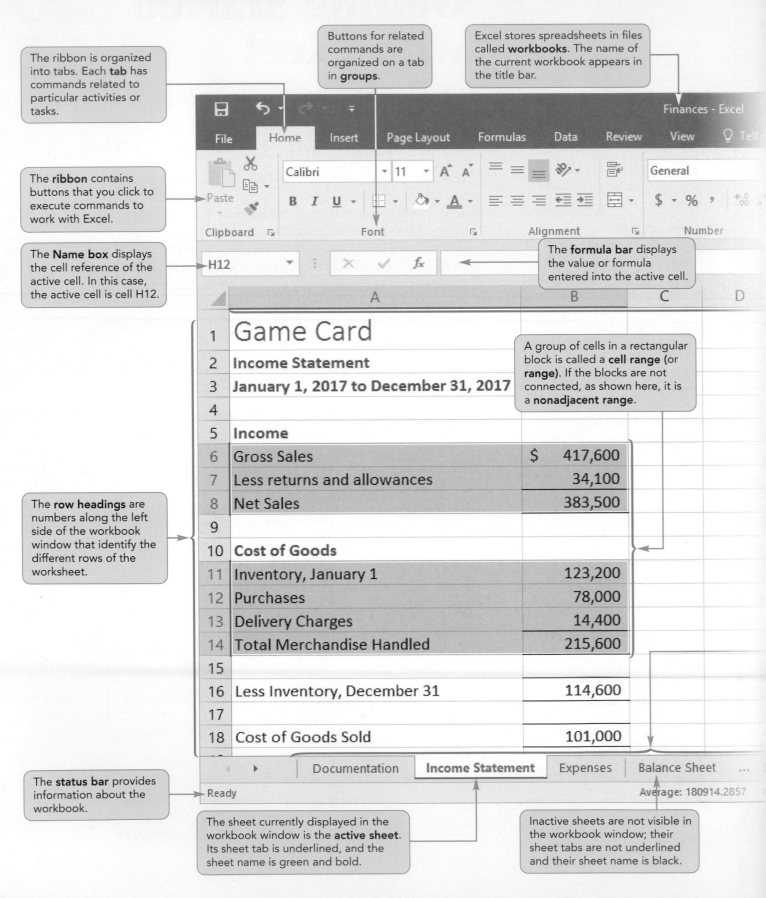

	A	B	C	D
1	Game Card			
2	Income Statement			
3	January 1, 2017 to December 31, 2017			
4				
5	Income			
6	Gross Sales	$ 417,600		
7	Less returns and allowances	34,100		
8	Net Sales	383,500		
9				
10	Cost of Goods			
11	Inventory, January 1	123,200		
12	Purchases	78,000		
13	Delivery Charges	14,400		
14	Total Merchandise Handled	215,600		
15				
16	Less Inventory, December 31	114,600		
17				
18	Cost of Goods Sold	101,000		

Documentation   **Income Statement**   Expenses   Balance Sheet   ...

Ready   Average: 180914.2857

The Excel Workbook

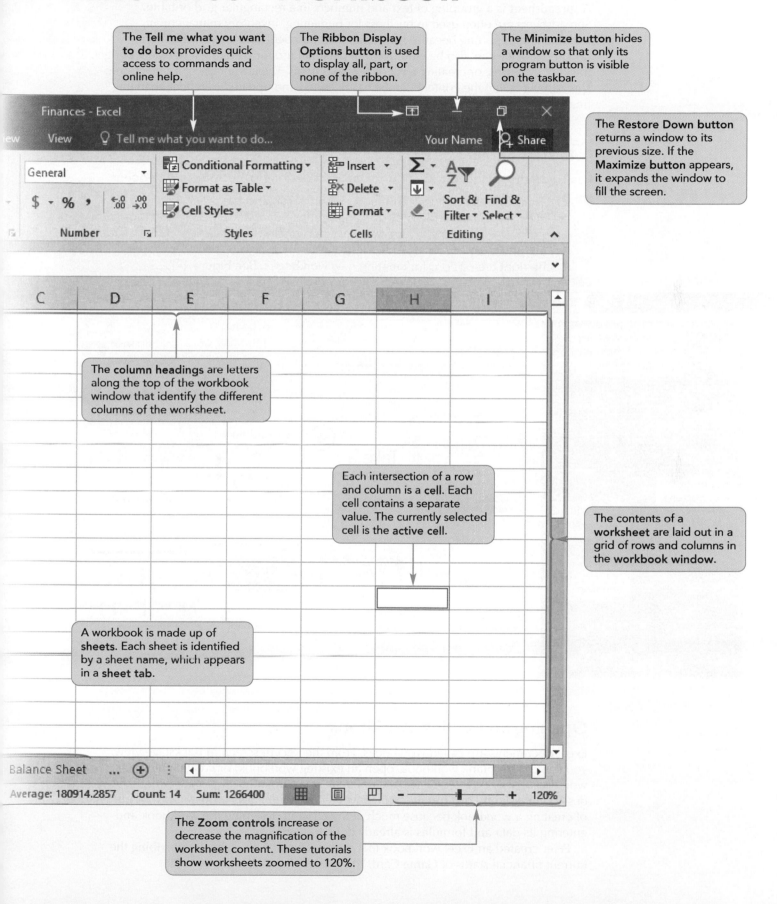

The **Tell me what you want to do** box provides quick access to commands and online help.

The **Ribbon Display Options button** is used to display all, part, or none of the ribbon.

The **Minimize button** hides a window so that only its program button is visible on the taskbar.

The **Restore Down button** returns a window to its previous size. If the **Maximize button** appears, it expands the window to fill the screen.

The **column headings** are letters along the top of the workbook window that identify the different columns of the worksheet.

Each intersection of a row and column is a **cell**. Each cell contains a separate value. The currently selected cell is the **active cell**.

The contents of a **worksheet** are laid out in a grid of rows and columns in the **workbook window**.

A workbook is made up of **sheets**. Each sheet is identified by a sheet name, which appears in a **sheet tab**.

The **Zoom controls** increase or decrease the magnification of the worksheet content. These tutorials show worksheets zoomed to 120%.

Introducing Excel and Spreadsheets

A **spreadsheet** is a grouping of text and numbers in a rectangular grid or table. Spreadsheets are often used in business for budgeting, inventory management, and financial reporting because they unite text, numbers, and charts within one document. They can also be employed for personal use for planning a personal budget, tracking expenses, or creating a list of personal items. The advantage of an electronic spreadsheet is that the content can be easily edited and updated to reflect changing financial conditions.

To start Excel:

▶ 1. On the Windows taskbar, click the **Start** button ⊞. The Start menu opens.

▶ 2. Click **All Apps** on the Start menu, scroll the list, and then click **Excel 2016**. Excel starts and displays the Recent screen in Backstage view. **Backstage view** provides access to various screens with commands that allow you to manage files and Excel options. On the left is a list of recently opened workbooks. On the right are options for creating new workbooks. See Figure 1-1.

Figure 1-1	Recent screen in Backstage view

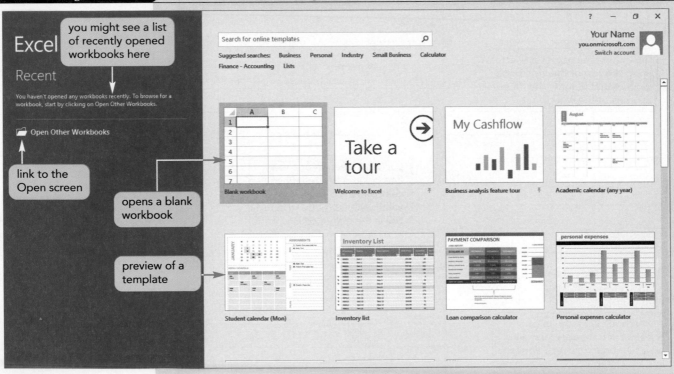

Opening an Existing Workbook

Excel documents are called workbooks. From the Recent screen in Backstage view, you can open a blank workbook, open an existing workbook, or create a new workbook based on a template. A **template** is a preformatted workbook with many design features and some content already filled in. Templates can speed up the process of creating a workbook because much of the effort in designing the workbook and entering its data and formulas is already done for you.

Peter created an Excel workbook that contains several worksheets describing the current financial status of Game Card. You will open that workbook now.

To open the Game Card financial status workbook:

1. In the navigation bar on the Recent screen, click the **Open Other Workbooks** link. The Open screen is displayed and provides access to different locations where you might store files. The Recent Workbooks list shows the workbooks that were most recently opened on your computer.

2. Click the **Browse** button. The Open dialog box appears.

3. Navigate to the **Excel1 > Module** folder included with your Data Files.

   Trouble? If you don't have the starting Data Files, you need to get them before you can proceed. Your instructor will either give you the Data Files or ask you to obtain them from a specified location (such as a network drive). If you have any questions about the Data Files, see your instructor or technical support person for assistance.

4. Click **Finances** in the file list to select it.

5. Click the **Open** button. The workbook opens in Excel.

   Trouble? If you don't see the full ribbon as shown in the Session 1.1 Visual Overview, the ribbon may be partially or fully hidden. To pin the ribbon so that the tabs and groups are fully displayed and remain visible, click the Ribbon Display Options button ⬒, and then click Show Tabs and Commands.

6. If the Excel window doesn't fill the screen, click the **Maximize** button ☐ in the upper-right corner of the title bar. See Figure 1-2.

Figure 1-2   Finances workbook

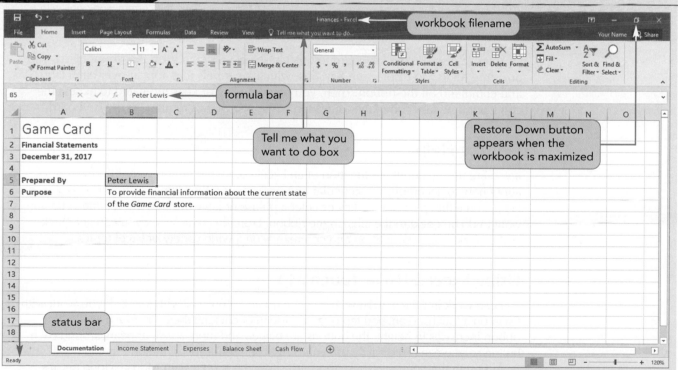

Using Keyboard Shortcuts to Work Faster

Keyboard shortcuts can help you work faster and more efficiently because you can keep your hands on the keyboard. A **keyboard shortcut** is a key or combination of keys that you press to access a feature or perform a command. Excel provides keyboard shortcuts for many commonly used commands. For example, Ctrl+S is the keyboard shortcut for the Save command, which means you hold down the Ctrl key while you press the S key to save the workbook. (Note that the plus sign is not pressed; it is used to indicate that an additional key is pressed.) When available, a keyboard shortcut is listed next to the command's name in a ScreenTip. A **ScreenTip** is a box with descriptive text about a command that appears when you point to a button on the ribbon. Figure 1-3 lists some of the keyboard shortcuts commonly used in Excel. The modules in this text show the corresponding keyboard shortcuts for accomplishing an action when available.

Figure 1-3   **Excel keyboard shortcuts**

Press	To	Press	To
Alt	Display the Key Tips for the commands and tools on the ribbon	Ctrl+V	Paste content that was cut or copied
Ctrl+A	Select all objects in a range	Ctrl+W	Close the current workbook
Ctrl+C	Copy the selected object(s)	Ctrl+X	Cut the selected object(s)
Ctrl+G	Go to a location in the workbook	Ctrl+Y	Repeat the last command
Ctrl+N	Open a new blank workbook	Ctrl+Z	Undo the last command
Ctrl+O	Open a saved workbook file	F1	Open the Excel Help window
Ctrl+P	Print the current workbook	F5	Go to a location in the workbook
Ctrl+S	Save the current workbook	F12	Save the current workbook with a new name or to a new location

You can also use the keyboard to quickly select commands on the ribbon. First, you press the Alt key to display the **Key Tips**, which are labels that appear over each tab and command on the ribbon. Then, you press the key or keys indicated to access the corresponding tab, command, or button while your hands remain on the keyboard.

Getting Help

If you are unsure about the function of an Excel command or you want information about how to accomplish a particular task, you can use the Help system. To access Excel Help, you either press the F1 key or enter a phrase or keyword into the Tell me what you want to do box next to the tabs on the ribbon. From this search box you can get quick access to detailed information and commands on a wide variety of Excel topics.

Using Excel 2016 in Touch Mode

You can work in Office 2016 with a keyboard and mouse or with touch. If you work with Excel on a touchscreen, you tap objects instead of clicking them. In **Touch Mode**, the ribbon increases in height, the buttons are bigger, and more space appears around each button so you can more easily use your finger or a stylus to tap the button you need.

Although the figures in these modules show the screen with Mouse Mode on, it's helpful to learn how to move between Touch Mode and Mouse Mode. You'll switch to Touch Mode and then back to Mouse Mode. If you are using a touch device, please read these steps, but do not complete them so that you remain working in Touch Mode.

To switch between Touch Mode and Mouse Mode:

1. On the Quick Access Toolbar, click the **Customize Quick Access Toolbar** button ⯆. A menu opens, listing buttons you can add to the Quick Access Toolbar as well as other options for customizing the toolbar.

   Trouble? If the Touch/Mouse Mode command on the menu has a checkmark next to it, press the Esc key to close the menu, and then skip Step 2.

2. Click **Touch/Mouse Mode**. The Quick Access Toolbar now contains the Touch/Mouse Mode button 🖑, which you can use to switch between Mouse Mode, the default display, and Touch Mode.

3. On the Quick Access Toolbar, click the **Touch/Mouse Mode** button 🖑. A menu opens listing Mouse and Touch, and the icon next to Mouse is shaded to indicate it is selected.

   Trouble? If the icon next to Touch is shaded, press the Esc key to close the menu and continue with Step 5.

4. Click **Touch**. The display switches to Touch Mode with more space between the commands and buttons on the ribbon. See Figure 1-4.

| Figure 1-4 | Ribbon displayed in Touch Mode |

Touch/Mouse Mode button

Customize Quick Access Toolbar button

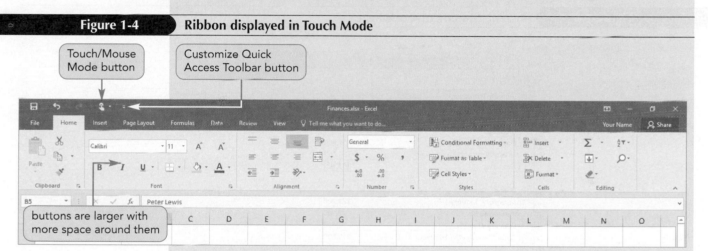

buttons are larger with more space around them

Next, you will switch back to Mouse Mode. If you are working with a touchscreen and want to use Touch Mode, skip Steps 5 and 6.

5. On the Quick Access Toolbar, click the **Touch/Mouse Mode** button 🖑, and then click **Mouse**. The ribbon returns to Mouse Mode, as shown earlier in Figure 1-2.

6. On the Quick Access Toolbar, click the **Customize Quick Access Toolbar** button ⯆, and then click **Touch/Mouse Mode** to deselect it. The Touch/Mouse Mode button is removed from the Quick Access Toolbar.

Exploring a Workbook

Workbooks are organized into separate pages called sheets. Excel supports two types of sheets: worksheets and chart sheets. A worksheet contains a grid of rows and columns into which you can enter text, numbers, dates, and formulas and display charts. A **chart sheet** contains a chart that provides a visual representation of worksheet data. The contents of a workbook are shown in the workbook window.

Changing the Active Sheet

The sheets in a workbook are identified in the sheet tabs at the bottom of the workbook window. The Finances workbook for Game Card includes five sheets labeled Documentation, Income Statement, Expenses, Balance Sheet, and Cash Flow. The sheet currently displayed in the workbook window is the active sheet, which in this case is the Documentation sheet. To make a different sheet active and visible, you click its sheet tab. You can tell which sheet is active because its name appears in bold green.

If a workbook includes so many sheets that not all of the sheet tabs can be displayed at the same time in the workbook window, you can use the sheet tab scrolling buttons to scroll through the list of tabs. Scrolling the sheet tabs does not change the active sheet; it changes only which sheet tabs are visible.

You will view the different sheets in the Finances workbook.

To change the active sheet:

▶ **1.** Click the **Income Statement** sheet tab. The Income Statement worksheet becomes the active sheet, and its name is in bold green type. See Figure 1-5.

Figure 1-5 Income Statement worksheet

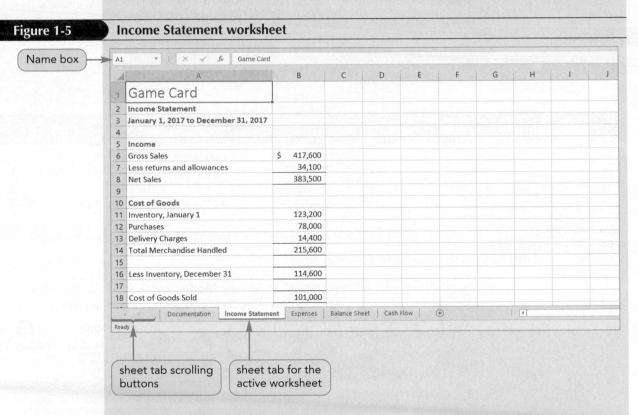

▶ **2.** Click the **Expenses** sheet tab to make it the active sheet. The Expenses sheet is an example of a chart sheet containing only an Excel chart. See Figure 1-6.

Figure 1-6   **Expenses chart sheet**

chart sheet contains a chart but no grid of text and data

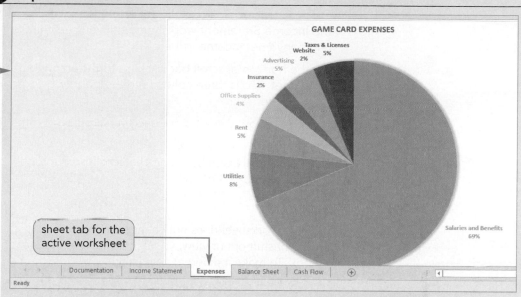

sheet tab for the active worksheet

3. Click the **Balance Sheet** sheet tab to make it the active sheet. Note that this sheet contains charts embedded into the grid of data values. A worksheet can contain data values, embedded charts, pictures, and other design elements.

4. Click the **Cash Flow** sheet tab. The worksheet with information about the company's cash flow is now active.

5. Click the **Income Statement** sheet tab to make the Income Statement worksheet the active sheet.

Navigating Within a Worksheet

A worksheet is organized into a grid of cells. Each cell is identified by a **cell reference**, which indicates the column and row in which the cell is located. For example, in Figure 1-5, the company name, Game Card, is in cell A1, which is the intersection of column A and row 1. The column letter always appears before the row number in any cell reference. The cell that is currently selected in the worksheet is referred to as the active cell. The active cell is highlighted with a thick green border, its cell reference appears in the Name box, and the corresponding column and row headings are highlighted. The active cell in Figure 1-5 is cell A1.

Row numbers range from 1 to 1,048,576, and column labels are letters in alphabetical order. The first 26 column headings range from A to Z. After Z, the next column headings are labeled AA, AB, AC, and so forth. Excel allows a maximum of 16,384 columns in a worksheet (the last column has the heading XFD). This means that you can create large worksheets whose content extends well beyond what is visible in the workbook window.

To move different parts of the worksheet into view, you can use the horizontal and vertical scroll bars located at the bottom and right edges of the workbook window, respectively. A scroll bar has arrow buttons that you can click to shift the worksheet one column or row in the specified direction, and a scroll box that you can drag to shift the worksheet in the direction you drag.

You will scroll the active worksheet so you can review the rest of the Game Card income statement.

To scroll through the Income Statement worksheet:

▶ 1. On the vertical scroll bar, click the **down arrow** button ▼ to scroll down the Income Statement worksheet until you see cell B36, which displays the company's net income value of $104,200.

▶ 2. On the horizontal scroll bar, click the **right arrow** button ▶ three times. The worksheet scrolls three columns to the right, moving columns A through C out of view.

▶ 3. On the horizontal scroll bar, drag the **scroll box** to the left until you see column A.

▶ 4. On the vertical scroll bar, drag the **scroll box** up until you see the top of the worksheet and cell A1.

Scrolling the worksheet does not change the location of the active cell. Although the active cell might shift out of view, you can always see the location of the active cell in the Name box. To make a different cell active, you can either click a new cell or use the keyboard to move between cells, as described in Figure 1-7.

Figure 1-7	Excel navigation keys

Press	To move the active cell
↑ ↓ ← →	Up, down, left, or right one cell
Home	To column A of the current row
Ctrl+Home	To cell A1
Ctrl+End	To the last cell in the worksheet that contains data
Enter	Down one row or to the start of the next row of data
Shift+Enter	Up one row
Tab	One column to the right
Shift+Tab	One column to the left
PgUp, PgDn	Up or down one screen
Ctrl+PgUp, Ctrl+PgDn	To the previous or next sheet in the workbook

You will use both your mouse and your keyboard to change the location of the active cell in the Income Statement worksheet.

To change the active cell:

▶ 1. Move your pointer over cell **A5**, and then click the mouse button. The active cell moves from cell A1 to cell A5. A green border appears around cell A5, the column heading for column A and the row heading for row 5 are both highlighted, and the cell reference in the Name box changes from A1 to A5.

▶ 2. Press the → key. The active cell moves one cell to the right to cell B5.

▶ 3. Press the **PgDn** key on your keyboard. The active cell moves down one full screen.

▶ 4. Press the **PgUp** key. The active cell moves up one full screen, returning to cell B5.

▶ 5. Press the **Ctrl+Home** keys. The active cell returns to the first cell in the worksheet, cell A1.

The mouse and keyboard provide quick ways to navigate the active worksheet. For larger worksheets that span several screens, you can move directly to a specific cell using the Go To command or by typing a cell reference in the Name box. You will try both of these methods.

To use the Go To dialog box and the Name box:

1. On the Home tab, in the Editing group, click the **Find & Select** button, and then click **Go To** on the menu that opens (or press the **Ctrl+G** keys). The Go To dialog box opens.

2. Type **B34** in the Reference box. See Figure 1-8.

Figure 1-8   **Go To dialog box**

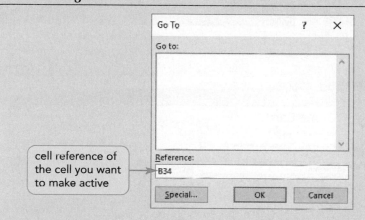

cell reference of the cell you want to make active

3. Click the **OK** button. Cell B34 becomes the active cell, displaying 182,000, which is the total expenses for Game Card. Because cell B34 is the active cell, its cell reference appears in the Name box.

4. Click in the Name box, type **A1**, and then press the **Enter** key. Cell A1 is again the active cell.

Selecting a Cell Range

Many tasks in Excel require you to work with a group of cells. A group of cells in a rectangular block is called a cell range (or simply a range). Each range is identified with a **range reference** that includes the cell reference of the upper-left cell of the rectangular block and the cell reference of the lower-right cell separated by a colon. For example, the range reference A1:G5 refers to all of the cells in the rectangular block from cell A1 through cell G5.

As with individual cells, you can select cell ranges using your mouse, the keyboard, or commands. You will select a range in the Income Statement worksheet.

TIP

You can also select a range by clicking its upper-left cell, holding down the Shift key as you click its lower-right cell, and then releasing the Shift key.

To select a cell range:

1. Click cell **A5** to select it, and without releasing the mouse button, drag down to cell **B8**.

2. Release the mouse button. The range A5:B8 is selected. The selected cells are highlighted and surrounded by a green border. The first cell you selected in the range, cell A5, is the active cell in the worksheet. The active cell in a selected range is white. The Quick Analysis button appears, providing options for working with the range; you will use this button in another module. See Figure 1-9.

Figure 1-9	Range A5:B8 selected

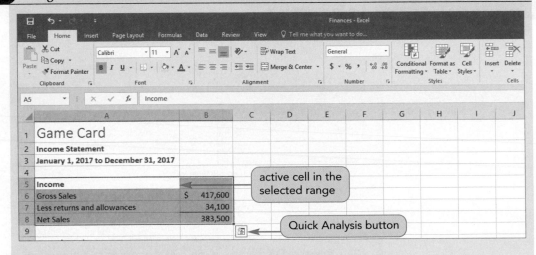

3. Click cell **A1** to deselect the range.

Another type of range is a nonadjacent range, which is a collection of separate rectangular ranges. The range reference for a nonadjacent range includes the range reference to each range separated by a comma. For example, the range reference A1:G5,A10:G15 includes two ranges—the first range is the rectangular block of cells from cell A1 to cell G5, and the second range is the rectangular block of cells from cell A10 to cell G15.

You will select a nonadjacent range in the Income Statement worksheet.

To select a nonadjacent range in the Income Statement worksheet:

1. Click cell **A5**, hold down the **Shift** key as you click cell **B8**, and then release the **Shift** key to select the range A5:B8.

2. Hold down the **Ctrl** key as you drag to select the range **A10:B14**, and then release the **Ctrl** key. The two separate blocks of cells in the nonadjacent range A5:B8,A10:B14 are selected. See Figure 1-10.

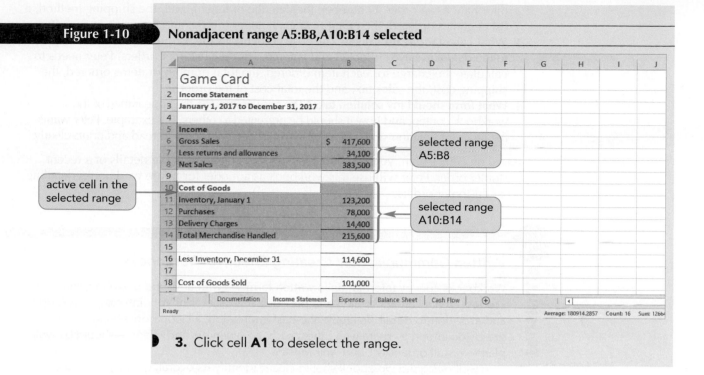

Figure 1-10   Nonadjacent range A5:B8,A10:B14 selected

3. Click cell **A1** to deselect the range.

Closing a Workbook

Once you are finished with a workbook you can close it. When you close a workbook, a dialog box might open, asking whether you want to save any changes you may have made to the document. If you have made changes that you want to keep, you should save the workbook. Since you have finished reviewing the financial workbook for Game Card, you will close it without saving any changes you may have inadvertently made to the document contents.

To close the workbook:

1. On the ribbon, click the **File** tab to display Backstage view, and then click **Close** in the navigation bar (or press the **Ctrl+W** keys).

2. If a dialog box opens, asking whether you want to save your changes to the workbook, click the **Don't Save** button. The workbook closes without saving any changes. Excel remains opens, ready for you to create or open another workbook.

Planning a Workbook

It's good practice to plan out your workbooks before you begin creating them. You can do this by using a planning analysis sheet, which includes the following questions that help you think about the workbook's purpose and how to achieve your desired results:

1. **What problems do I want to solve?** The answer identifies the goal or purpose of the workbook. For example, Peter wants you to record customer orders and be able to analyze details from these orders.

2. **What data do I need?** The answer identifies the type of data that you need to collect and enter into the workbook. For example, Peter needs customer contact

information, an order ID number, the date the order shipped, the shipping method, a list of games ordered, the quantity of each item ordered, and the price of each item.

3. **What calculations do I need?** The answer identifies the formulas you need to apply to the data you have collected and entered. For the customer orders, Peter needs to calculate the charge for each item ordered, the total number of items ordered, the shipping cost, the sales tax, and the total cost of the order.

4. **What form should my solution take?** The answer impacts the appearance of the workbook content and how it should be presented to others. For example, Peter wants the order information stored in a single worksheet that is easy to read and prints clearly.

Based on Peter's plan, you will create a workbook containing the details of a recent customer order. Peter will use this workbook as a model for future workbooks detailing other customer orders.

PROSKILLS

Written Communication: Creating Effective Workbooks

Workbooks convey information in written form. As with any type of writing, the final product creates an impression and provides an indicator of your interest, knowledge, and attention to detail. To create the best impression, all workbooks—especially those you intend to share with others such as coworkers and clients—should be well planned, well organized, and well written.

A well-designed workbook should clearly identify its overall goal and present information in an organized format. The data it includes—both the entered values and the calculated values—should be accurate. The process of developing an effective workbook includes the following steps:

- Determine the workbook's purpose, content, and organization before you start.
- Create a list of the sheets used in the workbook, noting each sheet's purpose.
- Insert a documentation sheet that describes the workbook's purpose and organization. Include the name of the workbook author, the date the workbook was created, and any additional information that will help others to track the workbook to its source.
- Enter all of the data in the workbook. Add labels to indicate what the values represent and, if possible, where they originated so others can view the source of your data.
- Enter formulas for calculated items rather than entering the calculated values into the workbook. For more complicated calculations, provide documentation explaining them.
- Test the workbook with a variety of values; edit the data and formulas to correct errors.
- Save the workbook and create a backup copy when the project is completed. Print the workbook's contents if you need to provide a hard-copy version to others or for your files.
- Maintain a history of your workbook as it goes through different versions, so that you and others can quickly see how the workbook has changed during revisions.

By including clearly written documentation, explanatory text, a logical organization, and accurate data and formulas, you will create effective workbooks that others can use easily.

Starting a New Workbook

You create new workbooks from the New screen in Backstage view. Similar to the Recent screen that opened when you started Excel, the New screen includes templates for a variety of workbook types. You can see a preview of what the different workbooks will look like. You will create a new workbook from the Blank workbook template, in which you can add all of the content and design Peter wants for the Game Card customer order worksheet.

To start a new, blank workbook:

1. On the ribbon, click the **File** tab to display Backstage view.

2. Click **New** in the navigation bar to display the New screen, which includes access to templates for a variety of workbooks.

TIP

You can also create a new, blank workbook by pressing the Ctrl+N keys.

3. Click the **Blank workbook** tile. A blank workbook opens.

   In these modules, the workbook window is zoomed to 120% for better readability. If you want to zoom your workbook window to match the figures, complete Step 4. If you prefer to work in the default zoom of 100% or at another zoom level, read but do not complete Step 4; you might see more or less of the worksheet on your screen, but this will not affect your work in the modules.

4. If you want your workbook window zoomed to 120% to match the figures, on the Zoom slider at the bottom-right of the program window, click the **Zoom In** button ⊞ twice to increase the percentage to 120%. The 120% magnification increases the size of each cell but reduces the number of worksheet cells visible in the workbook window. See Figure 1-11.

Figure 1-11   Blank workbook

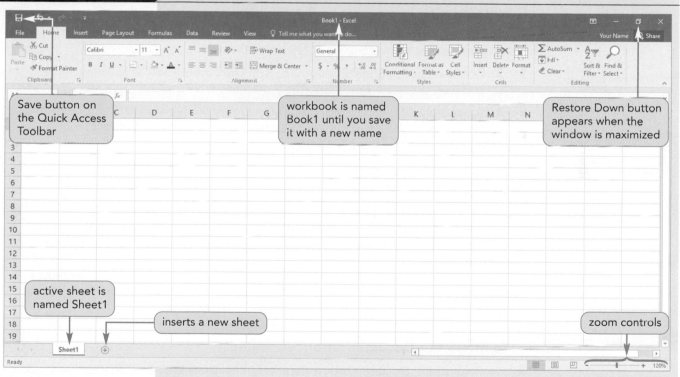

The name of the active workbook, Book1, appears in the title bar. If you open multiple blank workbooks, they are named Book1, Book2, Book3, and so forth until you save them with a more descriptive name.

Renaming and Inserting Worksheets

Blank workbooks open with a single blank worksheet named Sheet1. You can give sheets more descriptive and meaningful names. This is a good practice so that you and others can easily tell what a sheet contains. Sheet names cannot exceed 31 characters, but they can contain blank spaces and include uppercase and lowercase letters.

Because Sheet1 is not a very descriptive name, Peter wants you to rename the worksheet as Customer Order.

To rename the Sheet1 worksheet:

▶ **1.** Double-click the **Sheet1** tab. The Sheet1 label in the tab is selected.

▶ **2.** Type **Customer Order** as the new name, and then press the **Enter** key. The width of the sheet tab expands to fit the longer sheet name.

Many workbooks include multiple sheets so that data can be organized in logical groups. A common business practice is to include a worksheet named Documentation that contains a description of the workbook, the name of the person who prepared the workbook, and the date it was created.

Peter wants you to create two new worksheets. You will rename one worksheet as Documentation and the other worksheet as Customer Contact. The Customer Contact worksheet will be used to store the customer's contact information.

To insert and name the Documentation and Customer Contact worksheets:

▶ **1.** To the right of the Customer Order sheet tab, click the **New sheet** button ⊕. A new sheet named Sheet2 is inserted to the right of the Customer Order sheet.

▶ **2.** Double-click the **Sheet2** sheet tab, type **Documentation** as the new name, and then press the **Enter** key. The worksheet is renamed.

▶ **3.** To the right of the Documentation sheet, click the **New sheet** button ⊕, and then rename the inserted Sheet3 worksheet as **Customer Contact**.

Moving Worksheets

A good practice is to place the most important sheets at the beginning of the workbook (the leftmost sheet tabs) and less important sheets at the end (the rightmost sheet tabs). To change the placement of sheets in a workbook, you drag them by their sheet tabs to the new location.

Peter wants you to move the Documentation worksheet to the front of the workbook, so that it appears before the Customer Order sheet.

To move the Documentation worksheet:

▶ **1.** Point to the **Documentation** sheet tab. The sheet tab name changes to bold.

▶ **2.** Press and hold the mouse button. The pointer changes to ▽, and a small arrow appears in the upper-left corner of the tab.

▶ **3.** Drag to the left until the small arrow appears in the upper-left corner of the Customer Order sheet tab, and then release the mouse button. The Documentation worksheet is now the first sheet in the workbook.

TIP

To copy a sheet, hold down the Ctrl key as you drag and drop its sheet tab.

Deleting Worksheets

In some workbooks, you will want to delete an existing sheet. The easiest way to delete a sheet is by using a **shortcut menu**, which is a list of commands related to a selection that opens when you click the right mouse button. Peter asks you to include the customer's contact information on the Customer Order worksheet so all of the information is on one sheet.

To delete the Customer Contact worksheet from the workbook:

1. Right-click the **Customer Contact** sheet tab. A shortcut menu opens.

2. Click **Delete**. The Customer Contact worksheet is removed from the workbook.

Saving a Workbook

As you modify a workbook, you should save it regularly—every 10 minutes or so is a good practice. The first time you save a workbook, the Save As dialog box opens so you can name the file and choose where to save it. You can save the workbook on your computer or network or to your account on OneDrive.

To save your workbook for the first time:

1. On the Quick Access Toolbar, click the **Save** button 🖫 (or press the **Ctrl+S** keys). The Save As screen in Backstage view opens.

2. Click the **Browse** button. The Save As dialog box opens.

3. Navigate to the location specified by your instructor.

4. In the File name box, select **Book1** (the suggested name) if it is not already selected, and then type **Game Card**.

5. Verify that **Excel Workbook** appears in the Save as type box.

6. Click the **Save** button. The workbook is saved, the dialog box closes, and the workbook window reappears with the new filename in the title bar.

As you modify the workbook, you will need to resave the file. Because you already saved the workbook with a filename, the next time you save, the Save command saves the changes you made to the workbook without opening the Save As dialog box.

Entering Text, Dates, and Numbers

Workbook content is entered into worksheet cells. Those cells can contain text, numbers, or dates and times. **Text data** is any combination of letters, numbers, and symbols. Text data is often referred to as a **text string** because it contains a series, or string, of text characters. **Numeric data** is any number that can be used in a mathematical calculation. **Date** and **time data** are commonly recognized formats for date and time values. For example, Excel interprets the cell entry April 15, 2017 as a date and not as text. New data is placed into the active cell of the current worksheet. As you enter data, the entry appears in both the active cell and the formula bar. By default, text is left-aligned in cells, and numbers, dates, and times are right-aligned.

Entering Text

Text is often used in worksheets to label other data and to identify areas of a sheet. Peter wants you to enter some of the information from the planning analysis sheet into the Documentation sheet.

To enter text in the Documentation sheet:

▶ 1. Go to the **Documentation** sheet, and then click the **Ctrl+Home** keys to make sure cell A1 is the active cell.

▶ 2. Type **Game Card** in cell A1. As you type, the text appears in cell A1 and in the formula bar.

▶ 3. Press the **Enter** key twice. The text is entered into cell A1, and the active cell moves down two rows to cell A3.

▶ 4. Type **Author** in cell A3, and then press the **Tab** key. The text is entered and the active cell moves one column to the right to cell B3.

▶ 5. Type your name in cell B3, and then press the **Enter** key. The text is entered and the active cell moves one cell down and to the left to cell A4.

▶ 6. Type **Date** in cell A4, and then press the **Tab** key. The text is entered, and the active cell moves one column to the right to cell B4, where you would enter the date you created the worksheet. For now, you will leave the cell for the date blank.

▶ 7. Press the **Enter** key to make cell A5 the active cell, type **Purpose** in the cell, and then press the **Tab** key. The active cell moves one column to the right to cell B5.

▶ 8. Type **To record customer game orders** in cell B5, and then press the **Enter** key. Figure 1-12 shows the text entered in the Documentation sheet.

Figure 1-12   **Text entered in the Documentation sheet**

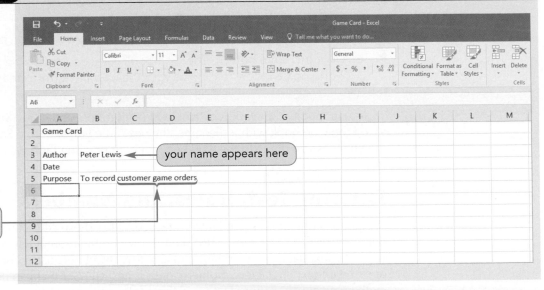

The text strings you entered in cells A1, B3, and B5 are so long that they cover the adjacent cells. Any text you enter in a cell that doesn't fit within that cell will cover the adjacent cells to the right as long as they are empty. If the adjacent cells contain data, only the text that fits into the cell is displayed. The rest of the text entry is hidden from view. The text itself is not affected. The complete text is still entered in the cell; it is just not displayed. (You will learn how to display all text in a cell in the next session.)

Undoing and Redoing an Action

As you enter data in a workbook, you might need to undo a previous action. Excel maintains a list of the actions you performed in the workbook during the current session, so you can undo most of your actions. You can use the Undo button on the Quick Access Toolbar or press the Ctrl+Z keys to reverse your most recent actions one at a time. If you want to undo more than one action, you can click the Undo button arrow and then select the earliest action you want to undo—all of the actions after the earliest action you selected are also undone.

You will undo the most recent change you made to the Documentation sheet—the text you entered into cell B5. Then you will enter more descriptive and accurate description of the worksheet's purpose.

To undo the text entry in cell B5:

1. On the Quick Access Toolbar, click the **Undo** button (or press the **Ctrl+Z** keys). The last action is reversed, removing the text you entered in cell B5.

2. In cell B5, type **To record purchases of board games from Game Card**, and then press the **Enter** key.

If you want to restore actions you have undone, you can redo them. To redo one action at a time, you can click the Redo button on the Quick Access Toolbar or press the Ctrl+Y keys. To redo multiple actions at once, you can click the Redo button arrow and then click the earliest action you want to redo. After you undo or redo an action, Excel continues the action list starting from any new changes you make to the workbook.

Editing Cell Content

As you continue to create your workbook, you might find mistakes you need to correct or entries that you want to change. To replace all of the content in a cell, you simply select the cell and then type the new entry to overwrite the previous entry. However, if you need to replace only part of a cell's content, you can work in **Edit mode**. To switch to Edit mode, you double-click the cell. A blinking insertion point indicates where the new content you type will be inserted. In the cell or formula bar, the pointer changes to an I-beam, which you can use to select text in the cell. Anything you type replaces the selected content.

Because customers can order more than just games from Game Card, Peter wants you to edit the text in cell B5. You will do that in Edit mode.

To edit the text in cell B5:

1. Double-click cell **B5** to select the cell and switch to Edit mode. A blinking insertion point appears within the text of cell B5. The status bar displays Edit instead of Ready to indicate that the cell is in Edit mode.

2. Press the **arrow keys** to move the insertion point directly to the left of the word "from" in the cell text.

3. Type **and other items** and then press the **spacebar**. The cell now reads "To record purchases of board games and other items from Game Card." See Figure 1-13.

Figure 1-13   **Edited text in the Documentation sheet**

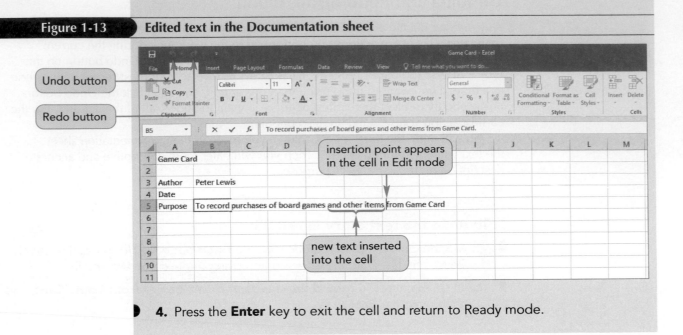

4. Press the **Enter** key to exit the cell and return to Ready mode.

Understanding AutoComplete

As you type text in the active cell, Excel tries to anticipate the remaining characters by displaying text that begins with the same letters as a previous entry in the same column. This feature, known as **AutoComplete**, helps make entering repetitive text easier. To accept the suggested text, press the Tab or Enter key. To override the suggested text, continue to type the text you want to enter in the cell. AutoComplete does not work with dates or numbers or when a blank cell is between the previous entry and the text you are typing.

Next, you will enter the contact information for Leslie Ritter, a customer from Brockton, Massachusetts, who recently placed an order with Game Card. You will enter this information on the Customer Order worksheet.

To enter Leslie Ritter's contact information:

1. Click the **Customer Order** sheet tab to make it the active sheet.

2. In cell A1, type **Customer Order** as the worksheet title, and then press the **Enter** key twice. The worksheet title is entered in cell A1, and the active cell becomes cell A3.

3. Type **Ship To** in cell A3, and then press the **Enter** key. The label is entered in the cell, and the active cell is now cell A4.

4. In the range A4:A10, enter the following labels, pressing the **Enter** key after each entry and ignoring any AutoComplete suggestions: **First Name**, **Last Name**, **Address**, **City**, **State**, **Postal Code**, and **Phone**.

5. Click cell **B4** to make that cell the active cell.

6. In the range B4:B10, enter the following contact information, pressing the **Enter** key after each entry and ignoring any AutoComplete suggestions: **Leslie**, **Ritter**, **805 Mountain St.**, **Brockton**, **MA**, **02302**, and **(508) 555-1072**. See Figure 1-14.

Figure 1-14   **Customer information entered in the Customer Order worksheet**

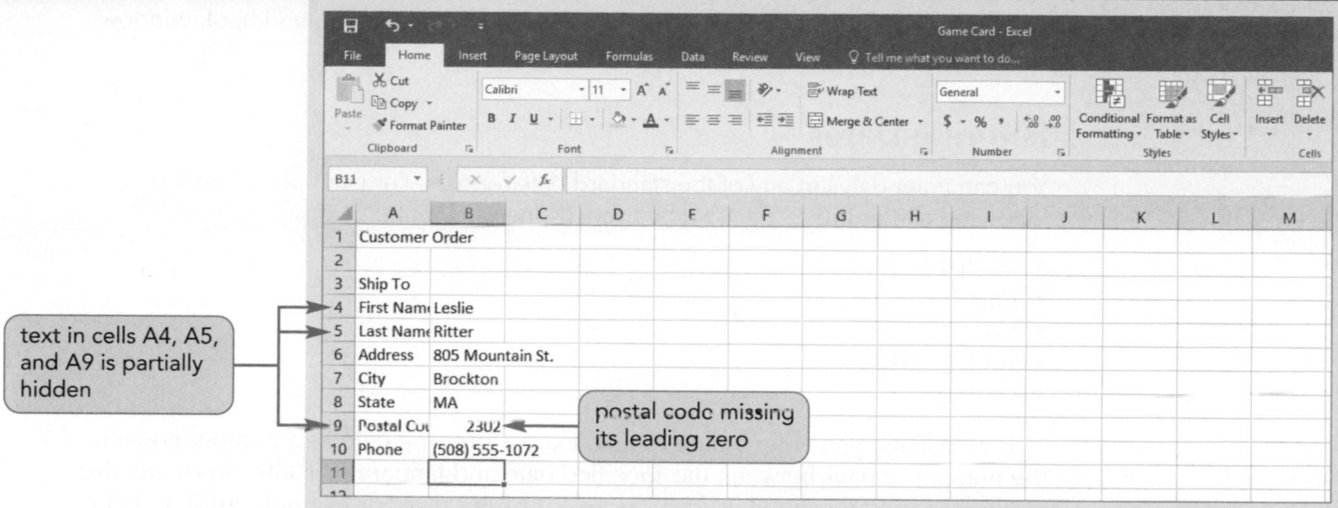

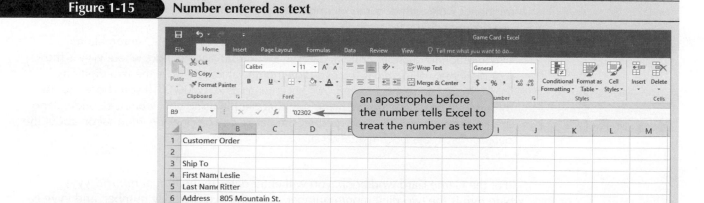

text in cells A4, A5, and A9 is partially hidden

postal code missing its leading zero

Displaying Numbers as Text

When you enter a number in a cell, Excel treats the entry as a number and ignores any leading zero. For example, in cell B9, the leading zero in the postal code 02302 is missing. Excel displays 2302 because it treats the postal code as a number, and 2302 and 02302 have the same value. To specify that a number entry should be considered text and all digits should be displayed, you include an apostrophe (') before the numbers.

To enter the postal code as text:

1. Click cell **B9** to select it. Notice that the postal code is right-aligned in the cell, unlike the other text entries, which are left-aligned—another indication that the entry is being treated as a number.

2. Type **'02302** in cell B9, and then press the **Enter** key. The text 02302 appears in cell B9 and is left-aligned in the cell, matching all of the other text entries.

3. Click cell **B9** to select it again. See Figure 1-15.

Figure 1-15   **Number entered as text**

an apostrophe before the number tells Excel to treat the number as text

green triangle flags a potential error

postal code is left-aligned in the cell

TIP

To remove a green triangle, click the cell, click the yellow caution icon that appears to the left of the cell, and then click Ignore Error.

Notice that a green triangle appears in the upper-left corner of cell B9. Excel uses green triangles to flag potential errors in cells. In this case, it is simply a warning that you entered a number as a text string. Because this is intentional, you do not have to edit the cell to fix the "error." Green triangles appear only in the workbook window and not in any printouts of the worksheet.

Entering Dates

You can enter dates in any of the standard date formats. For example, all of the following entries are recognized by Excel as the same date:

- 4/6/2017
- 4/6/17
- 4-6-2017
- April 6, 2017
- 6-Apr-17

Even though you enter a date as text, Excel stores the date as a number equal to the number of days between the specified date and January 0, 1900. Times are also entered as text and stored as fractions of a 24-hour day. For example April 4, 2017 @ 6:00 PM is stored by Excel as 42,842.75 which is 42,842 days after January 0, 1900 plus 3/4 of one day. Dates and times are stored as numbers so that Excel can easily perform date and time calculations, such as determining the elapsed time between one date and another.

Based on the default date format your computer uses, Excel might alter the format of a date after you type it. For example, if you enter the date 4/6/17 into the active cell, Excel might display the date with the four-digit year value, 4/6/2017; if you enter the text April 6, 2017, Excel might change the date format to 6-Apr-17. Changing the date or time format does not affect the underlying date or time value.

INSIGHT

International Date Formats

As business transactions become more international in scope, you may need to adopt international standards for expressing dates, times, and currency values in your workbooks. For example, a worksheet cell might contain 06/05/17. This format could be interpreted as any of the following dates: the 5th of June, 2017; the 6th of May, 2017; and the 17th of May, 2006.

The interpretation depends on which country the workbook has been designed for. You can avoid this problem by entering the full date, as in June 5, 2017. However, this might not work with documents written in foreign languages, such as Japanese, that use different character symbols.

To solve this problem, many international businesses adopt ISO (International Organization for Standardization) dates in the format *yyyy-mm-dd*, where *yyyy* is the four-digit year value, *mm* is the two-digit month value, and *dd* is the two-digit day value. So, a date such as June 5, 2017 is entered as 2017/06/05. If you choose to use this international date format, make sure that people using your workbook understand this format so they do not misinterpret the dates. You can include information about the date format in the Documentation sheet.

For the Game Card workbook, you will enter dates in the format *mm/dd/yyyy*, where *mm* is the two-digit month number, *dd* is the two-digit day number, and *yyyy* is the four-digit year number.

To enter the current date into the Documentation sheet:

▶ 1. Click the **Documentation** sheet tab to make the Documentation sheet the active worksheet.

▶ 2. Click cell **B4** to make it the active cell, type the current date in the *mm/dd/yyyy* format, and then press the **Enter** key. The date is entered in the cell.

   Trouble? Depending on your system configuration, Excel might change the date to the date format *dd-mmm-yy*. This difference will not affect your work.

▶ 3. Click the **Customer Order** sheet tab to return to the Customer Order worksheet.

The next part of the Customer Order worksheet will list the items that customer Leslie Ritter purchased from Game Card. As shown in Figure 1-16, the list includes identifying information about each item, including the item's price, and the quantity of each item ordered.

| Figure 1-16 | Customer order from Leslie Ritter |

Stock ID	Category	Manufacturer	Title	Players	Price	Qty
SG71	Strategy Game	Drebeck Brothers	Kings and Jacks: A Medieval Game of Deception	4	$39.95	2
FG14	Family Game	Misty Games	Twirple, Tweedle, and Twaddle	6	$24.55	1
PG05	Party Game	Parlor Vision	Trivia Connection	8	$29.12	1
SU38	Supplies	Parlor Vision	Box of Dice (10)		$9.95	3
SG29	Strategy Game	Drebeck Brothers	Solar Warfare	2	$35.15	1

You will enter the first four columns of the order into the worksheet.

To enter the first part of the customer order:

▶ 1. In the Customer Order worksheet, click cell **A12** to make it the active cell, type **Stock ID** as the column label, and then press the **Tab** key to move to cell B12.

▶ 2. In the range B12:D12, type the following labels, pressing the **Tab** key to move to the next cell: **Category**, **Manufacturer**, and **Title**.

▶ 3. Press the **Enter** key to go to the next row of the worksheet, making cell A13 the active cell.

▶ 4. In the range A13:D17, type the Stock ID, Category, Manufacturer, and Title text for the five items purchased by Leslie Ritter listed in Figure 1-16, pressing the **Tab** key to move from one cell to the next, and pressing the **Enter** key to move to a new row. Note that the text in some cells will be partially hidden; you will fix that problem shortly. See Figure 1-17.

Figure 1-17   **Partial customer order**

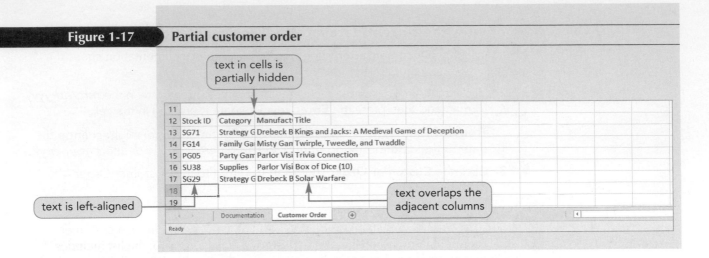

Entering Numbers

In Excel, numbers can be integers such as 378, decimals such as 1.95, or negatives such as –5.2. In the case of currency and percentages, you can include the currency symbol and percent sign when you enter the value. Excel treats a currency value such as $87.25 as the number 87.25, and a percentage such as 95% as the decimal 0.95. Much like dates, currency and percentages are formatted in a convenient way for you to read, but only the number is stored within the cell. This makes it easier to perform calculations with currency and percentage values.

You will complete Leslie Ritter's order by entering the players, price, and quantity values.

To enter the rest of the customer order:

1. In the range E12:G12, enter **Players**, **Price**, and **Qty** as the labels.

2. In cell E13, enter **4** as the number of players for the game Kings and Jacks.

3. In cell F13, enter **$39.95** as the price of the game. The game price is stored as a number but displayed with the $ symbol.

4. In cell G13, enter **2** as the quantity of the game ordered by Leslie.

5. In the range E14:G17, enter the remaining number of players, prices, and quantities shown earlier in Figure 1-16. See Figure 1-18.

Figure 1-18   **Completed customer order**

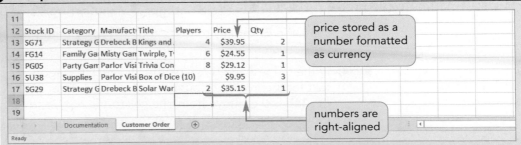

6. On the Quick Access Toolbar, click the **Save** button (or press the **Ctrl+S** keys) to save the workbook.

Resizing Columns and Rows

Much of the information in the Customer Order worksheet is difficult to read because of the hidden text. You can display all of the cell contents by changing the size of the columns and rows in the worksheet.

Changing Column Widths

Column widths are expressed as the number of characters the column can contain. The default column width is 8.43 standard-sized characters. In general, this means that you can type eight characters in a cell; any additional text is hidden or overlaps the adjacent cell. Column widths are also expressed in terms of pixels. A **pixel** is a single point on a computer monitor or printout. A column width of 8.43 characters is equivalent to 64 pixels.

INSIGHT

Setting Column Widths

On a computer monitor, pixel size is based on screen resolution. As a result, cell contents that look fine on one screen might appear very different when viewed on a screen with a different resolution. If you work on multiple computers or share your workbooks with others, you should set column widths based on the maximum number of characters you want displayed in the cells rather than pixel size. This ensures that everyone sees the cell contents the way you intended.

You will increase the width of column A so that the contact information labels in cells A4, A5, and A9 are completely displayed.

To increase the width of column A:

▶ **1.** Point to the **right border** of the column A heading until the pointer changes to ↔.

▶ **2.** Click and drag to the right until the width of the column heading reaches **15** characters, but do not release the mouse button. The ScreenTip that appears as you resize the column shows the new column width in characters and in pixels. See Figure 1-19.

Figure 1-19   **Width of column A increased to 15 characters**

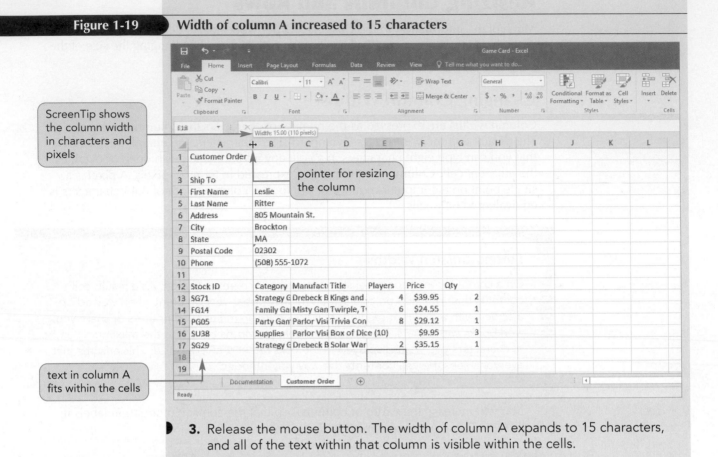

ScreenTip shows the column width in characters and pixels

pointer for resizing the column

text in column A fits within the cells

> ● **3.** Release the mouse button. The width of column A expands to 15 characters, and all of the text within that column is visible within the cells.

You will increase the widths of columns B and C to 18 characters so that their complete entries are visible. Rather than resizing each column separately, you can select both columns and adjust their widths at the same time.

To increase the widths of columns B and C:

> ● **1.** Click the **column B** heading. The entire column is selected.

> ● **2.** Hold down the **Ctrl** key, click the **column C** heading, and then release the **Ctrl** key. Both columns B and C are selected.

> ● **3.** Point to the **right border** of the column C heading until the pointer changes to ╬.

> ● **4.** Drag to the right until the column width changes to **18** characters, and then release the mouse button. Both column widths increase to 18 characters and display all of the entered text.

TIP

To select adjacent columns, you can also click and drag the pointer over multiple column headings.

Using the mouse to resize columns can be imprecise and a challenge to some users with special needs. The Format command on the Home tab gives you precise control over column width and row height settings. You will use the Format command to set the width of column D to exactly 25 characters so that the hidden text is visible.

To set the width of column D using the Format command:

1. Click the **column D** heading. The entire column is selected.

2. On the Home tab, in the Cells group, click the **Format** button, and then click **Column Width.** The Column Width dialog box opens.

3. Type **25** in the Column width box to specify the new column width.

4. Click the **OK** button. The width of column D changes to 25 characters.

5. Click cell **A12** to deselect column D. Figure 1-20 shows the revised column widths for the customer order columns.

Figure 1-20   **Resized columns**

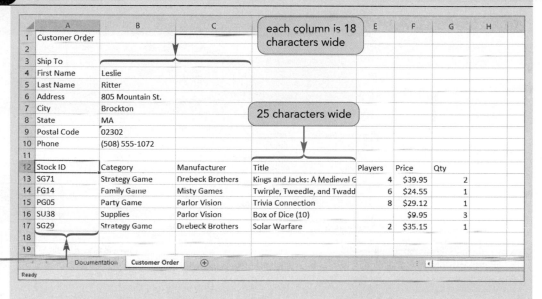

15 characters wide

Wrapping Text Within a Cell

TIP

If the row or column is blank, autofitting restores its default height or width.

Notice that 25 characters is not wide enough to display all of the characters in each cell of column D. Instead of manually resizing the column width or row height to fit it to the cell contents, you can autofit the column or row. **AutoFit** changes the column width or row height to display the longest or tallest entry within the column or row. You autofit a column or a row by double-clicking the right border of the column heading or the bottom border of the row heading.

To autofit the contents of column D:

1. Point to the **right border** of column D until the pointer changes to ✛.

2. Double-click the **right border** of the column D heading. The width of column D increases to about 43 characters so that the longest item title is completely visible.

Wrapping Text Within a Cell

Sometimes, resizing a column width to display all of the text entered in the cells results in a cell that is too wide to read or print nicely. Another way to display long text entries is to wrap text to a new line when it would otherwise extend beyond the cell boundaries. When text wraps within a cell, the row height increases so that all of the text within the cell is displayed.

You will resize column D and then wrap the text entries in the column.

To wrap text in column D:

1. Resize the width of column D to **25** characters.

2. Select the range **D13:D17**. These cells include the titles that extend beyond the column width.

3. On the Home tab, in the Alignment group, click the **Wrap Text** button. The Wrap Text button is toggled on, and text in the selected cells that exceeds the column width wraps to a new line.

4. Click cell **A12** to make it the active cell. See Figure 1-21.

Figure 1-21   **Text wrapped within cells**

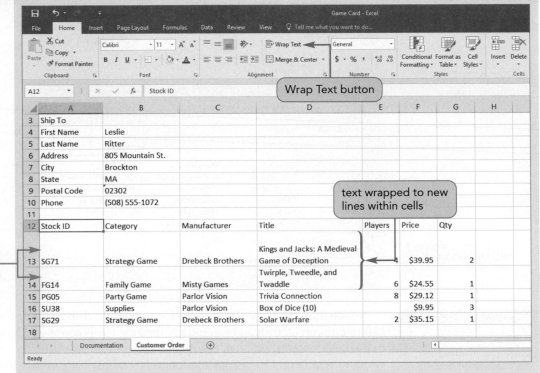

If you want to create a new line within a cell, press the Alt+Enter keys to move the insertion point to the next line within the cell. Whatever you type next will appear on the new line in the cell.

Changing Row Heights

The height of a row is measured in points or pixels. A **point** is approximately 1/72 of an inch. The default row height is 15 points, or 20 pixels. Row heights are set in the same way as column widths. You can drag the bottom border of the row heading to a new row height, specify a row height using the Format command, or autofit the row's height to match its content.

Peter notices that the height of row 13 is a little too tall for its contents. He asks you to change to it 30 points.

To change the height of row 13:

▶ **1.** Point to the **bottom border** of the row 13 heading until the pointer changes to ✛.

TIP

You can also set the row height by clicking the Format button in the Cells group on the Home tab and then using the Row Height command.

▶ **2.** Drag the **bottom border** down until the height of the row is equal to **30** points (or **40** pixels), and then release the mouse button. The height of row 13 is set to 30 points.

▶ **3.** Press the **Ctrl+S** keys to save the workbook.

You have entered most of the data for Leslie Ritter's order at Game Card. In the next session, you will calculate the total charge for the order and print the worksheet.

REVIEW

Session 1.1 Quick Check

1. What are the two types of sheets used in a workbook?
2. What is the cell reference for the cell located in the second column and fifth row of a worksheet?
3. What is the range reference for the block of cells C2 through D10?
4. What is the reference for the nonadjacent block of cells B5 through C10 and cells B15 through D20?
5. What keyboard shortcut makes the active cell to cell A1?
6. What is text data?
7. How do you enter a number so that Excel sees it as text?
8. Cell B2 contains the entry May 3, 2017. Why doesn't Excel consider this a text entry?
9. How do you autofit a column to match the longest cell entry?

Session 1.2 Visual Overview:

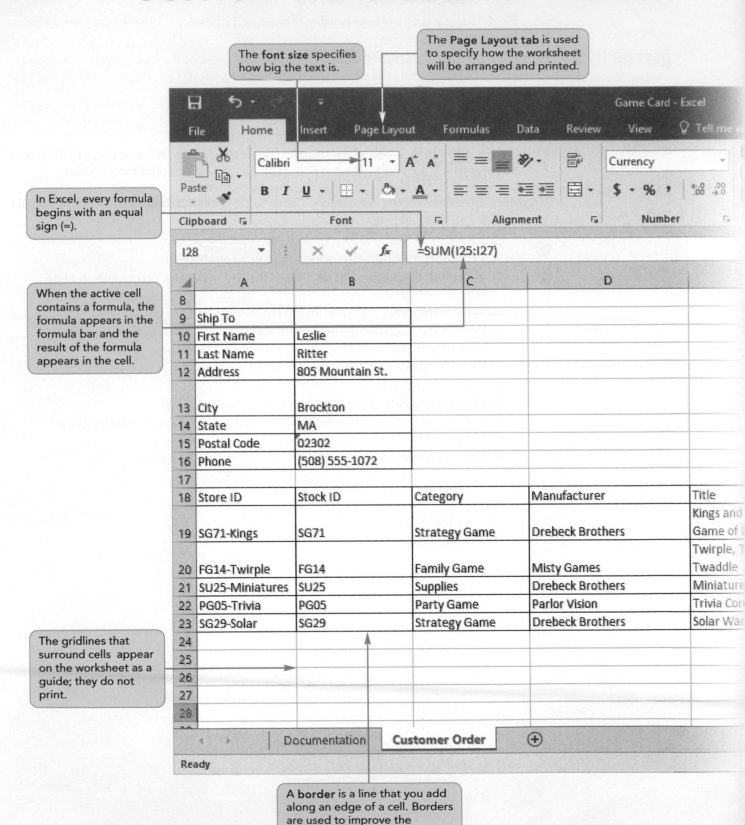

The **font size** specifies how big the text is.

The **Page Layout tab** is used to specify how the worksheet will be arranged and printed.

In Excel, every formula begins with an equal sign (=).

When the active cell contains a formula, the formula appears in the formula bar and the result of the formula appears in the cell.

The gridlines that surround cells appear on the worksheet as a guide; they do not print.

A **border** is a line that you add along an edge of a cell. Borders are used to improve the readability of the worksheet.

Game Card - Excel

File	Home	Insert	Page Layout	Formulas	Data	Review	View

Calibri 11

Currency

Clipboard · Font · Alignment · Number

I28 · fx =SUM(I25:I27)

	A	B	C	D
8				
9	Ship To			
10	First Name	Leslie		
11	Last Name	Ritter		
12	Address	805 Mountain St.		
13	City	Brockton		
14	State	MA		
15	Postal Code	02302		
16	Phone	(508) 555-1072		
17				
18	Store ID	Stock ID	Category	Manufacturer	Title
19	SG71-Kings	SG71	Strategy Game	Drebeck Brothers	Kings and Game of
20	FG14-Twirple	FG14	Family Game	Misty Games	Twirple, T Twaddle
21	SU25-Miniatures	SU25	Supplies	Drebeck Brothers	Miniature
22	PG05-Trivia	PG05	Party Game	Parlor Vision	Trivia Con
23	SG29-Solar	SG29	Strategy Game	Drebeck Brothers	Solar Wa
24				
25				
26				
27				
28				

Documentation | **Customer Order** | ⊕

Ready

Excel Formulas and Functions

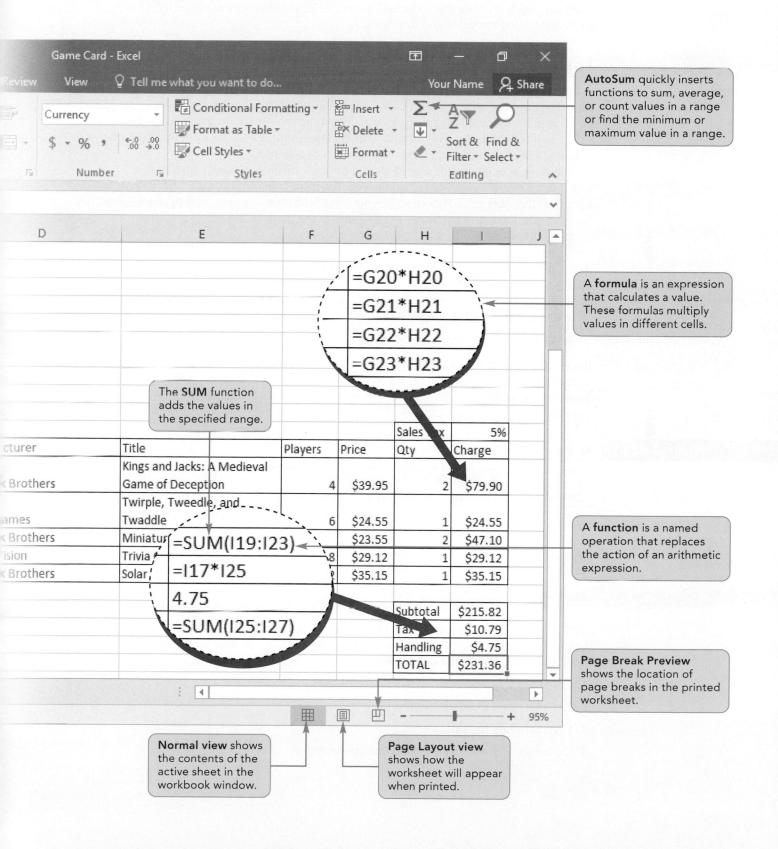

AutoSum quickly inserts functions to sum, average, or count values in a range or find the minimum or maximum value in a range.

=G20*H20
=G21*H21
=G22*H22
=G23*H23

A **formula** is an expression that calculates a value. These formulas multiply values in different cells.

The **SUM** function adds the values in the specified range.

=SUM(I19:I23)
=I17*I25
4.75
=SUM(I25:I27)

A **function** is a named operation that replaces the action of an arithmetic expression.

	Title	Players	Price	Qty	Charge
			Sales Tax		5%
cturer					
Brothers	Kings and Jacks: A Medieval Game of Deception	4	$39.95	2	$79.90
ames	Twirple, Tweedle, and Twaddle	6	$24.55	1	$24.55
Brothers	Miniatur		$23.55	2	$47.10
ision	Trivia	8	$29.12	1	$29.12
Brothers	Solar		$35.15	1	$35.15
				Subtotal	$215.82
				Tax	$10.79
				Handling	$4.75
				TOTAL	$231.36

Page Break Preview shows the location of page breaks in the printed worksheet.

95%

Normal view shows the contents of the active sheet in the workbook window.

Page Layout view shows how the worksheet will appear when printed.

Performing Calculations with Formulas

So far you have entered text, numbers, and dates in the worksheet. However, the main reason for using Excel is to perform calculations and analysis on data. For example, Peter wants the workbook to calculate the number of items that the customer ordered and how much revenue the order will generate. Such calculations are added to a worksheet using formulas and functions.

Entering a Formula

A formula is an expression that returns a value. In most cases, this is a number—though it could also be text or a date. In Excel, every formula begins with an equal sign (=) followed by an expression describing the operation that returns the value. If you don't begin the formula with the equal sign, Excel assumes that you are entering text and will not treat the cell contents as a formula.

A formula is written using **operators** that combine different values, resulting in a single value that is then displayed in the cell. The most common operators are **arithmetic operators** that perform addition, subtraction, multiplication, division, and exponentiation. For example, the following formula adds 3 and 8, returning a value of 11:

=3+8

Most Excel formulas contain references to cells rather than specific values. This allows you to change the values used in the calculation without having to modify the formula itself. For example, the following formula returns the result of adding the values stored in cells C3 and D10:

=C3+D10

If the value 3 is stored in cell C3 and the value 8 is stored in cell D10, this formula would also return a value of 11. If you later changed the value in cell C3 to 10, the formula would return a value of 18. Figure 1-22 describes the different arithmetic operators and provides examples of formulas.

Figure 1-22   Arithmetic operators

Operation	Arithmetic Operator	Example	Description
Addition	+	=B1+B2+B3	Adds the values in cells B1, B2, and B3
Subtraction	–	=C9-B2	Subtracts the value in cell B2 from the value in cell C9
Multiplication	*	=C9*B9	Multiplies the values in cells C9 and B9
Division	/	=C9/B9	Divides the value in cell C9 by the value in cell B9
Exponentiation	^	=B5^3	Raises the value of cell B5 to the third power

If a formula contains more than one arithmetic operator, Excel performs the calculation based on the **order of operations**, which is the sequence in which operators are applied in a calculation:

1. Calculate any operations within parentheses

2. Calculate any exponentiations (^)

3. Calculate any multiplications (*) and divisions (/)

4. Calculate any additions (+) and subtractions (–)

For example, the following formula returns the value 23 because multiplying 4 by 5 takes precedence over adding 3:

=3+4*5

If a formula contains two or more operators with the same level of priority, the operators are applied in order from left to right. In the following formula, Excel first multiplies 4 by 10 and then divides that result by 8 to return the value 5:

=4*10/8

When parentheses are used, the value inside them is calculated first. In the following formula, Excel calculates (3+4) first, and then multiplies that result by 5 to return the value 35:

=(3+4)*5

Figure 1-23 shows how slight changes in a formula affect the order of operations and the result of the formula.

Figure 1-23 **Order of operations applied to Excel formulas**

Formula	Order of Operations	Result
=50+10*5	10*5 calculated first and then 50 is added	100
=(50+10)*5	(50+10) calculated first and then 60 is multiplied by 5	300
=50/10–5	50/10 calculated first and then 5 is subtracted	0
=50/(10–5)	(10–5) calculated first and then 50 is divided by that value	10
=50/10*5	Two operators are at same precedence level, so the calculation is done left to right with 50/10 calculated first and that value is then multiplied by 5	25
=50/(10*5)	(10*5) is calculated first and then 50 is divided by that value	1

Peter wants the Customer Order worksheet to include the total amount charged for each item ordered. The charge is equal to the number of each item ordered multiplied by each item's price. You already entered this information in columns F and G. Now you will enter a formula to calculate the charge for each set of items ordered in column H.

To calculate the charge for the first item ordered:

1. If you took a break after the previous session, make sure the Game Card workbook is open and the Customer Order worksheet is active.

2. Click cell **H12** to make it the active cell, type **Charge** as the column label, and then press the **Enter** key. The label text is entered in cell H12, and cell H13 is now the active cell.

3. Type **=F13*G13** (the price of the Kings and Jacks game multiplied by the number of that game ordered). As you type the formula, a list of Excel function names appears in a ScreenTip, which provides a quick method for entering functions. The list will close when you complete the formula. You will learn more about Excel functions shortly. Also, after you type each cell reference, Excel color codes each cell reference and its cell. See Figure 1-24.

Figure 1-24   **Formula being entered in a cell**

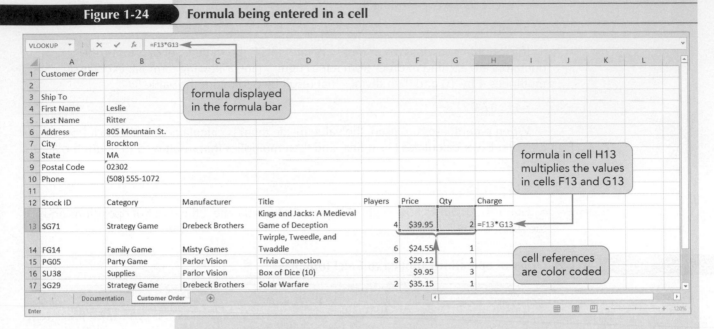

4. Press the **Enter** key. The formula is entered in cell H13 displaying the value $79.90. The result is displayed as currency because cell F13, which is referenced in the formula, contains a currency value.

5. Click cell **H13** to make it the active cell. Note that the cell displays the result of the formula, and the formula bar displays the formula you entered.

For the first item, you entered the formula by typing each cell reference in the expression. You can also insert a cell reference by clicking the cell as you type the formula. This technique reduces the possibility of error caused by typing an incorrect cell reference. You will use this method to enter the formula to calculate the charge for the second item on the order.

To enter a formula using the mouse:

1. Click cell **H14** to make it the active cell.

2. Type **=**. The equal sign indicates that you are entering a formula. Any cell you click from now on inserts the cell reference of the selected cell into the formula until you complete the formula by pressing the Enter or Tab key.

> Be sure to type = first; otherwise, Excel will not recognize the entry as a formula.

3. Click cell **F14**. The cell reference is inserted into the formula in the formula bar. At this point, any cell you click changes the cell reference used in the formula. The cell reference isn't locked until you type an operator.

4. Type ***** to enter the multiplication operator. The cell reference for cell F14 is locked in the formula, and the next cell you click will be inserted after the operator.

5. Click cell **G14** to enter its cell reference in the formula. The formula is complete.

6. Press the **Enter** key. Cell H14 displays the value $24.55, which is the charge for the second item ordered.

Copying and Pasting Formulas

Sometimes you will need to repeat the same formula throughout a worksheet. Rather than retyping the formula, you can copy a formula from one cell and paste it into another cell. When you copy a formula, Excel places the formula into the **Clipboard**, which is a temporary storage location for text and graphics. When you paste, Excel takes the formula from the Clipboard and inserts it into the selected cell or range. Excel adjusts the cell references in the formula to reflect the formula's new location in the worksheet. This occurs because you usually want to copy the actions of a formula rather than the specific value the formula generates. In this case, the formula's action is to multiply the price of the item ordered by the quantity. By copying and pasting the formula, you can quickly repeat that action for every item listed in the worksheet.

You will copy the formula you entered in cell H14 to the range H15:H17 to calculate the charges on the remaining three items in Leslie Ritter's order. By copying and pasting the formula, you will save time and avoid potential mistakes from retyping the formula.

To copy and paste the formula:

1. Click cell **H14** to select the cell that contains the formula you want to copy.

2. On the Home tab, in the Clipboard group, click the **Copy** button (or press the **Ctrl+C** keys). Excel copies the formula to the Clipboard. A blinking green box surrounds the cell being copied.

3. Select the range **H15:H17**. You want to paste the formula into these cells.

4. In the Clipboard group, click the **Paste** button (or press the **Ctrl+V** keys). Excel pastes the formula into the selected cells, adjusting each formula so that the charge calculated for each ordered item is based on the corresponding values within that row. A button appears below the selected range, providing options for pasting formulas and values. See Figure 1-25.

Figure 1-25   **Copied and pasted formula**

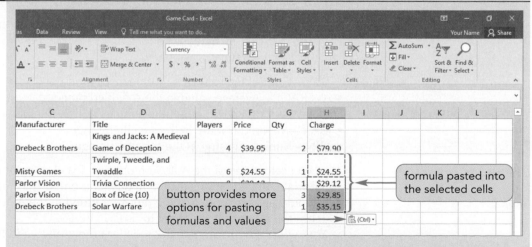

5. Click cell **H15** and verify that the formula =F15*G15 appears in the formula bar. The formula was updated to reflect the cell references in the corresponding row.

6. Click the other cells in column H, and verify that the corresponding formulas are entered in those cells.

Simplifying Formulas with Functions

In addition to cell references and operators, formulas can also contain functions. A function is a named operation that replaces the arithmetic expression in a formula. Functions are used to simplify long or complex formulas. For example, to add the values from cells A1 through A10, you could enter the following long formula:

```
=A1+A2+A3+A4+A5+A6+A7+A8+A9+A10
```

Or, you could use the SUM function to calculate the sum of those cell values by entering the following formula:

```
=SUM(A1:A10)
```

In both instances, Excel adds the values in cells A1 through A10, but the SUM function is faster and simpler to enter and less prone to a typing error. You should always use a function, if one is available, in place of a long, complex formula. Excel supports more than 300 different functions from the fields of finance, business, science, and engineering, including functions that work with numbers, text, and dates.

Introducing Function Syntax

Every function follows a set of rules, or **syntax**, which specifies how the function should be written. The general syntax of all Excel functions is

```
FUNCTION(arg1,arg2,…)
```

where *FUNCTION* is the function name, and *arg1*, *arg2*, and so forth are values used by that function. For example, the SUM function shown above uses a single argument, A1:A10, which is the range reference of the cells whose values will be added. Some functions do not require any arguments and are entered as *FUNCTION()*. Functions without arguments still require the opening and closing parentheses but do not include a value within the parentheses.

Entering Functions with AutoSum

A fast and convenient way to enter commonly used functions is with AutoSum. The AutoSum button includes options to insert the following functions into a select cell or cell range:

- SUM—Sum of the values in the specified range
- AVERAGE—Average value in the specified range
- COUNT—Total count of numeric values in the specified range
- MAX—Maximum value in the specified range
- MIN—Minimum value in the specified range

After you select one of the AutoSum options, Excel determines the most appropriate range from the available data and enters it as the function's argument. You should always verify that the range included in the AutoSum function matches the range that you want to use.

You will use AutoSum to enter the SUM function to add the total charges for Leslie Ritter's order.

To use AutoSum to enter the SUM function:

▶ 1. Click cell **G18** to make it the active cell, type **Subtotal** as the label, and then press the **Tab** key to make cell H18 the active cell.

2. On the Home tab, in the Editing group, click the **AutoSum button arrow**. The button's menu opens and displays five common functions: Sum, Average, Count Numbers, Max (for maximum), and Min (for minimum).

3. Click **Sum** to enter the SUM function. The formula =SUM(H13:H17) is entered in cell H18. The cells being summed are selected and highlighted on the worksheet so you can quickly confirm that Excel selected the appropriate range from the available data. A ScreenTip appears below the formula describing the function's syntax. See Figure 1-26.

Figure 1-26   **SUM function being entered with AutoSum button**

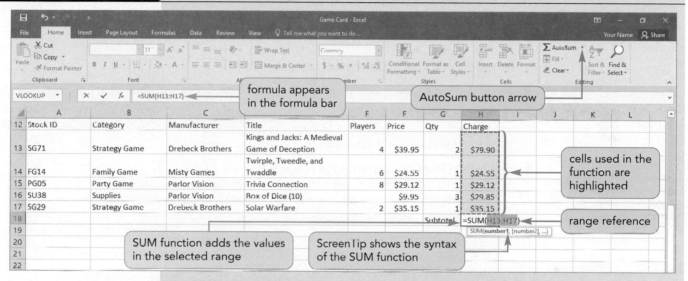

4. Press the **Enter** key to accept the formula. The subtotal of the charges on the order returned by the SUM function is $198.57.

AutoSum makes entering a commonly used formula such as the SUM function fast and easy. However, AutoSum can determine the appropriate range reference to include only when the function is adjacent to the cells containing the values you want to summarize. If you need to use a function elsewhere in the worksheet, you will have to select the range reference to include or type the function yourself.

Each purchase made at Game Card is subject to a 5 percent sales tax and, in the case of online orders, a $4.75 handling fee. You will add these to the Customer Order worksheet so you can calculate the total charge for Leslie Ritter's order.

To add the sales tax and handling fee to the worksheet:

1. Click cell **G11**, type **Sales Tax** as the label, and then press the **Tab** key to make cell H11 the active cell.

2. In cell H11, type **5%** as the sales tax rate, and then press the **Enter** key. The sales tax rate is entered in the cell and can be used in other calculations. The value is displayed with the % symbol but is stored as the equivalent decimal value 0.05.

3. Click cell **G19** to make it the active cell, type **Tax** as the label, and then press the **Tab** key to make cell H19 the active cell.

4. Type **=H11*H18** as the formula to calculate the sales tax on the customer order, and then press the **Enter** key. The formula multiplies the sales tax value in cell H11 by the order subtotal value in cell H18. The value $9.93 is displayed in cell H19, which is 5 percent of the subtotal value of $198.57.

5. In cell G20, type **Handling** as the label, and then press the **Tab** key to make cell H20 the active cell. You will enter the handling fee in this cell.

6. Type **$4.75** as the handling fee, and then press the **Enter** key.

The last part of the customer order is to calculate the total cost by adding the subtotal, the tax, and the handling fee. Rather than using AutoSum, you will type the SUM function so you can enter the correct range reference for the function. You can type the range reference or select the range in the worksheet. Remember that you must type parentheses around the range reference.

To calculate the total order cost:

1. In cell G21, type **TOTAL** as the label, and then press the **Tab** key.

2. Type **=SUM(** in cell H21 to enter the function name and the opening parenthesis. As you begin to type the function, a ScreenTip lists the names of all functions that start with S.

3. Type **H18:H20** to specify the range reference of the cells you want to add. The cells referenced in the function are selected and highlighted on the worksheet so you can quickly confirm that you entered the correct range reference.

Make sure the cell reference in the function matches the range you want to calculate.

4. Type **)** to complete the function, and then press the **Enter** key. The value of the SUM function appears in cell H21, indicating that the total charge for the order is $213.25.

5. Click cell **H21** to select the cell and its formula. See Figure 1-27.

Figure 1-27   **Total charge calculated for the order**

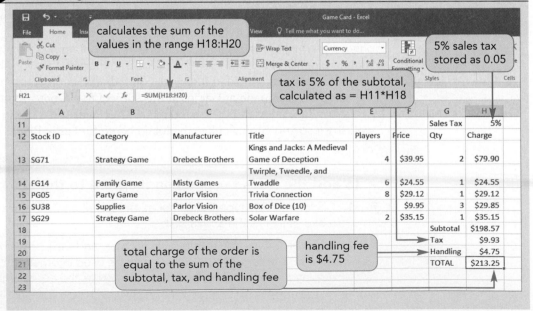

The SUM function makes it simple to quickly add the values in a group of cells.

PROSKILLS

Problem Solving: Writing Effective Formulas

You can use formulas to quickly perform calculations and solve problems. First, identify the problem you need to solve. Then, gather the data needed to solve the problem. Finally, create accurate and effective formulas that use the data to answer or resolve the problem. Follow these guidelines:

- **Keep formulas simple.** Use functions in place of long, complex formulas whenever possible. For example, use the SUM function instead of entering a formula that adds individual cells, which makes it easier to confirm that the formula is making an accurate calculation as it provides answers needed to evaluate the problem.

- **Do not hide data values within formulas.** The worksheet displays formula results, not the actual formula. For example, to calculate a 5 percent interest rate on a currency value in cell A5, you could enter the formula =0.05*A5. However, this doesn't show how the value is calculated. A better approach places the value 0.05 in a cell accompanied by a descriptive label and uses the cell reference in the formula. If you place 0.05 in cell A6, the formula =A6*A5 would calculate the interest value. Other people can then easily see the interest rate as well as the resulting interest, ensuring that the formula is solving the right problem.

- **Break up formulas to show intermediate results.** When a worksheet contains complex computations, other people can more easily comprehend how the formula results are calculated when different parts of the formula are distinguished. For example, the formula =SUM(A1:A10)/SUM(B1:B10) calculates the ratio of two sums but hides the two sum values. Instead, enter each SUM function in a separate cell, such as cells A11 and B11, and use the formula =A11/B11 to calculate the ratio. Other people can see both sums and the value of their ratio in the worksheet and better understand the final result, which makes it more likely that the best problem resolution will be selected.

- **Test formulas with simple values.** Use values you can calculate in your head to confirm that your formula works as intended. For example, using 1s or 10s as the input values lets you easily figure out the answer and verify the formula.

Finding a solution to a problem requires accurate data and analysis. With workbooks, this means using formulas that are easy to understand, clearly showing the data being used in the calculations, and demonstrating how the results are calculated. Only then can you be confident that you are choosing the best problem resolution.

Modifying a Worksheet

As you develop a worksheet, you might need to modify its content and structure to create a more logical organization. Some ways you can modify a worksheet include moving cells and ranges, inserting rows and columns, deleting rows and columns, and inserting and deleting cells.

Moving and Copying a Cell or Range

One way to move a cell or range is to select it, position the pointer over the bottom border of the selection, drag the selection to a new location, and then release the mouse button. This technique is called **drag and drop** because you are dragging the range and dropping it in a new location. If the drop location is not visible, drag the selection to the edge of the workbook window to scroll the worksheet, and then drop the selection.

You can also use the drag-and-drop technique to copy cells by pressing the Ctrl key as you drag the selected range to its new location. A copy of the original range is placed in the new location without removing the original range from the worksheet.

Moving or Copying a Cell or Range

- Select the cell or range you want to move or copy.
- Move the pointer over the border of the selection until the pointer changes shape.
- To move the range, click the border and drag the selection to a new location (or to copy the range, hold down the Ctrl key and drag the selection to a new location).

or

- Select the cell or range you want to move or copy.
- On the Home tab, in the Clipboard group, click the Cut or Copy button (or right-click the selection, and then click Cut or Copy on the shortcut menu, or press the Ctrl+X or Ctrl+C keys).
- Select the cell or the upper-left cell of the range where you want to paste the content.
- In the Clipboard group, click the Paste button (or right-click the selection and then click Paste on the shortcut menu, or press the Ctrl+V keys).

Peter wants the subtotal, tax, handling, and total values in the range G18:H21 moved down one row to the range G19:H22 to set those calculations off from the list of items in the customer order. You will use the drag-and-drop method to move the range.

To drag and drop the range G18:H21:

1. Select the range **G18:H21**. These are the cells you want to move.

2. Point to the **bottom border** of the selected range so that the pointer changes to ⛶.

3. Press and hold the mouse button to change the pointer to ⇖, and then drag the selection down one row. Do not release the mouse button. A ScreenTip appears, indicating that the new range of the selected cells will be G19:H22. A dark green border also appears around the new range. See Figure 1-28.

Figure 1-28 **Range being moved**

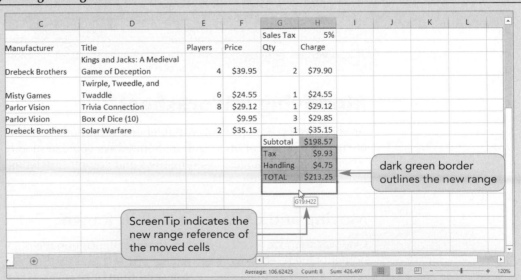

4. Make sure the ScreenTip displays the range G19:H22, and then release the mouse button. The selected cells move to their new location.

Some people find dragging and dropping a select cell range difficult and awkward, particularly if the selected range is large or needs to move a long distance in the worksheet. In those situations, it is often more efficient to cut or copy and paste the cell contents. Cutting moves the selected content, whereas copying duplicates the selected content in the new location.

Peter wants the worksheet to include a summary of the customer order starting in row 3. You will cut the customer contact information and the item listing from range A3:A22 and paste it into range A9:H28, freeing up space for the order information.

To cut and paste the customer contact information:

1. Click cell **A3** to select it.

2. Press the **Ctrl+Shift+End** keys to extend the selection to the last cell in the lower-right corner of the worksheet (cell H22).

3. On the Home tab, in the Clipboard group, click the **Cut** button (or press the **Ctrl+X** keys). The range is surrounded by a moving border, indicating that it has been cut.

4. Click cell **A9** to select it. This is the upper-left corner of the range where you want to paste the range that you cut.

5. In the Clipboard group, click the **Paste** button (or press the **Ctrl+V** keys). The range A3:H22 is pasted into the range A9:H28. Note that the cell references in the formulas were automatically updated to reflect the new location of those cells in the worksheet.

Using the COUNT Function

Sometimes you will want to know how many unique items are included in a range, such as the number of different items in the customer order. To calculate that value, you use the COUNT function

=COUNT(*range*)

TIP

To count cells containing non-numeric values, use the COUNTA function.

where *range* is the range of cells containing numeric values to be counted. Note that any cell in the range containing a non-numeric value is not counted in the final tally.

You will include the count of the number of different items from the order in the summary information. The summary will also display the order ID (a unique number assigned by Game Card to identify the order), the shipping date, and the type of delivery (overnight, two-day, or standard) in the freed-up space at the top of the worksheet. In addition, Peter wants the total charge for the order to be displayed with the order summary so that he does not have to scroll to the bottom of the worksheet to find that value.

To add the order summary:

1. Click cell **A3**, type **Order ID** as the label, press the **Tab** key, type **C10489** in cell B3, and then press the **Enter** key. The order ID is entered, and cell A4 is the active cell.

2. Type **Shipping Date** as the label in cell A4, press the **Tab** key, type **4/3/2017** in cell B4, and then press the **Enter** key. The shipping date is entered, and cell A5 is the active cell.

3. Type **Delivery** as the label in cell A5, press the **Tab** key, type **standard** in cell B5, and then press the **Enter** key. The delivery type is entered, and cell A6 is the active cell.

4. Type **Items Ordered** as the label in cell A6, and then press the **Tab** key. Cell B6 is the active cell. Now you will enter the COUNT function to determine the number of different items ordered.

5. In cell B6, type **=COUNT(** to begin the function.

6. With the insertion point still blinking in cell B6, select the range **G19:G23**. The range reference is entered as the argument for the COUNT function.

7. Type **)** to complete the function, and then press the **Enter** key. Cell B6 displays the value 5, indicating that five items were ordered by Leslie Ritter. Cell A7 is the active cell.

8. Type **Total Charge** as the label in cell A7, and then press the **Tab** key to make cell B7 the active cell.

9. Type **=** to start the formula, and then click cell **H28** to enter its cell reference in the formula in cell B7. The formula you created, =H28, tells Excel to display the contents of cell H28 in the current cell.

10. Press the **Enter** key to complete the formula. The total charge of $213.25 appears in cell B7. See Figure 1-29.

Figure 1-29	Customer order summary

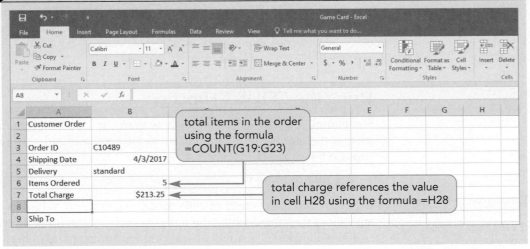

Inserting a Column or Row

You can insert a new column or row anywhere within a worksheet. When you insert a new column, the existing columns are shifted to the right, and the new column has the same width as the column directly to its left. When you insert a new row, the existing rows are shifted down, and the new row has the same height as the row above it. Because inserting a new row or column moves the location of the other cells in the worksheet, any cell references in a formula or function are updated to reflect the new layout.

Inserting or Deleting a Column or Row

To insert a column or row:
- Select the column(s) or row(s) where you want to insert the new column(s) or row(s). Excel will insert the same number of columns or rows as you select to the left of the selected columns or above the selected rows.
- On the Home tab, in the Cells group, click the Insert button (or right-click a column or row heading or selected column and row headings, and then click Insert on the shortcut menu; or press the Ctrl+Shift+= keys).

To delete a column or row:
- Select the column(s) or row(s) you want to delete.
- On the Home tab, in the Cells group, click the Delete button (or right-click a column or row heading or selected column and row headings, and then click Delete on the shortcut menu; or press the Ctrl+- keys).

Peter informs you that the customer order report for Leslie Ritter is missing an item. You need to insert a new row directly above the entry for the Trivia Connection game in which you'll write the details of the missing item.

To insert a row for the missing order item:

1. Click the **row 21** heading to select the entire row.

2. On the Home tab, in the Cells group, click the **Insert** button (or press the **Ctrl+Shift+=** keys). A new row is inserted below row 20 and becomes the new row 21.

3. Enter **SU25** in cell A21, enter **Supplies** in cell B21, enter **Drebeck Brothers** in cell C21, enter **Miniatures Set (12)** in cell D21, leave cell E21 blank, enter **$23.55** in cell F21, and then enter **2** in cell G21.

4. Click cell **H20** to select the cell with the formula for calculating the item charge, and then press the **Ctrl+C** keys to copy the formula in that cell.

5. Click cell **H21** to select the cell where you want to insert the formula, and then press the **Ctrl+V** keys to paste the formula into the cell.

6. Click cell **H26**. See Figure 1-30.

Figure 1-30   New row inserted into the worksheet

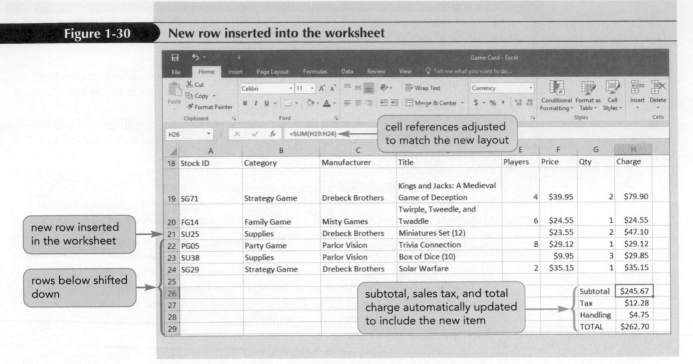

Notice that the formula in cell H26 is now =SUM(H19:H24). The range reference was updated to reflect the inserted row. Also, the tax amount increased to $12.28 based on the new subtotal value of $245.67, and the total charge increased to $262.70 because of the added item. Also, the result of the COUNT function in cell B6 increased to 6 to reflect the item added to the order.

Deleting a Row or Column

You can also delete rows or columns from a worksheet. **Deleting** removes the data from the row or column as well as the row or column itself. The rows below the deleted row shift up to fill the vacated space. Likewise, the columns to the right of the deleted column shift left to fill the vacated space. Also, all cell references in the worksheet are adjusted to reflect the change. You click the Delete button in the Cells group on the Home tab to delete selected rows or columns.

Deleting a column or row is not the same as clearing a column or row. **Clearing** removes the data from the selected row or column but leaves the blank row or column in the worksheet. You press the Delete key to clear the contents of the selected row or column, which leaves the worksheet structure unchanged.

Leslie Ritter did not order the box of dice created by Parlor Vision. Peter asks you to delete the row containing this item from the report.

To delete the row containing the box of dice from the order:

▶ **1.** Click the **row 23** heading to select the entire row.

▶ **2.** On the Home tab, in the Cells group, click the **Delete** button (or press the **Ctrl+-** keys). Row 23 is deleted, and the rows below it shift up to fill the space.

All of the cell references in the worksheet are again updated automatically to reflect the impact of deleting row 23. The subtotal value in cell H25 is now $215.82, which is the sum of the range H19:H23. The sales tax in cell H26 decreases to $10.79. The total cost of the order decreases to $231.36. Also, the result of the COUNT function in cell B6 decreases to 5 to reflect the item deleted from the order. As you can see, one of the great advantages of using Excel is that it modifies the formulas to reflect the additions and deletions you make to the worksheet.

Inserting and Deleting a Range

You can also insert or delete cell ranges within a worksheet. When you use the Insert button to insert a range of cells, the existing cells shift down when the selected range is wider than it is long, and they shift right when the selected range is longer than it is wide, as shown in Figure 1-31. When you use the Insert Cells command, you specify whether the existing cells shift right or down, or whether to insert an entire row or column into the new range.

Figure 1-31   Cells inserted into a worksheet

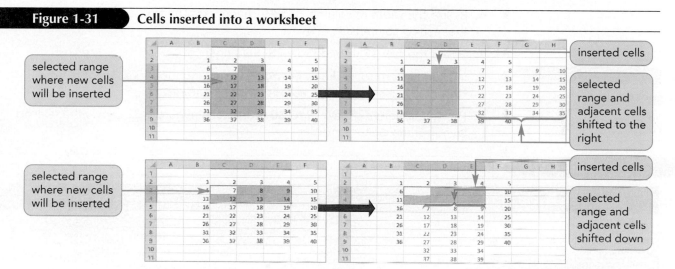

The process works in reverse when you delete a range. As with deleting a row or column, the cells adjacent to the deleted range either move up or left to fill in the space vacated by the deleted cells. The Delete Cells command lets you specify whether you want to shift the adjacent cells left or up or whether you want to delete the entire column or row.

When you insert or delete a range, cells that shift to a new location adopt the width of the columns they move into. As a result, you might need to resize columns and rows in the worksheet.

REFERENCE

Inserting or Deleting a Range

- Select a range that matches the range you want to insert or delete.
- On the Home tab, in the Cells group, click the Insert button or the Delete button.

or

- Select the range that matches the range you want to insert or delete.
- On the Home tab, in the Cells group, click the Insert button arrow and then click Insert Cells, or click the Delete button arrow and then click Delete Cells (or right-click the selected range, and then click Insert or Delete on the shortcut menu).
- Click the option button for the direction to shift the cells, columns, or rows.
- Click the OK button.

Peter wants you to insert a range into the worksheet for the ID that Game Card uses to identify the items it stocks in its store. You will insert these new cells into the range A17:A28, shifting the adjacent cells to the right.

To insert a range for the store IDs:

1. Select the range **A17:A28**.

2. On the Home tab, in the Cells group, click the **Insert button arrow**. A menu of insert options appears.

3. Click **Insert Cells**. The Insert dialog box opens.

4. Verify that the **Shift cells right** option button is selected.

5. Click the **OK** button. New cells are inserted into the selected range, and the adjacent cells move to the right. The cell contents do not fit well in the columns and rows they shifted into, so you will resize the columns and rows.

6. Resize the width of column E to **25** characters. The text is easier to read in the resized columns.

7. Select the row **19** through row **23** headings.

TIP

You can also autofit by double-clicking the bottom border of row 23.

8. In the Cells group, click the **Format** button, and then click **AutoFit Row Height**. The selected rows autofit to their contents.

9. Resize the height of row 19 to **30 (40 pixels)**. Figure 1-32 shows the revised layout of the customer order.

Figure 1-32   Range added to worksheet

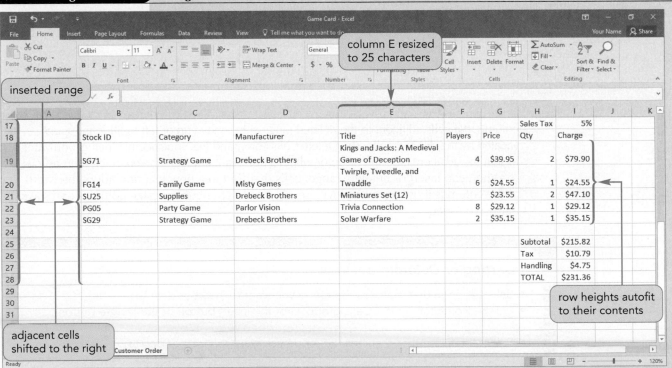

Notice that even though the customer orders will be entered only in the range A18:A23 you selected the range A17:A28 to retain the layout of the page design. Selecting the additional rows ensures that the sales tax and summary values still line up with the Qty and Charge columns. Whenever you insert a new range, be sure to consider its impact on the layout of the entire worksheet.

Hiding and Unhiding Rows, Columns, and Worksheets

Workbooks can become long and complicated, filled with formulas and data that are important for performing calculations but are of little interest to readers. In those situations, you can simplify these workbooks for readers by hiding rows, columns, and even worksheets. Although the contents of hidden cells cannot be seen, the data in those cells is still available for use in formulas and functions throughout the workbook.

Hiding a row or column essentially decreases that row height or column width to 0 pixels. To a hide a row or column, select the row or column heading, click the Format button in the Cells group on the Home tab, point to Hide & Unhide on the menu that appears, and then click Hide Rows or Hide Columns. The border of the row or column heading is doubled to mark the location of hidden rows or columns.

A worksheet often is hidden when the entire worksheet contains data that is not of interest to the reader and is better summarized elsewhere in the document. To hide a worksheet, make that worksheet active, click the Format button in the Cells group on the Home tab, point to Hide & Unhide, and then click Hide Sheet.

Unhiding redisplays the hidden content in the workbook. To unhide a row or column, click in a cell below the hidden row or to the right of the hidden column, click the Format button, point to Hide & Unhide, and then click Unhide Rows or Unhide Columns. To unhide a worksheet, click the Format button, point to Hide & Unhide, and then click Unhide Sheet. The Unhide dialog box opens. Click the sheet you want to unhide, and then click the OK button. The hidden content is redisplayed in the workbook.

Although hiding data can make a worksheet and workbook easier to read, be sure never to hide information that is important to the reader.

Peter wants you to add the store ID used by Game Card to identify each item it sells. You will use Flash Fill to create these unique IDs.

Using Flash Fill

Flash Fill enters text based on patterns it finds in the data. As shown in Figure 1-33, Flash Fill generates customer names from the first and last names stored in the adjacent columns in the worksheet. To enter the rest of the names, you press the Enter key; to continue typing the names yourself, you press the Esc key.

Figure 1-33   **Text being entered with Flash Fill**

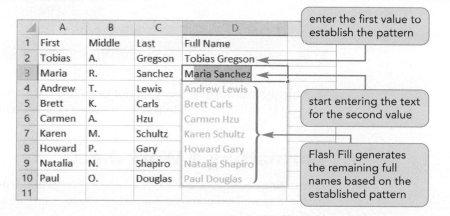

	A	B	C	D
1	First	Middle	Last	Full Name
2	Tobias	A.	Gregson	Tobias Gregson
3	Maria	R.	Sanchez	Maria Sanchez
4	Andrew	T.	Lewis	Andrew Lewis
5	Brett	K.	Carls	Brett Carls
6	Carmen	A.	Hzu	Carmen Hzu
7	Karen	M.	Schultz	Karen Schultz
8	Howard	P.	Gary	Howard Gary
9	Natalia	N.	Shapiro	Natalia Shapiro
10	Paul	O.	Douglas	Paul Douglas
11				

enter the first value to establish the pattern

start entering the text for the second value

Flash Fill generates the remaining full names based on the established pattern

Flash Fill works best when the pattern is clearly recognized from the values in the data. Be sure to enter the data pattern in the column or row right next to the related data. The data used to generate the pattern must be in a rectangular grid and cannot have blank columns or rows.

The store IDs used by Game Card combines the Stock ID and the first name of the item. For example, the Kings and Jacks game has a Stock ID of SG71, so its Store ID is SG71-Kings. Rather than typing this for every item in the customer order, you'll use Flash Fill to complete the data entry.

To enter the Store IDs using Flash Fill:

▶ **1.** Click cell **A18**, type **Store ID** as the label, and then press the **Enter** key. The label is entered in cell A18, and cell A19 is now the active cell.

▶ **2.** Type **SG71-Kings** as the Store ID, and then press **Enter** to make cell A20 active.

▶ **3.** Type **FG** in cell A20. As soon as you complete those two characters Flash Fill generates the remaining entries in the column based on the pattern you entered. See Figure 1-34.

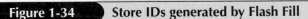

| Figure 1-34 | Store IDs generated by Flash Fill |

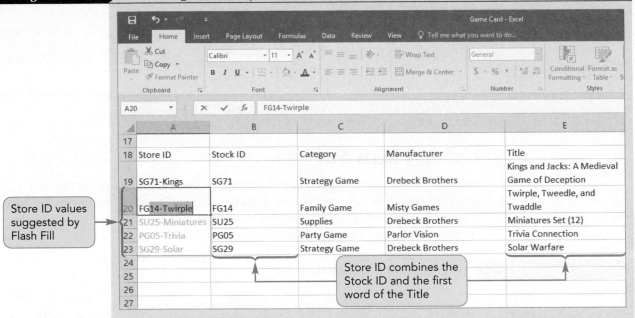

Store ID values suggested by Flash Fill

Store ID combines the Stock ID and the first word of the Title

▶ **4.** Press the **Enter** key to accept the suggested entries.

Note that Flash Fill enters text, not formulas. If you edit or replace an entry originally used by Flash Fill, the content generated by Flash Fill will not be updated.

Formatting a Worksheet

Formatting changes a workbook's appearance to make the content of a worksheet easier to read. Two common formatting changes are adding cell borders and changing the font size of text.

Adding Cell Borders

Sometimes you want to include lines along the edges of cells to enhance the readability of rows and columns of data. You can do this by adding a border to the left, top, right, or bottom edge of a cell or range. You can also specify the thickness of and the number of lines in the border. This is especially helpful when a worksheet is printed because the gridlines that surround the cells are not printed by default; they appear on the worksheet only as a guide.

Peter wants to add borders around the cells that contain content in the Customer Order worksheet to make the content easier to read.

To add borders around the worksheet cells:

1. Select the range **A3:B7**. You will add borders around all of the cells in the selected range.

2. On the Home tab, in the Font group, click the **Borders button arrow** ⊞ ▾, and then click **All Borders**. Borders are added around each cell in the range. The Borders button changes to reflect the last selected border option, which in this case is All Borders. The name of the selected border option appears in the button's ScreenTip.

3. Select the nonadjacent range **A9:B16,H17:I17**. You will add borders around each cell in the selected range.

4. In the Font group, click the **All Borders** button ⊞ to add borders to all of the cells in the selected range.

5. Select the nonadjacent range **A18:I23,H25:I28**, and then click the **All Borders** button ⊞ to add borders to all of the cells in the selected range.

6. Click cell **A28** to deselect the cells. Figure 1-35 shows the borders added to the worksheet cells.

Figure 1-35   Borders added to cells

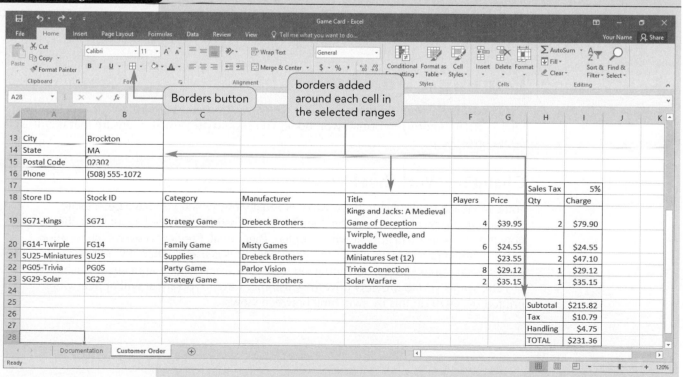

Changing the Font Size

Changing the size of text in a sheet provides a way to identify different parts of a worksheet, such as distinguishing a title or section heading from data. The size of the text is referred to as the font size and is measured in points. The default font size for worksheets is 11 points, but it can be made larger or smaller as needed. You can resize text in selected cells using the Font Size button in the Font group on the Home tab. You can also use the Increase Font Size and Decrease Font Size buttons to resize cell content to the next higher or lower standard font size.

Peter wants you to increase the size of the worksheet title to 26 points to make it more prominent.

To change the font size of the worksheet title:

1. Click cell **A1** to select the cell containing the worksheet title.

2. On the Home tab, in the Font group, click the **Font Size button arrow** ``11 ▾`` to display a list of font sizes, and then click **28**. The worksheet title changes to 28 points. See Figure 1-36.

| Figure 1-36 | Font size of the cell increased |

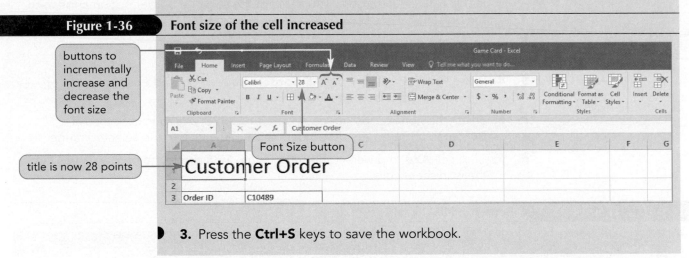

buttons to incrementally increase and decrease the font size

Font Size button

title is now 28 points

Customer Order

3. Press the **Ctrl+S** keys to save the workbook.

Printing a Workbook

Now that you have finished the workbook, Peter wants you to print a copy of Leslie Ritter's order. Before you print a workbook, you should preview it to ensure that it will print correctly.

Changing Worksheet Views

You can view a worksheet in three ways. Normal view, which you have been using throughout this module, shows the contents of the worksheet. Page Layout view shows how the worksheet will appear when printed. Page Break Preview displays the location of the different page breaks within the worksheet. This is useful when a worksheet will span several printed pages, and you need to control what content appears on each page.

Peter wants you to preview how the Customer Order worksheet will appear when printed. You will do this by switching between views.

To switch the Customer Order worksheet to different views:

1. Click the **Page Layout** button on the status bar. The page layout of the worksheet appears in the workbook window.

2. On the Zoom slider, click the **Zoom Out** button until the percentage is **50%**. The reduced magnification makes it clear that the worksheet will spread over two pages when printed. See Figure 1-37.

Figure 1-37   Worksheet in Page Layout view

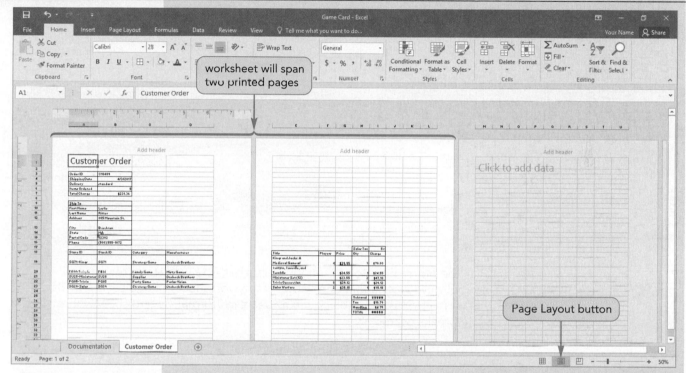

3. Click the **Page Break Preview** button on the status bar. The view switches to Page Break Preview, which shows only those parts of the current worksheet that will print. A dotted blue border separates one page from another.

4. Zoom the worksheet to **70%** so that you can more easily read the contents of the worksheet. See Figure 1-38.

TIP

You can relocate a page break by dragging the dotted blue border in the Page Break Preview window.

Figure 1-38   **Worksheet in Page Break Preview**

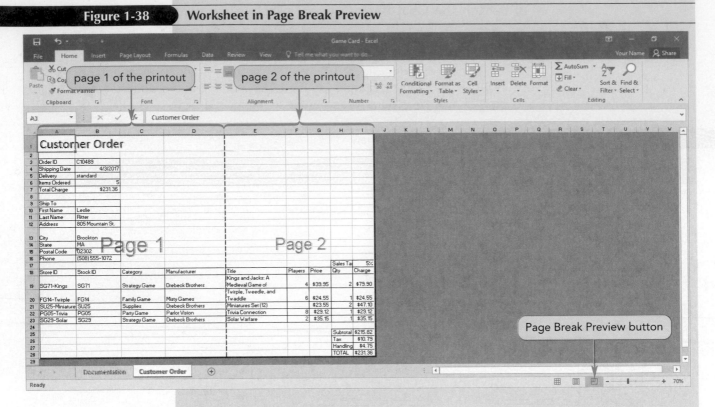

5. Click the **Normal** button ⊞ on the status bar. The worksheet returns to Normal view. Notice that after viewing the worksheet in Page Layout or Page Break Preview, a dotted black line appears in Normal view to show where the page breaks occurs.

Changing the Page Orientation

Page orientation specifies in which direction content is printed on the page. In **portrait orientation**, the page is taller than it is wide. In **landscape orientation**, the page is wider than it is tall. By default, Excel displays pages in portrait orientation. Changing the page orientation affects only the active sheet or sheets.

As you saw in Page Layout view and Page Break Preview, the Customer Order worksheet will print on two pages—columns A through D will print on the first page, and columns E through I will print on the second page, although the columns that print on each page may differ slightly depending on the printer. Peter wants the entire worksheet to print on a single page, so you'll change the page orientation from portrait to landscape.

To change the page orientation of the worksheet:

1. On the ribbon, click the **Page Layout** tab. The tab includes options for changing how the worksheet is arranged.

2. In the Page Setup group, click the **Orientation** button, and then click **Landscape**. The worksheet switches to landscape orientation.

3. Click the **Page Layout** button 🔲 on the status bar to switch to Page Layout view. The worksheet will still print on two pages.

Setting the Scaling Options

You can force the printout to a single page by **scaling** the printed output. There are several options for scaling your printout. You can scale the width or the height of the printout so that all of the columns or all of the rows fit on a single page. You can also scale the printout to fit the entire worksheet (both columns and rows) on a single page. If the worksheet is too large to fit on one page, you can scale the print to fit on the number of pages you select. You can also scale the worksheet to a percentage of its size. For example, scaling a worksheet to 50% reduces the size of the sheet by half when it is sent to the printer. When scaling a printout, make sure that the worksheet is still readable after it is resized. Scaling affects only the active worksheet, so you can scale each worksheet to best fit its contents.

Peter asks you to scale the printout so that all of the Customer Order worksheet fits on one page in landscape orientation.

To scale the printout of the Customer Order worksheet:

1. On the Page Layout tab, in the Scale to Fit group, click the **Width** arrow, and then click **1 page** on the menu that appears. All of the columns in the worksheet now fit on one page.

   If more rows are added to the worksheet, Peter wants to ensure that they still fit within a single sheet.

2. In the Scale to Fit group, click the **Height** arrow, and then click **1 page**. All of the rows in the worksheet now fit on one page. See Figure 1-39.

Figure 1-39   **Printout scaled to fit on one page**

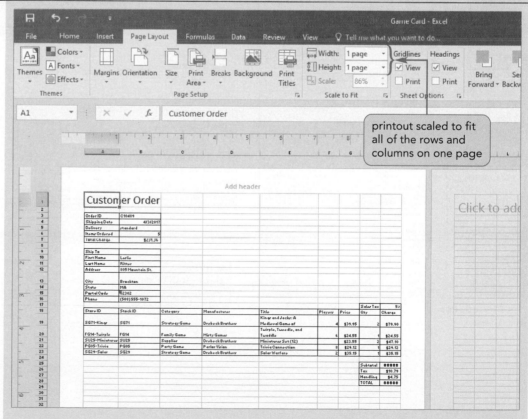

printout scaled to fit all of the rows and columns on one page

Setting the Print Options

TIP

To print the gridlines or the column and row headings, click the corresponding Print check box in the Sheet Options group on the Page Layout tab.

You can print the contents of a workbook by using the Print screen in Backstage view. The Print screen provides options for choosing where to print, what to print, and how to print. For example, you can specify the number of copies to print, which printer to use, and what to print. You can choose to print only the selected cells, only the active sheets, or all of the worksheets in the workbook that contain data. The printout will include only the data in the worksheet. The other elements in the worksheet, such as the row and column headings and the gridlines around the worksheet cells, will not print by default. The preview shows you exactly how the printed pages will look with the current settings. You should always preview before printing to ensure that the printout looks exactly as you intended and avoid unnecessary reprinting.

Peter asks you to preview and print the customer order workbook now.

Note: Check with your instructor first to make sure you should complete the steps for printing the workbook.

To preview and print the workbook:

1. On the ribbon, click the **File** tab to display Backstage view.

2. Click **Print** in the navigation bar. The Print screen appears with the print options and a preview of the Customer Order worksheet printout. See Figure 1-40.

Figure 1-40 **Print screen in Backstage view**

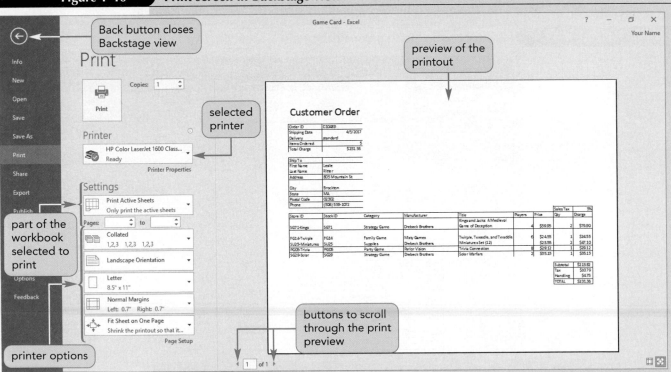

> **3.** Click the **Printer** button, and then click the **printer** to which you want to print, if it is not already selected. By default, Excel will print only the active sheet.

> **4.** In the Settings options, click the top button, and then click **Print Entire Workbook** to print all of the sheets in the workbook—in this case, both the Documentation and the Customer Order worksheets. The preview shows the first sheet in the workbook—the Documentation worksheet. Note that this sheet is still in the default portrait orientation.

> **5.** Below the preview, click the **Next Page** button ▶ to view the Customer Order worksheet. As you can see, the Customer Order worksheet will print on a single page in landscape orientation.

> **6.** If you are instructed to print, click the **Print** button to send the contents of the workbook to the specified printer. If you are not instructed to print, click the **Back** button ⬅ in the navigation bar to exit Backstage view.

Viewing Worksheet Formulas

Most of the time, you will be interested in only the final results of a worksheet, not the formulas used to calculate those results. However, in some cases, you might want to view the formulas used to develop the workbook. This is particularly useful when you encounter unexpected results and you want to examine the underlying formulas, or you want to discuss your formulas with a colleague. You can display the formulas instead of the resulting values in cells.

If you print the worksheet while the formulas are displayed, the printout shows the formulas instead of the values. To make the printout easier to read, you should print the worksheet gridlines as well as the row and column headings so that cell references in the formulas are easy to find in the printed version of the worksheet.

You will look at the Customer Order worksheet with the formulas displayed.

To display the cell formulas:

> **1.** Make sure the Customer Order worksheet is in Page Layout view.

TIP

You can also display formulas in a worksheet by clicking the Show Formulas button in the Formula Auditing group on the Formulas tab.

> **2.** Press the **Ctrl+`** keys (the grave accent symbol ` is usually located above the Tab key). The worksheet changes to display all of the formulas instead of the resulting values. Notice that the columns widen to display all of the formula text in the cells.

> **3.** Look at the entry in cell B4. The underlying numeric value of the shipping date (42828) is displayed instead of the formatted date value (4/3/2017). See Figure 1-41.

Figure 1-41   Worksheet with formulas displayed

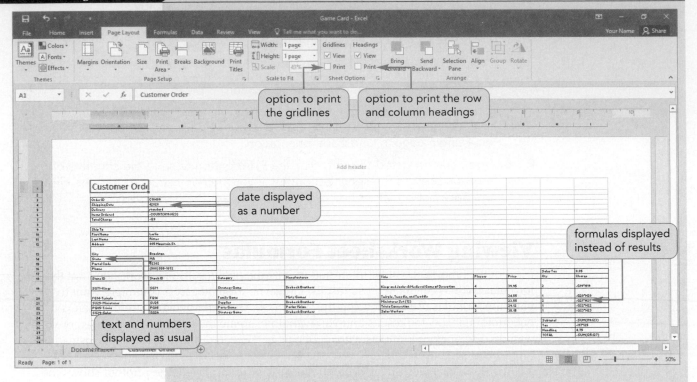

It's good practice to hide the formulas when you are done reviewing them.

4. Press the **Ctrl+`** keys to hide the formulas and display the resulting values.

5. Click the **Normal** button ⊞ on the status bar to return the workbook to Normal view.

Saving a Workbook with a New Filename

Whenever you click the Save button on the Quick Access Toolbar or press the Ctrl+S keys, the workbook file is updated to reflect the latest content. If you want to save a copy of the workbook with a new filename or to a different location, you need to use the Save As command. When you save a workbook with a new filename or to a different location, the previous version of the workbook remains stored as well.

You have completed the customer order workbook for Game Card. Peter wants to use the workbook as a model for other customer order reports. You will save the workbook with a new filename to avoid overwriting the Leslie Ritter order. Then you'll clear the information related to that order, leaving the formulas intact. This new, revised workbook will then be ready for the next customer order.

To save the workbook with a new filename:

1. Press the **Ctrl+S** keys to save the workbook. This ensures that the final copy of the workbook contains the formatted version of Leslie Ritter's order.

2. On the ribbon, click the **File** tab to display Backstage view, and then click **Save As** on the navigation bar. The Save As screen is displayed.

TIP

Save the workbook with the new name before making changes to avoid inadvertently saving your edits to the wrong file.

3. Click the **Browse** button. The Save As dialog box opens so you can save the workbook with a new filename or to a new location.

4. Navigate to the location specified by your instructor.

5. In the File name box, type **Game Card Order** as the new filename.

6. Click the **Save** button. The workbook is saved with the new filename, and you are returned to the workbook window.

7. Select the range **B3:B5**, right-click the selected range to open the shortcut menu, and then click **Clear Contents** to clear the contents of the order ID, shipping date, and delivery cells.

8. Select the nonadjacent range **B10:B16,A19:H23**, and then press the **Delete** key to clear the contact information for Leslie Ritter and the list of items she ordered.

9. Select cell **I27**, and then clear the handling fee.

10. Click cell **A3** to make that cell the active cell the next time this workbook is opened.

11. Press the **Ctrl+S** keys to save the workbook.

12. Click the **Close** button ☒ on the title bar (or press the **Ctrl+W** keys). The workbook closes, and the Excel program closes.

Peter is pleased with the workbook you created. With the calculations already in place in the new workbook, he will be able to quickly enter new customer orders and see the calculated charges without having to recreate the worksheet.

Session 1.2 Quick Check

REVIEW

1. What formula would you enter to add the values in cells C1, C2, and C3? What function would you enter to achieve the same result?

2. What formula would you enter to count how many numeric values are in the range D21:D72?

3. If you insert cells into the range C1:D10, shifting the cells to the right, what is the new location of the data that was previously in cell F4?

4. Cell E11 contains the formula =SUM(D1:D20). How does this formula change if a new row is inserted above row 5?

5. Describe four ways of viewing the content of a workbook in Excel.

6. How are page breaks indicated in Page Break Preview?

7. What orientation would you use to make the printed page wider than it is tall?

8. How do you display the formulas used in a worksheet instead of the formula results?

Review Assignments

There are no Data Files needed for the Review Assignment.

Game Card also buys and resells used games and gaming supplies. Peter wants to use Excel to record recent used purchases made by the store. The workbook should list every item the company has ordered, provide information about the item, and calculate the total order cost. Complete the following:

1. Create a new, blank workbook, and then save the workbook as **Game List** in the location specified by your instructor.
2. Rename the Sheet1 worksheet as **Documentation**, and then enter the data shown in Figure 1-42 in the specified cells.

Figure 1-42   Documentation sheet data

Cell	Text
A1	Game Card
A3	Author
A4	Date
A5	Purpose
B3	*your name*
B4	*current date*
B5	To record game acquisitions for Game Card

3. Set the font size of the title text in cell A1 to **28** points.
4. Add a new worksheet after the Documentation sheet, and then rename the sheet as **Game Purchases**.
5. In cell A1, enter the text **Game Purchases**. Set the font size of this text to **28** points.
6. In cell A3, enter the text **Date** as the label. In cell B3, enter the date **4/3/2017**.
7. In the range A5:F10, enter the data shown in Figure 1-43.

Figure 1-43   Game list

Purchase Number	Category	Manufacturer	Title	Players	Cost
83	Strategy Game	Drebeck Brothers	Secrets of Flight: Building an Airforce	6	$29.54
84	Family Game	Parlor Vision	Brain Busters and Logic Gaming	8	$14.21
85	Strategy Game	Aspect Gaming	Inspection Deduction	3	$18.91
86	Party Game	Miller Games	Bids and Buys	8	$10.81
87	Family Game	Aspect Gaming	Buzz Up	4	$21.43

8. Insert cells into the range A5:A10, shifting the other cells to the right.
9. In cell A5, enter **Stock ID** as the label. In cell A6, enter **SG83** as the first Stock ID, and then type **FG** in cell A7, allowing Flash Fill to enter the remaining Stock IDs.
10. Set the width of column A to **12** characters, columns B through D to **18** characters, and column E to **25** characters.
11. Wrap text in the range E6:E10 so that the longer game titles appear on multiple lines within the cells.

12. Autofit the heights of rows 5 through 10.

13. Move the game list in the range A5:G10 to the range A8:G13.

14. In cell F15, enter **TOTAL** as the label. In cell G15, enter a formula with the SUM function to calculate the sum of the costs in the range G9:G13.

15. In cell A4, enter **Total Items** as the label. In cell B4, enter a formula with the COUNT function to count the number of numeric values in the range G9:G13.

16. In cell A5, enter **Total Cost**. In cell B5, enter a formula to display the value from cell G15.

17. In cell A6, enter **Average Cost** as the label. In cell B6, enter a formula that divides the total cost of the purchased games (listed in cell B5) by the number of games purchased (listed in cell B4).

18. Add borders around each cell in the nonadjacent range A3:B6,A8:G13,F15:G15.

19. For the Game Purchases worksheet, change the page orientation to landscape and scale the worksheet to print on a single page for both the width and the height. If you are instructed to print, print the entire workbook.

20. Display the formulas in the Game Purchases worksheet. If you are instructed to print, print the entire worksheet.

21. Save and close the workbook.

Case Problem 1

Data File needed for this Case Problem: Donation.xlsx

Henderson Pediatric Care Center   Kari Essen is a fundraising coordinator for the Pediatric Care Center located in Henderson, West Virginia. Kari is working on a report detailing recent donations to the center and wants you to enter this data into an Excel workbook. Complete the following:

1. Open the **Donation** workbook located in the Excel1 > Case1 folder included with your Data Files. Save the workbook as **Donation List** in the location specified by your instructor.

2. In the Documentation sheet, enter your name in cell B3 and the date in cell B4.

3. Increase the font size of the text in cell A1 to 28 points.

4. Add a new sheet to the end of the workbook, and rename it as **Donor List**.

5. In cell A1 of the Donor List worksheet, enter **Donor List** as the title, and then set the font size to 28 points.

6. In the range A6:H13, enter the donor information shown in Figure 1-44. Enter the ZIP code data as text rather than as numbers.

Figure 1-44   **Donation list**

Last Name	First Name	Street	City	State	ZIP	Phone	Donation
Robert	Richards	389 Felton Avenue	Miami	FL	33127	(305) 555-5685	$150
Barbara	Hopkins	612 Landers Street	Caledonia	IL	61011	(815) 555-5865	$75
Daniel	Vaughn	45 Lyman Street	Statesboro	GA	30461	(912) 555-8564	$50
Parker	Penner	209 South Street	San Francisco	CA	94118	(415) 555-7298	$250
Kenneth	More	148 7th Street	Newberry	IN	47449	(812) 555-8001	$325
Robert	Simmons	780 10th Street	Houston	TX	77035	(713) 555-5266	$75
Donna	Futrell	834 Kimberly Lane	Ropesville	TX	79358	(806) 555-6186	$50

7. Set the width of columns A through D to 25 characters. Set the width of column G to 15 characters.

8. In cell A2, enter the text **Total Donors**. In cell A3, enter the text **Total Donations**. In cell A4, enter the text **Average Donation**.

9. In cell B2, enter a formula that counts how many numeric values are in the range H7:H13.

10. In cell B3, enter a formula that calculates the sum of the donations in the range H7:H13.

11. In cell B4, enter a formula that calculates the average donation by dividing the value in cell B3 by the value in cell B2.

12. Add borders around the nonadjacent range A2:B4,A6:H13.

13. Set the page orientation of the Donor List to landscape.

14. Scale the worksheet to print on a single page for both the width and the height. If you are instructed to print the worksheet, print the Donor List sheet.

15. Display the formulas in the Donor List worksheet. If you are instructed to print, print the worksheet.

16. Save and close the workbook.

Case Problem 2

CREATE

Data File needed for this Case Problem: Balance.xlsx

Scott Kahne Tool & Die   Cheryl Hippe is a financial officer at Scott Kahne Tool & Die, a manufacturing company located in Mankato, Minnesota. Every month the company publishes a balance sheet, a report that details the company's assets and liabilities. Cheryl asked you to create the workbook with the text and formulas for this report. Complete the following:

1. Open the **Balance** workbook located in the Excel1 > Case2 folder included with your Data Files. Save the workbook as **Balance Sheet** in the location specified by your instructor.

2. In the Documentation sheet, enter your name in cell B3 and the date in cell B4.

3. Go to the Balance Sheet worksheet. Set the font size of the title in cell A1 to 28 points.

4. In cell A2, enter the text **Statement for March 2017**.

5. Set the width of columns A and E to 30 characters. Set the width of columns B, C, F, and G to 12 characters. Set the width of column D to 4 characters. (*Hint:* Hold down the Ctrl key as you click the column headings to select both adjacent and nonadjacent columns.)

6. Set the font size of the text in cells A4, C4, E4, and G4 to 18 points.

7. Set the font size of the text in cells A5, E5, A11, E11, A14, E15, A19, E20, and A24 to 14 points.

8. Enter the values shown in Figure 1-45 in the specified cells.

Figure 1-45   **Assets and liabilities**

Current Assets	Cell	Value
Cash	B6	$123,000
Accounts Receivable	B7	$75,000
Inventories	B8	$58,000
Prepaid Insurance	B9	$15,000
Long-Term Investments	**Cell**	**Value**
Available Securities	B12	$29,000
Tangible Assets	**Cell**	**Value**
Land	B15	$49,000
Building and Equipment	B16	$188,000
Less Accumulated Depreciation	B17	-$48,000
Intangible Assets	**Cell**	**Value**
Goodwill	B20	$148,000
Other Assets	B22	$14,000
Current Liabilities	**Cell**	**Value**
Accounts Payable	F6	$62,000
Salaries	F7	$14,000
Interest	F8	$12,000
Notes Payable	F9	$38,000
Long-Term Liabilities	**Cell**	**Value**
Long-Term Notes Payable	F12	$151,000
Mortgage	F13	$103,000
Stockholders' Equity	**Cell**	**Value**
Capital Stock	F16	$178,000
Retained Earnings	F17	$98,000
Comprehensive Income/Loss	F18	-$5,000

9. In cell C9, enter a formula to calculate the sum of the Current Assets in the range B6:B9.

10. In cell C12, enter a formula to display the value of B12.

11. In cell C17, enter a formula to calculate the sum of the Tangible Assets in the range B15:B17.

12. In cells C20 and C22, enter formulas to display the values of cells B20 and B22, respectively.

13. In cell C24, enter a formula to calculate the total assets in the balance sheet by adding cells C9, C12, C17, C20, and C22. Set the font size of the cell to 14 points.

14. In cell G9, enter a formula to calculate the sum of the Current Liabilities in the range F6:F9.

15. In cell G13, enter a formula to calculate the sum of the Long-Term Liabilities in the range F12:F13.

16. In cell G18, enter a formula to calculate the sum of the Stockholders' Equity in the range F16:F18.

17. In cell G20, calculate the Total Liabilities and Equity for the company by adding the values of cells G9, G13, and G18. Set the font size of the cell to 14 points.

18. Check your calculations. In a balance sheet the total assets (cell C24) should equal the total liabilities and equity (cell G20).

19. Set the page layout orientation to landscape and the Balance Sheet worksheet to print to one page for both the width and height.

20. Preview the worksheet on the Print screen in Backstage view, and then save and close the workbook.

Case Problem 3

Data File needed for this Case Problem: FTP.xslx

Succeed Gym Allison Palmer is the owner of Succeed Gym, an athletic club in Austin, Texas, that specializes in coaching men and women aspiring to participate in triathlons, marathons, and other endurance sports. During the winter, Allison runs an indoor cycling class in which she tracks the progress of each student's fitness. One measure of fitness is FTP (Functional Threshold Power). Allison has recorded FTP levels from her students over five races and wants you to use the functions described in Figure 1-46 to analyze this data so that she can track the progress of her class and of individual students.

Figure 1-46 **Excel functions**

Function	Description
=AVERAGE(*range*)	Calculates the average of the values from the specified *range*
=MEDIAN(*range*)	Calculates the median or midpoint of the values from the specified *range*
=MIN(*range*)	Calculates the minimum of the values from the specified *range*
=MAX(*range*)	Calculates the maximum of the values from the specified *range*

Complete the following:

1. Open the **FTP** workbook located the Excel1 > Case3 folder included with your Data Files. Save the workbook as **FTP Report** in the location specified by your instructor.
2. In the Documentation sheet, enter your name in cell B3 and the date in cell B4.
3. Go to the Race Results worksheet. Change the font size of the title in cell A1 to 28 points.
4. Set the width of column A and B to 15 characters. Set the width of column I to 2 characters.
5. In the range J4:M4, enter the labels **Median**, **Average**, **Min**, and **Max**.
⊕ **Explore** 6. In cell J5, use the MEDIAN function to calculate the median (midpoint) of the FTP values of races 1 through 5 for Diana Bartlett in the range D5:H5. Copy the formula in cell J5 to the range J6:J28 to calculate the median FTP values for the other riders.
⊕ **Explore** 7. In cell K5, use the AVERAGE function to calculate the average the FTP value for races 1 through 5 for Diana Bartlett. Copy the formula to calculate the averages for the other riders.
⊕ **Explore** 8. In cell L5, use the MIN function to return the minimum FTP value for Diana Bartlett. Copy the formula to calculate the minimums for the other riders.
⊕ **Explore** 9. In cell M5, use the MAX function to return the maximum FTP value for Diana Bartlett. Copy the formula to calculate the maximums for the other riders.
10. In the range C30:C33, enter the labels **Median**, **Average**, **Min**, and **Max** to record summary information for each of the five races.
11. In cell D30, use the MEDIAN function to calculate the median FTP value from the range D5:D28. Copy the formula to the range E30:H30 to determine the median values for the other four races.
12. In the range D31:H31, use the AVERAGE function to calculate the average FTP value for each race.
13. In the range D32:H32, use the MIN function to calculate the minimum value for each race.
14. In the range D33:H33, use the MAX function to calculate the maximum FTP value for each race.
15. Move the range A4:M33 to the range A10:M39 to create space for additional summary calculations at the top of the worksheet.

16. In the range A3:A7, enter the labels **Class Size**, **Class Average**, **Class Median**, **Class Minimum**, and **Class Maximum**.

✛ **Explore** 17. In cell B3, use the COUNTA function to count the number of entries in the range A11:A34.

18. In cell B4, use the AVERAGE function to calculate the average of all FTP values in the range D11:H34.

19. In cell B5, use the MEDIAN function to calculate the median of all FTP values in the range D11:H34.

20. In cell B6, use the MIN function to calculate the minimum FTP value in the range D11:H34.

21. In cell B7, use the MAX function to calculate the maximum FTP value in the range D11:H34.

22. Set the page layout orientation for the Race Results worksheet to portrait and scale the worksheet so that its width and height fit on one page.

23. View the worksheet in Page Layout view, return to Normal view, and then save and close the workbook.

Case Problem 4

TROUBLESHOOT

Data File needed for this Case Problem: Service.xlsx

Welch Home Appliance Repair   Stefan Welch is the owner of Welch Home Appliance Repair in Trenton, New Jersey. Stefan wants to use Excel to record data from his service calls to calculate the total charge on each service call and the total charges from all service calls within a given period. Unfortunately, the workbook he has created contains several errors. He has asked you to fix the errors and complete the workbook. Complete the following:

1. Open the **Service** workbook located in the Excel1 > Case4 folder included with your Data Files. Save the workbook as **Service Calls** in the location specified by your instructor.

2. In the Documentation sheet, enter your name in cell B3 and the date in cell B4.

3. Go to the Call Sheet worksheet. Insert cells in the range A7:A27, shifting the other cells to the right.

4. In cell A7, enter **Cust ID** as the label. In cell A8, enter **Jensen-5864** (the customer's last name and last four digits on the phone number) as the customer ID for Patricia Jensen. Use Flash Fill to enter in the remaining customer IDs in the column.

5. Resize the columns of the Call Sheet worksheet so that all of the column labels and the cell contents are completely displayed.

⚙ **Troubleshoot** 6. There is a problem with the some of the customer ZIP codes. New Jersey ZIP codes begin with a 0, and these leading zeros are not showing up in the contact information. Revise the text of the ZIP code values to correct this problem.

⚙ **Troubleshoot** 7. The formula in cell L8 that calculates the total number of billable hours for the first customer is not correct. Instead of showing the number of hours, it displays the value as a percentage of a day. Fix this problem by revising the formula so that it multiplies the difference between the value in K8 and J8 by 24. (*Hint:* Use parentheses to enclose the expression that calculates the difference between starting and ending times so that the difference is calculated first.)

8. Copy the formula you entered for cell L8 to calculate the total billable hours for the rest of the entries in column L.

9. The total charge for each service call is equal to the hourly rate multiplied by the number of hours plus the charge for parts. In cell O8, enter a formula to calculate the total service charge for the first customer, and then copy that formula to calculate the rest of the service charges in column O.

10. In cell B4, enter a formula that uses the COUNT function to count the total number of service calls.

⚙ **Troubleshoot** 11. In cell B5, Stefan entered a formula to calculate the total charges from all of the service calls. Examine the formula, and correct the expression so that it adds all of the service call charges.

12. Insert two new rows above row 5.
13. In cell A5, enter the label **Total Hours**. In cell B5, enter function to calculate the total number of hours from all of the service calls.
14. In cell A6, enter the label **Average Charge**. In cell B6, enter a formula that calculates the average charge per call by dividing the total charges by the total number of calls.
15. Add borders around the cells in the nonadjacent range A4:B7,A9:O29.
16. Set the page layout of the Call Sheet worksheet so that it prints on a single page in landscape orientation.
17. View the worksheet in Page Break Preview, return to Normal view, and then save and close the workbook.

Formatting Workbook Text and Data

Creating a Sales Report

OBJECTIVES

Session 2.1
- Change fonts, font style, and font color
- Add fill colors and a background image
- Create formulas to calculate sales data
- Format numbers as currency and percentages
- Format dates and times
- Align, indent, and rotate cell contents
- Merge a group of cells

Session 2.2
- Use the AVERAGE function
- Apply cell styles
- Copy and paste formats with the Format Painter
- Find and replace text and formatting
- Change workbook themes
- Highlight cells with conditional formats
- Format a worksheet for printing
- Set the print area, insert page breaks, add print titles, create headers and footers, and set margins

Case | *Morning Bean*

Carol Evans is a sales manager at Morning Bean, a small but growing chain of shops specializing in coffee, tea, and other hot drinks. Carol needs to develop a workbook for the upcoming sales conference that will provide information on sales and profits for stores located in the Northwest region of the country. Carol already started the workbook by entering sales data for the previous years. She wants you to use this financial data to calculate summary statistics and then format the workbook before it's distributed to stockholders attending the conference.

EXCEL

STARTING DATA FILES

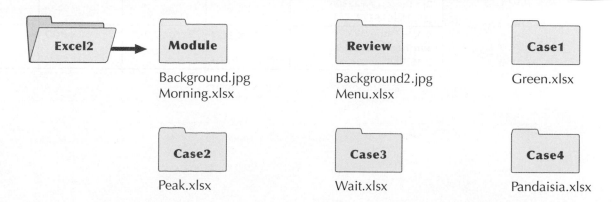

Excel2 → **Module**

Background.jpg
Morning.xlsx

Review

Background2.jpg
Menu.xlsx

Case1

Green.xlsx

Case2

Peak.xlsx

Case3

Wait.xlsx

Case4

Pandaisia.xlsx

Session 2.1 Visual Overview:

The Font group has buttons for setting the font, font size, font color, and **font style**, such as **bold**, *italic*, or underline.

You can format text strings within a cell in Edit mode.

Accounting format lines up numbers in a column by their currency symbol and decimal point; negative numbers are in parentheses.

A **font** is a set of characters that employ the same typeface, such as Arial, Times New Roman, and Courier.

You can **merge**, or combine, several cells into one cell. This content is centered in the merged range A11:A13.

You can rotate content in a cell.

The Alignment group has buttons for setting horizontal and vertical alignment, orientation, and indents; wrapping text in cells; and merging cells.

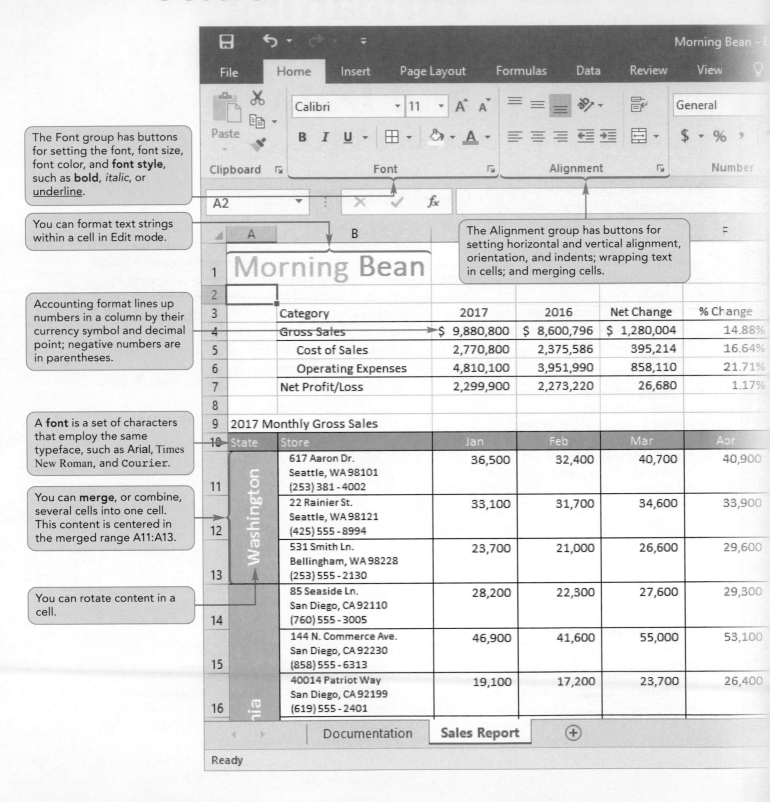

Category	2017	2016	Net Change	% Change
Gross Sales	$ 9,880,800	$ 8,600,796	$ 1,280,004	14.88%
Cost of Sales	2,770,800	2,375,586	395,214	16.64%
Operating Expenses	4,810,100	3,951,990	858,110	21.71%
Net Profit/Loss	2,299,900	2,273,220	26,680	1.17%

2017 Monthly Gross Sales

State	Store	Jan	Feb	Mar	Apr
Washington	617 Aaron Dr. Seattle, WA 98101 (253) 381 - 4002	36,500	32,400	40,700	40,900
	22 Rainier St. Seattle, WA 98121 (425) 555 - 8994	33,100	31,700	34,600	33,900
	531 Smith Ln. Bellingham, WA 98228 (253) 555 - 2130	23,700	21,000	26,600	29,600
California	85 Seaside Ln. San Diego, CA 92110 (760) 555 - 3005	28,200	22,300	27,600	29,300
	144 N. Commerce Ave. San Diego, CA 92230 (858) 555 - 6313	46,900	41,600	55,000	53,100
	40014 Patriot Way San Diego, CA 92199 (619) 555 - 2401	19,100	17,200	23,700	26,400

Documentation | **Sales Report** | ⊕

Ready

Formatting a Worksheet

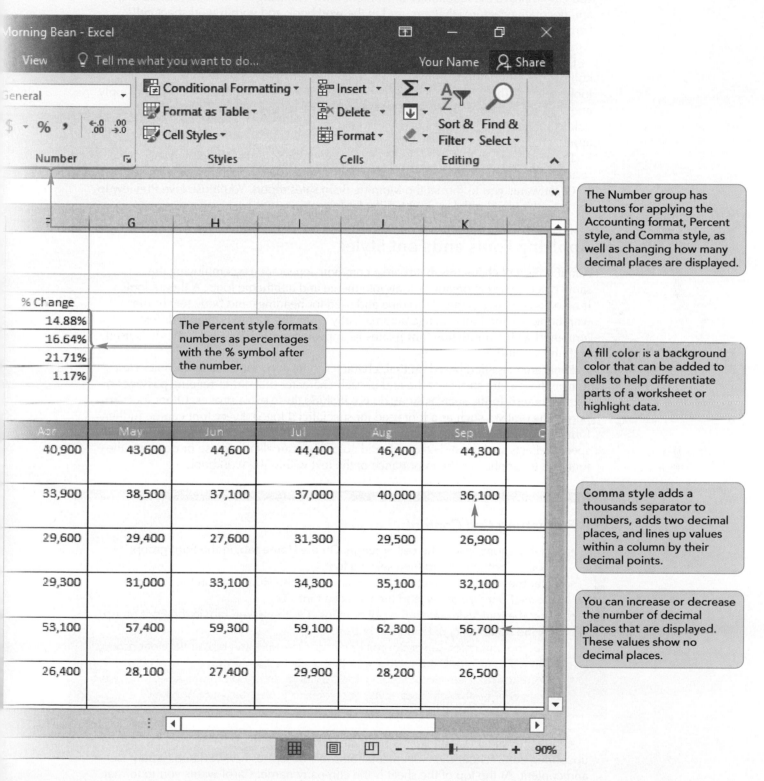

The Number group has buttons for applying the Accounting format, Percent style, and Comma style, as well as changing how many decimal places are displayed.

The Percent style formats numbers as percentages with the % symbol after the number.

A fill color is a background color that can be added to cells to help differentiate parts of a worksheet or highlight data.

Comma style adds a thousands separator to numbers, adds two decimal places, and lines up values within a column by their decimal points.

You can increase or decrease the number of decimal places that are displayed. These values show no decimal places.

Formatting Cell Text

You can improve the readability of workbooks by choosing the fonts, styles, colors, and decorative features that are used in the workbook and within worksheet cells. Formatting changes only the appearance of the workbook data—it does not affect the data itself.

Excel organizes complementary formatting options into themes. A **theme** is a collection of formatting for text, colors, and effects that give a workbook a unique look and feel. The Office theme is applied to workbooks by default, but you can apply another theme or create your own. You can also add formatting to a workbook using colors, fonts, and effects that are not part of the current theme. Note that a theme is applied to the entire workbook and can be shared between workbooks.

To help you choose the best formatting for your workbooks, **Live Preview** shows the results of each formatting option before you apply it to your workbook.

Carol wants you to format the Morning Bean sales report. You'll use Live Preview to see how the workbook looks with different formatting options.

Applying Fonts and Font Styles

A font is a set of characters that share a common appearance by employing the same typeface. Excel organizes fonts into theme and nontheme fonts. A **theme font** is associated with a particular theme and used for headings and body text in the workbook. Theme fonts change automatically when the theme is changed. Text formatted with a **nontheme font** retains its appearance no matter what theme is used with the workbook.

Fonts are classified based on their character style. **Serif fonts**, such as Times New Roman, have extra strokes at the end of each character that aid in reading passages of text. **Sans serif fonts**, such as Arial, do not include these extra strokes. Other fonts are purely decorative, such as a font used for specialized logos. Every font can be further formatted with a font style such as *italic*, **bold**, or ***bold italic***; with underline; and with special effects such as ~~strikethrough~~ and color. You can also increase or decrease the font size to emphasize the importance of the text within the workbook.

REFERENCE

Formatting Cell Content

- To set the font, select the cell or range. On the Home tab, in the Font group, click the Font arrow, and then select a font.
- To set the font size, select the cell or range. On the Home tab, in the Font group, click the Font Size arrow, and then select a font size.
- To set the font style, select the cell or range. On the Home tab, in the Font group, click the Bold, Italic, or Underline button.
- To set the font color, select the cell or range. On the Home tab, in the Font group, click the Font Color button arrow, and then select a theme or nontheme color.
- To format a text selection, double-click the cell to enter Edit mode, select the text to format, change the font, size, style, or color, and then press the Enter key.

Carol already entered the data and some formulas in her workbook for the upcoming conference. The Documentation sheet describes her workbook's purpose and content. At the top of the sheet is the company name. Carol wants you to format the name in large, bold letters using the default heading font from the Office theme.

To the format the company name:

1. Open the **Morning** workbook located in the **Excel2 > Module** folder included with your Data Files, and then save the workbook as **Morning Bean** in the location specified by your instructor.

2. In the Documentation sheet, enter your name in cell B4 and the date in cell B5.

3. Click cell **A1** to make it the active cell.

4. On the Home tab, in the Font group, click the **Font button arrow** to display a gallery of fonts available on your computer. Each name is displayed in its font. The first two fonts listed are the theme fonts for headings and body text–Calibri Light and Calibri.

5. Scroll down the Fonts gallery until you see Bauhaus 93 in the All Fonts list, and then point to **Bauhaus 93** (or another font). Live Preview shows the effect of the Bauhaus 93 font on the text in cell A1. See Figure 2-1.

Figure 2-1　　**Font gallery**

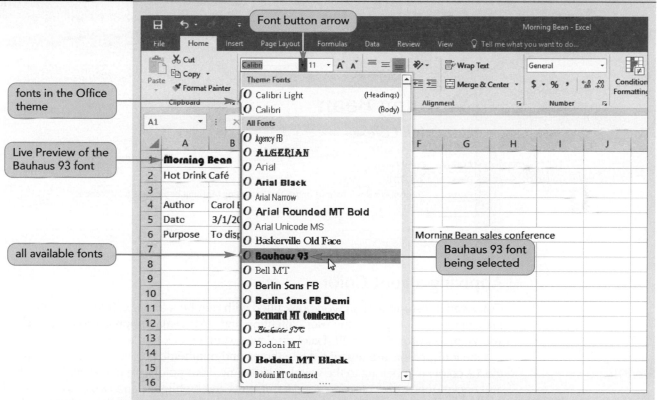

- Font button arrow
- fonts in the Office theme
- Live Preview of the Bauhaus 93 font
- all available fonts
- Morning Bean sales conference
- Bauhaus 93 font being selected

6. Point to three other fonts in the list to see the Live Preview of how the text in cell A1 would look with that font.

7. Click **Calibri Light** in the Theme Fonts list. The company name in cell A1 changes to the Calibri Light Font, the default headings font in the current theme.

8. In the Font group, click the **Font Size button arrow** 11 ▾ to display a list of font sizes, point to **26** to preview the text in that font size, and then click **26**. The company name changes to 26 points.

9. In the Font group, click the **Bold** button B (or press **Ctrl+B** keys). The text changes to bold.

▶ **10.** Click cell **A2** to make it the active cell. The cell with the company description is selected.

▶ **11.** In the Font group, click the **Font Size button arrow** `11 ▾`, and then click **18**. The company description changes to 18 points.

▶ **12.** In the Font group, click the **Italic** button `I` (or press the **Ctrl+I** keys). The company description in cell A2 is italicized.

▶ **13.** Select the range **A4:A6**, and then press the **Ctrl+B** keys. The text in the selected range changes to bold.

▶ **14.** Click cell **A7** to deselect the range. See Figure 2-2.

Figure 2-2	Formatted text in the Documentation sheet

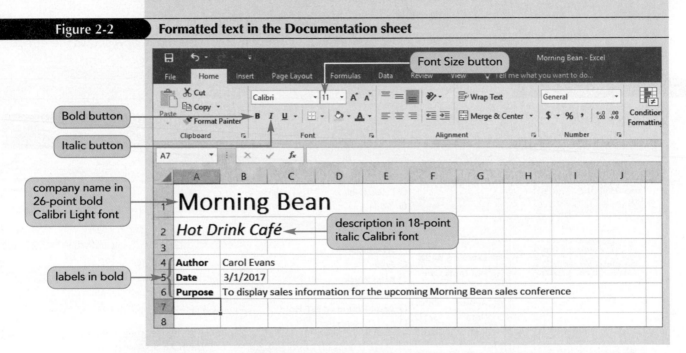

Applying a Font Color

Color can transform a plain workbook filled with numbers and text into a powerful presentation that captures the user's attention and adds visual emphasis to the points you want to make. By default, Excel displays text in a black font color.

Like fonts, colors are organized into theme and nontheme colors. **Theme colors** are the 12 colors that belong to the workbook's theme. Four colors are designated for text and backgrounds, six colors are used for accents and highlights, and two colors are used for hyperlinks (followed and not followed links). These 12 colors are designed to work well together and to remain readable in all combinations. Each theme color has five variations, or accents, in which a different tint or shading is applied to the theme color.

Ten **standard colors**—dark red, red, orange, yellow, light green, green, light blue, blue, dark blue, and purple—are always available regardless of the workbook's theme. You can open an extended palette of 134 standard colors. You can also create a custom color by specifying a mixture of red, blue, and green color values, making available 16.7 million custom colors—more colors than the human eye can distinguish. Some dialog boxes have an automatic color option that uses your Windows default text and background colors, usually black text on a white background.

INSIGHT

Creating Custom Colors

Custom colors let you add subtle and striking colors to a formatted workbook. To create custom colors, you use the **RGB Color model** in which each color is expressed with varying intensities of red, green, and blue. RGB color values are often represented as a set of numbers in the format

(red, green, blue)

where **red** is an intensity value assigned to red light, **green** is an intensity value assigned to green light, and **blue** is an intensity value assigned to blue light. The intensities are measured on a scale of 0 to 255—0 indicates no intensity (or the absence of the color) and 255 indicates the highest intensity. So, the RGB color value (255, 255, 0) represents a mixture of high-intensity red (255) and high-intensity green (255) with the absence of blue (0), which creates the color yellow.

To create colors in Excel using the RGB model, click the More Colors option located in a color menu or dialog box to open the Colors dialog box. In the Colors dialog box, click the Custom tab, and then enter the red, green, and blue intensity values. A preview box shows the resulting RGB color.

Carol wants the company name and description in the Documentation sheet to stand out. You will change the text in cell A1 and cell A2 to green.

To change the font color of the company name and description:

1. Select the range **A1:A2**.

2. On the Home tab, in the Font group, click the **Font Color button arrow** to display the gallery of theme and standard colors.

3. In the Standard Colors section, point to the **Green** color (the sixth color). The color name appears in a ScreenTip, and you see a Live Preview of the text with the green font color. See Figure 2-3.

Figure 2-3   **Font Color gallery**

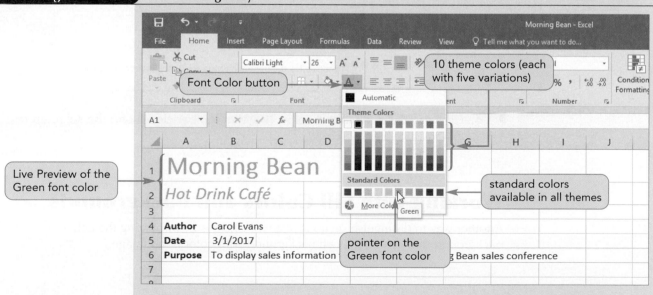

4. Click the **Green** color. The company name and description change to green.

Formatting Text Selections Within a Cell

In Edit mode, you can select and format selections of text within a cell. You can make these changes to selected text from the ribbon or from the Mini toolbar. The **Mini toolbar** contains buttons for common formatting options used for that selection. These same buttons appear on the ribbon.

Carol asks you to format the company name in cell A1 so that the text "Morning" appears in gold.

To format part of the company name in cell A1:

▶ **1.** Double-click cell **A1** to select the cell and enter Edit mode (or click cell **A1** and press the **F2** key). The status bar shows Edit to indicate that you are working with the cell in Edit mode. The pointer changes to the I-beam pointer.

▶ **2.** Drag the pointer over the word **Morning** to select it. A Mini toolbar appears above the selected text with buttons to change the font, size, style, and color of the selected text in the cell. In this instance, you want to change the font color.

▶ **3.** On the Mini toolbar, click the **Font Color button arrow** 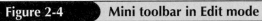, and then in the Themes Colors section, point to the **Gold, Accent 4** color (the eighth color). Live Preview shows the color of the selected text as gold. See Figure 2-4.

| Figure 2-4 | Mini toolbar in Edit mode |

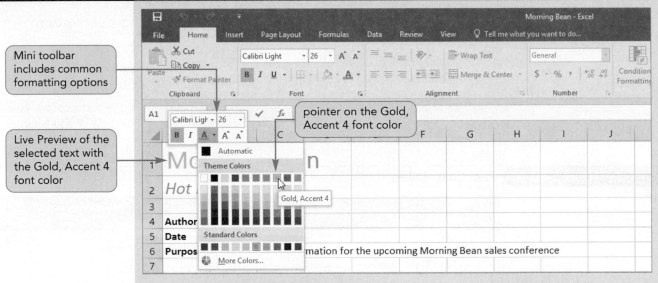

Mini toolbar includes common formatting options

pointer on the Gold, Accent 4 font color

Live Preview of the selected text with the Gold, Accent 4 font color

▶ **4.** Click the **Gold, Accent 4** color. The Mini toolbar closes and the selected text changes to the gold color.

Working with Fill Colors and Backgrounds

Another way to distinguish sections of a worksheet is by formatting the cell background. You can fill the cell background with color or an image.

Changing a Fill Color

TIP

To change a sheet tab's color, right-click its tab, point to Tab Color, and then click a color.

By default, worksheet cells do not include any background color. But background colors, also known as fill colors, can be helpful for distinguishing different parts of a worksheet or adding visual interest. The same selection of colors used to format the color of cell text can be used to format the cell background.

INSIGHT

Using Color to Enhance a Workbook

When used wisely, color can enhance any workbook. However, when used improperly, color can distract the user, making the workbook more difficult to read. As you format a workbook, keep in mind the following tips:

- Use colors from the same theme to maintain a consistent look and feel across the worksheets. If the built-in themes do not fit your needs, you can create a custom theme.
- Use colors to differentiate types of cell content and to direct users where to enter data. For example, format a worksheet so that formula results appear in cells without a fill color and users enter data in cells with a light gray fill color.
- Avoid color combinations that are difficult to read.
- Print the workbook on both color and black-and-white printers to ensure that the printed copy is readable in both versions.
- Understand your printer's limitations and features. Colors that look good on your monitor might not look as good when printed.
- Be sensitive to your audience. About 8 percent of all men and 0.5 percent of all women have some type of color blindness and might not be able to see the text when certain color combinations are used. Red-green color blindness is the most common, so avoid using red text on a green background or green text on a red background.

Carol wants you to change the background color of the range A4:A6 in the Documentation sheet to green and the font color to white.

To change the font and fill colors in the Documentation sheet:

1. Select the range **A4:A6**.

2. On the Home tab, in the Font group, click the **Fill Color button arrow** 🖉 ▾, and then click the **Green** color (the sixth color) in the Standard Colors section.

3. In the Font group, click the **Font Color button arrow** 🅰 ▾, and then click the **White, Background 1** color (the first color) in the Theme Colors section. The labels are formatted as white text on a green background.

4. Select the range **B4:B6**, and then format the cells with the **Green** font color and the **White, Background 1** fill color.

5. Increase the width of column B to **30** characters, and then wrap the text within the selected range.

6. Select the range **A4:B6**, and then add all borders around each of the selected cells.

7. Click cell **A7** to deselect the range. See Figure 2-5.

Figure 2-5   **Font and fill colors in the Documentation sheet**

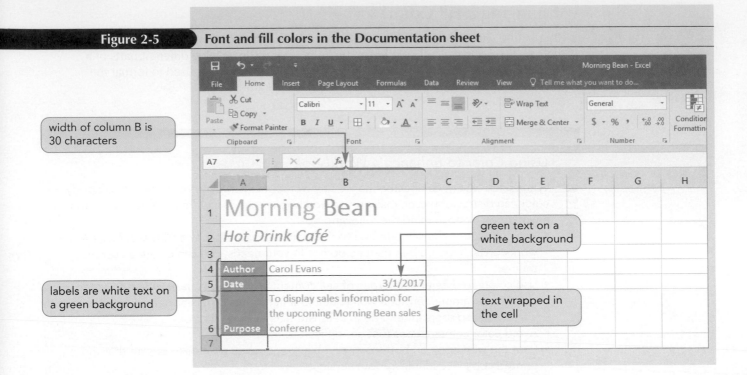

width of column B is
30 characters

green text on a
white background

labels are white text on
a green background

text wrapped in
the cell

Adding a Background Image

Another way to add visual interest to worksheets is with a background image. Many background images are based on textures such as granite, wood, or fibered paper. The image does not need to match the size of the worksheet; a smaller image can be repeated until it fills the entire sheet. Background images do not affect any cell's format or content. Fill colors added to cells appear on top of the image, covering that portion of the image.

Carol has provided an image that she wants you to use as the background of the Documentation sheet.

To add a background image to the Documentation sheet:

1. On the ribbon, click the **Page Layout** tab to display the page layout options.

2. In the Page Setup group, click the **Background** button. The Insert Pictures dialog box opens with options to search for an image file on your computer or local network, or use the Bing Image Search tool.

3. Click the **Browse** button next to the From a file label. The Sheet Background dialog box opens.

4. Navigate to the **Excel2 > Module** folder included with your Data Files, click the **Background** JPEG image file, and then click the **Insert** button. The image is added to the background of the Documentation sheet. The Background button changes to the Delete Background button, which you can click to remove background image. See Figure 2-6.

Figure 2-6   Background image added to the Documentation sheet

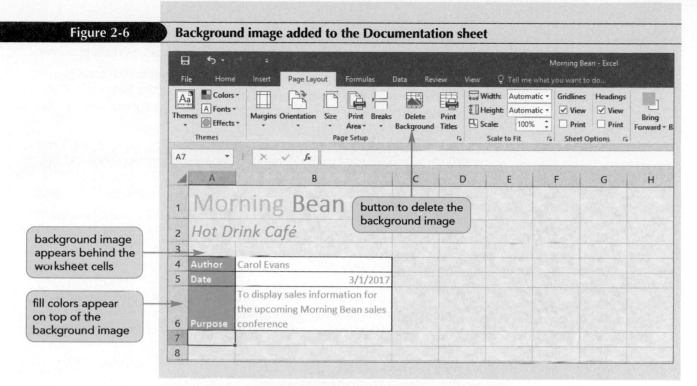

You've completed the formatting the Documentation sheet. Next, you'll work on the Sales Report worksheet.

Using Functions and Formulas to Calculate Sales Data

In the Sales Report worksheet, you will format the data on the gross sales from each of Morning Bean's 20 stores. The worksheet is divided into two areas. The table at the bottom of the worksheet displays gross sales for the past year for each month by store. The section at the top of the worksheet summarizes the sales over the past two years. Carol has compiled the following sales data:

- **Gross Sales**—the total amount of sales at all of the stores
- **Cost of Sales**—the cost of creating Morning Bean products
- **Operating Expenses**—the cost of running the individual stores including the employment and insurance costs
- **Net Profit/Loss**—the difference between the income from the gross sales and the total cost of sales and operating expenses
- **Units Sold**—the total number of menu items sold by Morning Bean during the year
- **Customers Served**—the total number of customers served by Morning Bean during the year

Carol wants you to calculate these sales statistics for the entire company and for each individual store. First, you will calculate Morning Bean's total gross sales from the past year and the company's overall net profit and loss.

To calculate Morning Bean's sales and profit/loss:

▶ **1.** Click the **Sales Report** sheet tab to make the Sales Report worksheet active.

▶ **2.** Click cell **C6**, type the formula **=SUM(C27:N46)** to calculate the total gross sales from all stores in the previous year, and then press the **Enter** key. Cell C6 displays 9880800, indicating that Morning Bean's total gross sales for the year were more than $9.8 million.

▶ **3.** In cell **C9**, enter the formula **=C6-(C7+C8)** to calculate the current year's net profit/loss, which is equal to the difference between the gross sales and the sum of the cost of sales and operating expenses. Cell C9 displays 2299900, indicating that the company's net profit for the year was close to $2.3 million.

▶ **4.** Copy the formula in cell **C9**, and then paste it into cell **D9** to calculate the net profit/loss for the previous year. Cell D9 displays 2273220, indicating that the company's net profit for that year was a little less than $2.3 million.

Morning Bean's net profit increased from the previous year, but it also opened two new stores during that time. Carol wants to investigate the sales statistics on a per-store basis by dividing the statistics you just calculated by the number of stores.

To calculate the per-store statistics:

▶ **1.** In cell **C16**, enter the formula **=C6/C23** to calculate the gross sales per store for the year. The formula returns 494040, indicating each Morning Bean store had, on average, almost $500,000 in gross sales during the year.

▶ **2.** In cell **C17**, enter the formula **=C7/C23** to calculate the cost of sales per store for the year. The formula returns the value 138540, indicating each Morning Bean store had a little more than $138,000 in sales cost.

▶ **3.** In cell **C18**, enter the formula **=C8/C23** to calculate the operating expenses per store for the year. The formula returns the value 240505, indicating that operating expense of a typical store was a little more than $240,000.

▶ **4.** In cell **C19**, enter the formula **=C9/C23** to calculate the net profit/loss per store for the year. The formula returns the value 114995, indicating that the net profit/loss of a typical store was about $115,000.

▶ **5.** In cell **C21**, enter the formula **=C11/C23** to calculate the units sold per store for the year. The formula returns the value 72655, indicating that a typical store sold more than 72,000 units.

▶ **6.** In cell **C22**, enter the formula **=C12/C23** to calculate the customers served per store during the year. The formula returns the value 10255, indicating that a typical store served more than 10,000 customers.

▶ **7.** Copy the formulas in the range **C16:C22** and paste them into the range **D16:D22**. The cell references in the formulas change to calculate the sales data for the previous year.

▶ **8.** Click cell **B24** to deselect the range. See Figure 2-7.

Figure 2-7 **Overall and per-store sales statistics**

	A	B	C	D	E	F	G	H
5		Category	2017	2016	Net Change	% Change		
6		Gross Sales	9880800	8600796				
7		Cost of Sales	2770800	2375586				
8		Operating Expenses	4810100	3951990				
9		Net Profit/Loss	2299900	2273220				
10								
11		Units Sold	1453100	1245600				
12		Customers Served	205100	189990				
13								
14		Sales Statistics per Store						
15		Category	2017	2016	Net Change	% Change		
16		Gross Sales	494040	477822				
17		Cost of Sales	138540	131977				
18		Operating Expenses	240505	219555				
19		Net Profit/Loss	114995	126290				
20								
21		Units Sold	72655	69200				
22		Customers Served	10255	10555				
23		Stores	20	18				

overall sales statistics

per-store sales statistics calculated by dividing the overall statistics by the number of stores

number of stores in the current and previous years

Documentation   Sales Report

Ready

Carol also wants to report how the company's sales and expenses have changed from the previous year to the current year. To do this, you will calculate the net change in the sales statistics as well as the percent change. The percent change is calculated using the following formula:

$$\text{percent change} = \frac{\text{current year value} - \text{previous year value}}{\text{previous year value}}$$

You will calculate the net change and percentage for all of the statistics in the Sales Report worksheet.

To calculate the net and percent changes:

1. In cell **E6**, enter the formula **=C6–D6** to calculate the difference in gross sales between the previous year and the current year. The formula returns 1280004, indicating that gross sales increased by about $1.28 million.

2. In cell **F6**, enter the formula **=(C6–D6)/D6** to calculate the percent change in gross sales from the previous year to the current year. The formula returns 0.1488239, indicating an increase in gross sales of about 14.88 percent.

   Next, you'll copy and paste the formulas in cells E6 and F6 to the rest of the sales data to calculate the net change and percent change from the previous year to the current year.

3. Select the range **E6:F6**, and then copy the selected range. The two formulas are copied to the Clipboard.

4. Select the nonadjacent range **E7:F9,E11:F12,E16:F19,E21:F23**, and then paste the formulas from the Clipboard into the selected range. The net and percent changes are calculated for the remaining sales data.

5. Click cell **B24** to deselect the range, and then scroll the worksheet up to display row 5. See Figure 2-8.

Be sure to include the parentheses as shown to calculate the percent change correctly.

Figure 2-8 **Net change and percent change from 2016 to 2017**

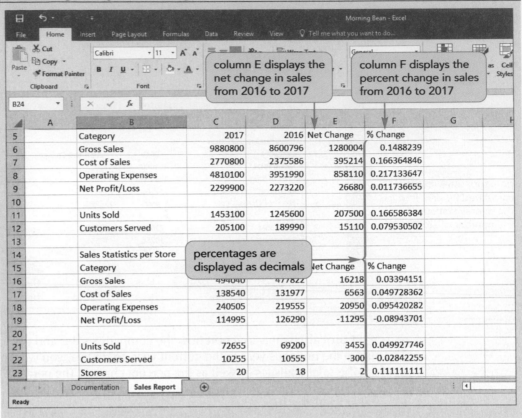

The bottom part of the worksheet contains the sales for each cafe from the current year. You will use the SUM function to calculate the total gross sales for each store during the entire year, the total monthly sales of all 20 stores, and the total gross sales of all stores and months.

To calculate different subtotals of the gross sales:

1. Click in the **Name** box to select the current cell reference, type **O26**, and then press the **Enter** key. Cell O26 is selected.

2. Type **TOTAL** as the label, and then press the **Enter** key. Cell O27 is now the active cell.

3. On the ribbon, click the **Home** tab, if necessary.

4. In the Editing group, click the **AutoSum** button, and then press the **Enter** key to accept the suggested range reference and enter the formula =SUM(C27:N27) in cell O27. The cell displays 370000, indicating gross sales in 2017 for the 85 Seaside Lane store in San Diego were $370,000.

5. Copy the formula in cell **O27**, and then paste that formula into the range **O28:O46** to calculate the total sales for each of the remaining 19 stores in the Morning Bean chain.

6. Click cell **B47**, type **TOTAL** as the label, and then press the **Tab** key. Cell C47 is now the active cell.

7. Select the range **C47:O47** so that you can calculate the total monthly sales for all of the stores.

8. On the Home tab, in the Editing group, click the **AutoSum** button to calculate the total sales for each month as well as the total sales for all months. For example, cell C47 displays 710900, indicating that monthly sales from all stores in January were $710,900.

9. Click cell **O48** to deselect the range. See Figure 2-9.

Figure 2-9 **Gross sales by store and month**

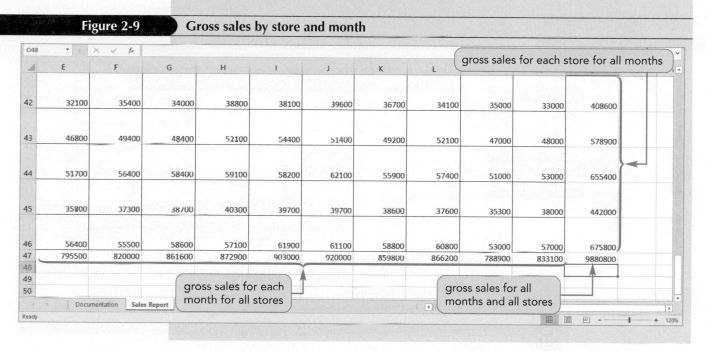

The Sales Report worksheet contains a lot of information that is difficult to read in its current form. You can improve the readability of the data by adding number formats.

Formatting Numbers

The goal in formatting any workbook is to make the content easier to interpret. For numbers, this can mean adding a comma to separate thousands, setting the number of decimal places, and using percentage and currency symbols to make numbers easier to read and understand. Changing the number format does not affect the value itself, only how that value is displayed in the worksheet.

Applying Number Formats

Cells start out formatted with the **General format**, which, for the most part, displays numbers exactly as they are typed. If a value is calculated from a formula or function, the General format displays as many digits after the decimal point as will fit in the cell and rounds the last digit. Calculated values that are too large to fit into the cell are displayed in scientific notation.

The General format is fine for small numbers, but some values require additional formatting to make the numbers easier to interpret. For example, you might want to:

- Change the number of digits displayed to the right of the decimal point
- Add commas to separate thousands in large numbers
- Include currency symbols to numbers to identify the monetary unit being used
- Identify percentages using the % symbol

TIP

To apply the Currency format, click the Number Format button arrow and click Currency, or press the Ctrl+Shift+$ keys.

Excel supports two monetary formats—currency and accounting. Both formats add a thousands separator to the currency values and display two digits to the right of the decimal point. However, the **Currency format** places a currency symbol directly to the left of the first digit of the currency value and displays negative numbers with a negative sign. The **Accounting format** fixes a currency symbol at the left edge of the column, and displays negative numbers within parentheses and zero values with a dash. It also slightly indents the values from the right edge of the cell to allow room for parentheses around negative values. Figure 2-10 compares the two formats.

Figure 2-10   Currency and Accounting number formats

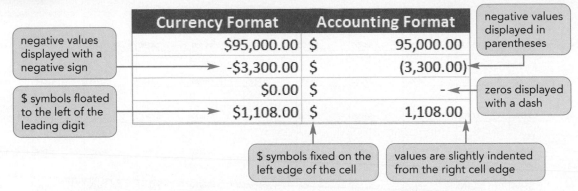

When choosing between the Currency format and the Accounting format for your worksheets, you should consider accounting principles that govern how financial data should be formatted and displayed.

PROSKILLS

Written Communication: Formatting Monetary Values

Spreadsheets commonly include monetary values. To make these values simpler to read and comprehend, keep in mind the following guidelines when formatting the currency data in a worksheet:

- **Format for your audience.** For general financial reports, round values to the nearest hundred, thousand, or million. Investors are generally more interested in the big picture than in exact values. However, for accounting reports, accuracy is important and often legally required. So, for those reports, be sure to display the exact monetary value.

- **Use thousands separators.** Large strings of numbers can be challenging to read. For monetary values, use a thousands separator to make the amounts easier to comprehend.

- **Apply the Accounting format to columns of monetary values.** The Accounting format makes columns of numbers easier to read than the Currency format. Use the Currency format for individual cells that are not part of long columns of numbers.

- **Use only two currency symbols in a column of monetary values.** Standard accounting format displays one currency symbol with the first monetary value in the column and optionally displays a second currency symbol with the last value in that column. Use the Accounting format to fix the currency symbols, lining them up within the column.

Following these standard accounting principles will make your financial data easier to read both on the screen and in printouts.

Carol wants you to format the gross sales amounts in the Accounting format so that they are easier to read.

To format the gross sales in the Accounting format:

1. Select the range **C6:E6** containing the gross sales.

2. On the Home tab, in the Number group, click the **Accounting Number Format** button $. The numbers are formatted in the Accounting format. You cannot see the format because the cells display ##########.

TIP

You can click the Accounting Number Format button arrow, and then click a different currency symbol.

The cells display ########## because the formatted numbers don't fit into the columns. One reason for this is that monetary values, by default, show both dollars and cents in the cell. However, you can increase or decrease the number of decimal places displayed in a cell. The displayed value might then be rounded. For example, the stored value 11.7 will appear in the cell as 12 if no decimal places are displayed to the right of the decimal point. Changing the number of decimal places displayed in a cell does not change the value stored in the cell.

Because the conference attendees are interested only in whole dollar amounts, Carol wants you to hide the cents values of the gross sales by decreasing the number of decimal places to zero.

To decrease the number of decimal places displayed in the gross sales:

1. Make sure the range **C6:E6** is still selected.

2. On the Home tab, in the Number group, click the **Decrease Decimal** button .00→.0 twice. The cents are hidden for gross sales.

3. Click cell **C4** to deselect the range. See Figure 2-11.

Figure 2-11   Formatted gross sales values

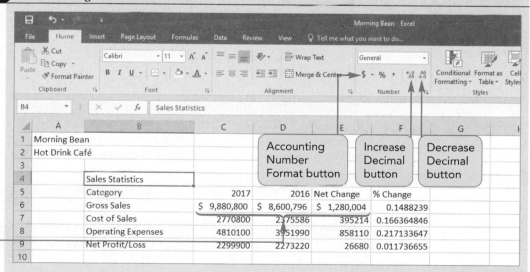

gross sales displayed in the Accounting format with no decimal places

---

The Comma style is identical to the Accounting format except that it does not fix a currency symbol to the left of the number. The advantage of using the Comma style and the Accounting format together is that the numbers will be aligned in the column.

Carol asks you to apply the Comma style to the remaining sales statistics.

To apply the Comma style to the sales statistics:

▶ **1.** Select the nonadjacent range **C7:E9,C11:E12** containing the sales figures for all stores in 2016 and 2017.

▶ **2.** On the Home tab, in the Number group, click the **Comma Style** button ⟨,⟩. In some instances, the number is now too large to be displayed in the cell.

▶ **3.** In the Number group, click the **Decrease Decimal** button ⟨.00→.0⟩ twice to remove two decimal places. Digits to the right of the decimal point are hidden for all of the selected cells, and all of the numbers are now visible.

▶ **4.** Click cell **C13** to deselect the range. See Figure 2-12.

Figure 2-12　　**Formatted sales values**

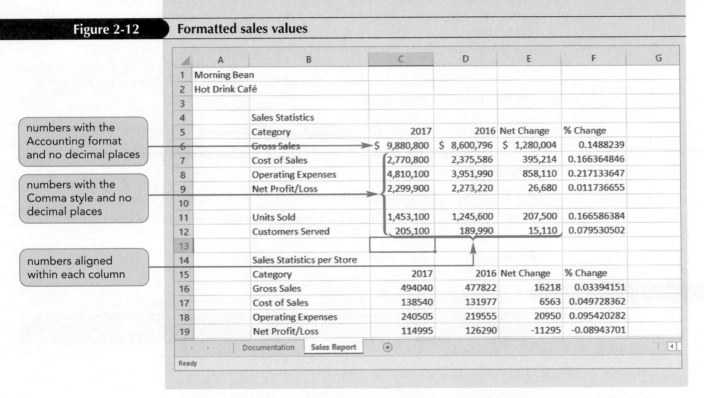

numbers with the Accounting format and no decimal places

numbers with the Comma style and no decimal places

numbers aligned within each column

	A	B	C	D	E	F	G
1	Morning Bean						
2	Hot Drink Café						
3							
4		Sales Statistics					
5		Category	2017	2016	Net Change	% Change	
6		Gross Sales	$ 9,880,800	$ 8,600,796	$ 1,280,004	0.1488239	
7		Cost of Sales	2,770,800	2,375,586	395,214	0.166364846	
8		Operating Expenses	4,810,100	3,951,990	858,110	0.217133647	
9		Net Profit/Loss	2,299,900	2,273,220	26,680	0.011736655	
10							
11		Units Sold	1,453,100	1,245,600	207,500	0.166586384	
12		Customers Served	205,100	189,990	15,110	0.079530502	
13							
14		Sales Statistics per Store					
15		Category	2017	2016	Net Change	% Change	
16		Gross Sales	494040	477822	16218	0.03394151	
17		Cost of Sales	138540	131977	6563	0.049728362	
18		Operating Expenses	240505	219555	20950	0.095420282	
19		Net Profit/Loss	114995	126290	-11295	-0.08943701	

Documentation　　**Sales Report**　　⊕

Ready

The Percent style formats numbers as percentages with no decimal places so that a number such as 0.124 appears as 12%. You can always change how many decimal places are displayed in the cell if that is important to show with your data.

Carol wants you to format the percent change from the 2016 to 2017 sales statistics with a percent symbol to make the percent values easier to read.

To format the percent change values as percentages:

▶ **1.** Select the nonadjacent range **F6:F9,F11:F12** containing the percent change values.

▶ **2.** On the Home tab, in the Number group, click the **Percent Style** button ⟨%⟩ (or press the **Ctrl+Shift+%** keys). The values are displayed as percentages with no decimal places.

▶ **3.** In the Number group, click the **Increase Decimal** button ⟨←.0 .00⟩ twice. The displayed number includes two decimal places.

▶ **4.** Click cell **F13** to deselect the range. See Figure 2-13.

Figure 2-13   **Formatted percent change values**

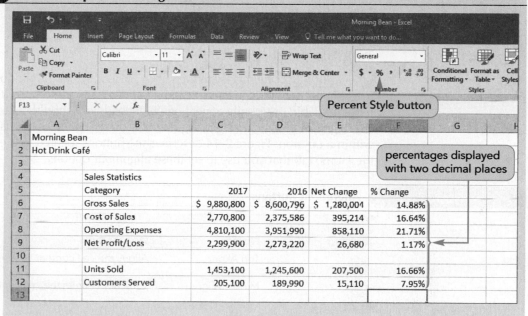

With the data reformatted, the worksheet clearly shows that Morning Bean's gross sales increased from 2016 to 2017 by almost 15 percent, but the company's net profit increased by only 1.17 percent due to increasing expenses in sales costs and operations of 16.64 percent and 21.71 percent, respectively. This type of information is very important to Morning Bean investors and to the company executives as plans are made for the upcoming year.

Formatting Dates and Times

TIP

To view the underlying date and time value, apply the General format to the cell or display the formulas instead of the formula results.

Because Excel stores dates and times as numbers and not as text, you can apply different date formats without affecting the underlying date and time value. The abbreviated format, *mm/dd/yyyy*, entered in the Documentation sheet is referred to as the **Short Date** format. You can also apply a **Long Date format** that displays the day of the week and the full month name in addition to the day of the month and the year. Other built-in formats include formats for displaying time values in 12- or 24-hour time format.

Carol asks you to change the date in the Documentation sheet to the Long Date format.

To format the date in the Long Date format:

1. Go to the **Documentation** sheet, and then select cell **B5**.

2. On the Home tab, in the Number group, click the **Number Format button arrow** to display a list of number formats, and then click **Long Date**. The date is displayed with the weekday name, month name, day, and year. Notice that the date in the formula bar did not change because you changed only the display format, not the date value.

Formatting Worksheet Cells

You can format the appearance of individual cells by modifying the alignment of text within the cell, indenting cell text, or adding borders of different styles and colors.

Aligning Cell Content

By default, text is aligned with the left edge of the cell, and numbers are aligned with the right edge. You might want to change the alignment to make the text and numbers more readable or visually appealing. In general, you should center column titles, left-align other text, and right-align numbers to keep their decimal places lined up within a column. Figure 2-14 describes the buttons located in the Alignment group on the Home tab that you use to set these alignment options.

Figure 2-14	Alignment buttons

Button	Name	Description
	Top Align	Aligns the cell content with the cell's top edge
	Middle Align	Vertically centers the cell content within the cell
	Bottom Align	Aligns the cell content with the cell's bottom edge
	Align Left	Aligns the cell content with the cell's left edge
	Center	Horizontally centers the cell content within the cell
	Align Right	Aligns the cell content with the cell's right edge
	Decrease Indent	Decreases the size of the indentation used in the cell
	Increase Indent	Increases the size of the indentation used in the cell
	Orientation	Rotates the cell content to any angle within the cell
	Wrap Text	Forces the cell text to wrap within the cell borders
	Merge & Center	Merges the selected cells into a single cell

The date in the Documentation sheet is right-aligned within cell B5 because Excel treats dates and times as numbers. Carol wants you to left-align the date from the Documentation sheet and center the column titles in the Sales Report worksheet.

To left-align the date and center the column titles:

▶ **1.** In the Documentation sheet, make sure cell **B5** is still selected.

▶ **2.** On the Home tab, in the Alignment group, click the **Align Left** button ⊟. The date shifts to the left edge of the cell.

▶ **3.** Go to the **Sales Report** worksheet.

▶ **4.** Select the range **C5:F5** containing the column titles.

▶ **5.** In the Alignment group, click the **Center** button ⊟. The column titles are centered in the cells.

Indenting Cell Content

Sometimes you want a cell's content moved a few spaces from the cell's left edge. This is particularly useful to create subsections in a worksheet or to set off some entries from others. You can increase the indent to shift the contents of a cell away from the left edge of the cell, or you can decrease the indent to shift a cell's contents closer to the left edge of the cell.

Carol wants you to indent the Cost of Sales and Operating Expenses labels in the sales statistics table from the other labels because they represent expenses to the company.

To indent the expense categories:

▶ **1.** Select the range **B7:B8** containing the expense categories.

▶ **2.** On the Home tab, in the Alignment group, click the **Increase Indent** button ⊞ twice to indent each label two spaces in its cell.

Adding Borders to Cells

Borders are another way to make financial data easier to interpret. Common accounting practices provide guidelines on when to add borders to cells. In general, a single black border should appear above a subtotal, a single bottom border should be added below a calculated number, and a double black bottom border should appear below the total.

Carol wants you to follow common accounting practices in the Sales Report worksheet. You will add borders below the column titles and below the gross sales values. You will add a top border to the net profit/loss values. Finally, you will add a top and bottom border to the Units Sold and Customers Served rows.

To add borders to the sales statistics data:

▶ **1.** Select the range **B5:F5** containing the cell headings.

▶ **2.** On the Home tab, in the Font group, click the **Borders button arrow** ⊞ ▾, and then click **Bottom Border**. A border is added below the column titles.

▶ **3.** Select the range **B6:F6** containing the gross sales amounts.

▶ **4.** In the Font group, click the **Bottom Border** button ⊞ to add a border below the selected gross sales amounts.

▶ **5.** Select the range **B9:F9**, click the **Borders button arrow** ⊞ ▾, and then click **Top Border** to add a border above the net profit/loss amounts.

   The Units Sold and Customers Served rows do not contain monetary values as the other rows do. You will distinguish these rows by adding a top and bottom border.

▶ **6.** Select the range **B11:F12**, click the **Borders button arrow** ⊞ ▾, and then click **Top and Bottom Border** to add a border above the number of units sold and below the number of customers served.

▶ **7.** Click cell **B3** to deselect the range. See Figure 2-15.

Figure 2-15   **Borders, indents, and alignment added to the sales data**

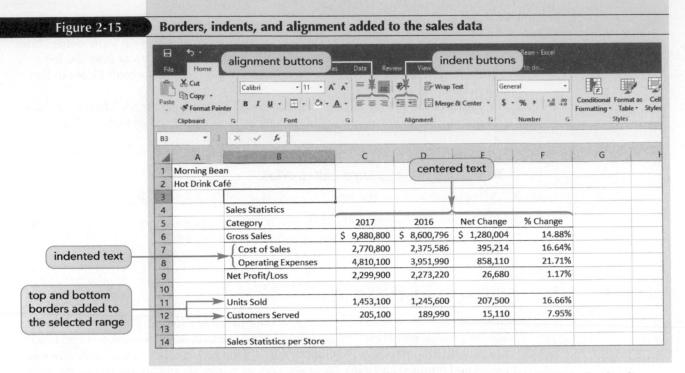

You can apply multiple formats to the same cell to create the look that best fits the data. For example, one cell might be formatted with a number format, alignments, borders, indents, fonts, font sizes, and so on. The monthly sales data needs to be formatted with number styles, alignments, indents, and borders. You'll add these formats now.

To format the monthly sales table:

1. Click in the **Name** box, type **C27:O47**, and then press the **Enter** key. The range C27:O47, containing the monthly gross sales for each store, is selected.

2. On the Home tab, in the Number group, click the **Comma Style** button ⟩ to add a thousands separator to the values.

3. In the Number group, click the **Decrease Decimal** button ⊞ twice to hide the cents from the sales results.

4. In the Alignment group, click the **Top Align** button ☰ to align the sales numbers with the top of each cell.

5. Select the range **C26:O26** containing the labels for the month abbreviations and the TOTAL column.

6. In the Alignment group, click the **Center** button ☰ to center the column labels.

7. Select the range **B27:B46** containing the store addresses.

8. Reduce the font size of the store addresses to **9** points.

9. In the Alignment group, click the **Increase Indent** button ⊞ to indent the store addresses.

10. In the Alignment group, click the **Top Align** button ☰ to align the addresses at the top of each cell.

11. Select the range **B47:O47** containing the monthly totals.

12. In the Font group, click the **Borders button arrow** ⊞ ▾, and then click **All Borders** to add borders around each monthly totals cell.

13. Select the range **O26:O46** containing the annual totals for each restaurant, and then click the **All Borders** button ⊞ to add borders around each restaurant total.

14. Click cell **A24** to deselect the range. See Figure 2-16.

Figure 2-16   **Formatted monthly gross sales**

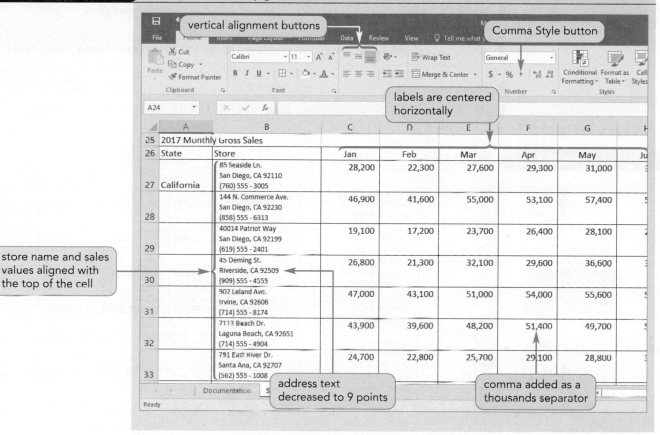

Merging Cells

You can merge, or combine, several cells into one cell. A merged cell contains two or more cells with a single cell reference. When you merge cells, only the content from the upper-left cell in the range is retained. The cell reference for the merged cell is the upper-left cell reference. So, if you merge cells A1 and A2, the merged cell reference is cell A1. After you merge cells, you can align the content within the merged cell. The Merge & Center button in the Alignment group on the Home tab includes the following options:

- **Merge & Center**—merges the range into one cell and horizontally centers the content
- **Merge Across**—merges each row in the selected range across the columns in the range
- **Merge Cells**—merges the range into a single cell but does not horizontally center the cell content
- **Unmerge Cells**—reverses a merge, returning the merged cell to a range of individual cells

The first column of the monthly sales data lists the states in which Morning Bean has stores. You will merge the cells for each state name into a single cell.

To merge the state name cells:

1. Select the range **A27:A33** containing the cells for the California stores. You will merge these seven cells into a single cell.

2. On the Home tab, in the Alignment group, click the **Merge & Center** button. The range A27:A33 merges into one cell with the cell reference A27, and the text is centered and bottom-aligned within the cell.

3. Select the range **A34:A36**, and then click the **Merge & Center** button to merge and center the cells for stores in the state of Washington.

4. Select the range **A37:A40**, and then merge and center the cells for the Oregon stores.

5. Click cell **A41**, and then click the **Center** button ≡ to center the Idaho text horizontally in the cell.

6. Merge and center the range **A42:A43** containing the Nevada cells.

7. Merge and center the range **A44:A46** containing the Colorado cells. See Figure 2-17.

Figure 2-17   Merged cells

	A	B	C	D	E	F	G
40	Oregon	41033 Main St. Ashland, OR 97250 (541) 555 - 3134	47,900	46,000	54,900	53,700	57,5
41	Idaho	112 Reservoir Ln. Boise, ID 83702 (208) 555 - 2138	39,200	35,900	45,800	44,200	47,1
42		1688 Latrobe Ave. Las Vegas, NV 89102 (702) 555 - 7734	27,700	24,100	32,100	35,400	34,0
43	Nevada	4188 Starr Ln. Las Vegas, NV 89199 (702) 555 - 9148	39,400	40,700	46,800	49,400	48,4
44		881 Peak Dr. Denver, CO 80236 (303) 555 - 0444	47,500	44,700	51,700	56,400	58,4
45		105 Barwin St. Denver, CO 80290 (702) 555 - 6106	32,100	28,900	35,800	37,300	38,7
46	Colorado	5 Meggett Dr. Boulder, CO 80305 (303) 555 - 8103	49,700	45,900	56,400	55,500	58,6
47		TOTAL	710,900	648,900	795,500	820,000	861,6
48							

range A42:A43 merged into a single cell

range A44:A46 merged into a single cell

Documentation   Sales Report   ⊕

Ready

The merged cells make it easier to distinguish restaurants in each state. Next, you will rotate the cells so that the state name rotates up the merged cells.

Rotating Cell Contents

Text and numbers are displayed horizontally within cells. However, you can rotate cell text to any angle to save space or to provide visual interest to a worksheet. The state names at the bottom of the merged cells would look better and take up less room if they were rotated vertically within their cells. Carol asks you to rotate the state names.

To rotate the state names:

1. Select the merged cell **A27**.

2. On the Home tab, in the Alignment group, click the **Orientation** button ✏️▾ to display a list of rotation options, and then click **Rotate Text Up**. The state name rotates 90 degrees counterclockwise.

> **3.** In the Alignment group, click the **Middle Align** button  to vertically center the rotated text in the merged cell.

> **4.** Select the merged cell range **A34:A46**, and then repeat Steps 2 and 3 to rotate and vertically center the rest of the state names in their cells.

> **5.** Reduce the width of column A to **7** characters because the rotated state names take up less space.

> **6.** Select cell **A47**. See Figure 2-18.

| Figure 2-18 | Rotated cell content |

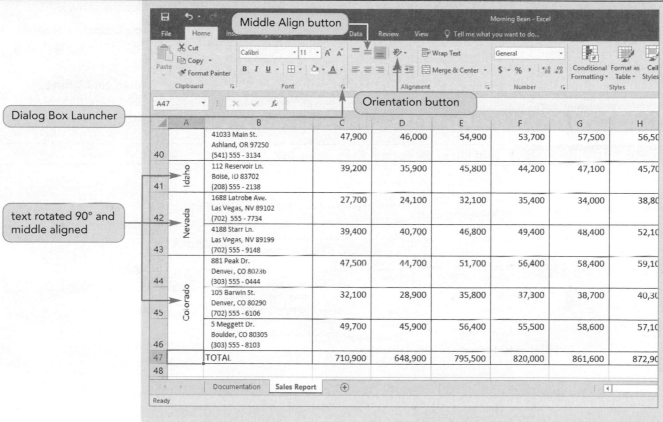

In addition to using the ribbon to apply formatting to a worksheet, you can also use the Format Cells dialog box to apply formatting.

Exploring the Format Cells Dialog Box

The buttons on the Home tab provide quick access to the most commonly used formatting choices. For more options, you can use the Format Cells dialog box. You can apply the formats in this dialog box to the selected worksheet cells. The Format Cells dialog box has six tabs, each focusing on a different set of formatting options, as described below:

- **Number**—provides options for formatting the appearance of numbers, including dates and numbers treated as text such as telephone or Social Security numbers
- **Alignment**—provides options for how data is aligned within a cell
- **Font**—provides options for selecting font types, sizes, styles, and other formatting attributes such as underlining and font colors

- **Border**—provides options for adding and removing cell borders as well as selecting a line style and color
- **Fill**—provides options for creating and applying background colors and patterns to cells
- **Protection**—provides options for locking or hiding cells to prevent other users from modifying their contents

Although you have applied many of these formats from the Home tab, the Format Cells dialog box presents them in a different way and provides more choices. You will use the Font and Fill tabs to format the column titles with a white font on a green background.

To use the Format Cells dialog box to format the column titles:

1. Select the range **A26:O26** containing the column titles for the table.

TIP

Clicking the Dialog Box Launcher in the Font, Alignment, or Number group opens the Format Cells dialog box with that tab displayed.

2. On the Home tab, in the Font group, click the **Dialog Box Launcher** located to the right of the group name (refer to Figure 2-18). The Format Cells dialog box opens with the Font tab displayed.

3. Click the **Color** box to display the available colors, and then click **White, Background 1** in the Theme Color section. The font is set to white. See Figure 2-19.

Figure 2-19   Font tab in the Format Cells dialog box

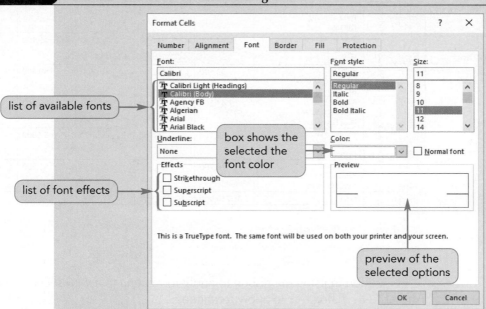

4. Click the **Fill** tab to display background options.

5. In the Background Color section, click the **green** standard color (the sixth color in the last row). The background is set to green, as you can see in the Sample box.

6. Click the **OK** button. The dialog box closes, and the font and fill options you selected are applied to the column titles.

You will also use the Format Cells dialog box to change the appearance of the row titles. You'll format them to be displayed in a larger white font on a gold background.

To format the row titles:

1. Select the range **A27:A46** containing the rotated state names.

2. Right-click the selected range, and then click **Format Cells** on the shortcut menu. The Format Cells dialog box opens with the last tab used displayed—in this case, the Fill tab.

3. In the Background Color section, click the **gold** theme color (the eighth color in the first row). Its preview is shown in the Sample box.

4. Click the **Font** tab to display the font formatting options.

5. Click the **Color** box, and then click the **White, Background 1** theme color to set the font color to white.

6. In the Size box, click **14** to set the font size to 14 points.

7. In the Font style box, click **Bold** to change the font to boldface.

8. Click the **OK** button. The dialog box closes, and the font and fill formats are applied to the state names.

9. Scroll up and click cell **A24** to deselect the A27:A46 range. See Figure 2-20.

Figure 2-20   **Formatted worksheet cells**

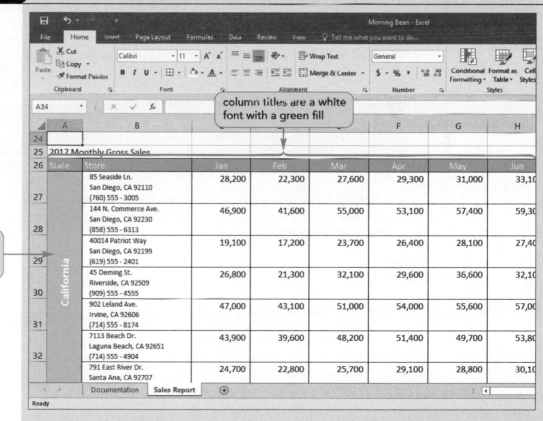

column titles are a white font with a green fill

row titles are 14-point white bold font with a gold fill

10. Save the workbook.

With the formats you have added to the Sales Report worksheet, readers will be able to more easily read and interpret the large table of store sales.

PROSKILLS

Written Communication: Formatting Workbooks for Readability and Appeal

Designing a workbook requires the same care as designing any written document or report. A well-formatted workbook is easy to read and establishes a sense of professionalism with readers. Do the following to improve the appearance of your workbooks:

- **Clearly identify each worksheet's purpose.** Include column or row titles and a descriptive sheet name.
- **Include only one or two topics on each worksheet.** Don't crowd individual worksheets with too much information. Place extra topics on separate sheets. Readers should be able to interpret each worksheet with a minimal amount of horizontal and vertical scrolling.
- **Place worksheets with the most important information first in the workbook.** Position worksheets summarizing your findings near the front of the workbook. Position worksheets with detailed and involved analysis near the end as an appendix.
- **Use consistent formatting throughout the workbook.** If negative values appear in red on one worksheet, format them in the same way on all sheets. Also, be consistent in the use of thousands separators, decimal places, and percentages.
- **Pay attention to the format of the printed workbook.** Make sure your printouts are legible with informative headers and footers. Check that the content of the printout is scaled correctly to the page size and that page breaks divide the information into logical sections.

Excel provides many formatting tools. However, too much formatting can be intrusive, overwhelm data, and make the document difficult to read. Remember that the goal of formatting is not simply to make a "pretty workbook" but also to accentuate important trends and relationships in the data. A well-formatted workbook should seamlessly convey your data to the reader. If the reader is thinking about how your workbook looks, it means he or she is not thinking about your data.

You have completed much of the formatting that Carol wants in the Sales Report worksheet for the Morning Bean sales conference. In the next session, you will explore other formatting options.

REVIEW

Session 2.1 Quick Check

1. What is the difference between a serif font and a sans serif font?

2. What is the difference between a theme color and a standard color?

3. A cell containing a number displays #######. Why does this occur, and what can you do to fix it?

4. What is the General format?

5. Describe the differences between Currency format and Accounting format.

6. The range B3:B13 is merged into a single cell. What is its cell reference?

7. How do you format text so that it is set vertically within the cell?

8. Where can you access all the formatting options for worksheet cells?

Session 2.2 Visual Overview:

The Page Layout tab has options for setting how the worksheet will print.

The Format Painter copies and pastes formatting from one cell or range to another without duplicating any data.

Print titles are rows and/or columns that are included on every page of the printout. In this case, the text in rows 1 and 2 will print on every page.

A manual page break is a page break that you set to indicate where a new page of the printout should start and is identified by a solid blue line.

| File | Home | Insert | Page Layout | Formulas | Data | Review | View |

Tw Cen MT | 26 | General

A1 — Morning Bean

	A	B	C	D	E	F	G
1	**Morning Bean**						
2	*Hot Drink Café*						
3							
4		Sales Statistics					
5		Category	2017	2016	Net Change	% Change	
6		Gross Sales	$ 9,880,800	$ 8,600,796	$ 1,280,004	14.88%	
7		Cost of Sales	2,770,800	2,375,586	395,214	16.64%	
8		Operating Expenses	4,810,100	3,951,990	858,110	21.71%	
9		Net Profit/Loss	2,299,900	2,273,220	26,680	1.17%	
10							
11		Units Sold	1,453,100	1,245,600	207,500	16.66%	
12		Customers Served	215,100	189,990	25,110	13.22%	
13							
14		Sales Statistics per Store					
15		Category	2017	2016	Net Change	% Change	
16		Gross Sales	$ 494,040	$ 477,822	$ 16,218	3.39%	
17		Cost of Sales	138,540	131,977	6,563	4.97%	
18		Operating Expenses	240,505	219,555	20,950	9.54%	
19		Net Profit/Loss	114,995	126,290	(11,295)	-8.94%	
20							
21		Units Sold	72,655	69,200	3,455	4.99%	
22		Customers Served	10,755	10,555	200	1.89%	
23		Stores	20	18	2	11.11%	
24							
25		2017 Monthly Gross Sales					
26	State	Store	Jan	Feb	Mar	Apr	May
27		85 Seaside Lane San Diego, CA 92110 (760) 555 - 3005	28,200	22,300	27,600	29,300	31,
28		144 N. Commerce Avenue San Diego, CA 92230 (858) 555 - 6313	46,900	41,600	55,000	53,100	57,
		40014 Patriot Way	19,100	17,200	23,700	26,400	28

Page 1

Documentation | **Sales Report** | +

Ready

Designing a Printout

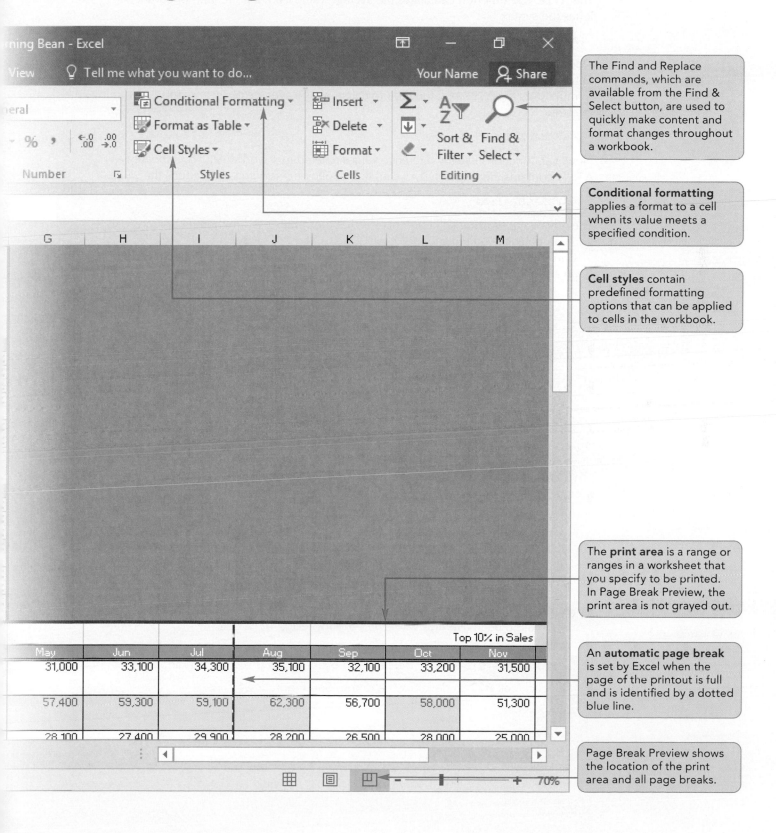

The Find and Replace commands, which are available from the Find & Select button, are used to quickly make content and format changes throughout a workbook.

Conditional formatting applies a format to a cell when its value meets a specified condition.

Cell styles contain predefined formatting options that can be applied to cells in the workbook.

The **print area** is a range or ranges in a worksheet that you specify to be printed. In Page Break Preview, the print area is not grayed out.

An **automatic page break** is set by Excel when the page of the printout is full and is identified by a dotted blue line.

Page Break Preview shows the location of the print area and all page breaks.

	May	Jun	Jul	Aug	Sep	Oct	Nov
	31,000	33,100	34,300	35,100	32,100	33,200	31,500
	57,400	59,300	59,100	62,300	56,700	58,000	51,300
	28,100	27,400	29,900	28,200	26,500	28,000	25,000

Top 10% in Sales

Calculating Averages

The **AVERAGE function** calculates the average value from a collection of numbers. It has the syntax

```
AVERAGE(number1,number2,number3,…)
```

where *number1*, *number2*, *number3*, and so forth are either numbers or cell references to the cells or a range where the numbers are stored. For example, the following formula uses the AVERAGE function to calculate the average of 1, 2, 5, and 8, returning the value 4:

```
=AVERAGE(1,2,5,8)
```

However, functions usually reference values entered in a worksheet. So, if the range A1:A4 contains the values 1, 2, 5, and 8, the following formula also returns the value 4:

```
=AVERAGE(A1:A4)
```

The advantage of using cell references is that the values used in the function are visible and can be easily edited.

Carol wants you to calculate the average monthly sales for each of the 20 Morning Bean stores. You will use the AVERAGE function to calculate these values.

To calculate the average monthly sales for each store:

1. If you took a break after the previous session, make sure the Morning Bean workbook is open and the Sales Report worksheet is active.

2. In cell **P26**, enter **AVERAGE** as the column title. The cell is formatted with a green fill and white font color, matching the other column titles.

3. In cell **P27**, enter the formula **=AVERAGE(C27:N27)** to calculate the average of the monthly gross sales values entered in the range C27:N27. The formula returns the value 30,833, which is the average monthly gross sales for the store on 85 Seaside Lane in San Diego, California.

4. Copy the formula in cell **P27**, and then paste the copied formula in the range **P28:P47** to calculate the average monthly gross sales for each of the remaining Morning Bean stores as well as the average monthly sales from all stores. The average monthly gross sales for individual stores range from $25,408 to $56,317. The monthly gross sales from all stores is $823,400.

5. Select the range **P27:P47**. You will format this range of sales statistics.

6. On the Home tab, in the Alignment group, click the **Top Align** button ≡ to align each average value with the top edge of its cell.

7. In the Font group, click the **Borders button arrow** ⊞ ▾, then click **All Borders** to add borders around every cell in the selected range.

8. Click cell **P27** to deselect the range. See Figure 2-21.

Figure 2-21   Average sales results

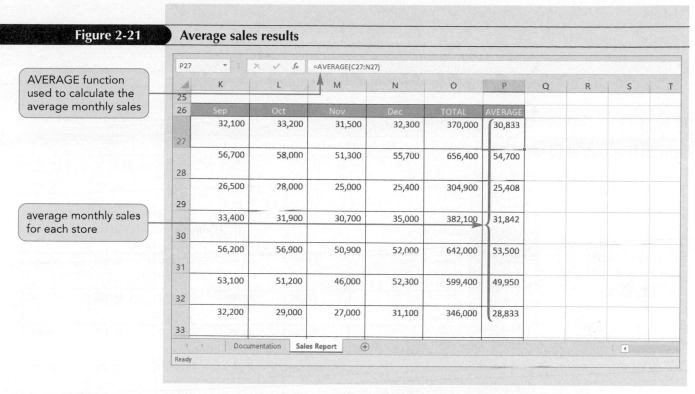

AVERAGE function used to calculate the average monthly sales

average monthly sales for each store

With so many values in the data, Carol wants you to insert double borders around the sales values for each state. The Border tab in the Format Cells dialog box provides options for changing the border style and color and placement.

To add a double border to the state results:

1. Select the range **A27:N33** containing the California monthly sales totals.
2. Open the Format Cells dialog box, and then click the **Border** tab.
3. In the Line section, click the **double line** in the lower-right corner of the Style box.
4. In the Presets section, click the **Outline** option. The double border appears around the selected cells in the Border preview. See Figure 2-22.

Figure 2-22   Border tab in the Format Cells dialog box

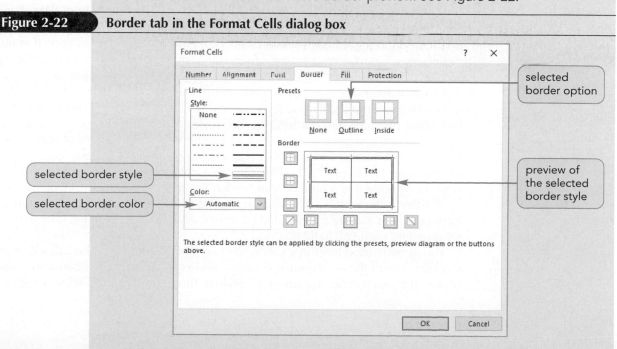

selected border option

selected border style

selected border color

preview of the selected border style

5. Click the **OK** button. The selected border is applied to the California monthly sales.

6. Repeat Steps 2 through 5 to apply double borders to the ranges **A34:N36**, **A37:N40**, **A41:N41**, **A42:N43**, and **A44:N46**.

7. Click cell **A48** to deselect the range. See Figure 2-23.

Figure 2-23 ▶ **Worksheet with font, fill, and border formatting**

double borders around each state's sales row

	A	B	C	D	E	F	G
40		41033 Main St. Ashland, OR 97250 (541) 555 - 3134	47,900	46,000	54,900	53,700	57,500
41	Idaho	112 Reservoir Ln. Boise, ID 83702 (208) 555 - 2138	39,200	35,900	45,800	44,200	47,100
42	Nevada	1688 Latrobe Ave. Las Vegas, NV 89102 (702) 555 - 7734	27,700	24,100	32,100	35,400	34,000
43		4188 Starr Ln. Las Vegas, NV 89199 (702) 555 - 9148	39,400	40,700	46,800	49,400	48,400
44	Colorado	881 Peak Dr. Denver, CO 80236 (303) 555 - 0444	47,500	44,700	51,700	56,400	58,400
45		105 Barwin St. Denver, CO 80290 (702) 555 - 6106	32,100	28,900	35,800	37,300	38,700
46		5 Meggett Dr. Boulder, CO 80305 (303) 555 - 8103	49,700	45,900	56,400	55,500	58,600
47		TOTAL	710,900	648,900	795,500	820,000	861,600

Documentation | Sales Report ⊕   Ready

Another way to format worksheet cells is with styles.

Applying Cell Styles

A workbook often contains several cells that store the same type of data. For example, each worksheet might have a cell displaying the sheet title, or a range of financial data might have several cells containing totals and averages. It is good design practice to apply the same format to worksheet cells that contain the same type of data.

One way to ensure that similar data is displayed consistently is with styles. A **style** is a collection of formatting options that include a specified font, font size, font styles, font color, fill color, and borders. The Cell Styles gallery includes a variety of built-in styles that you can use to format titles and headings, different types of data such as totals or calculations, and cells that you want to emphasize. For example, you can use the Heading 1 style to display sheet titles in a bold, blue-gray, 15-point Calibri font with no fill color and a blue bottom border. You can then apply the Heading 1 style to all titles in the workbook. If you later revise the style, the appearance of any cell formatted with that style is updated automatically. This saves you the time and effort of reformatting each cell individually.

You already used built-in styles when you formatted data in the Sales Report worksheet with the Accounting, Comma, and Percent styles. You can also create your own cell styles by clicking New Cell Style at the bottom of the Cell Styles gallery.

Applying a Cell Style

- Select the cell or range to which you want to apply a style.
- On the Home tab, in the Styles group, click the Cell Styles button.
- Point to each style in the Cell Styles gallery to see a Live Preview of that style on the selected cell or range.
- Click the style you want to apply to the selected cell or range.

Carol wants you to add more color and visual interest to the Sales Report worksheet. You'll use the styles in the Cell Styles gallery to do this.

To apply cell styles to the Sales Report worksheet:

1. Click cell **B4** containing the text "Sales Statistics."

2. On the Home tab, in the Styles group, click the **Cell Styles** button. The Cell Styles gallery opens.

3. Point to the **Heading 1** style in the Titles and Headings section. Live Preview shows cell B4 in a 15-point, bold font with a solid blue bottom border. See Figure 2-24.

Figure 2-24   **Cell Styles gallery**

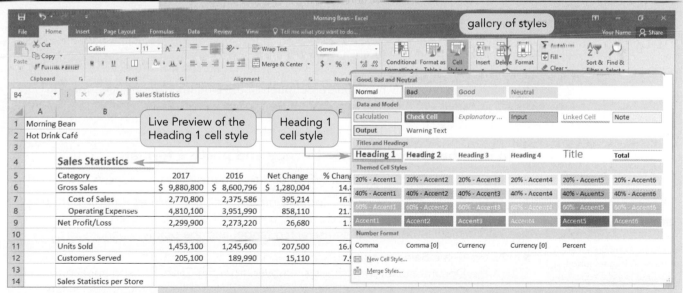

4. Move the pointer over different styles in the Cell Styles gallery to see cell B4 with a Live Preview of each style.

5. Click the **Title** style. The Title style—18-point, Blue-Gray, Text 2 Calibri Light font—is applied to cell B4.

6. Select the range **B5:F5** containing the column titles for the Sales Statistics data.

7. In the Styles group, click the **Cell Styles** button, and then click the **Accent4** style in the Themed Cell Styles section of the Cell Styles gallery.

8. Click cell **A25** containing the text "2017 Monthly Gross Sales," and then apply the **Title** cell style to the cell.

9. Click cell **A3**. See Figure 2-25.

| Figure 2-25 | Cell styles applied to the worksheet |

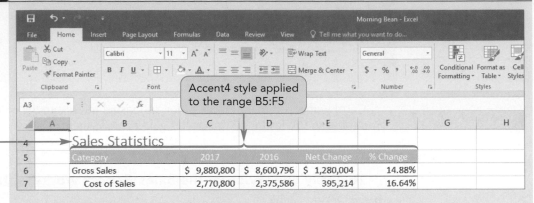

Title style applied to cell B4

Accent4 style applied to the range B5:F5

Copying and Pasting Formats

Large workbooks often use the same formatting on similar data throughout the workbook, sometimes in widely scattered cells. Rather than repeating the same steps to format these cells, you can copy the format of one cell or range and paste it to another.

Copying Formats with the Format Painter

The Format Painter provides a fast and efficient way of copying and pasting formats, ensuring that a workbook has a consistent look and feel. The Format Painter does not copy formatting applied to selected text within a cell, and it does not copy data.

Carol wants the Sales Report worksheet to use the same formats you applied to the Morning Bean company name and description in the Documentation sheet. You will use the Format Painter to copy and paste the formats.

To use the Format Painter to copy and paste a format:

1. Go to the **Documentation** worksheet, and then select the range **A1:A2**.

2. On the Home tab, in the Clipboard group, click the **Format Painter** button. The formats from the selected cells are copied to the Clipboard, a flashing border appears around the selected range, and the pointer changes to ⊹ 🖌.

3. Go to the **Sales Report** worksheet, and then click cell **A1**. The formatting from the Documentation worksheet is removed from the Clipboard and applied to the range A1:A2. Notice that gold font color you applied to the text selection "Morning" was not included in the pasted formats.

4. Double-click cell **A1** to enter Edit mode, select **Morning**, and then change the font color to the **Gold, Accent 4** theme color. The format for the company title now matches what you applied earlier in the Documentation sheet.

5. Press the **Enter** key to exit Edit mode and select cell A2.

> **TIP**
>
> To paste the same format multiple times, double-click the Format Painter button. Click the button again or press the Esc key to turn it off.

You can use the Format Painter to copy all of the formats within a selected range and then apply those formats to another range that has the same size and shape by clicking the upper-left cell of the range. Carol wants you to copy all of the formats that you applied to the Sales Statistics data to the sales statistics per store data.

To copy and paste multiple formats:

1. Select the range **B4:F12** in the Sales Report worksheet.

2. On the Home tab, in the Clipboard group, click the **Format Painter** button.

3. Click cell **B14**. All of the number formats, cell borders, fonts, and fill colors are pasted in the range B14:F22.

4. Select the range **C23:E23**. You'll format this data.

5. On the Home tab, in the Number group, click the **Comma Style** button ⟨ , ⟩ , and then click the **Decrease Decimal** button [.00→.0] twice to remove the decimal places to the right of the decimal point. The numbers are now vertically aligned in their columns.

6. Click cell **F23**.

7. In the Number group, click the **Percent Style** button [%] to change the number to a percentage, and then click the **Increase Decimal** button [←.0 .00] twice to display two decimal places in the percentage. The value is now formatted to match the other percentages.

8. Click cell **B24**. See Figure 2-26.

TIP

If the range you paste the formats in is bigger than the range you copied, Format Painter will repeat the copied formats to fill the pasted range.

Figure 2-26   **Formatting copied and pasted between ranges**

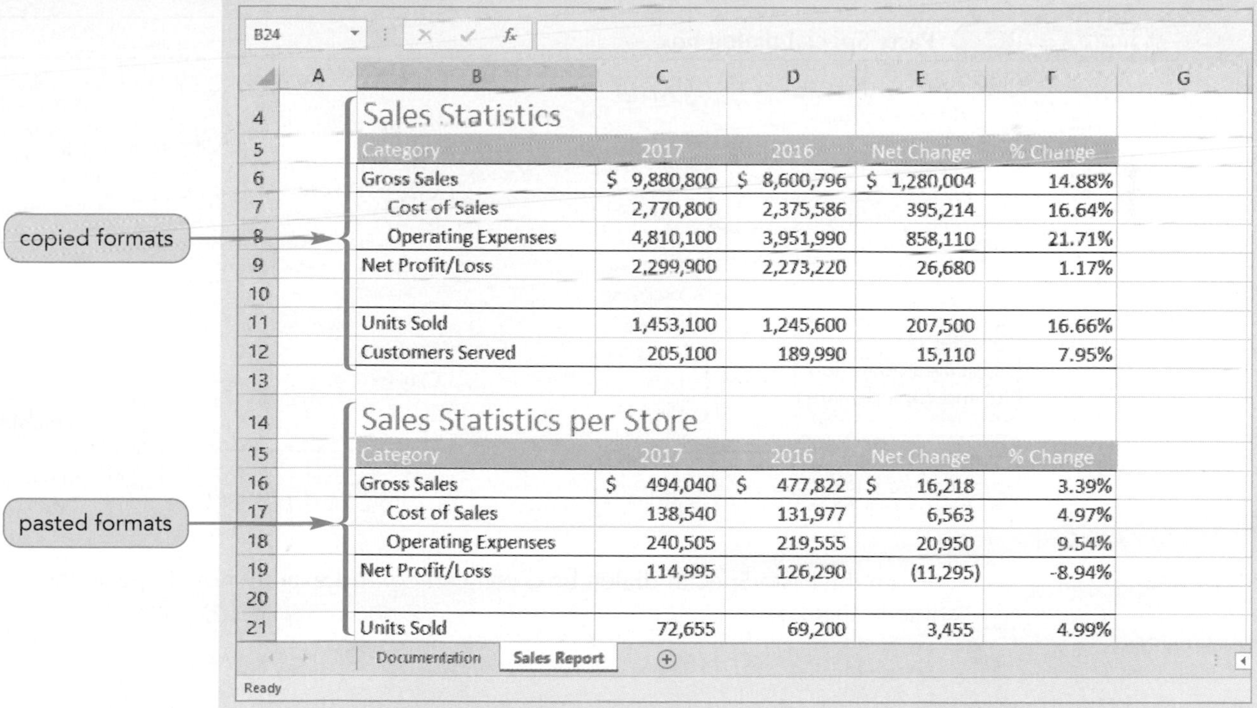

Copying Formats with the Paste Options Button

Another way to copy and paste formats is with the Paste Options button [📋 (Ctrl)▾], which provides options for pasting only values, only formats, or some combination of values and formats. Each time you paste, the Paste Options button appears in the lower-right corner of the pasted cell or range. You click the Paste Options button to open a list of pasting options, shown in Figure 2-27, such as pasting only the values or only the formatting. You can also click the Transpose button to paste the column data into a row, or to paste the row data into a column.

Figure 2-27 **Paste Options button**

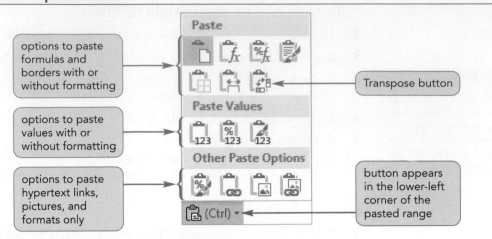

options to paste formulas and borders with or without formatting

Transpose button

options to paste values with or without formatting

options to paste hypertext links, pictures, and formats only

button appears in the lower-left corner of the pasted range

Copying Formats with Paste Special

The Paste Special command provides another way to control what you paste from the Clipboard. To use Paste Special, select and copy a range, select the range where you want to paste the Clipboard contents, click the Paste button arrow in the Clipboard group on the Home tab, and then click Paste Special to open the dialog box shown in Figure 2-28.

Figure 2-28 **Paste Special dialog box**

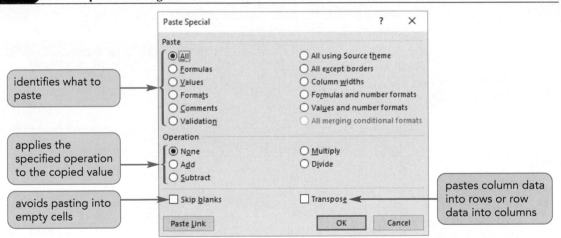

identifies what to paste

applies the specified operation to the copied value

avoids pasting into empty cells

pastes column data into rows or row data into columns

From the Paste Special dialog box, you can control exactly how to paste the copied range.

Finding and Replacing Text and Formats

The Find and Replace commands let you make content and design changes to a worksheet or the entire workbook quickly. The Find command searches through the current worksheet or workbook for the content or formatting you want to locate, and the Replace command then substitutes it with the new content or formatting you specify.

The Find and Replace commands are versatile. You can find each occurrence of the search text one at a time and decide whether to replace it. You can highlight all occurrences of the search text in the worksheet. Or, you can replace all occurrences at once without reviewing them.

Carol wants you to replace all the street title abbreviations (such as Ave.) in the Sales Report with their full names (such as Avenue). You will use Find and Replace to make these changes.

To find and replace the street title abbreviations:

1. On the Home tab, in the Editing group, click the **Find & Select** button, and then click **Replace** (or press the **Ctrl+H** keys). The Find and Replace dialog box opens.

2. Type **Ave.** in the Find what box.

3. Press the **Tab** key to move the insertion point to the Replace with box, and then type **Avenue**. See Figure 2-29.

Figure 2-29   Find and Replace dialog box

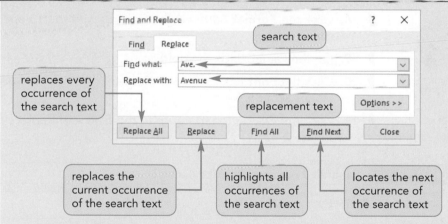

4. Click the **Replace All** button to replace all occurrences of the search text without reviewing them. A dialog box opens, reporting that three replacements were made in the worksheet.

5. Click the **OK** button to return to the Find and Replace dialog box.

   Next, you will replace the other street title abbreviations.

6. Repeat Steps 2 through 5 to replace all occurrences of each of the following: **St.** with **Street**, **Ln.** with **Lane,** and **Dr.** with **Drive**.

7. Click the **Close** button to close the Find and Replace dialog box.

8. Scroll through the Sales Report worksheet to verify that all street title abbreviations were replaced with their full names.

The Find and Replace dialog box can also be used to replace one format with another or to replace both text and a format simultaneously. Carol wants you to replace all occurrences of the white text on a gold fill in the Sales Report worksheet with blue text on a gold fill. You'll use the Find and Replace dialog box to make this formatting change.

To replace white text with blue text:

▶ 1. On the Home tab, in the Editing group, click the **Find & Select** button, and then click **Replace** (or press the **Ctrl+H** keys). The Find and Replace dialog box opens.

▶ 2. Delete the search text from the Find what and Replace with boxes, leaving those two boxes empty. By not specifying a text string to find and replace, the dialog box will search through all cells regardless of their content.

▶ 3. Click the **Options** button to expand the dialog box.

▶ 4. Click the **Format** button in the Find what row to open the Find Format dialog box, which is similar to the Format Cells dialog box you used earlier to format a range.

▶ 5. Click the **Font** tab to make it active, click the **Color** box, and then click the **White, Background 1** theme color.

▶ 6. Click the **Fill** tab, and then in the Background Color section, click the **gold** color (the eighth color in the first row).

▶ 7. Click the **OK** button to close the Find Format dialog box and return to the Find and Replace dialog box.

▶ 8. Click the **Format** button in the Replace with row to open the Replace Format dialog box.

▶ 9. On the Fill tab, click the **gold** color.

▶ 10. Click the **Font** tab, click the **Color** box, and then click **Blue** in the Standard Colors section.

▶ 11. Click the **OK** button to return to the Find and Replace dialog box. See Figure 2-30.

Figure 2-30 **Expanded Find and Replace dialog box**

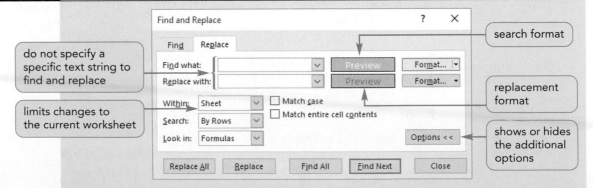

▶ **12.** Click the **Replace All** button to replace all occurrences of white text on a gold fill in the Sales Report worksheet with blue text on a gold fill. A dialog box opens, reporting that 16 replacements were made.

▶ **13.** Click the **OK** button to return to the Find and Replace dialog box.

It is a good idea to clear the find and replace formats after you are done so that they won't affect any future searches and replacements. Carol asks you to remove the formats from the Find and Replace dialog box.

To clear the options from the Find and Replace dialog box:

▶ **1.** In the Find and Replace dialog box, click the **Format button arrow** in the Find what row, and then click **Clear Find Format**. The search format is removed.

▶ **2.** Click the **Format button arrow** in the Replace with row, and then click **Clear Replace Format**. The replacement format is removed.

▶ **3.** Click the **Close** button. The Find and Replace dialog box closes.

Another way to make multiple changes to the formats used in your workbook is through themes.

Working with Themes

Recall that a theme is a coordinated selection of fonts, colors, and graphical effects that are applied throughout a workbook to create a specific look and feel. When you switch to a different theme, the theme-related fonts, colors, and effects change throughout the workbook to reflect the new theme. The appearance of nontheme fonts, colors, and effects remains unchanged no matter which theme is applied to the workbook.

Most of the formatting you have applied to the Sales Report workbook is based on the Office theme. Carol wants you to change the theme to see how it affects the workbook's appearance.

To change the workbook's theme:

▶ **1.** On the ribbon, click the **Page Layout** tab.

▶ **2.** In the Themes group, click the **Themes** button. The Themes gallery opens. Office—the current theme—is the default.

▶ **3.** Point to different themes in the Themes gallery using Live Preview to preview the impact of each theme on the fonts and colors used in the worksheet.

▶ **4.** Click the **Droplet** theme to apply that theme to the workbook. See Figure 2-31.

Figure 2-31 Live Preview of the Droplet theme

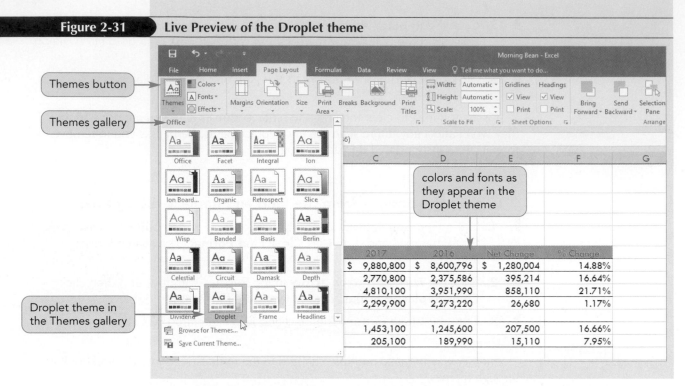

Changing the theme made a significant difference in the worksheet's appearance. The most obvious changes to the worksheet are the fill colors and the fonts. Only formatting options directly tied to a theme change when you select a different theme. Any formatting options you selected that were not theme-based remain unaffected by the change. For example, using a standard color or a nontheme font will not be affected by the choice of theme. In the Sales Report worksheet, the standard green color used for the font of the company description and the fill of the column title cells in the 2017 Monthly Gross Sales data didn't change because that green is not a theme color.

INSIGHT

Sharing Styles and Themes

Using a consistent look and feel for all the files you create in Microsoft Office is a simple way to project a professional image. This consistency is especially important when a team is collaborating on a set of documents. When all team members work from a common set of style and design themes, readers will not be distracted by inconsistent or clashing formatting.

To quickly copy the styles from one workbook to another, open the workbook with the styles you want to copy, and then open the workbook in which you want to copy those styles. On the Home tab, in the Styles group, click the Cell Styles button, and then click Merge Styles. The Merge Styles dialog box opens, listing the currently open workbooks. Select the workbook with the styles you want to copy, and then click the OK button to copy those styles into the current workbook. If you modify any styles, you must copy the styles to the other workbook; Excel does not update styles between workbooks.

Because other Office files, including those created with Word or PowerPoint, use the same file format for themes, you can create one theme to use with all your Office files. To save a theme, click the Themes button in the Themes group on the Page Layout tab, and then click Save Current Theme. The Save Current Theme dialog box opens. Select a save location, type a name in the File name box, and then click the Save button. If you saved the theme file in a default Theme folder, the theme appears in the Themes gallery and affects any Office file that uses that theme.

Highlighting Data with Conditional Formats

Conditional formatting is often used to help analyze data. Conditional formatting applies formatting to a cell when its value meets a specified condition. For example, conditional formatting can be used to format negative numbers in red and positive numbers in black. Conditional formatting is dynamic, which means that the formatting can change when the cell's value changes. Each conditional format has a set of rules that define how the formatting should be applied and under what conditions the format will be changed.

Excel has four types of conditional formatting—data bars, highlighting, color scales, and icon sets. In this module, you will use conditional formatting to highlight cells.

Highlighting Cells Based on Their Values

Cell highlighting changes the cell's font color or fill color based on the cell's value, as described in Figure 2-32. You can enter a value or a cell reference if you want to compare other cells with the value in a certain cell.

Figure 2-32   Highlight Cells rules

Rule	Highlights Cell Values
Greater Than	Greater than a specified number
Less Than	Less than a specified number
Between	Between two specified numbers
Equal To	Equal to a specified number
Text that Contains	That contain specified text
A Date Occurring	That contain a specified date
Duplicate Values	That contain duplicate or unique values

Carol wants to highlight important trends and sales values in the Sales Report worksheet. She asks you to highlight sales statistics that show a negative net change or negative percent change from the previous year to the current year. You will use conditional formatting to highlight the negative values in red.

To highlight negative values in red:

1. In the Sales Report worksheet, select the range **E6:F12,E16:F22** containing the net and percent changes overall and per store from the previous year to the current year.

2. On the ribbon, click the **Home** tab.

3. In the Styles group, click the **Conditional Formatting** button, and then point to **Highlight Cells Rules** to display a menu of the available rules.

4. Click **Less Than**. The Less Than dialog box opens so you can select the value and formatting to highlight negative values.

5. Make sure the value in the first box is selected, and then type **0** so that cells in the selected range that contain values that are less than 0 are formatted with a light red fill and dark red text. Live Preview shows the conditional formatting applied to the cells with negative numbers. See Figure 2-33.

Figure 2-33   Live Preview of the Less Than conditional format

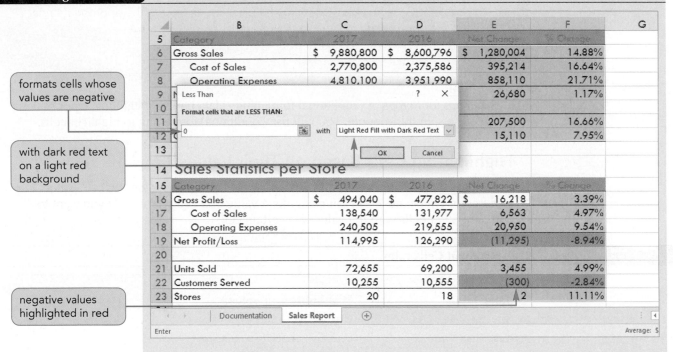

6. Click the **OK** button to apply the highlighting rule.

The conditional formatting highlights that Morning Bean showed a decline from the previous year to the current year for two statistics: The net profit per store declined $11,295 or 8.94 percent, and the number of customers served per store declined by 300 persons or 2.84 percent. These declines occurred because the two new stores that Morning Bean opened in 2017 are still finding a market, resulting in lower profit and customer served per store for the entire franchise.

Conditional formatting is dynamic, which means that changes in the values affect the format of those cells. The total number of customers served in 2017 was incorrectly entered in cell C12 as 205,100. The correct value is 215,100. You will make this change and view its impact on the cells highlighted with conditional formatting.

To view the impact of changing values on conditional formatting:

1. Click cell **C12** to select it.

2. Type **215,100** as the new value, and then press the Enter key. The conditional formatting changes based on the new value. See Figure 2-34.

Figure 2-34 **Cells with conditional formatting**

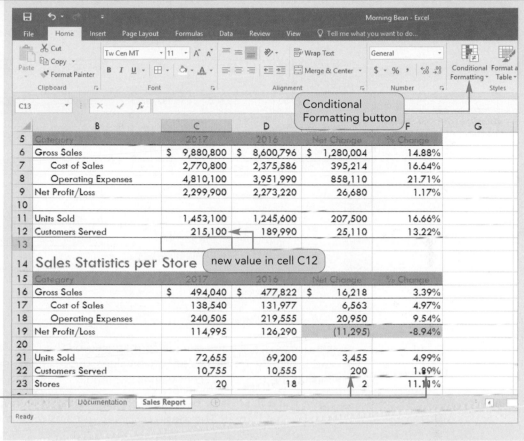

cells E22 and F22 are no longer formatted with red

By changing the value in cell C12 to 215,100, the net change in customers served per store in cell E22 is now 200 and the percentage change in cell F22 is now 1.89%. Because both of these values are now positive, the cells are no longer highlighted in red.

Highlighting Cells with a Top/Bottom Rule

Another way of applying conditional formatting is with the Quick Analysis tool. The **Quick Analysis tool**, which appears whenever you select a range of cells, provides access to the most common tools for data analysis and formatting. The Formatting category includes buttons for the Greater Than and Top 10% conditional formatting rules. You can highlight cells based on their values in comparison to other cells. For example, you can highlight cells with the 10 highest or lowest values in a selected range, or you can highlight the cells with above-average values in a range.

Carol wants to know which stores and which months rank in the top 10 percent of sales. She wants to use this information to identify the most successful stores and learn which months those stores show the highest sales volume. You'll highlight those values using the Quick Analysis tool.

To use a Top/Bottom Rule to highlight stores with the highest average sales:

▶ 1. Select the range **C27:N46** containing the monthly sales values for each of the 20 Morning Bean stores.

▶ 2. Click the **Quick Analysis** button, and then point to **Top 10%**. Live Preview formats the cells in the top 10 percent with red font and a red fill. See Figure 2-35.

Figure 2-35 Quick Analysis tool applying conditional formatting

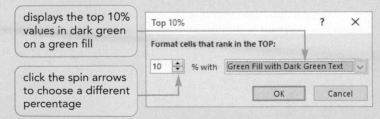

	J	K	L	M	N	O	P
	51,400	49,200	52,100	47,000	48,000	578,900	48,242
43							
	62,100	55,900	57,400	51,000	53,000	655,400	54,617
44							
	39,700	38,600	37,600	35,300	38,000	442,000	36,833
45							
	61,100	58,800	60,800	53,000	57,000		
46							
47	920,000	859,800	866,200	788,900	833,100	9,880,800	823,400

months with the top 10 percent in sales

Quick Analysis button

Quick Analysis categories

Formatting | Charts | Totals | Tables | Sparklines

Data Bars | Color... | Icon Set | Greater... | Top 10% | Clear...

pointer on the Top 10 percent formatting options

Conditional Formatting uses rules to highlight interesting data.

Documentation **Sales Report**

Ready Average: 41,170

Carol doesn't like the default format used by the Quick Analysis tool because red is usually applied to negative values and results. Instead, she wants to format the top 10 percent values in green.

3. Press the **Esc** key to close the Quick Analysis tool without applying the conditional format. The range C27:N46 remains selected.

   Trouble? If the conditional formatting was applied to the worksheet, press the Ctrl+Z keys to undo the format, and then continue with Step 4.

4. On the Home tab, in the Styles group, click the **Conditional Formatting** button, and then point to **Top/Bottom Rules** to display a list of available rules.

5. Click **Top 10%** to open the Top 10% dialog box.

6. Click the **with** arrow box and click **Green Fill with Dark Green Text** to apply green to cells with sales value in the top 10 percent. See Figure 2-36.

Figure 2-36 Top 10% dialog box

displays the top 10% values in dark green on a green fill

click the spin arrows to choose a different percentage

Top 10% ? ✕

Format cells that rank in the TOP:

10 ⬍ % with Green Fill with Dark Green Text ⌄

OK Cancel

7. Click the **OK** button, and then click cell **A24** to deselect the cells. Monthly sales that rank in the top 10 percent are formatted with green.

8. Zoom the worksheet to **40%** so you can view all of the monthly gross sales and more easily see the sales pattern. See Figure 2-37.

Figure 2-37   **Top 10 percent highlighted with green conditional formatting**

top 10 percent sales occur between May and October and are found in six stores

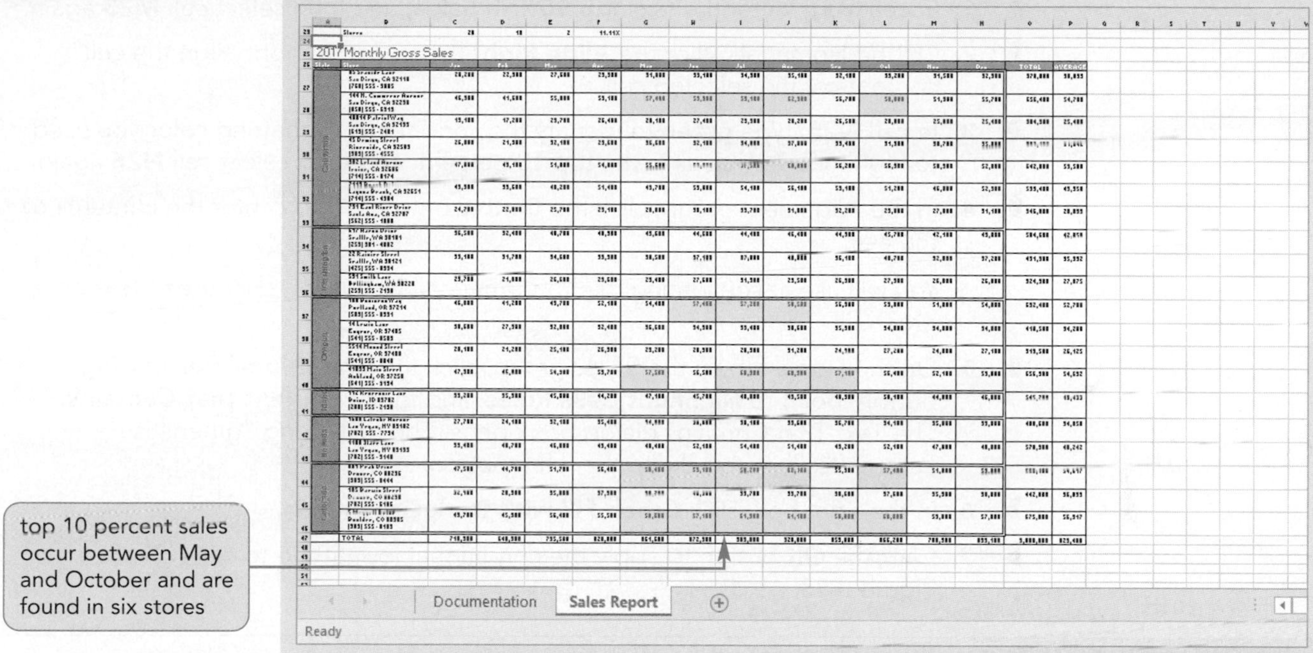

9. Return the zoom to **120%** or whatever zoom is appropriate for your monitor.

The top 10 percent in monthly sales comes from six stores located in San Diego, Irvine, Portland, Ashland, Denver, and Boulder. The highest sales appear to be centered around the months from May to October. This information will be valuable to Carol as she compares the sales performance of different stores and projects monthly cash flows for the company.

Other Conditional Formatting Options

To create dynamic conditional formats that are based on cell values rather than a constant value, you can enter a cell reference in the conditional format dialog box. For example, you can highlight all cells whose value is greater than the value in cell B10. For this type of conditional format, enter the formula =$B$10 in the conditional formatting dialog box. Note that the $ character keeps the cell reference from changing if that formula moves to another cell.

You can remove a conditional format at any time without affecting the underlying data by selecting the range containing the conditional format, clicking the Conditional Formatting button, and then clicking the Clear Rules command. A menu opens, providing options to clear the conditional formatting rules from the selected cells or the entire worksheet. You can also click the Quick Analysis button that appears in the lower-right corner of the selected range and then click the Clear Format button in the Formatting category. Note that you might see only "Clear..." as the button name.

Creating a Conditional Formatting Legend

When you use conditional formatting to highlight cells in a worksheet, the purpose of the formatting is not always immediately apparent. To ensure that everyone knows why certain cells are highlighted, you should include a **legend**, which is a key that identifies each format and its meaning.

Carol wants you to add a legend to the Sales Report worksheet to document the two conditional formatting rules you created in the worksheet.

To create a conditional formatting legend:

▶ 1. In cell **M25**, enter the text **Top 10% in Sales**, and then select cell **M25** again.

▶ 2. On the Home tab, click the **Align Right** button ☰ to right-align the cell contents of the selected cell.

▶ 3. In cell **N25**, type **green** to identify the conditional formatting color you used to highlight the values in the top 10 percent, and then select cell **N25** again.

▶ 4. In the Alignment group, click the **Center** button ☰ to center the contents of the cell.

You will use a highlighting rule to format cell N25 using dark green text on a green fill.

▶ 5. On the Home tab, in the Styles group, click the **Conditional Formatting** button, point to **Highlight Cells Rules**, and then click **Text that Contains**. The Text That Contains dialog box opens. The text string "green" is automatically entered into the left input box.

▶ 6. In the right box, click **Green Fill with Dark Green Text**.

▶ 7. Click the **OK** button to apply the conditional formatting to cell N25. See Figure 2-38.

Figure 2-38   **Conditional formatting legend**

legend explains the purpose of the conditional formatting

	J	K	L	M	N	O	P	Q
22								
23								
24								
25				Top 10% in Sales	green			
26	Aug	Sep	Oct	Nov	Dec	TOTAL	AVERAGE	
	35,100	32,100	33,200	31,500	32,300	370,000	30,833	
27								
	62,300	56,700	58,000	51,300	55,700	656,400	54,700	
28								
	28,200	26,500	28,000	25,000	25,400	304,900	25,408	
29								
	37,800	33,400	31,900	30,700	35,000	382,100	31,842	
30								
	60,800	56,200	56,900	50,900	52,000	642,000	53,500	
31								
	56,100	53,100	51,200	46,000	52,300	599,400	49,950	

Documentation   **Sales Report**   ⊕

Ready

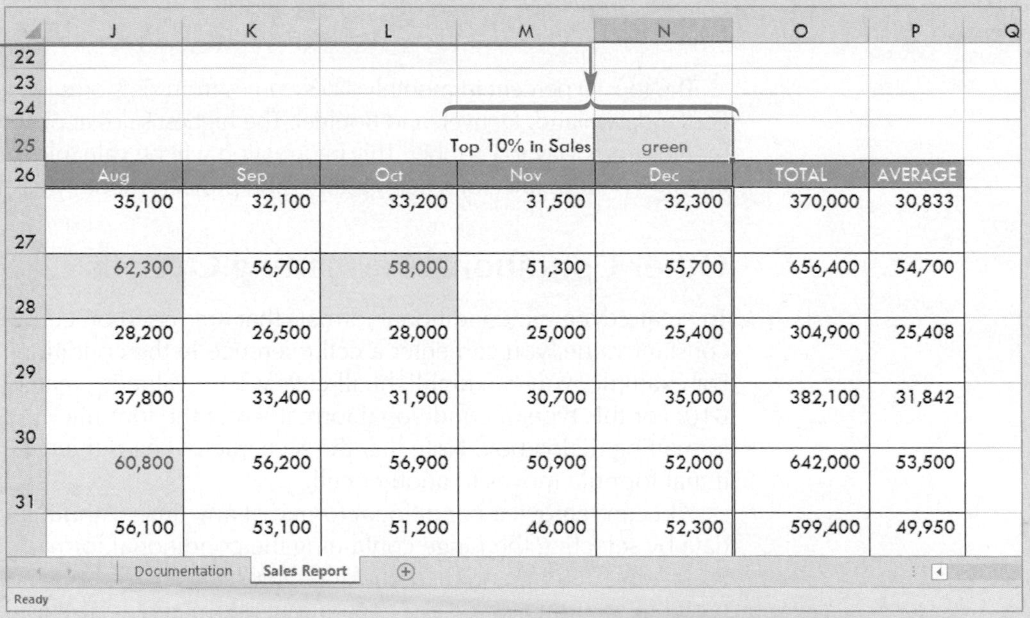

You've completed formatting the appearance of the workbook for the computer screen. Next you'll explore how to format the workbook for the printer.

PROSKILLS

Written Communication: Using Conditional Formatting Effectively

Conditional formatting is an excellent way to highlight important trends and data values to clients and colleagues. However, be sure to use it judiciously. Overusing conditional formatting might obscure the very data you want to emphasize. Keep in mind the following tips as you make decisions about what to highlight and how it should be highlighted:

- **Document the conditional formats you use.** If a bold, green font means that a sales number is in the top 10 percent of all sales, include that information in a legend in the worksheet.
- **Don't clutter data with too much highlighting.** Limit highlighting rules to one or two per data set. Highlights are designed to draw attention to points of interest. If you use too many, you will end up highlighting everything—and, therefore, nothing.
- **Use color sparingly in worksheets with highlights.** It is difficult to tell a highlight color from a regular fill color, especially when fill colors are used in every cell.
- **Consider alternatives to conditional formats.** If you want to highlight the top 10 sales regions, it might be more effective to simply sort the data with the best-selling regions at the top of the list.

Remember that the goal of highlighting is to provide a strong visual clue to important data or results. Careful use of conditional formatting helps readers to focus on the important points you want to make rather than distracting them with secondary issues and facts.

Formatting a Worksheet for Printing

You should format any worksheets you plan to print so that they are easy to read and understand. You can do this using the print settings, which enable you to set the page orientation, the print area, page breaks, print titles, and headers and footers. Print settings can be applied to an entire workbook or to individual sheets. Because other people will likely see your printed worksheets, you should format the printed output as carefully as you format the electronic version.

Carol wants you to format the Sales Report worksheet so she can distribute the printed version at the upcoming sales conference.

Using Page Break Preview

Page Break Preview shows only those parts of the active sheet that will print and how the content will be split across pages. A dotted blue border indicates a page break, which separates one page from another. As you format the worksheet for printing, you can use this view to control what content appears on each page.

Carol wants to know how the Sales Report worksheet would print in portrait orientation and how many pages would be required. You will look at the worksheet in Page Break Preview to find these answers.

To view the Sales Report worksheet in Page Break Preview:

▶ 1. Click the **Page Break Preview** button 🔲 on the status bar. The worksheet switches to Page Break Preview.

▶ 2. Change the zoom level of the worksheet to **30%** so you can view the entire contents of this large worksheet. See Figure 2-39.

Figure 2-39   Sales Report worksheet in Page Break preview

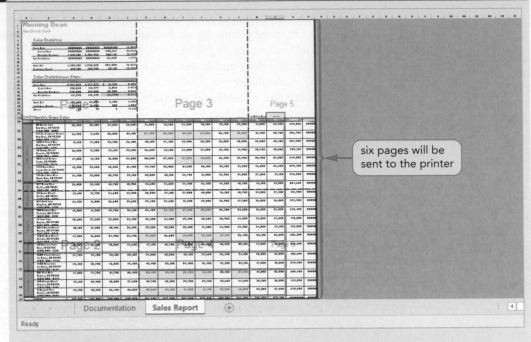

Trouble? If you see a different page layout or the worksheet is split onto a different number of pages, don't worry. Each printer is different, so the layout and pages might differ from what is shown in Figure 2-39.

Page Break Preview shows that a printout of the Sales Report worksheet requires six pages in portrait orientation, and that pages 3 and 5 would be mostly blank. Note that each printer is different, so your Page Break Preview might show a different number of pages. With this layout, each page would be difficult to interpret because the data is separated from the descriptive labels. Carol wants you to fix the layout so that the contents are easier to read and understand.

Defining the Print Area

By default, all cells in a worksheet containing text, formulas, or values are printed. If you want to print only part of a worksheet, you can set a print area, which is the region of the worksheet that is sent to the printer. Each worksheet has its own print area. Although you can set the print area in any view, Page Break Preview shades the areas of the worksheet that are not included in the print area, making it simple to confirm what will print.

Carol doesn't want the empty cells in the range G1:P24 to print, so you will set the print area to exclude those cells.

To set the print area of the Sales Report worksheet:

1. Change the zoom level of the worksheet to **80%** to make it easier to select cells and ranges.

2. Select the nonadjacent range **A1:F24,A25:P47** containing the cells with content.

3. On the ribbon, click the **Page Layout** tab.

> **4.** In the Page Setup group, click the **Print Area** button, and then click **Set Print Area**. The print area changes to cover only the nonadjacent range A1:F24,A25:P47. The rest of the worksheet content is shaded to indicate that it will not be part of the printout.

> **5.** Click cell **A1** to deselect the range.

> **6.** Change the zoom level to **50%** so you can view more of the worksheet. See Figure 2-40.

Figure 2-40   Print area set for the Sales Report worksheet

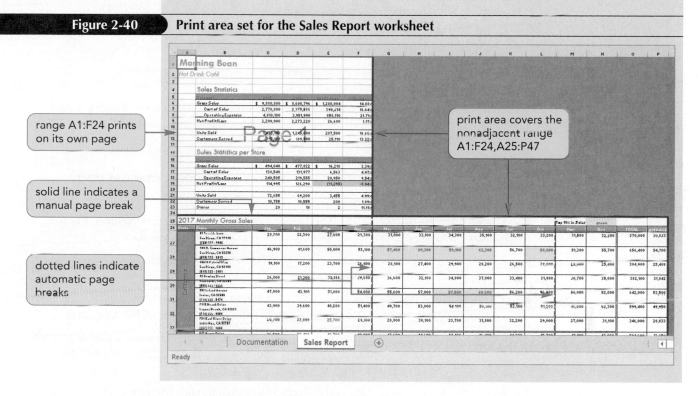

range A1:F24 prints on its own page

solid line indicates a manual page break

dotted lines indicate automatic page breaks

print area covers the nonadjacent range A1:F24,A25:P47

Inserting Page Breaks

Often, the contents of a worksheet will not fit onto a single printed page. When this happens, Excel prints as much of the content that fits on a single page without resizing, and then inserts automatic page breaks to continue printing the remaining worksheet content on successive pages. The resulting printouts might split worksheet content in awkward places, such as within a table of data.

TIP

When you remove a page break, Excel will automatically rescale the printout to fit into the allotted pages.

To split the printout into logical segments, you can insert manual page breaks. Page Break Preview identifies manual page breaks with a solid blue line and automatic page breaks with a dotted blue line. When you specify a print area for a nonadjacent range, as you did for the Sales Report worksheet, you also insert manual page breaks around the adjacent ranges. So a manual page break already appears in the print area you defined (see Figure 2-40). You can remove a page break in Page Break Preview by dragging it out of the print area.

Inserting and Removing Page Breaks

To insert a page break:
- Click the first cell below the row where you want to insert a page break, click a column heading, or click a row heading.
- On the Page Layout tab, in the Page Setup group, click the Breaks button, and then click Insert Page Break.

To remove a page break:
- Select any cell below or to the right of the page break you want to remove.
- On the Page Layout tab, in the Page Setup group, click the Breaks button, and then click Remove Page Break.

or
- In Page Break Preview, drag the page break line out of the print area.

The Sales Report worksheet has automatic page breaks along columns F and L. Carol wants you to remove these automatic page breaks from the Sales Report worksheet.

To remove the automatic page breaks and insert manual page breaks:

1. Point to the dotted blue page break directly to the right of column L in the 2017 Monthly Gross Sales table until the pointer changes to ↔.

2. Drag the page break to the right and out of the print area. The page break is removed from the worksheet.

3. Point to the page break that is located in column F so that the pointer changes to ↔, and then drag the page break to the right and out of the print area.

4. Click the **I** column heading to select the entire column. You will add a manual page break between columns H and I to split the monthly gross sales data onto two pages so the printout will be larger and easier to read.

5. On the Page Layout tab, in the Page Setup group, click the **Breaks** button, and then click **Insert Page Break**. A manual page break is added between columns H and I, forcing the monthly gross sales onto a new page after the June data.

6. Click cell **A1** to deselect the column. The printout of the Sales Report worksheet is now limited to three pages. However, the gross sales data in the range A25:P47 is split across pages. See Figure 2-41.

Figure 2-41	Manual page break in the print area

manual page break splits the data into two pages

Adding Print Titles

It is a good practice to include descriptive information such as the company name, logo, and worksheet title on each page of a printout in case a page becomes separated from the other pages. You can repeat information, such as the company name, by specifying which rows or columns in the worksheet act as print titles. If a worksheet contains a large table, you can print the table's column headings and row headings on every page of the printout by designating those columns and rows as print titles.

In the Sales Report worksheet, the company name appears on the first page of the printout but does not appear on subsequent pages. Also, the descriptive row titles for the monthly sales table in column A do not appear on the third page of the printout. You will add print titles to fix these issues.

To set the print titles:

TIP

You can also open the Page Setup dialog box by clicking the Dialog Box Launcher in the Page Setup group on the Page Layout tab.

1. On the Page Layout tab, in the Page Setup group, click the **Print Titles** button. The Page Setup dialog box opens with the Sheet tab displayed.

2. In the Print titles section, click the **Rows to repeat at top** box, move the pointer over the worksheet, and then select the range **A1:A2**. A flashing border appears around the first two rows of the worksheet to indicate that the contents of the first two rows will be repeated on each page of the printout. The row reference $1:$2 appears in the Rows to repeat at top box.

3. Click the **Columns to repeat at left** box, and then select columns A and B from the worksheet. The column reference $A:$B appears in the Columns to repeat at left box. See Figure 2-42.

Figure 2-42	Sheet tab in the Page Setup dialog box

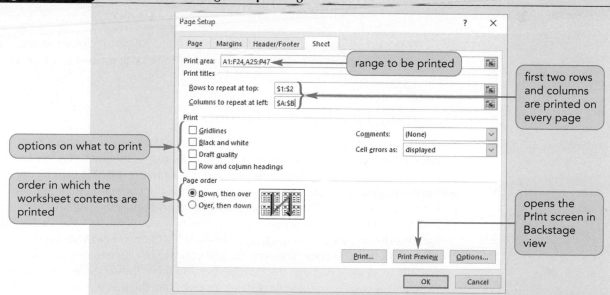

You will next rescale the worksheet so that it doesn't appear too small in the printout.

4. In the Page Setup dialog box, click the **Page** tab.

5. In the Scaling section, change the Adjust to amount to **60%** of normal size.

6. Click the **Print Preview** button to preview the three pages of printed material on the Print screen in Backstage view.

7. Verify that each of the three pages has the Morning Bean title at the top of the page and that the state and store names appear in the leftmost columns of pages 2 and 3. See Figure 2-43.

Figure 2-43 **Print titles on page 3 of the printout**

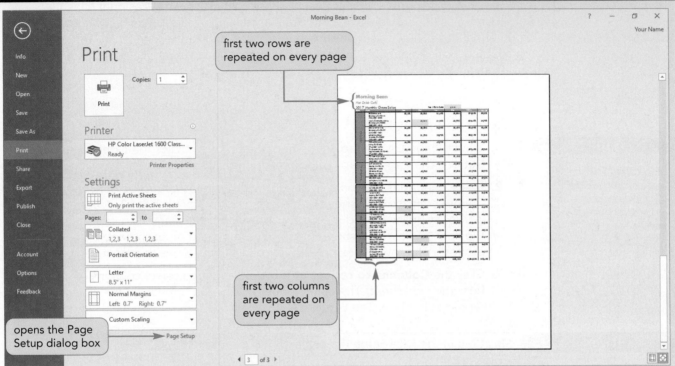

Trouble? If your printout doesn't fit on three pages, reduce the scaling factor from 60 percent to a slightly lower percentage until it does fit on three pages.

Designing Headers and Footers

You can also use headers and footers to repeat information on each printed page. A **header** appears at the top of each printed page; a **footer** appears at the bottom of each printed page. Headers and footers contain helpful and descriptive text that is usually not found within the worksheet, such as the workbook's author, the current date, or the workbook's filename. If the printout spans multiple pages, you can display the page number and the total number of pages in the printout to help ensure you and others have all the pages.

Each header and footer has three sections—a left section, a center section, and a right section. Within each section, you type the text you want to appear, or you insert elements such as the worksheet name or the current date and time. These header and footer elements are dynamic; if you rename the worksheet, for example, the name is automatically updated in the header or footer. Also, you can create one set of headers and footers for even and odd pages, and you can create another set for the first page in the printout.

Carol wants the printout to display the workbook's filename in the header's left section, and the current date in the header's right section. She wants the center footer to display the page number and the total number of pages in the printout, and the right footer to display your name as the workbook's author.

To set up the page header:

1. Near the bottom of the Print screen, click the **Page Setup** link. The Page Setup dialog box opens.

2. Click the **Header/Footer** tab to display the header and footer options.

3. Click the **Different first page** check box to select it. This lets you create one set of headers and footers for the first page, and one set for the rest of the pages.

4. Click the **Custom Header** button to open the Header dialog box. The dialog box contains two tabs—Header and First Page Header—because you selected the Different first page option.

TIP

You can create or edit headers and footers in Page Layout view by clicking in the header/footer section and using the tools on the Design tab.

5. On the Header tab, in the Left section box, type **Filename:**, press the **spacebar**, and then click the **Insert File Name** button 📄. The code &[File], which displays the filename of the current workbook, is added to the left section of the header.

6. Press the **Tab** key twice to move to the right section of the header, and then click the **Insert Date** button 📅. The code &[Date] is added to the right section of the header. See Figure 2-44.

Figure 2-44   **Header dialog box**

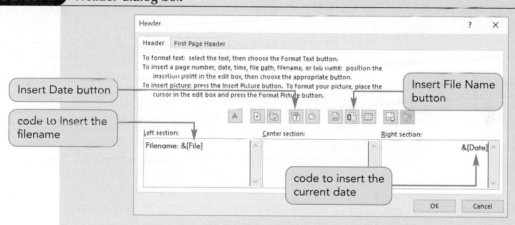

7. Click the **OK** button to return to the Header/Footer tab in the Page Setup dialog box.

You did not define a header for the first page of the printout, so no header information will be added to that page. Next, you will format the footer for all pages of the printout.

To create the page footer:

1. On the Header/Footer tab of the Page Setup dialog box, click the **Custom Footer** button. The Footer dialog box opens.

2. On the Footer tab, click the **Center section** box, type **Page**, press the **spacebar**, and then click the **Insert Page Number** button 📄. The code &[Page], which inserts the current page number, appears after the label "Page."

3. Press the **spacebar**, type **of**, press the **spacebar**, and then click the **Insert Number of Pages** button 📄. The code &[Pages], which inserts the total number of pages in the printout, is added to the Center section box. See Figure 2-45.

Figure 2-45 Footer dialog box

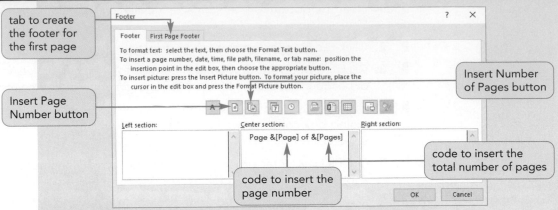

tab to create the footer for the first page

Insert Page Number button

Insert Number of Pages button

code to insert the total number of pages

code to insert the page number

▶ **4.** Click the **First Page Footer** tab so you can create the footer for the first page of the printout.

▶ **5.** Click the **Right section** box, type **Prepared by:**, press the **spacebar**, and then type your name.

▶ **6.** Click the **OK** button to return to the Page Setup dialog box.

You will leave the Page Setup dialog box so you can finish formatting the printout by setting the page margins.

Setting the Page Margins

A **margin** is the space between the page content and the edges of the page. By default, Excel sets the page margins to 0.7 inch on the left and right sides, and 0.75 inch on the top and bottom; and it allows for 0.3-inch margins around the header and footer. You can reduce or increase these margins as needed by selecting predefined margin sizes or setting your own.

Carol's reports need a wider margin along the left side of the page to accommodate the binding. She asks you to increase the left margin for the printout from 0.7 inch to 1 inch.

To set the left margin:

▶ **1.** Click the **Margins** tab in the Page Setup dialog box to display options for changing the page margins.

▶ **2.** Double-click the **Left** box to select the setting, and then type **1** to increase the size of the left margin to 1 inch. See Figure 2-46.

TIP

To select preset margins, click the Margins button in the Page Setup group on the Page Layout tab.

Figure 2-46   Margins tab in the Page Setup dialog box

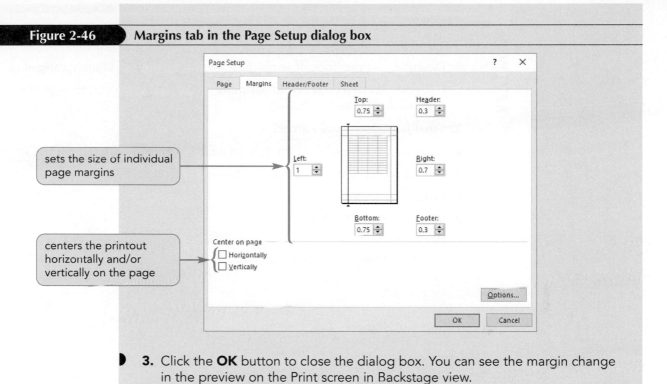

sets the size of individual page margins

centers the printout horizontally and/or vertically on the page

3. Click the **OK** button to close the dialog box. You can see the margin change in the preview on the Print screen in Backstage view.

Now that you have formatted the printout, you can print the final version of the worksheet.

To save and print the workbook:

1. With the workbook still in the Print screen in Backstage view, click the first box in the Settings section, and then click **Print Entire Workbook**.

Both the Sales Report worksheet and the Documentation sheet appear in the preview. As you can see, the printout will include a header with the filename and date on every page except the first page and a footer with your name on the first page and the page number along with the total number of pages on subsequent pages.

2. If you are instructed to print, print the entire workbook.

3. Click the **Back** button ⊖ from the Backstage View navigation bar to return to the workbook window.

4. Click the **Normal** button ▦ on the status bar to return the view of the workbook to normal.

5. Save the workbook, and then close it.

Carol is pleased with the worksheet's appearance and the layout of the printout. The formatting has made the contents easier to read and understand.

REVIEW

Session 2.2 Quick Check

1. Describe two methods of applying the same format to different ranges.

2. Red is a standard color. What happens to red text when you change the workbook's theme?

3. What is a conditional format?

4. How would you highlight the top 10 percent values of the range A1:C20?

5. How do you insert a manual page break in a worksheet?

6. What is a print area?

7. What are print titles?

8. Describe how to add the workbook filename to the center section of the footer on every page of the printout.

Review Assignments

Data Files needed for the Review Assignments: Menu.xlsx, Background2.jpg

Carol created a workbook that tracks the sales of individual items from the Morning Bean menu to share at an upcoming conference. She has already entered most of the financial formulas but wants you to calculate some additional values. She also asks you to format the workbook so that it will look professional and be easy to read and understand. Complete the following:

1. Open the **Menu** workbook located in the Excel2 > Review folder included with your Data Files, and then save the workbook as **Menu Sales** in the location specified by your instructor.

2. In the Documentation sheet, enter your name in cell B4 and the date in cell B5.

3. Change the theme of the workbook to Retrospect.

4. Make the following formatting changes to the Documentation sheet:

   a. Set the background image to the **Background2** JPEG file located in the Excel2 > Review folder.

   b. Format the text in cell A1 in a 26-point bold Calibri Light.

   c. In cell A1, change the font color of the word "Morning" to the Orange, Accent 1 theme color and change the font color of the word "Bean" to the Brown, Accent 3 theme color.

   d. Format the text in cell A2 in 18-point, italic, and change the font color to the Brown, Accent 3 theme color.

   e. Format the range A4:A6 with the Accent 3 cell style.

   f. Change the font color of the range B4:B6 to the Brown, Accent 3 theme color, and change the fill color to the White, Background 1 theme color.

   g. In cell B5, format the date in the Long Date format and left-align the cell contents.

5. Use the Format Painter to copy the formatting in the range A1:A2 in the Documentation sheet and paste it to the same range in the Menu Items worksheet. Change the font colors in cell A1 of the Menu Items worksheet to match the colors used in cell A1 of the Documentation sheet.

6. Apply the Title cell style to cells B4, B12, and A20.

7. Make the following changes to the Units Sold table in the range B5:F10:

   a. Apply the Accent3 cell style to the headings in the range B5:F5. Center the headings in the range C5:F5.

   b. In cell C6, use the SUM function to calculate the total number of specialty drinks sold by the company (found in the range C22:N31 in the Units Sold per Month table). In cell C7, use the SUM function to calculate the total number of smoothies sold (in the range C32:N36). In cell C8, use the SUM function calculate the total number of sandwiches sold (in the range C37:N41). In cell C9, calculate the total number of soups sold (in the range C42:N45).

   c. In cell C10, use the SUM function to calculate the total units sold from all menu types in 2017 (based on the range C6:C9). Copy the formula to cell D10 to calculate the total units sold in 2016.

   d. In each cell of the range E6:E10, calculate the change in units sold between the 2017 and 2016 values. In each cell of the range F6:F10, calculate the percent change from 2016 to 2017. (*Hint*: The percent change is the net change divided by the 2016 value.)

   e. Format the range C6:E10 with the Comma style and no decimal places.

   f. Format the range F6:F10 with the Percent style and two decimal places.

   g. Add a top border to the range B10:F10.

8. Make the following changes to the Gross Sales table in the range B13:F18:

   a. In cells C18 and D18, use the SUM function to calculate the totals of the 2017 and 2016 sales.

   b. In the range E14:F18, enter formulas to calculate the net change and the percent change in sales.

   c. Use the Format Painter to copy the formatting from the range B5:F10 to the range B13:F18.

   d. Format the ranges C14:E14 and C18:E18 with Accounting format and no decimal places.

9. Make the following changes to the Units Sold per Month table in the range A21:O46:

   a. In the range O22:O45, use the SUM function to calculate the total units sold for each menu item. In the range C46:O46, use the SUM function to calculate the total items sold per month and overall.

   b. Format the headings in the range A21:O21 with the Accent3 cell style. Center the headings in the range C21:O21.

   c. Format the units sold values in the range C22:O46 with the Comma style and no decimal places.

   d. Change the fill color of the subtotals in the range O22:O45,C46:N46 to the White, Background 1, Darker 15% theme color (the first color in the third row).

   e. Merge each of the menu categories in the ranges A22:A31, A32:A36, A37:A41, and A42:A45 into single cells. Rotate the text of the cells up, and middle-align the cell contents.

   f. Format cell A22 with the Accent1 cell style. Format cell A32 with the Accent2 cell style. Format cell A37 with the Accent3 cell style. Format cell A42 with the Accent4 cell style. Change the font size of these four merged cells to 14 points.

   g. Add thick outside borders around each category of menu item in the ranges A22:O31, A32:O36, A37:O41, and A42:O45.

10. Use conditional formatting to highlight negative values in the range E6:F10,E14:F18 with a light red fill with dark red text to highlight which menu categories showed a decrease in units sold or gross sales from 2016 to 2017.

11. Use conditional formatting to format cells that rank in the top 10 percent of the range C22:N45 with a green fill with dark green text to highlight the menu items and months that are in the top 10 percent of units sold.

12. Create a legend for the conditional formatting you added to the worksheet. In cell O20, enter the text **Top Sellers**. Add thick outside borders around the cell, and then use conditional formatting to display this text with a green fill with dark green text.

13. Set the following print formats for the Menu Items worksheet:

   a. Set the print area to the nonadjacent range A1:F19,A20:O46.

   b. Switch to Page Break Preview, and then remove any automatic page breaks in the Units Sold per Month table. Insert a manual page break to separate the June and July sales figures. The printout of the Menu Sales worksheet should fit on three pages.

   c. Scale the printout to 70 percent.

   d. Create print titles that repeat the first three rows at the top of the sheet and the first two columns at the left of the sheet.

   e. Increase the left margin of the printout from 0.7 inch to 1 inch.

   f. Create headers and footers for the printout with a different first page.

   g. For the first page header, print **Prepared by** followed by your name in the right section. For every other page, print **Filename:** followed by the filename in the left section and the date in the right section. (*Hint*: Use the buttons in the Header dialog box to insert the filename and date.)

   h. For every footer, including the first page, print **Page** followed by the page number and then **of** followed by the total number of pages in the printout in the center section.

   i. Preview the printout to verify that the company name and description appear on every page of the Menu Items worksheet printout and that the menu category and menu item name appear on both pages with the Units Sold table. If you are instructed to print, print the entire workbook in portrait orientation.

14. Save the workbook, and then close it.

Case Problem 1

APPLY

Data File needed for this Case Problem: Green.xlsx

Green Clean Homes   Sean Patel is developing a business plan for Green Clean Homes, a new professional home cleaning service in Toledo, Ohio. As part of his business plan, Sean needs to predict the company's annual income and expenses. You will help him finalize and format the Excel workbook containing the projected income statement. Complete the following:

1. Open the **Green** workbook located in the Excel2 > Case1 folder, and then save the workbook as **Green Clean** in the location specified by your instructor.
2. In the Documentation sheet, enter your name in cell B3 and the date in cell B4.
3. Display the date in cell B4 in the Long Date format and left-aligned.
4. Change the theme of the workbook to Facet.
5. Make the following formatting changes to the Documentation sheet:
   a. Merge and center cells A1 and B1.
   b. Apply the Accent2 cell style to the merged cell A1 and to the range A3:A5.
   c. In cell A1, set the font size to 22 points and bold the text. Italicize the word "Clean" in the company name.
   d. Add borders around each cell in the range A3:B5. Top-align the text in the range A3:B5.
   e. Change the font color of the text in the range B3:B5 to Dark Green, Accent 2.
6. In the Income Statement worksheet, merge and center the range A1:C1, and then apply the Accent2 cell style to the merged cell. Change the font size to 24 points and the text style to bold. Italicize the word "Clean" within the company name.
7. Make the following changes to the Income Statement worksheet:
   a. Format the range A3:C3 with the Heading 1 cell style.
   b. Format the range A4:C4,A9:C9 with the 40% - Accent1 cell style.
   c. Format cell B5 in the Accounting style with no decimal places.
   d. Format cell B6 and the range B10:B17 in the Comma style with no decimal places.
8. Add the following calculations to the workbook:
   a. In cell C7, calculate the gross profit, which is equal to the gross sales minus the cost of sales.
   b. In cell C18, calculate the company's total operating expenses, which is equal to the sum of the values in the range B10:B17. Format the value in the Accounting format with no decimal places.
   c. In cell C20, calculate the company's operating profit, which is equal to its gross profit minus its total operating expenses.
   d. In cell C21, calculate the company's incomes taxes by multiplying its total operating profit by the corporate tax rate (cell G25). Format the value in the Accounting format with no decimal places.
   e. In cell C22, calculate the company's net profit, which is equal to the total operating profit minus the income taxes.
9. Finalize the formatting of the Projected Income statement by adding the following:
   a. Add a bottom border to the ranges A6:C6, A17:C17, and A20:C20. Add a single top border and a double bottom border to the range A22:C22.
   b. Indent the expenses categories in the range A10:A17 twice.
10. Format the Financial Assumptions section as follows:
   a. Add borders around all of the cells in the range E4:G25.
   b. Format the range E3:G3 with the Heading 1 cell style.
   c. Merge the cells in the ranges E4:E7, E9:E13, E14:E15, E16:E18, and E20:E22.
   d. Top-align and left-align the range E4:E25.
   e. Change the fill color of the range E4:F25 to Green, Accent 1, Lighter 60%.

11. Use conditional formatting to highlight the net profit (cell C22) if its value is less than $50,000 with a light red fill with dark red text.

12. Change the value in cell G9 from 4 to **5**. Observe the impact that hiring another cleaner has on the projected net profit for the company in cell C22.

13. Format the printed version of the Income Statement worksheet as follows:

   a. Add a manual page break between columns D and E.

   b. For the first page, add a header that prints **Prepared by** followed by your name in the left section of the header and the current date in the right section of the header. Do not display header text on any other page.

   c. For every page, add a footer that prints the workbook filename in the left section, **Page** followed by the page number in the center section, and the worksheet name in the right section.

   d. Set the margins to 1 inch on all four sides of the printout, and center the contents of the worksheet horizontally within the printed page.

14. If you are instructed to print, print the entire contents of the workbook in portrait orientation.

15. Save and close the workbook.

Case Problem 2

APPLY

Data File needed for this Case Problem: Peak.xlsx

Peak Bytes   Peter Taylor is an engineer at Peak Bytes, an Internet service provider located in Great Falls, Montana. Part of Peter's job is to track the over-the-air connection speeds from the company's transmitters. Data from an automated program recording Internet access times has been entered into a workbook, but the data is difficult to interpret. He wants you to edit the workbook so that the data is easier to read and the fast and slow connection times are quickly visible. He also wants the workbook to provide summary statistics on the connection speeds. Complete the following:

1. Open the **Peak** workbook located in the Excel2 > Case2 folder, and then save the workbook as **Peak Bytes** in the location specified by your instructor.

2. In the Documentation sheet, enter your name in cell B3 and the date in cell B4.

3. Apply the Banded theme to the workbook.

4. Format the Documentation sheet as follows:

   a. Apply the Title cell style to cell A1. Change the font style to bold and the font size to 24 points.

   b. Add borders around the range A3:B5.

   c. Apply the Accent4 cell style to the range A3:A5.

   d. Top-align the contents in the range A3:B5.

5. In the Speed Test worksheet, move the data from the range A1:D97 to the range A12:D108.

6. Copy cell A1 from the Documentation sheet, and paste it into cell A1 of the Speed Test worksheet.

7. In cell A2, enter **Internet Speed Test Results**. Apply the Heading 1 cell style to the range A2:D2.

8. In cell A4, enter **Date** and format it using the Accent4 cell style. In cell B4, enter **4/8/2017** and format it using the Long Date format. Add a border around the cells in the range A4:B4.

9. Format the data in the Speed Test worksheet as follows:

   a. In the range A13:A108, format the numeric date and time values with the Time format. (*Hint*: The Time format is in the Number Format box in the Number group on the Home tab.)

   b. In the range C13:D108, show the numbers with three decimal places.

   c. In the range A12:D12, apply the Accent4 cell style and center the text.

   d. In the range A12:D108, add borders around all of the cells.

10. Create a table of summary statistics for the Internet Speed Test as follows:

   a. Copy the headings in the range B12:D12, and paste them into the range B6:D6.

   b. In cell A7, enter **Average**. In cell A8, enter **Minimum**. In cell A9, enter **Maximum**. Format the range A7:A9 with the Accent4 cell style.

c. In cell B7, use the AVERAGE function to calculate the average ping value of the values in the range B13:B108. In cell B8, use the MIN function to calculate the minimum ping value of the values in the range B13:B108. In cell B9, use the MAX function to calculate the maximum ping value of the values in the range B13:B108.

d. Copy the formulas from the range B7:B9 to the range C7:D9 to calculate summary statistics for the download and upload speeds from the Internet test.

e. Format the values in the range B7,C7:D9 to show two decimal places.

f. Add borders around all of the cells in the range A6:D9.

11. Use conditional formatting to highlight ping values greater than 70 in the range B13:B108 with a light red fill with dark red text to highlight times when the Internet usually appears to be slow.

12. Use conditional formatting to highlight upload values less than 3.5 in the range C13:C108 with a light red fill with dark red text.

13. Use conditional formatting to highlight download values less than 2 in the range D13:D108 with a light red fill with dark red text.

14. In cell D11, enter the text **Slow Connection**. Use conditional formatting to display this text string with a light red fill with dark red text. Center the text, and add a border around cell D11.

15. Set the print titles to repeat the first 12 rows at the top of every page of the printout.

16. For the first page of the printout, add a header that prints **Prepared by** followed by your name in the left section of the header and the current date in the right section of the header. Do not display header text on any other page.

17. For every page, add a footer that prints the workbook filename in the left section, **Page** followed by the page number followed by **of** followed by the number of pages in the center section, and then the worksheet name in the right section.

18. If you are instructed to print, print the entire contents of the workbook in portrait orientation.

19. Save and close the workbook.

Case Problem 3

Data File needed for this Case Problem: Wait.xlsx

YuriTech   Kayla Schwartz is the customer service manager at YuriTech, an electronics and computer firm located in Scottsdale, Arizona. Kayla is analyzing the calling records for technical support calls to YuriTech to determine which times are understaffed, resulting in unacceptable wait times. She has compiled several months of data and calculated the average wait times in one-hour intervals for each day of the week. You will format Kayla's workbook to make it easier to determine when YuriTech should hire more staff to assist with customer support requests. Complete the following:

1. Open the **Wait** workbook located in the Excel2 > Case3 folder, and then save the workbook as **Wait Times** in the location specified by your instructor.

2. In the Documentation sheet, enter your name in cell B3 and the date in cell B4.

3. Apply the Ion theme to the workbook.

4. Format the Documentation sheet as follows:

a. Format the title in cell A1 using a 36-point Impact font with the Purple, Accent 6 font color.

b. Format the range A3:A5 with the Accent6 cell style.

c. Add a border around the cells in the range A3:B5. Wrap the text within each cell, and top-align the cell text.

5. Copy the format you used in cell A1 of the Documentation sheet, and paste it to cell A1 of the Wait Times worksheet.

6. Format the text in cell A2 with 14-point bold font and the Purple, Accent6 font color.

7. In the range A14:H39, format the average customer wait times for each hour and day of the week data as follows:

   a. Merge and center the range A14:H14, and apply the Title cell style to the merged contents.

   b. Change the number format of the data in the range B16:H39 to show one decimal place.

   c. Format the column and row labels in the range A15:H15,A16:A39 with the Accent6 cell style. Center the column headings in the range B15:H15.

8. In cell B5, enter the value **22** as an excellent wait time. In cell B6, enter **34** as a good wait time. In cell B7, enter **45** as an acceptable wait time. In cell B8, enter **60** as a poor wait time. In cell B9, enter **78** as a very poor wait time. In cell B10, enter **90** as an unacceptable wait time.

9. In the range A4:C10, apply the following formats to the wait time goals:

   a. Merge and center the range A4:C4, and apply the Accent6 cell style to the merged cells.

   b. Add borders around the cells in the range A4:C10.

10. In cell E4, enter the label **Average Wait Time (All Days)**. In cell E7, enter the label **Average Wait Time (Weekdays)**. In cell E10, enter the label **Average Wait Time (Weekends)**.

11. Merge and center the range E4:F6, wrap the text in the merged cell, center the cell content both horizontally and vertically, and then apply the Accent6 cell style to the merged cell.

12. Copy the format from the merged cell E4:F6 to cells E7 and E10.

13. In cell G4, enter a formula to calculate the average of the wait times in the range B16:H39. In cell G7, enter a formula to calculate the average weekday wait times in the range C16:G39. In cell G10, calculate the average weekend rate times in the range B16:B39,H16:H39.

14. Merge and center the ranges G4:G6, G7:G9, and G10:G12, and then center the calculated averages vertically within each merged cell.

15. Add borders around the cells in the range E4:G12.

16. Change the fill color of the range A5:C5 to a medium green, the fill color of the range A6:C6 to a light green, the fill color of the range A7:C7 to a light gold, the fill color of the range A8:C8 to a light red, and the fill color of the range A9:C9 to a medium red. Format the range A10:C10 with white text on a black background.

⊕ **Explore** 17. Use conditional formatting to highlight cells with custom formats as follows:

   a. Select the range G4:G12,B16:H39. Use conditional formatting to highlight cells with values less than 22 with a custom format that matches the fill color used in the range A5:C5.

   b. Use conditional formatting to highlight cells with values greater than 90 in the range G4:G12,B16:H39 with a custom format of a white font on a black fill.

   c. Use conditional formatting to highlight cells with values between 22 and 34 in the range G4:G12,B16:H39 with a custom format that matches the fill color used in the range A6:C6.

   d. Use conditional formatting to highlight cells with values between 34 and 60 in the range G4:G12,B16:H39 with a light gold fill color that matches the cells in the range A7:C7.

   e. Use conditional formatting to highlight cells with values between 60 and 78 in the range G4:G12,B16:H39 with light red, matching the fill color of the cells in the range A8:C8.

   f. Use conditional formatting to highlight cells with values between 78 and 90 in the range G4:G12,B16:H39 with medium red, matching the fill color of the cells in the range A9:C9.

18. In cell A41, enter the label **Notes** and then format it with the Title cell style.

19. Merge the range A42:H50. Top- and left-align the contents of the cell. Turn on text wrapping within the merged cell. Add a thick outside border to the merged cell.

20. Within the merged cell in the range A42:H50, summarize your conclusions about the wait times. Answer whether the wait times are within acceptable limits on average for the entire week, on weekdays, and on weekends. Also indicate whether there are times during the week that customers are experience very poor to unacceptable delays.

21. Format the printed version of the Wait Times worksheet as follows:

    a. Scale the sheet so that it fits on a single page in portrait orientation.

    b. Center the sheet on the page horizontally and vertically.

c. Add the header **Prepared by** followed by your name in the right section.

d. Add a footer that prints the filename in the left section, the worksheet name in the center section, and the date in the right section.

22. If you are instructed to print, print the entire contents of the workbook.

23. Save and close the workbook.

Case Problem 4

CREATE

Data File needed for this Case Problem: Pandaisia.xlsx

Pandaisia Chocolates   Anne Ambrose is the owner and head chocolatier of Pandaisia Chocolates, a chocolate shop located in Essex, Vermont. Anne has asked you to create an Excel workbook in which she can enter customer orders. She wants the workbook to be easy to use and read. The final design of the order form is up to you. One possible solution is shown in Figure 2-47.

Figure 2-47   Pandaisia Chocolates order form

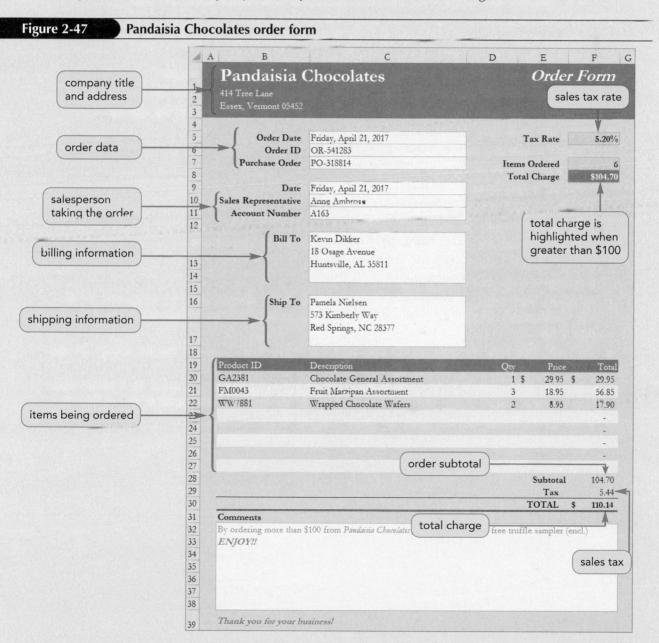

Complete the following:

1. Open the **Pandaisia** workbook located in the Excel2 > Case3 folder, and then save the workbook as **Pandaisia Order** in the location specified by your instructor.
2. In the Documentation sheet, enter your name in cell B3 and the date in cell B4.
3. Insert a worksheet named **Order Form** after the Documentation worksheet.
4. Enter the following information in the order form:
    - The title and address of Pandaisia Chocolates
    - The order date, order ID, and purchase order ID
    - The date, sales representative, and account number for the order
    - The billing address of the order
    - The shipping address of the order
    - A table listing every item ordered including the item's product ID, description, quantity ordered, price, and total charge for the item(s)
    - A comment box where Anne can insert additional information about the order
5. Include formulas in the order form to do the following:
    a. For each item ordered, calculate the cost of the item(s), which is equal to the quantity multiplied by the price.
    b. Calculate the subtotal of the costs for every item ordered by the customer.
    c. Calculate the sales tax for the order, which is equal to 5.2 percent times the subtotal value.
    d. Calculate the total cost of the order, which is equal to the subtotal plus the sale tax.
6. Format the order form by doing the following:
    a. Apply a different built-in Excel theme.
    b. Change the font colors and fill colors.
    c. Format a text string within a cell.
    d. Align content within cells.
    e. Format dates with the Long Date format.
    f. Apply the Percent, Accounting, and Currency formats as appropriate.
    g. Add borders around cells and ranges.
    h. Merge a range into a single cell.
7. Pandaisia Chocolates includes a free complimentary truffle sample for every order over $100. Use conditional formatting to highlight the total charge in bold colored font when it is greater than $100.
8. Test your order form by entering the data shown in Figure 2-47. Confirm that the charge on your order matches that shown in the figure.
9. Set up the print version of the order form so that it prints in portrait orientation on a single sheet. Add a header and/or footer that includes your name, the date, and the name of the workbook.
10. If you are instructed to print, print the entire contents of the workbook.
11. Save and close the workbook.

EXCEL

OBJECTIVES

Session 3.1
- Document formulas and data values
- Explore function syntax
- Insert functions from the Formula Library
- Perform a what-if analysis

Session 3.2
- AutoFill series and formulas
- Use relative and absolute cell references
- Use the Quick Analysis tool
- Work with dates and Date functions
- Find values with Lookup functions
- Work with Logical functions

Performing Calculations with Formulas and Functions

Calculating Farm Yield and Revenue

Case | *Wingait Farm*

Jane Wingait is the owner and operator of Wingait Farm, a small farm located outside of Cascade, Iowa. Jane's cash crop is corn, and she has planted almost 140 acres of the sweet corn variety for the past 11 years. Near harvest time every year Jane samples and analyzes a portion of her crop to estimate her farm's total yield for the year. She wants you to help her design an Excel workbook that will calculate her corn yield. As Jane prepares for next year's crop, she also wants to use Excel to track her corn's growth from planting to harvesting. As you create the workbook, you will explore how Jane can use Excel formulas to help her in running her farm.

STARTING DATA FILES

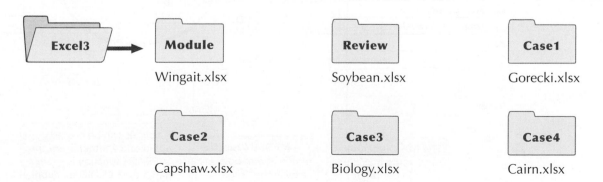

Excel3 →	Module	Review	Case1
	Wingait.xlsx	Soybean.xlsx	Gorecki.xlsx
	Case2	Case3	Case4
	Capshaw.xlsx	Biology.xlsx	Cairn.xlsx

Session 3.1 Visual Overview:

Functions are organized by category in the Function Library group. When you select a function, the Function Arguments dialog box opens.

The Insert Function button opens the Insert Function dialog box from which you can select a function.

The Input cell style can be used for data that is inserted by the user.

The Calculated cell style can be used for calculated values.

The **COUNT function** tallies how many cells in the specified range contain numbers or dates.

The **MIN function** returns the minimum value in the range.

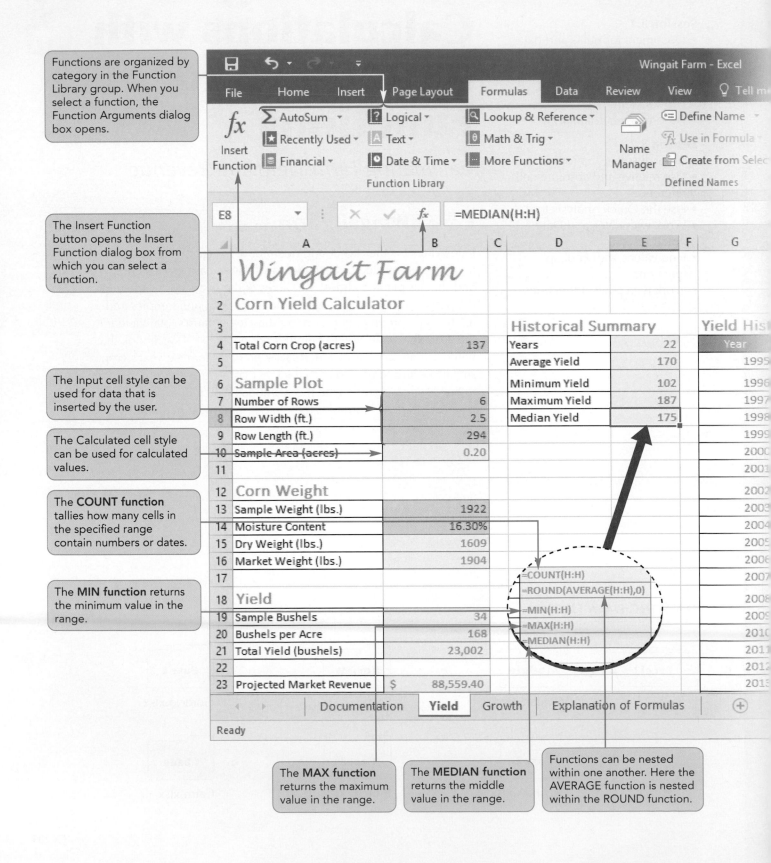

The MAX function returns the maximum value in the range.

The MEDIAN function returns the middle value in the range.

Functions can be nested within one another. Here the AVERAGE function is nested within the ROUND function.

Formulas and Functions

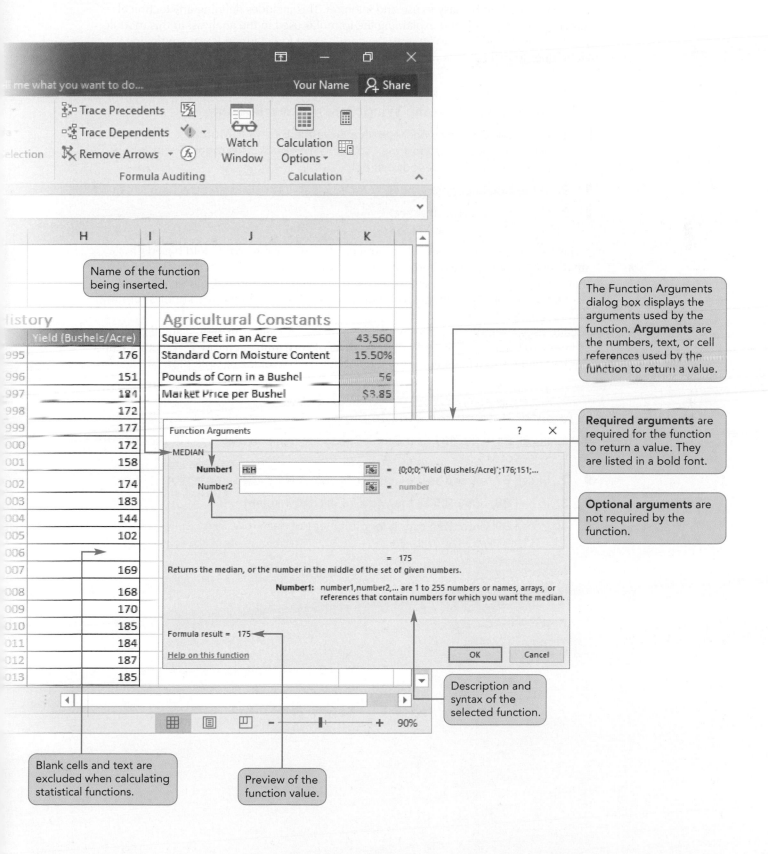

Name of the function being inserted.

The Function Arguments dialog box displays the arguments used by the function. **Arguments** are the numbers, text, or cell references used by the function to return a value.

Required arguments are required for the function to return a value. They are listed in a bold font.

Optional arguments are not required by the function.

Description and syntax of the selected function.

Preview of the function value.

Blank cells and text are excluded when calculating statistical functions.

Agricultural Constants

Square Feet in an Acre	43,560
Standard Corn Moisture Content	15.50%
Pounds of Corn in a Bushel	56
Market Price per Bushel	$3.85

History

	Yield (Bushels/Acre)
995	176
996	151
997	181
998	172
999	177
000	172
001	158
002	174
003	183
004	144
005	102
006	
007	169
008	168
009	170
010	185
011	184
012	187
013	185

Function Arguments

MEDIAN

Number1 H:H = {0;0;0;"Yield (Bushels/Acre)";176;151;...

Number2 = number

= 175

Returns the median, or the number in the middle of the set of given numbers.

Number1: number1,number2,... are 1 to 255 numbers or names, arrays, or references that contain numbers for which you want the median.

Formula result = 175

Help on this function

OK   Cancel

Trace Precedents
Trace Dependents
Remove Arrows
Formula Auditing

Watch Window

Calculation Options
Calculation

90%

Making Workbooks User-Friendly

Excel is a powerful application for interpreting a wide variety of data used in publications from financial reports to scientific articles. To be an effective tool for data analysis, a workbook needs to be easy to use and interpret. This includes defining any technical terms in the workbook and explaining the formulas used in the analysis. In this module, you'll create a workbook to analyze the corn harvest for a farm in Iowa, employing techniques to make the workbook easily accessible to other users.

To open and review the Wingait Farms workbook:

▶ **1.** Open the **Wingait** workbook located in the **Excel3 > Module** folder included with your Data Files, and then save the workbook as **Wingait Farm** in the location specified by your instructor.

▶ **2.** In the Documentation sheet, enter your name in cell B3 and the date in cell B4.

▶ **3.** Go to the **Yield** worksheet.

Jane uses the Yield worksheet to project her farm's entire corn yield based on a small sample of harvested corn. Information about the sample and the calculations that estimate the total yield will be entered in columns A and B. Columns D and E contain important agricultural constants that Jane will use in the workbook's formulas and functions.

Jane uses a sample plot to estimate the farm's total yield. This plot, a small portion of Jane's 137-acre farm, is laid out in six rows of corn with each row 294 feet long and 2.5 feet wide. You will enter information about the size of the sample plot.

To enter data on the sample plot:

▶ **1.** In cell **B4**, enter **137** as the total acreage of the farm that Jane devotes to sweet corn.

▶ **2.** In cell **B7**, enter **6** as the number of corn rows in the sample plot.

▶ **3.** In cell **B8**, enter **2.5** as the width of each row in feet.

▶ **4.** In cell **B9**, enter **294** as the length in feet of each row. See Figure 3-1.

Figure 3-1   Sample plot data entered

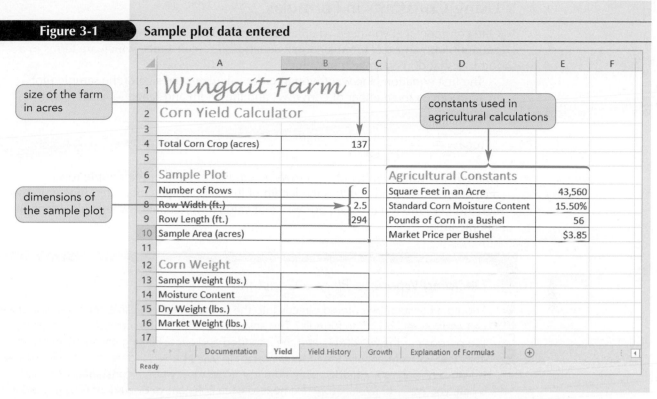

size of the farm in acres

dimensions of the sample plot

constants used in agricultural calculations

The width and length of the sample rows are measured in feet, but Jane needs the total area expressed in acres. To calculate the area of the sample being tested, you need to refer to the agricultural equations that Jane documented for you.

Documenting Formulas

Documenting the contents of a workbook helps to avoid errors and confusion. It also makes it easier for others to interpret the analysis in the workbook. For workbooks that include many calculations, such as the Wingait Farm workbook, it is helpful to explain the formulas and terms used in the calculations. Such documentation also can serve as a check that the equations are accurate.

Jane has included explanations of equations you'll use in developing her workbook. Before proceeding, you'll review this documentation.

To review the documentation in Wingait Farm workbook:

1. Go to the **Explanation of Formulas** worksheet.

2. Read the worksheet contents, reviewing the descriptions of common agricultural constants and formulas. As you continue developing the Wingait Farm workbook, you'll learn about these terms and formulas in more detail.

3. Go to the **Yield** worksheet.

Using Constants in Formulas

One common skill you need when creating a workbook is being able to translate an equation into an Excel formula. Some equations use **constants**, which are terms in a formula that don't change their value.

The first equation Jane wants you to enter calculates the size of the sample plot in acres, given the number of corn rows and the width and length of each row. The formula is

$$area = \frac{2 \times rows \times width \times length}{43560}$$

where *rows* is the number of corn rows, *width* is the width of the sample rows measured in feet, and *length* is the length of the sample rows measured in feet. In this equation, 43560 is a constant because that value never changes when calculating the sample area.

INSIGHT

Deciding Where to Place a Constant

Should a constant be entered directly into the formula or placed in a separate worksheet cell and referenced in the formula? The answer depends on the constant being used, the purpose of the workbook, and the intended audience. Placing constants in separate cells that you reference in the formulas can help users better understand the worksheet because no values are hidden within the formulas. Also, when a constant is entered in a cell, you can add explanatory text next to each constant to document how it is being used in the formula. On the other hand, you don't want a user to inadvertently change the value of a constant and throw off all the formula results. You will need to evaluate how important it is for other people to immediately see the constant and whether the constant requires any explanation for other people to understand the formula.

To convert the area equation to an Excel formula, you'll replace the *row*, *width*, and *length* values with references to the cells B7, B8, and B9, and you'll replace 43560 with a reference to cell E7. These cells provide the number of rows in the sample plot, the row width in feet, the row length in feet, and the number of square feet in one acre of land.

To calculate the area of the sample plot:

1. In cell **B10**, enter the formula **=2*B7*B8*B9/E7** to calculate the area of the sample plot. The formula returns 0.202479339.

   Trouble? If your result differs from 0.202479339, you probably entered the formula incorrectly. Edit the formula you entered in cell B10 as needed so that the numbers and cell references match those shown in the formula in Step 1.

   Jane does not need to see the acreage of the sample plot with eight decimal places.

2. Click cell **B10**, and then decrease the number of decimal places to **2**. The area of the sample plot is displayed as 0.20 acres. See Figure 3-2.

TIP

Decreasing the number decimals places rounds the displayed value; the stored value remains unchanged.

Figure 3-2   Calculated size of the sample plot in acres

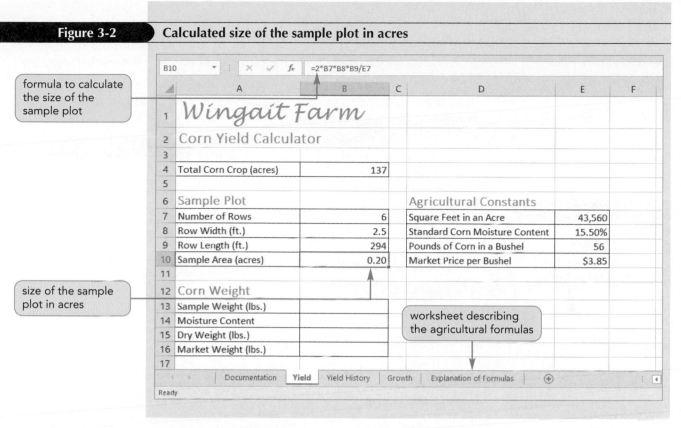

formula to calculate the size of the sample plot

size of the sample plot in acres

When Jane harvests the corn from the sample plot, she measures the total weight of the corn, which includes its moisture content. She then analyzes the corn to determine what percentage of its weight is due to moisture. The total weight of the corn is 1,922 pounds of which 16.3 percent is moisture. To sell the corn, Jane needs to calculate the dry weight of the corn without the moisture. She can do this with the formula

$$dry\ weight = total\ weight \times (1 - moisture)$$

where *total weight* is the weight of the corn and *moisture* is the percentage of the weight due to moisture. Market prices for corn are standardized at a moisture percentage of 15.5 percent, so to get the correct market weight of her corn, Jane uses the following formula:

$$market\ weight = \frac{dry\ weight}{1 - 0.155}$$

You will enter these two formulas in Jane's workbook to calculate the market weight of the corn she harvested from the sample plot.

To calculate the market weight of the corn:

1. In cell **B13**, enter **1922** as the total weight of the corn sample.

2. In cell **B14**, enter **16.3%** as the moisture content.

3. In cell **B15**, enter the formula **=B13*(1-B14)** to calculate the dry weight of the corn kernels. Based on the formula, the dry weight of the corn harvested from the sample plot is 1608.714 pounds.

Because the expression requires dividing by two terms, you must enclose those terms within parentheses.

4. In cell **B16**, enter the formula **=B15/(1-E8)** to calculate the market weight of the corn kernels using the dry weight value in cell B15 and the standard moisture content value in cell E8. Based on the formula, the market weight of the corn is 1903.80355 pounds.

Jane does not need to see such precise weight values, so you will reduce the number of decimal places displayed in the worksheet.

5. Select the range **B15:B16**, and then format the numbers with no decimals places to display the dry and market weights of 1609 and 1904 pounds, respectively. See Figure 3-3.

Figure 3-3	Calculated dry and market weights of the corn

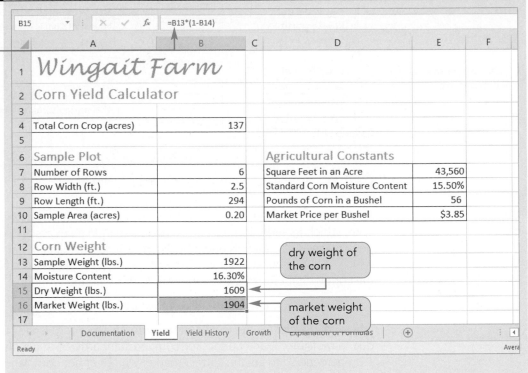

formula to calculate the dry corn weight

B15   fx   =B13*(1-B14)

dry weight of the corn

market weight of the corn

Corn is not sold by the pound but rather by the bushel where 1 bushel contains 56 pounds of corn. You will calculate the number of bushels of corn in the sample plot and then use this number to estimate the farm's total yield and revenue.

To project the farm's total yield and revenue:

1. In cell **B19**, enter the formula **=B16/E9** to convert the market weight to bushels. In this case, the market weight is equal to 33.99649197 bushels.

2. In cell **B19**, format the number with no decimals places. The number is rounded to 34 bushels.

3. In cell **B20**, enter the formula **=B19/B10** to divide the number of bushels in the sample plot by the size of the plot in acres. Based on this calculation, this year's crop has yielded 167.901042 bushels per acre.

4. In cell **B20**, format the number with no decimals places. This year's crop yielded about 168 bushels per acre.

   Assuming that the rest of the farm is as productive as the sample plot, you can calculate the total bushels that the farm can produce by multiplying the bushels per acre by the total acreage of the farm.

5. In cell **B21**, enter the formula **=B20*B4** to multiply the bushels per acre by the total acreage of the farm. Assuming that the rest of the farm is as productive as the sample plot, the total bushels that the farm can produce is 23002.44275 bushels.

6. Format cell B21 using the Comma style with no decimal places. Cell B21 displays 23,002.

7. In cell **B23**, enter the formula **=B21*E10** to calculate the revenue Jane can expect by selling all of the farm's corn at the market price of $3.85 per bushel.

8. Format cell B23 with the Accounting style. The formula result is displayed as $88,559.40. See Figure 3-4.

| Figure 3-4 | Projected yield and revenue from the corn harvest |

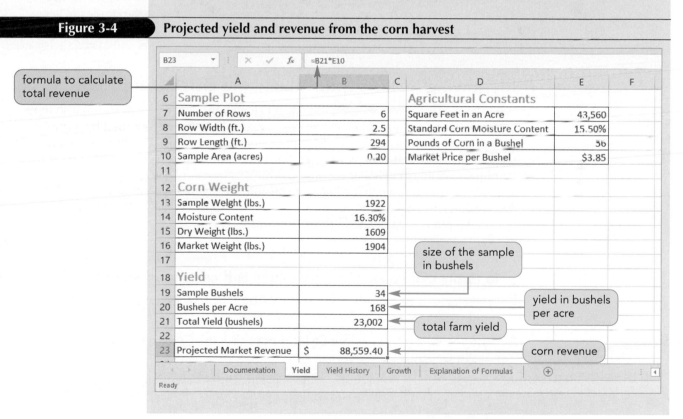

Based on your calculations, Jane projects an income of almost $90,000 from this year's corn crop.

Written Communication: Displaying Significant Digits

Excel stores numbers with up to 15 digits and displays as many digits as will fit into the cell. So even the result of a simple formula such as =10/3 will display 3.33333333333333 if the cell is wide enough.

A number with 15 digits is difficult to read, and calculations rarely need that level of accuracy. Many scientific disciplines, such as chemistry or physics, have rules for specifying exactly how many digits should be displayed with any calculation. These digits are called **significant digits** because they indicate the accuracy of the measured and calculated values. For example, an input value of 19.32 has four significant digits.

The rules are based on several factors and vary from one discipline to another. Generally, a calculated value should display no more digits than are found in any of the input values. For example, because the input value 19.32 has four significant digits, any calculated value based on that input should have no more than four significant digits. Showing more digits would be misleading because it implies a level of accuracy beyond that which was actually measured.

Because Excel displays calculated values with as many digits as can fit into a cell, you need to know the standards for your profession and change the display of your calculated values accordingly.

Identifying Notes, Input Values, and Calculated Values

When worksheets involve notes and many calculations, it is useful to distinguish input values that are used in formulas from calculated values that are returned by formulas. Formatting that clearly differentiates input values from calculated values helps others more easily understand the worksheet. Such formatting also helps prevent anyone from entering a value in a cell that contains a formula.

Jane wants to be sure that whenever she and her staff update the workbook, they can easily see where to enter data values. You will apply cell styles to distinguish between input and calculated values.

To apply cell styles to input values and calculated values:

▶ 1. Select the nonadjacent range **B4,B7:B9,B13:B14,E7:E10**. These cells contain the data that you entered for Jane.

▶ 2. On the Home tab, in the Styles group, click the **Cell Styles** button to open the Cell Styles gallery.

▶ 3. In the Data and Model section, click the **Input** cell style. The selected cells are formatted with a light blue font on an orange background, identifying those cells as containing input values.

▶ 4. Select the nonadjacent range **B10,B15:B16,B19:B21,B23**. These cells contain the formulas for calculating the weight, yield, and revenue values.

▶ 5. Format the selected cells with the **Calculation** cell style located in the Data and Model section of the Cell Styles gallery. The cells with the calculated values are formatted with a bold orange font on a light gray background.

▶ 6. Click cell **D12** to deselect the range. See Figure 3-5.

Figure 3-5 | Input and calculated values formatted with cell styles

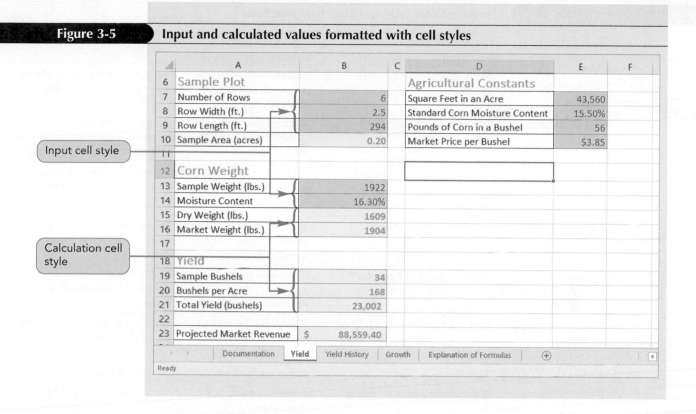

Input cell style

Calculation cell style

	A	B	C	D	E	F
6	Sample Plot			Agricultural Constants		
7	Number of Rows	6		Square Feet in an Acre	43,560	
8	Row Width (ft.)	2.5		Standard Corn Moisture Content	15.50%	
9	Row Length (ft.)	294		Pounds of Corn in a Bushel	56	
10	Sample Area (acres)	0.20		Market Price per Bushel	$3.85	
11						
12	Corn Weight					
13	Sample Weight (lbs.)	1922				
14	Moisture Content	16.30%				
15	Dry Weight (lbs.)	1609				
16	Market Weight (lbs.)	1904				
17						
18	Yield					
19	Sample Bushels	34				
20	Bushels per Acre	168				
21	Total Yield (bushels)	23,002				
22						
23	Projected Market Revenue	$ 88,559.40				

Documentation | **Yield** | Yield History | Growth | Explanation of Formulas | ⊕

Ready

Using Excel Functions

Excel functions can be used in place of long and complicated formulas to simplify your worksheet. Jane wants to compare the estimated yield for this year's crop to historic trends. To make that comparison, you'll work with some Excel functions.

Understanding Function Syntax

Before you use functions, you should understand the function syntax. Recall that the syntax of an Excel function follows the general pattern

    FUNCTION(argument1,argument2,...)

where FUNCTION is the name of the function, and argument1, argument2, and so forth are arguments used by the function. An argument can be any type of value including text, numbers, cell references, or even other formulas or functions. Not all functions require arguments.

Some arguments are optional and can be included with the function or omitted altogether. Most optional arguments will have default values, so that if you omit an argument value, Excel will automatically apply the default. The convention is to show optional arguments within square brackets along with the argument's default value (if any), as

    FUNCTION(argument1[,argument2=value2,...])

where argument1 is a required argument, argument2 is optional, and value2 is the default value for argument2. As you work with specific functions, you will learn which arguments are required and which are optional as well as any default values associated with those optional arguments.

Figure 3-6 describes some of the more commonly used Math, Trig, and Statistical functions and provides the syntax of those functions, including any optional arguments.

Figure 3-6   **Common Math, Trig, and Statistical functions**

Function	Description
AVERAGE(number1[,number2,...])	Calculates the average of a collection of numbers, where number1, number2, and so forth are numbers or cell references
COUNT(value1[,value2,...])	Counts how many cells in a range contain numbers, where value1, value2, and so forth are either numbers or cell references
COUNTA(value1[,value2,...])	Counts how many cells are not empty in ranges value1, value2, and so forth including both numbers and text entries
INT(number)	Displays the integer portion of number
MAX(number1[,number2,...])	Calculates the maximum value of a collection of numbers, where number1, number2, and so forth are either numbers or cell references
MEDIAN(number1[,number2,...])	Calculates the median, or middle, value of a collection of numbers, where number1, number2, and so forth are either numbers or cell references
MIN(number1[,number2,...])	Calculates the minimum value of a collection of numbers, where number1, number2, and so forth are either numbers or cell references
RAND()	Returns a random number between 0 and 1
ROUND(number,num_digits)	Rounds number to the number of digits specified by num_digits
SUM(number1[,number2,...])	Adds a collection of numbers, where number1, number2, and so forth are either numbers or cell references

Entering the COUNT function

The following COUNT function is used by Excel to count how many cells in a range contain numbers. The COUNT function syntax is

```
COUNT(value1[,value2,…])
```

where value1 is either a cell reference, range reference, or a number, and value2 and so on are optional arguments that provide additional cell references, range references, or numbers. There are no default values for the optional arguments.

The COUNT function does not include blank cells or cells that contain text in its tally. For example, the following function counts how many cells in the range A1:A10, the range C1:C5, and cell E5 contain numbers or dates:

```
COUNT(A1:A10,C1:C5,E5)
```

The COUNT function is especially helpful when data in the ranges are regularly updated.

INSIGHT

Counting Text

Excel has another important function for counting cells—the **COUNTA function**. This function counts the number of cells that contain any entries, including numbers, dates, or text. The syntax of the COUNTA function is

COUNTA(*value1*[,*value2*,...])

where *value1* is the first item or cell reference containing the entries you want to count. The remaining optional value arguments are used primarily when you want to count entries in nonadjacent ranges. The COUNTA function should be used for text data or for data in which you need to include blanks as part of the total.

You'll use the COUNT function to tally how many years of data are included in the corn yield history.

To count the number of years in the corn yield history:

1. Go to the **Yield History** worksheet, and then click cell **B5**. You'll enter the COUNT function in this cell.

2. Type **=COUNT(** to begin entering the COUNT function. The first argument, which is the only required argument, is the cell or range reference for the cells to be counted.

   The yield values are stored in the range E5:E27. Instead of referencing this range, you will use column E as the argument for the COUNT function because Jane plans to add data to this column each year as she continues to track the farm's annual corn yield.

3. Click the **E** column heading to select the entire column. The column reference E:E is inserted into the function as the first argument.

4. Type **)** to end the function, and then press the **Enter** key. The formula =COUNT(E:E) is entered in cell B5 and returns 22, which is the number of years for which Jane has corn yield data.

Nesting the ROUND and AVERAGE Functions

One function can be placed inside, or **nested**, within another function. When a formula contains more than one function, Excel first evaluates the innermost function and then moves outward to evaluate the next function. The inner function acts as an argument value for the outer function. For example, the following expression nests the AVERAGE function within the ROUND function.

ROUND(AVERAGE(A1:A100),0)

TIP

The ROUND function changes the value stored in the cell, not the number of decimal places displayed in the cell.

Excel first uses the AVERAGE function to calculate the average of the values in the range A1:A100 and then uses the ROUND function to round that average to the nearest integer (where the number of digits to the right of the decimal point is 0.)

One challenge of nested functions is being sure to include all of the parentheses. You can check this by counting the number of opening parentheses and making sure that number matches the number of closing parentheses. Excel also displays each level of nested parentheses in different colors to make it easier for you to match the opening and closing parentheses. If the number of parentheses doesn't match, Excel will not accept the formula and will provide a suggestion for how to rewrite the formula so the number of opening and closing parentheses does match.

Jane wants you to analyze the corn yield history at Wingait Farm. You'll use the COUNT function to tally the number of years in the historical sample and then use the AVERAGE function to calculate the average yield during those years. Because Jane doesn't need the exact corn yield values, you'll use the ROUND function to round that calculated average to the nearest integer.

To analyze the corn yield history:

1. Click cell **B6**. You want to enter the nested function in this cell.

2. Type **=ROUND(** to begin the formula with the ROUND function.

3. Type **AVERAGE(E:E)** to enter the AVERAGE function as the first argument of the ROUND function.

4. Type **,** (a comma) to separate the first and second arguments.

5. Type **0)** to specify the number of decimal places to include in the results. In this case, Jane doesn't want to include any decimal places.

6. Press the **Enter** key. The nested functions first calculate the average value of the numbers in column E and then round that number to the nearest integer. The formula returns 170, which is the average annual yield of Wingait Farm in bushels per acre rounded to the nearest integer. See Figure 3-7.

Figure 3-7 Nested functions calculate the average annual yield

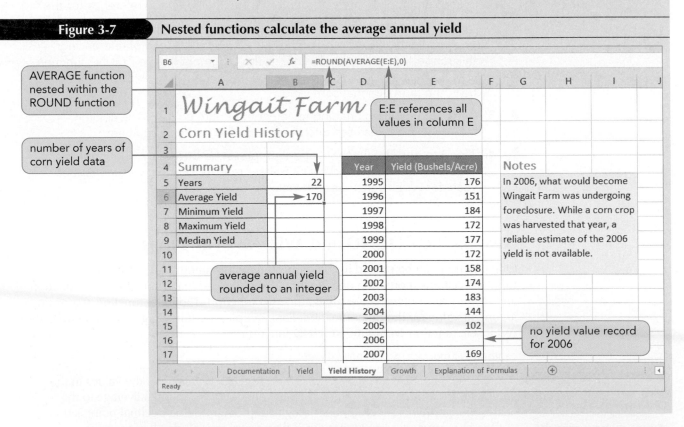

Based on values from 22 seasons of data, Jane expects her farm to yield 170 bushels of corn per acre each year.

Note that in 2006, no data on corn yield was available. Excel ignores nonnumeric data and blank cells when calculating statistical functions such as COUNT and AVERAGE. So, the count and average values in cells B5 and B6 represent only those years containing recorded corn yields. Keep in mind that a blank cell is not the same as a zero value in worksheet calculations. Figure 3-8 shows how function results differ when a zero replaces a blank in the selected range.

Figure 3-8   Calculations with blank cells and zero values

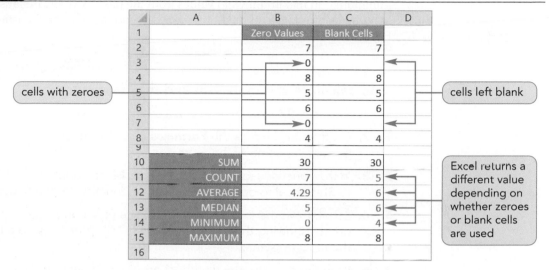

Whether you use a blank or zero depends on what you're trying to measure. For example, if Jane were to calculate average hours worked per day at the Wingait farm store, she could enter 0 for the holidays on which the store is closed, or she could enter a blank and thus calculate the average only for days in which the store is open.

Using the Function Library and the Insert Function Dialog Box

With so many Excel functions, it can difficult to locate the function you want to use for a particular application. Excel organizes its function into the 13 categories described in Figure 3-9. These function categories are available in the Function Library group on the Formulas tab and in the Insert Function dialog box.

Figure 3-9   Excel function categories

Category	Description
Compatibility	Functions from Excel 2010 or earlier, still supported to provide backward compatibility
Cube	Retrieve data from multidimensional databases involving online analytical processing (OLAP)
Database	Retrieve and analyze data stored in databases
Date & Time	Analyze or create date and time values and time intervals
Engineering	Analyze engineering problems
Financial	Analyze information for business and finance
Information	Return information about the format, location, or contents of worksheet cells
Logical	Return logical (true-false) values
Lookup & Reference	Look up and return data matching a set of specified conditions from a range
Math & Trig	Perform math and trigonometry calculations
Statistical	Provide statistical analyses of data sets
Text	Return text values or evaluate text
Web	Provide information on web-based connections

Once you select a function either from the Function Library or the Insert Function dialog box, the Function Arguments dialog box opens, listing all of the arguments associated with that function. Required arguments are in bold type; optional arguments are in normal type.

Jane wants to know the range of annual corn yields, so she asks you to calculate the minimum and maximum yield values from the past 23 years. Because minimums and maximums are statistical measures, you will find them in the Statistics category in the Function Library.

To calculate the minimum and maximum yield:

1. Click cell **B7** if necessary to make it the active cell.

2. On the ribbon, click the **Formulas** tab. The Function Library group has buttons for some of the more commonly used categories of functions.

3. In the Function Library group, click the **More Functions** button, and then point to **Statistical** to open a list of all of the functions in the Statistical category.

4. Scroll down the list, and click **MIN**. The Function Arguments dialog box opens, showing the arguments for the MIN function and a brief description of the function syntax.

5. With the entry for the Number1 argument highlighted, click the **E** column heading to select the entire column and insert the cell reference **E:E** into the Number1 input box. See Figure 3-10.

Figure 3-10	MIN function in the Function Arguments dialog box

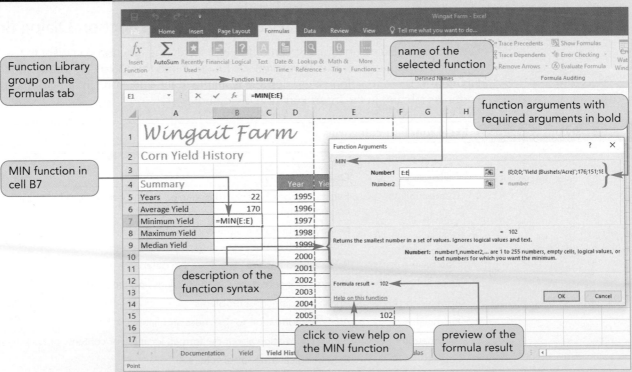

Trouble? You can click and drag the title bar in the Function Arguments dialog box to move it out of the way of the column E heading.

6. Click the **OK** button to insert the formula =MIN(E:E) into cell B7. The formula returns 102, which is the minimum value in column E.

7. Click cell **B8**, and then repeat Steps 3 through 6, selecting the **MAX** function from the Statistical category. The formula =MAX(E:E) entered in cell B8, and returns 187, which is the maximum value in column E. See Figure 3-11.

Figure 3-11 **Results of the MIN and MAX functions**

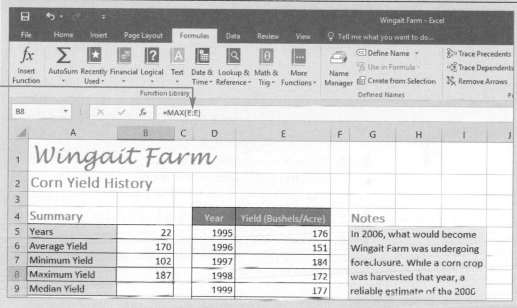

formula to calculate the maximum value in column E

Note that like the COUNT and AVERAGE functions, the MIN and MAX functions ignore cells with text or blank cells in the selected range.

The average is one way of summarizing data from a sample. However, averages are susceptible to the effects of extremely large or extremely small values. For example, imagine calculating the average net worth of 10 people when one of them is a billionaire. An average would probably not be a good representation of the typical net worth of that group. To avoid the effect of extreme values, statisticians often use the middle, or median, value in the sample.

Jane wants you to include the median corn yield value from the farm's history. Rather than inserting the function from the Function Library, you'll search for this function in the Insert Function dialog box.

To find the median corn yield:

1. Click cell **B9** to make it the active cell.

2. Click the **Insert Function** button f_x located to the left of the formula bar. The Insert Function dialog box opens.

3. In the Search for a function box, type **middle value** as the search description, and then click the **Go** button. A list of functions matching that description appears in the Select a function box. See Figure 3-12.

Figure 3-12 Search results in the Insert Function dialog box

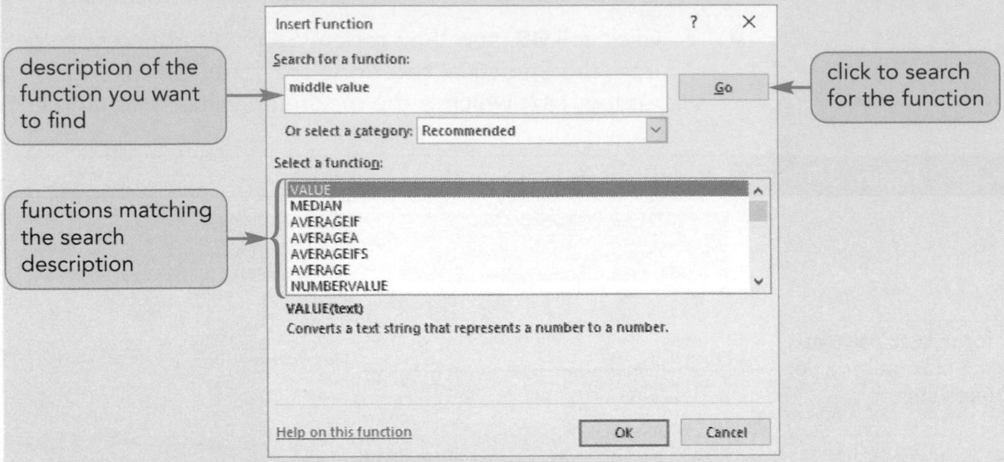

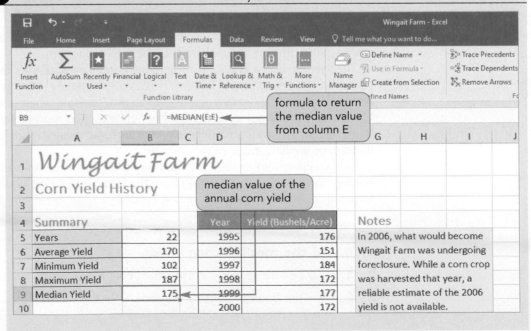

4. In the Select a function box, click **MEDIAN** to select that function, and then click the **OK** button. The Function Arguments dialog box opens with the insertion point in the Number1 box.

5. Click the **E** column heading to insert the reference E:E in the Number1 box.

6. Click the **OK** button. The formula =MEDIAN(E:E) is entered in cell B9. The formula returns 175, which is the middle value from the list of annual corn yields in the farm's history. See Figure 3-13.

Figure 3-13 Median function finds the middle corn yield value

The median estimate of 175 bushels per acre is higher than the average value of 170 bushels per acre. This is due in part to the extremely low yield of 102 bushels per acre in 2005, which brought the overall average value down. Because of this, 175 bushels per acre might be a more reliable estimate of the farm's productivity.

Methods of Rounding

For cleaner and neater workbooks, you will often want to round your values. There is little need for a large corporation to show revenue to the nearest cents at the annual stockholders' convention. Excel provides several methods for rounding data values. One method is to decrease the number of decimal places displayed in the cell, leaving the underlying value unchanged but rounding the displayed value to a specified number of digits.

Another approach is to use the ROUND function, which rounds the value itself to a specified number of digits. The ROUND function also accepts negative values for the number of digits in order to round the value to the nearest multiple of 10, 100, 1000, and so forth. The formula

```
=ROUND(5241,-2)
```

returns a value of 5200, rounding the value to the nearest hundred. For rounding to the nearest of multiple of a given number, use the function

```
MROUND(number,multiple)
```

where *number* is the number to be rounded and *multiple* is the multiple that the number should be rounded to. For example, the formula

```
=MROUND(5241,25)
```

rounds 5241 to the nearest multiple of 25, returning 5250. Remember though that when you use these rounding methods, you should always have access to the original, unrounded data, in case you need to audit your calculations in the future.

Next Jane wants to explore how to increase the farm's corn revenue in future seasons. You can explore the possibilities with a what-if analysis.

Performing What-If Analyses

A **what-if analysis** explores the impact that changing input values has on calculated values. For example, Jane wants to increase the farm's total revenue from corn, which you calculated as $88,559.40 for the current year, to at least $100,000. The most obvious way to increase the farm's corn revenue is to plant and then harvest more corn. Jane asks you to perform a what-if analysis to determine how many acres of corn would be needed to generate $100,000 of income, assuming conditions remain the same as the current year in which the farm yielded 168 bushels per acre at a selling price of $3.85 per bushel.

Using Trial and Error

One way to perform a what-if analysis is with **trial and error** where you change one or more of the input values to see how they affect the calculated results. Trial and error requires some guesswork as you estimate which values to change and by how much. You will use the trial and error to study the impact of changing the cornfield acreage on the total revenue generated for the farm.

To use trial and error to find how many acres of corn will generate $100,000 revenue:

   1. Go to the **Yield** worksheet containing calculations for determining the farm's current corn revenue.

2. In cell **B4**, change the farm acreage from 137 to **150**. Cell B23 shows that with 150 acres of corn sold at $3.85 per bushel, the farm's revenue from corn sales would increase from $88,559.40 to $96,962.85.

3. In cell **B4**, change the farm acreage from 150 to **175**. Cell B23 shows that if the farm plants 175 acres of corn, the revenue would increase to $113,123.33.

4. In cell **B4**, change the farm acreage back to **137**, which is the current acreage of corn on Wingait Farm.

To find the exact acreage that would result in $100,000 of revenue, you would have to continue trying different values in cell B4, gradually closing in on the correct value. This is why the method is called "trial and error." For some calculations, trial and error can be a very time-consuming way to locate the exact input value. A more direct approach to this problem is to use Goal Seek.

Using Goal Seek

Goal Seek automates the trial-and-error process by allowing you to specify a value for a calculated item, which Excel uses to determine the input value needed to reach that goal. In this case, because Jane wants $100,000 of revenue, the question that Goal Seek answers is: "How many acres of corn are needed to generate $100,000?" Goal Seek starts by setting the calculated value and automatically works backward to determine the correct input value.

REFERENCE

Performing What-If Analysis and Goal Seek

To perform a what-if analysis by trial and error:
- Change the value of a worksheet cell (the input cell).
- Observe its impact on one or more calculated cells (the result cells).
- Repeat until the desired results are achieved.

To perform a what-if analysis using Goal Seek:
- On the Data tab, in the Forecast group, click the What-If Analysis button, and then click Goal Seek.
- Select the result cell in the Set cell box, and then specify its value (goal) in the To value box.
- In the By changing cell box, specify the input cell.
- Click the OK button. The value of the input cell changes to set the value of the result cell.

You will use Goal Seek to find how much acreage Wingait Farms must plant with corn to achieve $100,000 of revenue.

To use Goal Seek to find how many acres of corn will generate $100,000 revenue:

1. On the ribbon, click the **Data** tab.

2. In the Forecast group, click the **What-If Analysis** button, and then click **Goal Seek**. The Goal Seek dialog box opens.

3. With Set cell box selected, click cell **B23** in the Yield worksheet. The cell reference $B$23 appears in the Set cell box. The set cell is the calculated value you want Goal Seek to change to meet your goal. (You'll learn about $ symbols in cell references in the next session.)

4. Press the **Tab** key to move the insertion point to the To value box, and then type **100000** indicating that you want Goal Seek to set the value in cell B23 value to 100,000.

5. Press the **Tab** key to move the insertion point to the By changing cell box.

   There are often many possible input values you can change to meet a goal. In this case, you want to change the size of the farm acreage in cell B4.

6. Click cell **B4**. The cell reference $B$4 appears in the By changing cell box. See Figure 3-14.

Figure 3-14	Goal Seek dialog box

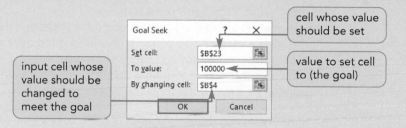

7. Click the **OK** button. The Goal Seek dialog box closes, and the Goal Seek Status dialog box opens, indicating that Goal Seek found a solution.

8. Click the **OK** button. The value in cell B4 changes to 154.6984204, and the value of cell B23 changes to $100,000.

If Jane increases the acreage devoted to corn production to almost 155 acres, the farm would produce a total revenue from corn of $100,000, assuming a yield of 168 bushels per acre sold at $3.85 per bushel. If the yield or market price increases, the revenue would also increase.

Interpreting Error Values

As you add formulas and values to a workbook, you might make a mistake such as mistyping a formula or entering data as the wrong type. When such errors occur, Excel displays an error value in the cell. An **error value** indicates that some part of a formula is preventing Excel from returning a value. Figure 3-15 lists the common error values you might see in place of calculated values from Excel formulas and functions. For example, the error value #VALUE! indicates that the wrong type of value is used in a function or formula.

Figure 3-15   **Excel error values**

Error Value	Description
#DIV/0!	The formula or function contains a number divided by 0.
#NAME?	Excel doesn't recognize text in the formula or function, such as when the function name is misspelled.
#N/A	A value is not available to a function or formula, which can occur when a workbook is initially set up prior to entering actual data values.
#NULL!	A formula or function requires two cell ranges to intersect, but they don't.
#NUM!	Invalid numbers are used in a formula or function, such as text entered in a function that requires a number.
#REF!	A cell reference used in a formula or function is no longer valid, which can occur when the cell used by the function was deleted from the worksheet.
#VALUE!	The wrong type of argument is used in a function or formula. This can occur when you reference a text value for an argument that should be strictly numeric.

Error values themselves are not particularly descriptive or helpful. To help you locate the error, an error indicator appears in the upper-left corner of the cell with the error value. When you point to the error indicator, a ScreenTip appears with more information about the source of the error. Although the ScreenTips provide hints as to the source of the error, you will usually need to examine the formulas in the cells with error values to determine exactly what went wrong.

Jane wants you to test the workbook. You'll change the value of cell B4 from a number to a text string, creating an error in the Yield worksheet.

To create an error value:

▶ **1.** In cell **B4**, enter the text string **137 acres**. After you press the Enter key, the #VALUE! error value appears in cells whose formulas use the value in cell B4 either directly or indirectly, indicating that the wrong type of argument is used in a function or formula. In the Yield worksheet, the value in cell B4 affects the values of cells B21 and B23. See Figure 3-16.

Figure 3-16   **Error value in the worksheet**

text string entered in cell B4

green triangle provides access to more information about the error

error value indicates the formula uses the wrong type of value

	A	B	C		E	F
4	Total Corn Crop (acres)	137 acres		text string entered in cell B4		
5						
6	Sample Plot			Agricultural Constants		
7	Number of Rows	6		Square Feet in an Acre	43,560	
8	Row Width (ft.)	2.5		Standard Corn Moisture Content	15.50%	
9	Row Length (ft.)	294		Pounds of Corn in a Bushel	56	
10	Sample Area (acres)	0.20		Market Price per Bushel	$3.85	
11						
12	Corn Weight					
13	Sample Weight (lbs.)	1922				
14	Moisture Content	16.30%				
15	Dry Weight (lbs.)	1609				
16	Market Weight (lbs.)	1904				
17						
18	Yield					
19	Sample Bushels	34				
20	Bushels per Acre	168				
21	Total Yield (bushels)	#VALUE!				

Documentation   Yield   Yield History   Growth

Ready

▶ 2. Click cell **B21**, and then point to the button that appears to the left of the cell. A ScreenTip appears, providing useful information about the cause of the error value. In this case, the ScreenTip is, "A value used in the formula is of the wrong data type."

▶ 3. Click cell **B4**, enter **137** to change the value back to the current acreage that Wingait Farm devotes to corn. After you press the Enter key, the error values disappear, the total yield in cell B21 returns to 23,002, and the projected revenue in cell B23 returns to $88,559.40.

▶ 4. Save the workbook.

So far, you have used formulas and functions to analyze the current and past season's crop yield at Wingait Farm. In the next session, you'll use additional formulas and functions to analyze the growth of Wingait Farm's corn crop from planting to harvesting.

Session 3.1 Quick Check

REVIEW

1. Convert the following equation into an Excel formula where the *radius* value is stored in cell E31 and the value of π is stored in cell D12:

$$area = \pi \times radius^2$$

2. In Excel, the PI() function returns the decimal value of π. Rewrite your answer for the previous formula using this function.

3. Write a formula to round the value in cell A5 to the fourth decimal place.

4. Write a formula to return the middle value from the values in the range Y1:Y100.

5. The range of a set of values is defined as the maximum value minus the minimum value. Write a formula to calculate the range of values in the range Y1:Y100 and then to round that value to the nearest integer.

6. Explain the difference between the COUNT function and the COUNTA function.

7. Stephen is entering hundreds of temperature values into an Excel worksheet for a climate research project, and he wants to speed up data entry by leaving freezing point values as blanks rather than typing zeroes. Explain why this will cause complications if he later tries to calculate the average temperature from those data values.

8. What is the difference between a what-if analysis by trial and error and by Goal Seek?

9. Cell B2 contains the formula =SUME(A1:A100) with the name of the SUM function misspelled as SUME. What error value will appear in the cell?

Session 3.2 Visual Overview:

The **VLOOKUP function** returns values from a vertical lookup table by specifying the value to be matched, the location of the lookup table, and the column containing the return values.

The **TODAY function** returns the current date.

A **relative cell reference** is used for references that change when the formula is moved to a new location. For example, E15 is a relative cell reference.

An **absolute cell reference** is used for references that do not change when the formula is moved to a new location. Absolute references have "$" before the row and column components. For example, $O$7 is an absolute cell reference.

Wingait Farm - Excel

File | Home | Insert | Page Layout | Formulas | Data | Review | View

B13   =VLOOKUP($B$12,$N$17:$O$19,2,FALSE)

=TODAY()

	A	B	C	D			G	H	I
1	Wingait Farm								
2	Corn Growth Calculator								
3									
4	Current Date	11/15/2017	Day			Tmin	Tmax	GDD	Cumu
5			Day 1	45	52	50	52	1.0	
6	Estimated Stage Dates		Day 2	42	64	50	64	7.0	
7	Planting Date	4/25/2017	Day 3	38	70	50	70	10.0	
8	Emergence	4/30/2017	Day 4	43	76	50	76	13.0	
9	First Leaf	5/3/2017	Day 5	47	74	50	74	12.0	
10			Day 6	45	74	50	74	12.0	
11	Hybrid Summary		Day 7	47	71	50	71	10.5	
12	Corn Hybrid	CS6489	Day 8	56	68	56	68	12.0	
13	Maturity (GDD)	2920	Day 9	60	85	60	85	22.5	
14			Day 10	61	71	61	71	16.0	
15	Harvesting			62		62	80	21.0	
16	Harvest Date	9/		79	65	79	22.0		
17				67	80	67	80	23.5	
18				56	70	56	70	13.0	
19				53	75	53	75	14.0	
20			Day 16	59	73	59	73	16.0	

=MAX(E14,$O
=MAX(E15,$O$7)
=MAX(E16,$O$7)
=MAX(E17,$O$7)
=MAX(E18,O

Documentation | Yield | Yield History | Growth | Explanation o ...

Ready

Cell References and Formulas

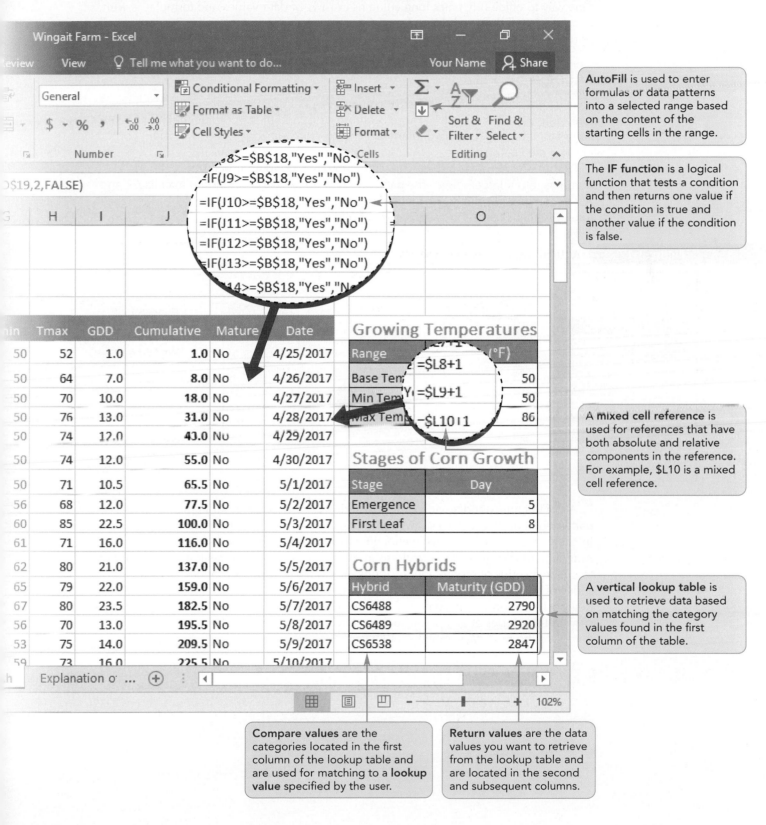

AutoFill is used to enter formulas or data patterns into a selected range based on the content of the starting cells in the range.

The **IF function** is a logical function that tests a condition and then returns one value if the condition is true and another value if the condition is false.

A **mixed cell reference** is used for references that have both absolute and relative components in the reference. For example, $L10 is a mixed cell reference.

A **vertical lookup table** is used to retrieve data based on matching the category values found in the first column of the table.

Compare values are the categories located in the first column of the lookup table and are used for matching to a **lookup value** specified by the user.

Return values are the data values you want to retrieve from the lookup table and are located in the second and subsequent columns.

AutoFilling Formulas and Data

One way to efficiently enter long columns or rows of data values and formulas is with AutoFill. AutoFill extends formulas or data patterns that were entered in a selected cell or range into adjacent cells. AutoFill is faster than copying and pasting.

Filling a Series

To extend a series of data values with a particular pattern, you enter enough values to establish the pattern, next you select those cells, and then you drag the fill handle across additional cells. The **fill handle** is the box that appears in the lower-right corner of a selected cell or range.

Figure 3-17 shows how AutoFill can be used to extend an initial series of odd numbers into a larger range. The pattern of odd numbers is established in cells A2 and A3. When the user drags the fill handle over the range A4:A9, Excel extends the series into those cells using the same pattern of odd numbers.

Figure 3-17 AutoFill used to extend a series

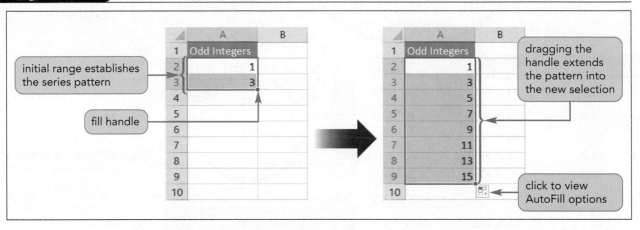

AutoFill can extend a wide variety of series, including dates and times and patterned text. Figure 3-18 shows some examples of series that AutoFill can generate. In each case, you must provide enough information for AutoFill to identify the pattern. AutoFill can recognize some patterns from only a single entry—such as Jan or January to create a series of month abbreviations or names, or Mon or Monday to create a series of the days of the week. A text pattern that includes text and a number such as Region 1, Region 2, and so on can also be automatically extended using AutoFill. You can start the series at any point, such as Weds, June, or Region 10, and AutoFill will complete the next days, months, or text.

Figure 3-18	Series patterns extended with AutoFill

Type	Initial Values	Extended Values
Numbers	1, 2, 3	4, 5, 6, ..
	2, 4, 6	8, 10, 12, ...
Dates and Times	Jan	Feb, Mar, Apr, ...
	January	February, March, April, ...
	15-Jan, 15-Feb	15-Mar, 15-Apr, 15-May, ...
	12/30/2017	12/31/2017, 1/1/2018, 1/2/2018, ...
	12/31/2017, 1/31/2018	2/29/2018, 3/31/2018, 4/30/2018, ...
	Mon	Tue, Wed, Thu, ...
	Monday	Tuesday, Wednesday, Thursday, ...
	11:00AM	12:00PM, 1:00PM, 2:00PM, ...
Patterned Text	1st period	2nd period, 3rd period, 4th period, ...
	Region 1	Region 2, Region 3, Region 4, ...
	Quarter 3	Quarter 4, Quarter 1, Quarter 2, ...
	Qtr3	Qtr4, Qtr1, Qtr2, ...

With AutoFill, you can quickly fill a range with a series of numbers, dates and times, and patterned text.

REFERENCE

Creating a Series with AutoFill

- Enter the first few values of the series into a range.
- Select the range, and then drag the fill handle of the selected range over the cells you want to fill.
- To copy only the formats or only the formulas, click the Auto Fill Options button and select the appropriate option.

or

- Enter the first few values of the series into a range.
- Select the entire range into which you want to extend the series.
- On the Home tab, in the Editing group, click the Fill button, and then click Down, Right, Up, Left, Series, or Justify to set the direction in which you want to extend the series.

Jane wants you to complete the worksheet she started to explore the growth of the Wingait Farm corn crop from planting through harvesting. You need to create a column that labels each day of corn growth starting with Day 1, Day2, and so forth through the end of the season. You will create these labels using AutoFill.

To use AutoFill to extend a series of labels:

TIP

You can also fill a series down by selecting the entire range including the initial cell(s) that establish the pattern, and then pressing the Ctrl+D keys.

1. If you took a break after the previous session, make sure the Wingait Farm workbook is open.

2. Go to the **Growth** worksheet.

3. In cell **D5**, enter the text string **Day 1**. This is the initial label in the series.

4. Click cell **D5** to select the cell, and then drag the **fill handle** (located in the bottom-right corner of the cell) down over the range **D5:D163**.

5. Release the mouse button. AutoFill enters the labels Day1 through Day 159 in the selected range. See Figure 3-19.

Figure 3-19   **Farm Day pattern extended with AutoFill**

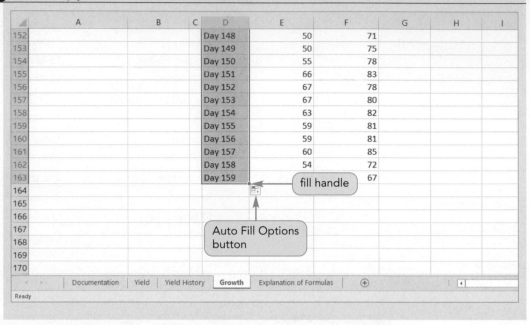

Exploring Auto Fill Options

By default, AutoFill copies both the content and the formatting of the original range to the selected range. However, sometimes you might want to copy only the content or only the formatting. The Auto Fill Options button that appears after you release the mouse button lets you specify what is copied. Figure 3-20 shows the Auto Fill Options menu for an extended series of patterned text.

Figure 3-20   **Auto Fill Options menu**

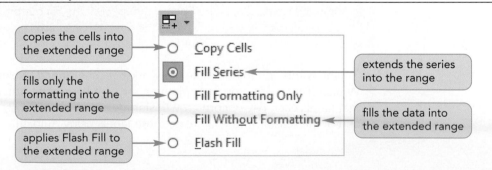

The Copy Cells option copies both the cell content and formatting but does not extend a series based on the initial values. The Fill Series option (the default) extends the initial series values into the new range. Other options allow you to fill in the values with or without the formatting used in the initial cells. Additional options (not shown in Figure 3-20) are provided when extending date values, allowing AutoFill to extend the initial dates by days, weekdays, months, or years.

The Series dialog box provides other options for how AutoFill is applied. To open the Series dialog box, click the Fill button in the Editing group on the Home tab, and then click Series. You can specify a linear or growth series for numbers; a date series for dates that increase by day, weekday, month, or year; or an AutoFill series for patterned text. With numbers, you can also specify the step value (how much each number increases over the previous entry) and a stop value (the endpoint for the entire series). See Figure 3-21.

Figure 3-21	Series dialog box

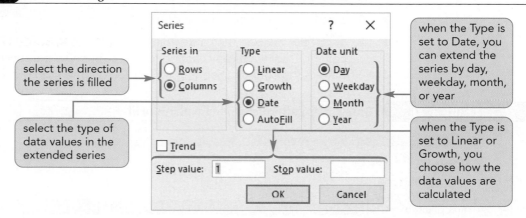

Filling Formulas

You can also use AutoFill to extend formulas into a range. AutoFill copies the formula in the initial cell or range into the extended range. Excel modifies the cell references in the formulas based on the location of the cells in the extended range.

Jane wants the Growth worksheet to include the date of each growing day starting from the planting date and extending to the last day of recorded data. Because dates are stored as numbers, you can fill in the calendar days by adding 1 to the date displayed in the previous row. Jane wants to use the date 4/15/2017 as the starting date of when the farm began planting corn.

To copy the formula with the dates for the growing season with AutoFill:

1. In cell **B7**, enter the date **4/15/2017** as the starting date of when the farm began planting corn.

2. In cell **L5**, enter the formula **=B7**. After you press the Enter key, cell L5 displays 4/15/2017, which is the first date of the growing season for corn.

3. In cell **L6**, enter the formula **=L5+1** to add one day to the date in cell L5. After you press the Enter key, the date 4/16/2017 appears in cell L6.

4. Click cell **L6** to select it, and then drag the fill handle over the range **L6:L163**. AutoFill copies the formula in cell L6 to the range L7:L163, increasing the date value by one day in each row.

AutoFill extends the formulas to display the date 4/16/2017 in cell L6 through the date 9/20/2017 in cell L163. Each date is calculated by increasing the value in the cell one row above it by one day. The formulas for these calculations are= L5+1 in cell L6, =L6+1 in cell L7, and so forth up to =L162+1 in cell L163.

Jane wants you to change the planting date to 4/25/2017, which is closer to the final date for planting corn at Wingait Farm.

To change the planting date:

1. Scroll to the top of the workbook.

2. In cell **B7**, change the value from 4/15/2017 to **4/25/2017**. The dates in column L automatically change to reflect the new planting date with the last date in the column changing to 9/30/2017. See Figure 3-22.

Figure 3-22　Date series pattern extended with AutoFill

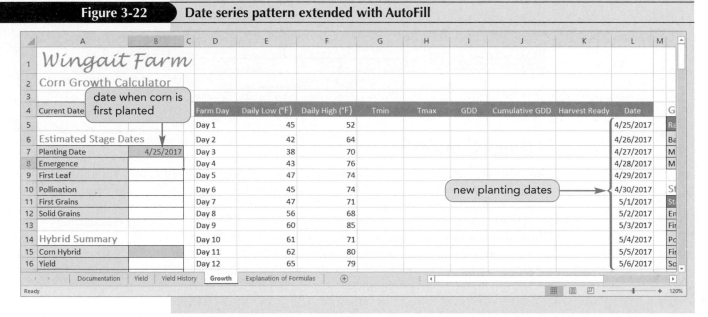

Jane wants to know when the corn crop will reach different stages of growth. In the range N11:O16 of the Growth worksheet, Jane created a table listing the number of days after planting that different growth milestones are reached. For example, the sprouts of the corn plant are often visible five days after planting (cell O12), the first small leaf appears eight days after planting (cell O13), and so forth. You will use the values in the range O12:O16 to estimate the calendar dates for when the first sprouts emerge, the first leaf appears, the corn begins to pollinate, the corn shows its first grains, and finally when the corn shows its solid grains or kernels.

To display the dates for corn growth milestones:

1. In cell **B8**, enter the formula **=B7+O12** to add the number of days until emergence to the planting date. The date 4/30/2017, which is the estimated date when the first corn sprouts will appear, is displayed in cell B8.

2. Click cell **B8** to select it, and then drag the fill handle over the range **B8:B12** to fill in the dates for the other growth milestones. See Figure 3-23.

Figure 3-23 Formula extended with AutoFill

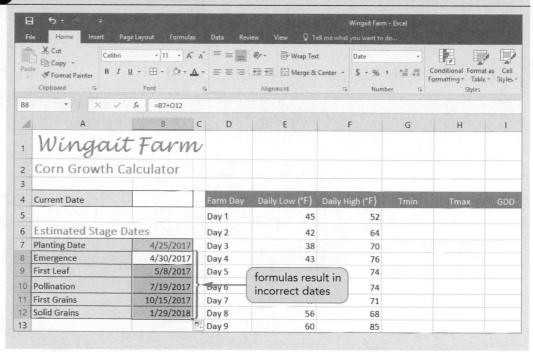

Something is wrong with the formulas that calculate the milestone dates. For example, the date for when the first corn kernels appear is January of the next year. To understand why the formulas resulted in incorrect dates, you need to look at the cell references.

Exploring Cell References

Excel has three types of cell references: relative, absolute, and mixed. Each type of cell reference in a formula is affected differently when the formula is copied and pasted to a new location.

Understanding Relative References

So far, all of the cell references you have worked with are relative cell references. When a formula includes a relative cell reference, Excel interprets the reference to each cell relative to the position of the cell containing the formula. For example, if cell A1 contains the formula =B1+B2, Excel interprets that formula as "Add the value of the cell one column to the right (B1) to the value of the cell one column to the right and one row down (B2)".

This relative interpretation of the cell reference is retained when the formula is copied to a new location. If the formula in cell A1 is copied to cell A3 (two rows down in the worksheet), the relative references also shift two rows down, resulting in the formula =B3+B4.

Figure 3-24 shows another example of how relative references change when a formula is pasted to new locations in the worksheet. In this figure, the formula =A3 entered in cell D6 displays 10, which is the number entered in cell A3. When pasted to a new location, each of the pasted formulas contains a reference to a cell that is three rows up and three rows to the left of the current cell's location.

Figure 3-24   Formulas using relative references

formula references a cell three rows up and three columns to the left of the active cell

when copied to new cells, each formula still references a cell three rows up and three columns to the left

values returned by each formula

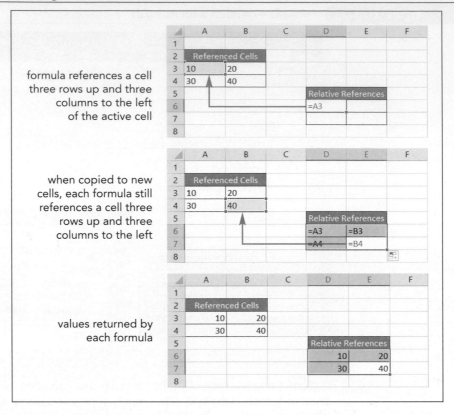

This explains what happened when you used AutoFill to copy the formula =B7+O12 in cell B8 into the range B9:B12. The formula in cell B9 became =B8+O13, the formula in cell B10 became =B9+O14, the formula in cell B11 became =B10+O15, and the formula in cell B12 became =B11+O16. In each case, the stage days were added to the date in the previous row, not the original planting date entered in cell B7. As a result, date calculation for the appearance of the first solid grains was pushed out to January of the following year.

To correct this, you need a cell reference that remains fixed on cell B7 no matter where the formula is pasted. This can be accomplished with an absolute reference.

Understanding Absolute References

An absolute reference is used for a cell reference that remains fixed even when that formula is copied to a new cell. Absolute references include $ (a dollar sign) before each column and row designation. For example, B8 is a relative reference to cell B8, while $B$8 is an absolute reference to that cell.

Figure 3-25 shows an example of how copying a formula with an absolute reference results in the same cell reference being pasted in different cells regardless of their position compared to the location of the original copied cell. In this example, the formula =$A$3 will always reference cell A3 no matter where the formula is copied to.

Figure 3-25   Formulas using absolute references

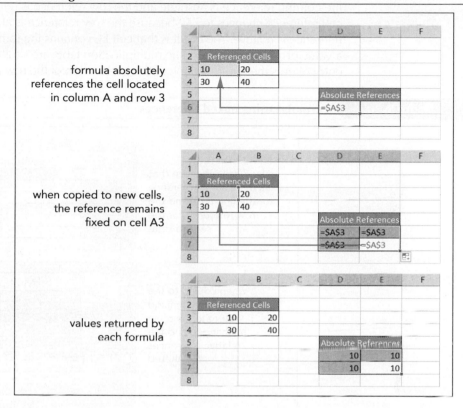

formula absolutely references the cell located in column A and row 3

when copied to new cells, the reference remains fixed on cell A3

values returned by each formula

Sometimes, you'll want only one part of the cell reference to remain fixed. This requires a mixed cell reference.

Understanding Mixed References

A mixed cell reference contains both relative and absolute components. For example, a mixed reference for cell A2 can be either $A2 where the column component is absolute and the row component is relative, or it can be entered as A$2 with a relative column component and a fixed row component. A mixed reference "locks" only one part of the cell reference. When you copy and paste a cell with a mixed reference to a new location, the absolute portion of the cell reference remains fixed, and the relative portion shifts along with the new location of the pasted cell.

Figure 3-26 shows an example of using mixed references to complete a multiplication table. The first cell in the table, cell B3, contains the formula =$A3*B$2, which multiplies the first column entry (cell A3) by the first row entry (cell B2), returning 1. When this formula is copied to another cell, the absolute portions of the cell references remain unchanged, and the relative portions of the references change. For example, if the formula is copied to cell E6, the first mixed cell reference changes to $A6 because the column reference is absolute and the row reference is relative, and the second cell reference changes to E$2 because the row reference is absolute and the column reference is relative. The result is that cell E6 contains the formula =$A6*E$2 and returns a value of 16. Other cells in the multiplication table are similarly modified so that each entry returns the multiplication of the intersection of the row and column headings.

Figure 3-26   **Formulas using mixed references**

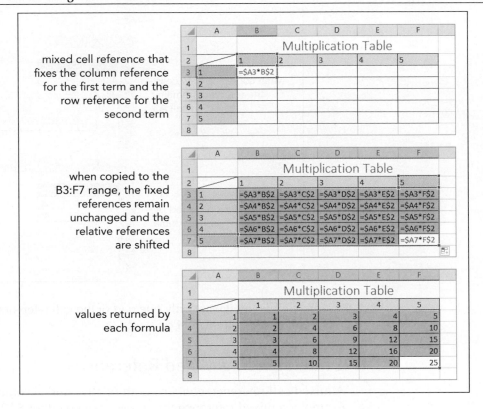

Changing Cell References in a Formula

You can quickly switch a cell reference from relative to absolute or mixed. Rather than retyping the formula, you can select the cell reference in Edit mode and then press the F4 key. As you press the F4 key, Excel cycles through the different reference types—starting with the relative reference, followed by the absolute reference, then to a mixed reference with an absolute row component followed by a mixed reference with an absolute column component.

To calculate the correct stage dates in the Growth worksheet, you will change the formula in cell B8 to use an absolute reference to cell B7 and then use AutoFill to copy that formula into range B9:B12.

To correct the stage dates formulas with absolute cell references:

1. Double-click cell **B8** to select it and enter Edit mode.

2. In cell B8, double-click the **B7** reference to select it, and then press the **F4** key. Excel changes the formula in cell B8 to =$B$7+O12.

3. Press the **Enter** key to enter the formula and exit Edit mode.

4. Click cell **B8** to select it, and then drag the fill handle over the range **B8:B12**. Figure 3-27 shows the revised dates for the different stages of corn growth.

| Figure 3-27 | Stage dates calculated with absolute cell references |

The revised dates for the different stages of the corn maturation are much more reasonable. For example, the date on which solid grains first appear is 8/9/2017, which is more in line with Jane's experience.

PROSKILLS

Problem Solving: When to Use Relative, Absolute, and Mixed References

Part of effective workbook design is knowing when to use relative, absolute, and mixed references. Use relative references when you want to apply the same formula with input cells that share a common layout or pattern. Relative references are commonly used when copying a formula that calculates summary statistics across columns or rows of data values. Use absolute references when you want your copied formulas to always refer to the same cell. This usually occurs when a cell contains a constant value, such as a tax rate, that will be referenced in formulas throughout the worksheet. Mixed references are seldom used other than when creating tables of calculated values such as a multiplication table in which the values of the formula or function can be found at the intersection of the rows and columns of the table.

Calendar days are one way of predicting crop growth, but Jane knows that five days of hot weather will result in more rapid growth than five mild days. A more accurate method to estimate growth is to calculate the crop's Growing Degree Days (GDD), which take into account the range of daily temperatures to which the crop is exposed. GDD is calculated using the formula

$$GDD = \frac{T_{max} + T_{min}}{2} - T_{base}$$

where T_{max} is the daily high temperature, T_{min} is the daily low temperature, and T_{base} is a baseline temperature for the region. For corn growing in Iowa, T_{min} and T_{max} are limited to the temperature range 50°F to 86°F with a baseline line temperature of 50°F. The limits are necessary because corn does not appreciably grow when the temperature falls below 50°F, nor does a temperature above 86°F increase the rate of growth.

Jane already retrieved meteorological data containing sample low and high temperatures for each day of the growing season in the Cascade, Iowa, region. She stored the limits of the corn's T_{min}, T_{max}, and T_{base} values in the Growth worksheet in the range N5:O8. You will use these values to calculate each day's GDD value for corn growth.

To calculate the GDD value:

▶ 1. Click cell **G5**, and then type the formula **=MAX(E5, $O$7)** to set the T_{min} value to either that day's minimum temperature or to 50°F, whichever is larger.

▶ 2. Press the **Tab** key. The formula returns a value of 50.

▶ 3. In cell H5, type the formula **=MIN(F5, $O$8)** to set the T_{max} value to that day's maximum temperature or to 86°F, whichever is smaller, and then press the **Tab** key. The formula returns a value of 52.

▶ 4. In cell I5, enter the formula **=(G5+H5)/2-$O$6** to calculate that day's GDD value using the T_{base} value of 50°F stored in cell O6. The formula returns 1.0, indicating that the GDD value for that day is 1.

Next you'll use AutoFill to copy these formulas into the range G5:I163. Because you used absolute references in the formulas, the copied formulas will continue to reference cells O7, O8, and O6 in the extended range.

▶ 5. Select the range **G5:I5**, and then drag the fill handle down to row **163**. Figure 3-28 shows the first several rows of GDD values for the corn crop's history.

Figure 3-28 GDD values for the corn crop

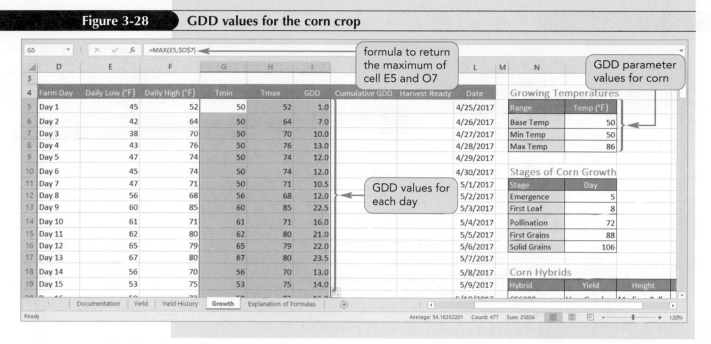

The first GDD values range between 1 and 22.5, but in July and August, GDD routinely reach the upper 20s and lower 30s, indicating that those hot days result in rapid corn growth.

Summarizing Data with the Quick Analysis Tool

The Quick Analysis tool can generate columns and rows of summary statistics and formulas that can be used for analyzing data. GDD is cumulative, which means that as the crop gains more Growing Degree Days, it continues to grow and mature. Jane needs you to calculate a running total of the GDD value for each day in the season. You will enter this calculation using the Quick Analysis tool.

To calculate a running total of GDD:

1. Select the range **I5:I163** containing the GDD values for day of the growing season.

2. Click the **Quick Analysis** button in the lower-right corner of the select range (or press the **Ctrl+Q** keys) to display the menu of Quick Analysis tools.

3. Click **Totals** from the list of tools. The Quick Analysis tools that calculate summary statistics for the selected data appear. See Figure 3-29.

Figure 3-29   Totals tools on the Quick Analysis tool

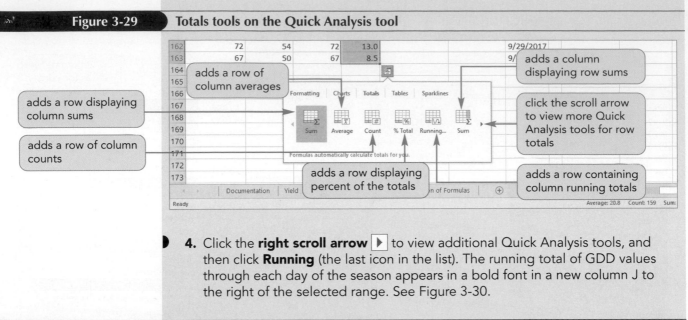

4. Click the **right scroll arrow** ▶ to view additional Quick Analysis tools, and then click **Running** (the last icon in the list). The running total of GDD values through each day of the season appears in a bold font in a new column J to the right of the selected range. See Figure 3-30.

Figure 3-30   Cumulative totals for the GDD values

Based on the running total in column J, Jane projects that by 9/30/2017, the corn crop will have a total of 3312 Growing Degree Days. To create the running total, the Quick Analysis tool added the following formula to cell J5 and then copied that formula over the range J5:J163:

=SUM($I$5:I5)

Note that this formula uses a combination of absolute and relative cell references. When copied to cell J6 the formula becomes

=SUM($I$5:I6)

and when copied to J7 the formula is

=SUM($I$5:I7)

In this formula, the starting cell of the range used with the SUM function is fixed at cell I5, but the ending cell is relative, causing the number of rows in the range to expand to match the cell selection. For the last date in row 163, the formula becomes:

=SUM($I$5:I163)

This approach shows how a combination of absolute and relative cell references expands the capability of Excel to create formulas for a variety of ranges.

Working with Dates and Date Functions

Excel has several functions that work with dates and times. These functions are particularly useful in workbooks that involve production schedules and calendars. Figure 3-31 describes some of the commonly used date and time functions.

Figure 3-31 Date functions

Function	Description
DATE(year,month,day)	Creates a date value for the date represented by the *year*, *month*, and *day* arguments
DAY(date)	Extracts the day of the month from *date*
MONTH(date)	Extracts the month number from *date* where 1=January, 2=February, and so forth
YEAR(date)	Extracts the year number from *date*
NETWORKDAYS(start,end[,holidays])	Calculates the number of whole working days between *start* and *end*; to exclude holidays, add the optional *holidays* argument containing a list of holiday dates to skip
WEEKDAY(date[,return_type])	Calculates the weekday from *date*, where 1=Sunday, 2=Monday, and so forth; to choose a different numbering scheme, set *return_type* to 1 (1=Sunday, 2=Monday, ...), 2 (1=Monday, 2=Tuesday, ...), or 3 (0=Monday, 1=Tuesday, ...)
WORKDAY(start,days[,holidays])	Returns the workday after *days* workdays have passed since the *start* date; to exclude holidays, add the optional *holidays* argument containing a list of holiday dates to skip
NOW( )	Returns the current date and time
TODAY( )	Returns the current date

Many workbooks include the current date so that any reports generated by the workbook are identified by date. To display the current date, you can use the TODAY function:

`TODAY( )`

TIP

To display the current date and time, which is updated each time the workbook is reopened, use the NOW function.

Note that although the TODAY function doesn't have any arguments, you still must include the parentheses for the function to work. The date displayed by the TODAY function is updated automatically whenever you reopen the workbook or enter a new calculation.

Jane wants the Growth worksheet to show the current date each time it is used or printed. You will use the TODAY function to display the current date in cell B4.

To display the current date:

1. Scroll to the top of the worksheet, and then click cell **B4**.

2. On the ribbon, click the **Formulas** tab.

3. In the Function Library group, click the **Date & Time** button to display the date and time functions.

4. Click **TODAY**. The Function Arguments dialog box opens and indicates that the TODAY function requires no arguments.

▶ **5.** Click the **OK** button. The formula =TODAY() is entered in cell B4, and the current date is displayed in the cell.

Note that Excel automatically formats cells containing the TODAY function to display the value in Short Date format.

INSIGHT

Date Calculations with Working Days

Businesspeople are often more interested in workdays rather than in all of the days of the week. For example, to estimate a delivery date in which packages are not shipped or delivered on weekends, it is more useful to know the date of the next weekday rather than the date of the next day.

To display the date of a weekday that is a specified number of weekdays past a start date, Excel provides the **WORKDAY function**

```
WORKDAY(start,days[,holidays])
```

where *start* is a start date, *days* is the number of workdays after that starting date, and *holidays* is an optional list of holiday dates to skip. For example, if cell A1 contains the date 12/20/2018, a Thursday, the following formula displays the date 1/2/2019, a Wednesday that is nine working days later:

```
=WORKDAY(A1,9)
```

The optional *holidays* argument references a series of dates that the WORKDAY function will skip in performing its calculations. So, if both 12/25/2018 and 1/1/2019 are entered in the range B1:B2 as holidays, the following function will return the date 1/4/2019, a Friday that is nine working days, excluding the holidays, after 12/20/2018:

```
=WORKDAY(A1,9,B1:B2)
```

To reverse the process and calculate the number of working days between two dates, use the NETWORKDAYS function

```
NETWORKDAYS(start,end[,holidays])
```

where *start* is the starting date and *end* is the ending date. So, if cell A1 contains the date 12/20/2018 and cell A2 contains the date 1/3/2019, the following function returns 9, indicating that there are nine working days between the start and ending, excluding the holidays specified in the range B1:B2:

```
=NETWORKDAYS(A1,A2,B1:B2)
```

For international applications in which the definition of working day differs between one country and another, Excel supports the WORKDAY.INTL function. See Excel Help for more information.

Corn seed is sold in a wide variety of hybrids used to create corn of different quality, size, resistance to parasites, and growth rates. Jane wants the Growth worksheet to display data about the corn hybrid she chose for Wingait Farm. You can retrieve that data using a lookup function.

Using Lookup Functions

A **lookup function** retrieves values from a table of data that match a specified condition. For example, a lookup function can be used to retrieve a tax rate from a tax table for a given annual income or to retrieve shipping rates for different delivery options.

The table that stores the data you want to retrieve is called a **lookup table**. The first row or column of the table contains compare values, which are the values that are being looked up. If the compare values are in the first row, the table is a **horizontal lookup table**; if the compare values are in the first column, the table is a vertical lookup table. The remaining rows or columns contain the return values, which are the data values being retrieved by the lookup function.

Figure 3-32 shows the range N19:Q27 in the Growth worksheet containing information about different corn hybrids. This information is a vertical lookup table because the first column of the table containing the names of the hybrids stores the compare values. The remaining columns containing type of yield, height of the corn stalk, and GDD units until the hybrid reaches maturity are the return values. To look up the Growing Degree Days required until the corn hybrid CS6478 reaches maturity, Excel scans the first column of the lookup table until it finds the entry for CS6478. Excel then moves to the right to the column containing information that needs to be returned.

Figure 3-32   **Finding an exact match from a lookup table**

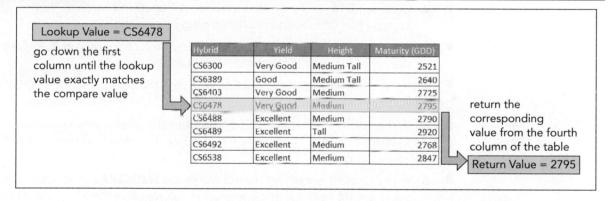

Lookup Value = CS6478

go down the first column until the lookup value exactly matches the compare value

Hybrid	Yield	Height	Maturity (GDD)
CS6300	Very Good	Medium Tall	2521
CS6389	Good	Medium Tall	2640
CS6403	Very Good	Medium	2725
CS6478	Very Good	Medium	2795
CS6488	Excellent	Medium	2790
CS6489	Excellent	Tall	2920
CS6492	Excellent	Medium	2768
CS6538	Excellent	Medium	2847

return the corresponding value from the fourth column of the table

Return Value = 2795

Lookup tables can be constructed for exact match or approximate match lookups. In an **exact match lookup**, the lookup value must exactly match one of the compare values in the first row or column of the lookup table. Figure 3-32 is an exact match lookup because the name of the corn hybrid must match one of the compare values in the table. An **approximate match lookup** is used when the lookup value falls within a range of compare values. You will work with exact match lookups in this module.

Finding an Exact Match with the VLOOKUP Function

To retrieve the return value from a vertical lookup table, you use the VLOOKUP function

VLOOKUP(*comp_value*,*table_array*,*col_index_num*[,*range_lookup*=TRUE])

where *comp_value* is the compare value to find in the first column of the lookup table, *table_array* is the range reference to the lookup table, and *col_index_num* is the number of the column in the lookup table that contains the return value. Keep in mind that *col_index_num* refers to the number of the column within the lookup table, not the worksheet column. So, a *col_index_num* of 2 refers to the lookup table's second column. Finally, *range_lookup* is an optional argument that specifies whether the lookup should be done as an exact match or an approximate match. For an exact match, you set the *range_lookup* value to FALSE. For approximate match lookups, you set the *range_lookup* value to TRUE. The default is to assume an approximate match.

For example, the following formula performs an exact match lookup using the text "CS6478" as the compare value and the data in the range N20:Q27 (shown in Figure 3-32) as the lookup table:

=VLOOKUP("CS6478",N20:Q27,4,FALSE)

The function looks through the compare values in the first column of the table to locate the "CS6478" entry. When the exact entry is found, the function returns the corresponding value in the fourth column of the table, which in this case is 2795.

Jane wants you to retrieve information about the CS6478 hybrid she uses at Wingait Farm and then display that information in the range B16:B18 on the Growth worksheet. You'll use a VLOOKUP function to retrieve yield information about the hybrid.

To use the VLOOKUP function to find yield information for hybrid CS6478:

1. In cell **B15**, enter the hybrid **CS6478**.

2. Click cell **B16**, and then click the **Insert Function** button f_x to the left of the formula bar. The Insert Function dialog box opens.

3. Click the **Or select a category** box, and then click **Lookup & Reference** in the list of function categories.

4. Scroll down the Select a function box, and then double-click **VLOOKUP**. The Function Arguments dialog box for the VLOOKUP function opens.

5. In the Lookup_value box, type **$B$15** as the absolute reference to the hybrid name, and then press the **Tab** key. The insertion point moves to the Table_array box.

6. In the Growth worksheet, select the range **N20:Q27** as the Table_array value, press the **F4** key to change the range reference to the absolute reference **$N$20:$Q$27**.

7. Press the **Tab** key. The insertion point moves to the Col_index_num box. Yield information is stored in the second column of the lookup table.

8. Type **2** in the Col_index_num box to return information from the second column of the lookup table, and then press the **Tab** key. The insertion point moves to the Range_lookup box.

9. Type **FALSE** in the Range_lookup box to perform an exact match lookup. See Figure 3-33.

Figure 3-33   **Function Arguments dialog box for the VLOOKUP function**

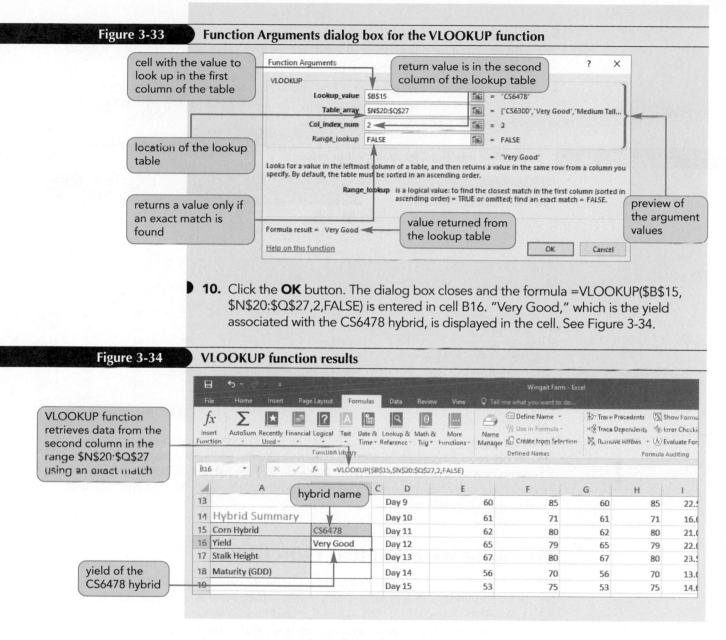

cell with the value to look up in the first column of the table

return value is in the second column of the lookup table

location of the lookup table

returns a value only if an exact match is found

value returned from the lookup table

preview of the argument values

10. Click the **OK** button. The dialog box closes and the formula =VLOOKUP($B$15, $N$20:$Q$27,2,FALSE) is entered in cell B16. "Very Good," which is the yield associated with the CS6478 hybrid, is displayed in the cell. See Figure 3-34.

Figure 3-34   **VLOOKUP function results**

VLOOKUP function retrieves data from the second column in the range $N$20:$Q$27 using an exact match

hybrid name

yield of the CS6478 hybrid

Jane wants to see the stalk height and the GDD information about the hybrid CS6478. You will use AutoFill to copy the VLOOKUP function into the other cells in the Hybrid Summary table.

To display other information about the hybrid CS6478:

1. Click cell **B16** to select it, and then drag the fill handle over the range **B16:B18** to copy the VLOOKUP formula into cells B17 and B18. The text "Very Good" appears in cells B17 and B18, because the formula is set up to retrieve text from the second column of the lookup table.

   You need to edit the formulas in cells B17 and B18 to retrieve information from the third and fourth columns of the lookup table, respectively.

> **2.** Double-click cell **B17** to enter into Edit mode, change the third argument from 2 to **3**, and then press the **Enter** key. The value Medium for the hybrid's stalk height appears in cell B17.

> **3.** Double-click cell **B18** to enter Edit mode, change the third argument from 2 to **4**, and then press the **Enter** key. The value 2795 for the hybrid's GDD appears in cell B18. See Figure 3-35.

Figure 3-35	VLOOKUP function results for other columns

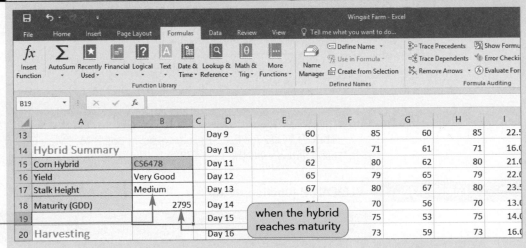

stalk height for the CS6478 hybrid

when the hybrid reaches maturity

Based on the values in the lookup table, the CS6478 hybrid will reach maturity and be ready for harvesting after 2795 Growing Degree Days. Jane wants you to add a column of values to the growth table that indicates for each date, whether the corn crop has reached maturity and is ready for harvesting. To create this column, you will need to use a logical function.

Working with Logical Functions

A **logical function** is a function that returns a different value depending on whether the given condition is true or false. That condition is entered as an expression, such as A5=3. If cell A5 is equal to 3, this expression and condition are true; if cell A5 is not equal to 3, this expression and condition are false. The most commonly used logical function is the IF function. The syntax of the IF function is

```
IF(condition,value_if_true,value_if_false)
```

where *condition* is an expression that is either true or false, *value_if_true* is the value returned by the function if the expression is true, and *value_if_false* is the value returned if the expression is false.

The value returned by the IF function can be a number, text, a date, a cell reference, or a formula. For example, the following formula tests whether the value in cell A1 is equal to the value in cell B1, returning 100 if those two cells are equal and 50 if they're not.

```
=IF(A1=B1,100,50)
```

TIP

To apply multiple logical conditions, you can nest one IF function within another.

In many cases, you will use cell references instead of values in the IF function. The following formula, for example, uses cell references, returning the value of cell C1 if A1 equals B1; otherwise, it returns the value of cell C2:

```
=IF(A1=B1,C1,C2)
```

The = symbol in these formulas is a **comparison operator** that indicates the relationship between two parts of the logical function's condition. Figure 3-36 describes other comparison operators that can be used within logical functions.

Figure 3-36   Logical comparison operators

Operator	Expression	Tests
=	A1 = B1	If the value in cell A1 is equal to the value in cell B1
>	A1 > B1	If the value in cell A1 is greater than the value in cell B1
<	A1 < B1	If the value in cell A1 is less than the value in cell B1
>=	A1 >= B1	If the value in cell A1 is greater than or equal to the value in cell B1
<=	A1 <= B1	If the value in cell A1 is less than or equal to the value in cell B1
<>	A1 <> B1	If the value in cell A1 is not equal to the value in cell B1

The IF function also works with text. For example, the following formula tests whether the value of cell A1 is equal to "yes":

```
=IF(A1="yes","done","restart")
```

If the condition is true (the value of cell A1 is equal to "yes"), then the formula returns the text "done"; otherwise, it returns the text "restart".

For each date in the growth record of the corn crop, Jane wants to know whether the cumulative GDD value is greater than or equal to the GDD value on which the hybrid reaches maturity and is ready for harvesting. If the crop is ready for harvesting, she wants the cell to display the text "Yes"; otherwise, it should display the text "No". You'll use the IF function to do this.

To enter the IF function to specify whether the corn is ready for harvesting:

1. Click cell **K5** to select it. You'll enter the IF function in this cell.

2. On the Formulas tab, in the Function Library group, click the **Logical** button to display the list of logical functions, and then click **IF**. The Function Arguments dialog box for the IF function opens.

3. In the Logical_test box, enter the expression **J5>=$B$18** to test whether the cumulative GDD value is greater than the maturity value in cell B18.

4. Press **Tab** key to move the insertion point to the Value_if_true box, and then type **"Yes"** as the value if the logical test is true.

5. Press **Tab** key to move the insertion point to the Value_if_false box, and then type **"No"** as the value if the logical test is false. See Figure 3-37.

Figure 3-37   **Function Arguments dialog box for the IF function**

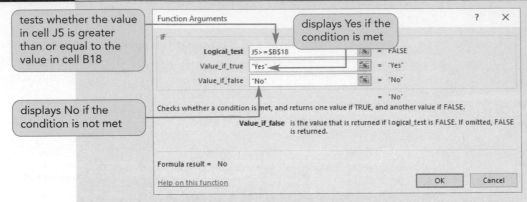

tests whether the value in cell J5 is greater than or equal to the value in cell B18

displays Yes if the condition is met

displays No if the condition is not met

6. Click the **OK** button. The formula =IF(J5>=$B$18,"Yes","No") is entered in cell K5. The cell displays the text "No," indicating that the crop is not harvest ready on this day (a logical result because this is the day when the farm starts planting the corn).

7. Click cell **K5**, and then drag fill handle to select the range **K5:K163**. The formula with the IF function is applied to the remaining days of the growing season. As shown in Figure 3-38, by the end of the growing season, the crop is ready for harvesting because the cumulative GDD value for the hybrid CS6478 has exceeded 2795.

Figure 3-38   **IF function evaluates whether the crop is harvest ready**

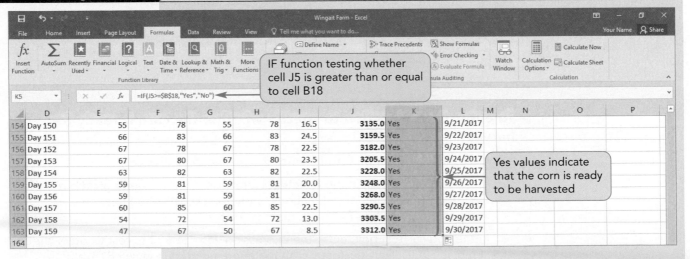

By scrolling up and down the Growth worksheet you can locate the row in which the value in the Harvest Ready column switches from No to Yes. For this data, the switch occurs in row 138 where the cumulative GDD value is equal to 2814, exceeding the minimum GDD value required for this particular hybrid to reach maturity.

Rather than scrolling through the worksheet, Jane wants the worksheet to display the calendar date on which the crop reaches maturity and is ready for harvesting. You can obtain this information by using columns K and L as a lookup table. Recall that Excel scans a lookup table from the top to the bottom and stops when it reaches the first value in the compare column that matches the lookup value. You can use this fact to find the first location in column K where the Harvest Ready value is equal to "Yes" and then apply the VLOOKUP function to return the corresponding calendar date in column L.

To display the harvest date for the corn crop:

1. Near the top of the worksheet, click cell **B21** to select it.

2. Click the **Insert Function** button f_x to the left of the formula bar. The Insert Function dialog box opens.

3. Click the **Or select a category box arrow**, and then click **Most Recently Used** to display a list of the functions you have used most recently.

4. Double-click **VLOOKUP** in the list. The Function Arguments dialog box for the VLOOKUP function opens.

5. In the Lookup_value box, type **"Yes"** and then press the **Tab** key. The insertion point moves to the Table_array box.

6. Select the **K** and **L** column headings to insert the reference K:L in the Table_array box, and then press the **Tab** key. The insertion point moves to the Col_index_num box.

7. Type **2** in the Col_index_num box to retrieve the value from the second column in the lookup table, and then press the **Tab** key. The insertion point moves to the Range_lookup box.

> Use FALSE to perform an exact match lookup.

8. Type **FALSE** in the Range_lookup box to apply an exact match lookup. See Figure 3-39.

Figure 3-39 Function Arguments for the VLOOKUP function

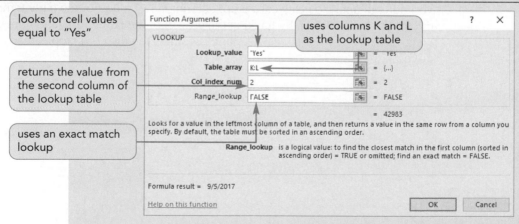

9. Click the **OK** button. The formula =VLOOKUP("Yes",K:L,2,FALSE) is entered in cell B21. The cell displays 9/5/2017, which is the date when the corn crop has reached maturity and is ready for harvesting to begin.

Jane can view the impact of different hybrids on the harvest date by changing the value of cell B15.

▶ **10.** Click cell **B15**, and then change the corn hybrid from CS6478 to **CS6489**. The results from the lookup and IF functions in the worksheet change to reflect the corn hybrid CS6489. This hybrid has excellent yield and tall stalks and is ready for harvesting on 9/10/2017, five days later than the corn hybrid CS6478. See Figure 3-40.

Figure 3-40   **Summary and harvesting data for the hybrid CS6489**

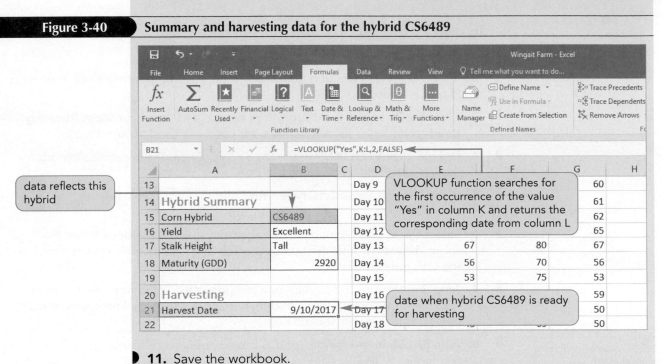

▶ **11.** Save the workbook.

You've completed your work on the Wingait Farm workbook. Jane will use this workbook to analyze next year's crop, entering new values for the daily temperatures and for the hybrid types. By tracking the growth of the corn crop, Jane hopes to more effectively increase her farm's yield and predict when the corn crop is ready for harvesting.

INSIGHT

Managing Error Values with the IF Function

An error value does not mean that you must correct the cell's formula or function. Some error values appear simply because you have not yet entered any data into the workbook. For example, if you use the VLOOKUP function without a lookup value, the #N/A error value appears because Excel cannot look up an empty value. However, as soon as you enter a lookup, the #N/A error value disappears, replaced with the result of the VLOOKUP function.

Error values of this type can make your workbook difficult to read and can confuse other users. One way to avoid error values resulting from missing input values is to nest formulas within an IF function. For example, the following formula first tests whether a value has been entered into cell B2 before attempting to use that cell as a lookup value in the VLOOKUP function:

```
=IF(B2="","",VLOOKUP(B2,$E1:$G$10,3,FALSE))
```

Note that "" is used to represent an empty text string or value. If the IF condition is true because no value has been entered into cell B2, the formula will return an empty text string instead of an error value, but if B2 has a value, the VLOOKUP function is applied using cell B2 as the lookup value. The result is a cleaner workbook that is easier for other people to read and use.

Jane appreciates all of the work you have done in developing the Wingait Farm workbook. She will continue to study the document and get back to you with future projects at the farm.

Session 3.2 Quick Check

REVIEW

1. If 4/30/2017 and 5/31/2017 are the initial values, what are the next two values AutoFill will insert?

2. You need to reference cell Q57 in a formula. What is its relative reference? What is its absolute reference? What are the two mixed references?

3. If cell R10 contains the formula =R1+R2, which is then copied to cell S20, what formula is entered in cell S20?

4. If cell R10 contains the formula =$R1+R$2, which is then copied to cell S20, what formula is entered in cell S20?

5. Explain how to use the Quick Analysis tool to calculate a running total of the values in the range D1:D10.

6. Write the formula to display the current date in the worksheet.

7. Write the formula to display a date that is four workdays after the date in cell A5. Do not assume any holidays in your calculation.

8. Write the formula to perform an exact match lookup with the lookup value from cell G5 using a vertical lookup table located in the range A1:F50. Return the value from the third column of the table.

9. If cell Q3 is greater than cell Q4, you want to display the text "OK"; otherwise, display the text "RETRY". Write the formula that accomplishes this.

Review Assignments

PRACTICE

Data File needed for the Review Assignments: Soybean.xlsx

Another cash crop grown at Wingait Farm is soybeans. Jane wants you to create a workbook for the soybean crop similar to the workbook you created for the corn crop. The workbook should estimate the total yield and revenue from a small plot sample and compare that yield to the farm's historic norms. The workbook should also track the soybean growth from planting to harvest. Complete the following:

1. Open the **Soybean** workbook located in the Excel3 > Review folder, and then save the workbook as **Soybean Crop** in the location specified by your instructor.
2. In the Documentation worksheet, enter your name in cell B3 and the date in cell B4.
3. The size of the soybean crop is **72** acres. Enter this value in cell B4 of the Yield worksheet.
4. The soybean sample comes from a plot of **4** rows each **7.5** inches wide and **21** inches long. Enter these values in the range B7:B9.
5. Within the plot, the farm has harvested **400** soybean pods with an average of **2.5** soybeans per pod. Enter these values in the B14:B15 range.
6. Apply the Input cell style to cells B4, B7:B9, and B14:B15.
7. Using the equations described in the Formulas worksheet, enter the following calculations:
   a. In cell B10, calculate the area of the plot sample in inches.
   b. In cell B11, convert the sample area to acres by dividing the value in cell B10 by the number of square inches in an acre (cell H4). Display the result to four decimal places.
   c. In cell B16, calculate the total number of seeds harvested in the sample.
   d. In cell B17, calculate the weight of the sample in pounds by dividing the number of seeds by the number of seeds in one pound (cell H5). Display the value to two decimal places.
   e. In cell B18, convert the weight to bushels by dividing the weight in pounds by the number of pounds of soybeans in one bushel (cell H6). Display the value to four decimal places.
   f. In cell B19, estimate the farm's soybean yield in bushels per acre by dividing the number of bushels in the plot sample by the area of the sample in acres. Display the value as an integer.
8. Calculate the following values for soybean yield and revenue:
   a. In cell B20, calculate the farm's average soybean yield using the values in column E. Use the ROUND function to round that average value to the nearest integer.
   b. In cell B21, calculate the farm's median soybean yield from the values in column E.
   c. In cell B24, calculate the farm's total production of soybeans in bushels by multiplying the bushels per acre value by the total number of acres that the farm devotes to soybeans. Display the value as an integer.
   d. In cell B25, calculate the total revenue from the soybean crop by multiplying the total bushels harvested by the current price per bushel (cell H7). Display the value using the Accounting format style.
9. Apply the Calculation style to the range B10:B11,B16:B21,B24:B25.
10. Use Goal Seek to determine what value in cell B4 (the number of acres devoted to soybeans) will result in a total soybean revenue of $40,000.
11. In the Growth worksheet, in cell B5, enter a formula with a function to display the current date.
12. Use AutoFill to insert the text strings Day 1 through Day 112 in the range D5:D116.
13. In cell G5, calculate the Growing Degree Days (GDD) for the first day of the season using the formula described in the Formulas worksheet and the temperature range values in the range L6:M9. (*Hint*: Use the same formula used in the tutorial for corn, but enter the T_{min}, T_{max}, and *base* values directly in the formula. Be sure to use absolute references for the temperature range values.)
14. Copy the formula in cell G5 to the range G5:G112.

15. Use the Quick Analysis tool to calculate the cumulative total of the GDD values from the range G5:G112, placing those values in the range H5:H112.

16. In cell B9, enter **5/12/2017**, which is the date the farm will start planting the soybean crop.

17. In cell J5, enter a formula to display the date from cell B9. In cell J6, enter a formula to increase the date in cell J5 by one day. Copy the formula in cell J6 to the range J6:J112 to enter the dates for the growing season.

18. In cell B8, enter **M070** as the maturity group for the current soybean hybrid.

19. In cell B10, use the VLOOKUP function to retrieve the cumulative GDD value for the M070 hybrid. (*Hint:* The range L12:M21 displays the cumulative GDD for each maturity group.)

20. In cell I5, enter an IF function that tests whether the cumulative GDD value in cell H5 is greater than the maturity value in cell B10. Use an absolute reference to cell B10. If the condition is true, return the text string "Ready"; otherwise, return the text "Not Ready". Copy the formula to the range I5:I112.

21. In cell B11, insert a VLOOKUP function using the values in the columns I and J that returns the date on which the Harvest Ready value is first equal to the text string "Ready".

22. In cell B12, calculate the number of days between planting and harvesting by subtracting the planting date (cell B9) from the harvest date (cell B11).

23. Save and close the workbook.

Case Problem 1

APPLY

Data File needed for this Case Problem: Gorecki.xlsx

Gorecki Construction Stefan Gorecki is the owner of Gorecki Construction, a small construction firm in Chester, Pennsylvania. He wants to use Excel to track his company's monthly income and expenses and then use that information to create a monthly budget. Stefan has already entered the raw data values but has asked to you to complete the workbook by adding the formulas and functions to perform the calculations. Complete the following:

1. Open the **Gorecki** workbook located in the Excel3 > Case1 folder, and then save the workbook as **Gorecki Budget** in the location specified by your instructor.

2. In the Documentation worksheet, enter your name in cell B3 and the date in cell B4.

3. The budget values are entered based on the end-of-month values. In the Monthly Budget worksheet, enter the date **31-Jan-18** in cell E4 and **28-Feb-18** in cell F4. Use AutoFill to fill in the remaining end-of-month date in the range G4:P4.

4. Calculate the company's total monthly income by selecting the range E6:P7 and using the Quick Analysis tool to insert the SUM function automatically into the range E8:P8.

5. Calculate the company's total cost of goods sold by selecting values in range E10:P11 and using the Quick Analysis tool to insert the SUM function automatically into the range E12:P12.

6. In the range E14:P14, calculate the company's monthly gross profit, which is equal to the difference between the monthly income and the monthly cost of goods sold.

7. Select the expenses entered in the range E17:P26, and use the Quick Analysis tool to insert the sum of the monthly expenses into the range E27:P27.

8. In the range E29:P29, calculate the company's net income equal to the difference between its gross profit and its total expenses.

9. Select the values in the range E29:P29, and then use the Quick Analysis tool to insert a running total of the company's net income into the range E30:P30.

10. Calculate the year-end totals for all financial categories by selecting the range E6:P29 and using the Quick Analysis tool to insert the sum of each row into the range Q6:Q29. Delete the content of any cells that do not contain financial figures.

11. Stefan wants the monthly averages of each financial category to be displayed in range B6:B29. Select cell B6, and then enter a formula that contains a nested function that first calculates the average of the values in the range E6:P6 and then uses the ROUND function to round that average to the nearest 10 dollars. (*Hint:* Use –1 for the value of the num_digits argument.) Use AutoFill to extend formula over the range B6:B29, deleting any cells corresponding to empty values.

12. Save and close the workbook.

Case Problem 2

Data File needed for this Case Problem: Capshaw.xlsx

Capshaw Family Dentistry   Carol Lemke is a new receptionist at Capshaw Dentistry in East Point, Georgia. She wants to get a rough estimate of what her take-home pay would be after deductions for federal and local taxes. She asks you to set up an Excel worksheet to perform the wage calculations for a sample two-week period. Carol already entered the work schedule and several tables containing the federal and state tax rates but needs you to insert the formulas. (*Note:* The tax rate tables and formulas used in this example are a simplified version of the tax code and should not be used to calculate actual taxes.) Complete the following:

1. Open the **Capshaw** workbook located in the Excel3 > Case2 folder, and then save the workbook as **Capshaw Wages** in the location specified by your instructor.

2. In the Documentation worksheet, enter your name in cell B3 and the date in cell B4.

3. In the Work Schedule worksheet, enter the following information in the range B5:B9: Name **Carol Lemke**; Hourly Rate **$16.25**; Federal Marital Status **Single**; State Marital Status **Single**; and Withholding Allowances **1**

4. In cell D6, enter the date **4/10/2017**. Use AutoFill to fill in the next day weekdays in the range D6:D15. (*Hint:* Click the AutoFill options button after dragging the fill handle, and then select the Fill Weekdays option button.)

5. In cell G6, calculate the total hours worked on the first day, which is equal to the difference between cell F6 and cell E6 multiplied by 24.

6. Carol will get overtime wages when she works more than eight hours in a day. Calculate the non-overtime hours in cell H6 by using the MIN function to return the minimum of the value in cell G6 and the value 8.

7. In cell I6, calculate the amount of overtime hours by using the IF function to test whether cell G6 is greater than 8. If it is, return the value cell G6 minus 8; otherwise, return the value 0.

8. In cell J6, calculate the salary due on the first day. The salary due is equal to the Straight Time worked multiplied by the hourly rate in cell B6 plus the Overtime multiplied by the hourly rate times 1.5 (Carol will receive time-and-a-half for each overtime hour.) Use an absolute reference to cell B6.

9. Select the range G6:J6, and then use AutoFill to copy the formulas into the range G7:J15 to calculate the salary for each of the ten days in the table.

10. In cell B11, calculate the total straight time hours worked by summing the values in column H. In cell B12, calculate the total overtime hours by summing the values in column I. In cell B13, calculate the total hours worked by summing the value in column G. In cell B14, calculate the total payments by summing the values in column J.

11. In cell B17, calculate the amount of federal tax by multiplying the Total Pay value in cell B14 by the appropriate federal tax rate for an employee with the marital status in cell B7 and withholding allowances in cell B9. (*Hint:* Use the VLOOKUP function with an exact match lookup for the lookup table in the range L6:W8. For the Col_index_num argument, use the value of cell B9 plus 2.)

12. In cell B18, calculate the Social Security tax equal to the value of cell B14 multiplied by the tax rate in cell M16.

13. In cell B19, calculate the Medicare tax equal to the value of cell B14 multiplied by the tax rate in cell M17.

14. In cell B20, calculate the amount of Georgia state tax by multiplying the value of cell B14 by the appropriate state tax rate in the range L12:W14 lookup table using the state marital status in cell B8 and the withholding allowance in cell B9. (*Hint*: Use the same type of VLOOKUP function as you did in Step 10 to retrieve the correct state tax rate.)

15. In cell B22, calculate the total deduction from pay by summing the values in the range B17:B20. In cell B23, calculate the withholding rate by dividing cell B22 by the total pay in cell B14.

16. In cell B24, calculate the take-home pay from subtracting the total withholding in cell B22 from cell B14.

17. Carol wants her take-home pay for the two weeks that she works in the sample schedule to be $1000. Use Goal Seek to find the hourly rate in cell B6 that will result in a take-home pay value of $1000.

18. Save and close the workbook.

Case Problem 3

CHALLENGE

Data File needed for this Case Problem: Biology.xlsx

Biology 221   Daivi Emani teaches biology and life sciences at Milford College in White Plains, New York. She wants to use Excel to track the test scores and calculate final averages for the students in her Biology 221 class. She has already entered the homework, quiz, and final exam scores for 66 students. The overall score is based on weighted average of the individual scores with homework accounting for 10 percent of the final grade, each of three quizzes accounting for 20 percent, and the final exam accounting for 30 percent. To calculate a weighted average you can use the SUMPRODUCT function

    SUMPRODUCT(*array1*,*array2*)

where *array1* is the range containing the weights assigned to each score and *array2* is the range containing the scores themselves.

Daivi also wants you to calculate each student's rank in the class based on the student's weighted average. Ranks are calculated using the RANK function

    RANK(*number*,*ref*[,*order*=0])

where *number* is the value to be ranked, *ref* is a reference to the range containing the values against which the ranking is done, and *order* is an optional argument that specifies whether to rank in descending order or ascending order. The default order value is 0 to rank the values in descending order.

Finally, you will create formulas that will look up information on a particular student based on that student's ID so that Daivi doesn't have to scroll through the complete class roster to find a particular student. Complete the following:

1. Open the **Biology** workbook located in the Excel3 > Case3 folder, and then save the workbook as **Biology Grades** in the location specified by your instructor.

2. In the Documentation worksheet, enter your name in cell B3 and the date in cell B4.

3. In the Biology Grades worksheet, in cell B5, calculate the number of students in the class by using the COUNTA function to count up the student IDs in the H column and subtracting 1 from that value (so as to not include cell H2 in the count).

4. In the range B8:F8, enter the weight values **10%**, **20%**, **20%**, **20%**, and **30%**.

5. In the range B9:F9, calculate the average of the numbers in columns K, L, M, N, and O.

6. In the range B10:F10, calculate the minimum values in the corresponding student score columns.

7. In the range B11:F11, use the MEDIAN function to calculate the midpoint of each of the student scores.

8. In the range B12:F12, calculate the maximum values for each of the student scores.

⊕ **Explore** 9. In cell P3, use the SUMPRODUCT function to calculate the weighted average of the scores for the first student in the list. Use an absolute reference to the range B8:F8 for the *array1* argument, and use the relative reference to the student scores in the range K3:O3 for the *array2* argument.

⊕ **Explore** 10. In cell Q3, use the RANK function to calculate the first student's rank in class. Use cell P3 for the *number* argument and column P for the *ref* argument. You do not to specify a value for the *order* argument.

11. Calculate the weighted average and ranks for all of the students by using AutoFill to copy the formulas in the range P3:Q3 to the range P3:Q68.

12. In cell B15, enter the student ID **602-1-99** for Lawrence Fujita.

13. In cell B16, use the VLOOKUP function with the student ID from cell B15 to look up the first name of the student matching that ID. Use the range H:Q as the reference to the lookup table, and retrieve the third column from the table.

14. In the range B17:B24, use lookup functions to retrieve the other data for the student ID entered in cell B15.

15. Test the VLOOKUP function by adding other student IDs in cell B15 to confirm that you can retrieve the record for any student in class based on his or her student ID.

16. Manuel Harmon was not able to take the final exam because of a family crisis. Daivi is scheduling a makeup exam for him. A weighted average of 92.0 will give Manuel an A for the course. Use Goal Seek to determine what grade he would need on the final to get an A for the course.

17. Save and close the workbook.

Case Problem 4

Data File needed for this Case Problem: Cairn.xlsx

Cairn Camping Supplies   Diane Cho is the owner of Cairn Camping Supplies, a small camping store she runs out of her home in Fort Smith, Arkansas. To help her manage her inventory and orders, she wants to develop an Excel worksheet for recording orders. The worksheet needs to calculate the cost of each order, including the cost of shipping and sales tax. Shipping costs vary based on whether the customer wants to use standard, three-day, two-day, or overnight shipping. Diane will also offer free shipping for orders that are more than $250. The shipping form worksheet will use lookup functions so that Diane can enter each product's ID code and have the name and price of the product automatically entered into the form. To keep the worksheet clean without distracting error values when no input values have been entered, you'll use IF functions to test whether the user has entered a required value first before applying a formula using that value. Complete the following:

1. Open the **Cairn** workbook located in the Excel3 > Case4 folder, and then save the workbook as **Cairn Camping** in the location specified by your instructor.

2. In the Documentation worksheet, enter your name in cell B3 and the date in cell B4.

3. In the Order Form worksheet, enter the following sample order data: Customer **Dixie Kaufmann**; Order Number **381**; Order Date **4/5/2018**; Street **414 Topeak Lane**; City **Fort Smith**; State **AK**; ZIP **72914**; Phone **(479) 555-2081**; and Delivery Type **3 Day**.

⊕ **Explore** 4. In cell B17, calculate the number of delivery days for the order. Insert an IF function that first tests whether the value in cell B16 is equal to an empty text string (""). If it is, return an empty text string; otherwise, apply a lookup function to retrieve the lookup value from the table in the range F5:H8 using the value of cell B16 as the lookup value.

⊕ **Explore** 5. In cell B18, estimate the date of weekday delivery by inserting an IF function that tests whether cell B16 is equal to an empty text string. If it is, return an empty text string, otherwise apply the WORKDAY function using the values in cell B6 as the starting date and cell B17 as the number of days.

6. In cell D13, enter **p4981** as the initial item ordered by the customer. In cell G13, enter **2** as the number of items ordered.

7. In cell E13, enter an IF function that tests whether the value in cell D13 is equal to an empty text string. If true, return an empty text string. If false, apply the VLOOKUP function to return the name of the product ID entered into cell D13.

8. In cell F13, enter another IF function that tests whether the value in cell D13 is equal to an empty text string. If true, return an empty text string. If false, return the price of the product ID entered in cell D13.

9. In cell H13, enter another IF function to test whether the value in cell D13 is equal to an empty text string. If true, return an empty text string; otherwise, calculate the value of the price of the item multiplied by the number of items ordered.

10. Copy the formula in the range E13:F13 to the range E13:F20. Use AutoFill to copy the formula from cell H13 into the range H13:H20.

11. In cell H22, calculate the sum of the values in the range H13:H20.

12. In cell H23, calculate the sales tax equal to the total cost of the items ordered multiplied by the sales tax rate in cell G10.

13. In cell H24, calculate the shipping cost of the order by inserting an IF function that tests whether the value of cell B16 is an empty text string. If it is, return the value 0; otherwise, use a lookup function to return the shipping cost for the indicated shipping method.

14. In cell H25, insert an IF function that tests whether the value of cell H22 is greater than 250 (the minimum order needed to qualify for free shipping). If it is, return a value of cell H24; otherwise, return a value of 0.

15. In cell H27, calculate the total cost of the order by summing the values in the range H22:H24 and subtracting the value of cell H25.

16. Complete the customer order by adding the following items: Item **t7829** and Qty **1**; Item **led7331** and Qty **3**; and Item **sb8502** and Qty **5**.

17. Confirm that your worksheet correctly calculates the total cost, and then save your workbook.

18. Save the workbook as **Cairn Order Form** in the location specified by your instructor.

19. Create a blank order form sheet by deleting the input values in the ranges B4:B6, B9:B13, B16, D13:D16, G13:G16. Do *not* delete any formulas in the worksheet. Confirm that the worksheet does not show any error values when the input data is removed.

20. Save and close the workbook.

OBJECTIVES

Session 4.1
- Use the PMT function to calculate a loan payment
- Create an embedded pie chart
- Apply styles to a chart
- Add data labels to a pie chart
- Format a chart legend
- Create a clustered column chart
- Create a stacked column chart

Session 4.2
- Create a line chart
- Create a combination chart
- Format chart elements
- Modify the chart's data source
- Create a histogram and Pareto chart
- Add sparklines to a worksheet
- Format cells with data bars

Analyzing and Charting Financial Data

Preparing a Business Plan

Case | *Backspace Gear*

Haywood Mills is the owner of Backspace Gear, a new business in Kennewick, Washington, that manufactures backpacks for work, school, travel, and camping. Haywood has been working from a small shop making specialized packs for friends and acquaintances and wants to expand his business and his customer base. To do that, he needs to secure a business loan. Part of the process of securing a loan is to present a business plan that shows the current state of the market and offers projections about the company's future growth and earnings potential.

In addition to financial tables and calculations, Haywood's presentation needs to include charts and graphics that show a visual picture of the company's current financial status and where he hopes to take it. Haywood has asked for your help in creating the Excel charts and financial calculations he needs to include in his business plan.

STARTING DATA FILES

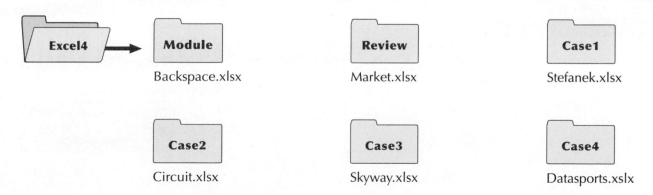

Excel4 →	Module	Review	Case1
	Backspace.xlsx	Market.xlsx	Stefanek.xlsx
	Case2	Case3	Case4
	Circuit.xlsx	Skyway.xlsx	Datasports.xslx

Session 4.1 Visual Overview:

A **data series** contains the actual values that are plotted or displayed on the chart. This data series shows the total number of each type of backpack.

The **category values** are the groups or categories to which the data series values belong. These category values show the different backpack types.

Each chart has a **data source**, which is the range that contains the data to display in the chart. The data source in the range A4:B10 is used in the pie chart.

A **chart**, or **graph**, is a visual representation of a set of data values. Charts show trends or relationships that may not be readily apparent from numbers alone.

The **chart area** contains the chart and all of the other chart elements.

A **data label** is text associated with an individual data marker, such as the percentage value next to a pie slice.

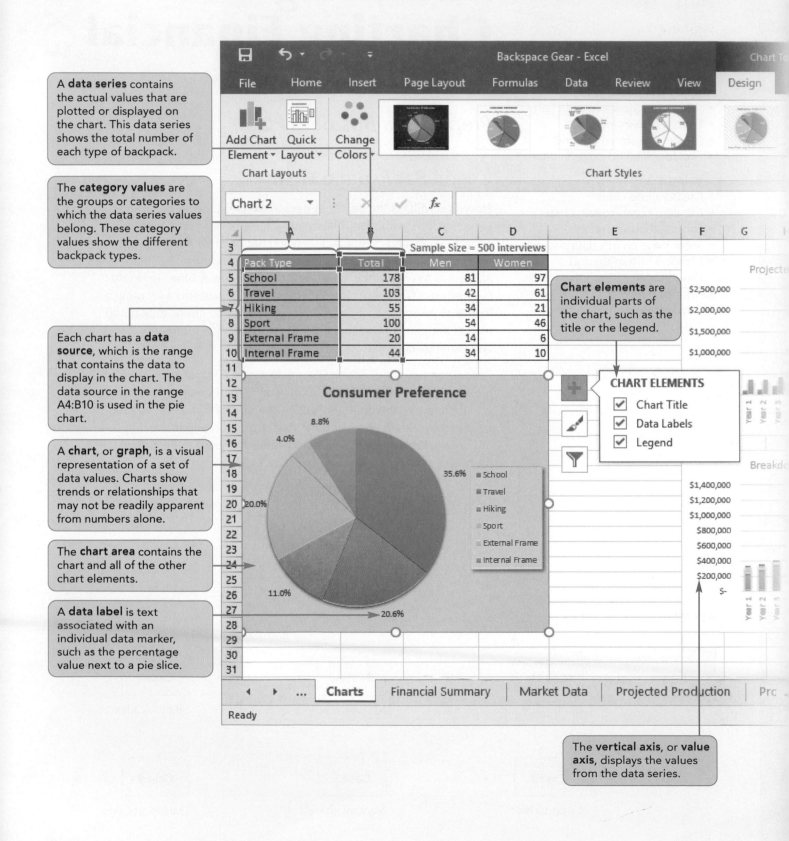

Chart elements are individual parts of the chart, such as the title or the legend.

CHART ELEMENTS
- ✓ Chart Title
- ✓ Data Labels
- ✓ Legend

The **vertical axis**, or **value axis**, displays the values from the data series.

Chart Elements

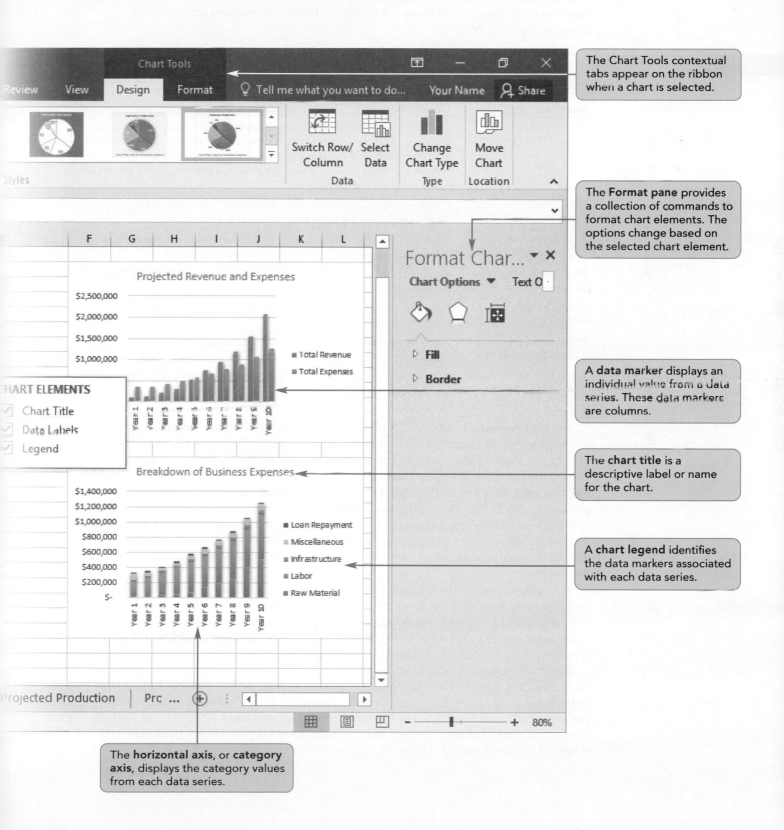

The Chart Tools contextual tabs appear on the ribbon when a chart is selected.

The **Format pane** provides a collection of commands to format chart elements. The options change based on the selected chart element.

A **data marker** displays an individual value from a data series. These data markers are columns.

The **chart title** is a descriptive label or name for the chart.

A **chart legend** identifies the data markers associated with each data series.

The **horizontal axis**, or **category axis**, displays the category values from each data series.

Introduction to Financial Functions

Financial functions are used to analyze loans, investments, and business statistics. Figure 4-1 lists some of the many Excel financial functions that are often used in business applications.

Figure 4-1   **Financial functions for loans and investments**

Function	Description
FV(rate,nper,pmt [,pv=0][,type=0])	Calculates the future value of an investment, where *rate* is the interest rate per period, *nper* is the total number of periods, *pmt* is the payment in each period, *pv* is the present value of the investment, and *type* indicates whether payments should be made at the end of the period (0) or the beginning of the period (1)
PMT(rate,nper,pv [,fv=0][,type=0])	Calculates the payments required each period on a loan or an investment, where *fv* is the future value of the investment
IPMT(rate,per,nper, pv[,fv=0][,type=0])	Calculates the amount of a loan payment devoted to paying the loan interest, where *per* is the number of the payment period
PPMT(rate,per,nper, pv[,fv=0][,type=0])	Calculates the amount of a loan payment devoted to paying off the principal of a loan
PV(rate,nper,pmt [,fv=0][,type=0])	Calculates the present value of a loan or an investment based on periodic, constant payments
NPER(rate,pmt,pv [,fv=0][,type=0])	Calculates the number of periods required to pay off a loan or an investment
RATE(nper,pmt,pv [,fv=0][,type=0])	Calculates the interest rate of a loan or an investment based on periodic, constant payments

The **PMT function** is used to calculate the payments required to completely repay a mortgage or other type of loan. Before you can use the PMT function, you need to understand some of the concepts and definitions associated with loans. The cost of a loan to the borrower is largely based on three factors—the principal, the interest, and the time required to repay the loan. **Principal** is the amount of the loan. **Interest** is the amount added to the principal by the lender. You can think of interest as a kind of "user fee" because the borrower is paying for the right to use the lender's money. Generally, interest is expressed at an annual percentage rate, or APR. For example, an 8 percent APR means that the annual interest rate on the loan is 8 percent of the amount owed to the lender.

An annual interest rate is divided by the number of payments per year (often monthly or quarterly). So, if the 8 percent annual interest rate is paid monthly, the resulting monthly interest rate is 1/12 of 8 percent, or about 0.67 percent per month. If payments are made quarterly, then the interest rate per quarter would be 1/4 of 8 percent, or 2 percent per quarter.

The third factor in calculating the cost of a loan is the time required to repay the loan, which is specified as the number of payment periods. The number of payment periods is based on the length of the loan multiplied by the number of payments per year. For example, a 10-year loan that is paid monthly has 120 payment periods (that is, 10 years $\times$ 12 months per year). If that same 10-year loan is paid quarterly, it has 40 payment periods (10 years $\times$ 4 quarters per year).

Using the PMT Function

To calculate the costs associated with a loan, such as the one that Haywood needs to fund the startup costs for Backspace Gear, you need the following information:

- The annual interest rate
- The number of payment periods per year
- The length of the loan in terms of the total number of payment periods
- The amount being borrowed
- When loan payments are due

The PMT function uses this information to calculate the payment required in each period to pay back the loan. The PMT function syntax is

```
PMT(rate,nper,pv[,fv=0][,type=0])
```

where *rate* is the interest rate for each payment period, *nper* is the total number of payment periods required to repay the loan, and *pv* is the present value of the loan or the amount that needs to be borrowed. The PMT function has two optional values—*fv* and *type*. The *fv* value is the future value of the loan. Because the intent with most loans is to repay them completely, the future value is equal to 0 by default. The *type* value specifies when the interest is charged on the loan, either at the end of the payment period (*type=0*), which is the default, or at the beginning of the payment period (*type=1*).

For example, you can use the PMT function to calculate the monthly payments required to repay a car loan of $15,000 over a five-year period at an annual interest rate of 9 percent. The *rate*, or interest rate per period value, is equal to 9 percent divided by 12 monthly payments, or 0.75 percent per month. The *nper*, or total number of payments value, is equal to 12 × 5 (12 monthly payments over five years) or 60 payments. The *pv*, or present value of the loan, is 15,000. In this case, because the loan will be repaid completely and payments will be made at the end of the month, you can accept the defaults for the *fv* and *type* values. The resulting PMT function can be written as

```
PMT(0.09/12, 5*12, 15000)
```

returning the value –311.38, or a monthly loan payment of $311.38. The PMT function returns a negative value because the monthly loan payments are treated as an expense to the borrower.

Rather than entering the argument values directly in the PMT function, you should include the loan terms in worksheet cells that are referenced in the function. This makes it clear what values are being used in the loan calculation. It also makes it easier to perform a what-if analysis exploring other loan options.

Haywood wants to borrow $150,000 to help start up his new business at a 6 percent annual interest rate. He plans to repay the loan in 10 years with monthly payments. You will calculate the amount of his monthly loan payment.

To enter the terms of the loan:

▶ 1. Open the **Backspace** workbook located in the **Excel4 > Module** folder included with your Data Files, and then save the workbook as **Backspace Gear** in the location specified by your instructor.

▶ 2. In the Documentation sheet, enter your name in cell B3 and the date in cell B4.

▶ 3. Go to the **Business Loan** worksheet. You'll use this worksheet to calculate the monthly payments that will be due on Haywood's loan.

▶ 4. In cell **B4**, enter **$150,000** as the loan amount.

▶ 5. In cell **B5**, enter **6.00%** as the annual interest rate.

6. In cell **B6**, enter **12** as the number of payments per year, indicating that the loan will be repaid monthly.

7. In cell **B7**, enter the formula **=B5/B6** to calculate the interest rate per period. In this case, the 6 percent interest rate is divided by 12 payments per year, returning a monthly interest rate of 0.50 percent.

8. In cell **B8**, enter **10** as the number of years in the loan.

9. In cell **B9**, enter **=B6*B8** to multiply the number of payments per year by the number of years in the loan, returning a value of 120 payments needed to repay the loan.

Next, you will use the PMT function to calculate the monthly payment needed to repay the loan in 10 years.

To calculate the monthly payment:

1. Select cell **B11** to make it the active cell. You will enter the PMT function in this cell.

2. On the ribbon, click the **Formulas** tab.

3. In the Function Library group, click the **Financial** button, and then scroll down and click **PMT** in the list of financial functions. The Function Arguments dialog box opens.

4. With the insertion point in the Rate box, click cell **B7** in the worksheet to enter the reference to the cell with the interest rate per month.

> **TIP**
>
> For the Rate argument, you must enter the interest rate per payment, not the annual interest rate.

5. Click in the **Nper** box, and then click cell **B9** in the worksheet to enter the reference to the cell with the total number of monthly payments required to repay the loan.

6. Click in the **Pv** box, and then click cell **B4** in the worksheet to enter the reference to the cell with the present value of the loan. See Figure 4-2.

Figure 4-2   Function Arguments dialog box for the PMT function

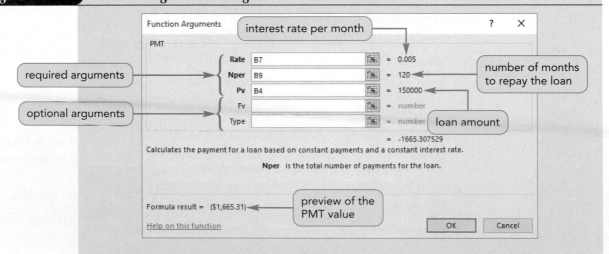

7. Click the **OK** button. The monthly payment amount ($1,665.31) appears in cell B11. The number is displayed in parentheses and in a red font to indicate a negative value because that is the payment that Backspace Gear must make rather than income it receives.

8. In cell B12, enter the formula **=B6*B11** to multiply the number of payments per year by the monthly payment amount, calculating the total payments for the entire year. The annual payments would be ($19,983.69), shown as a negative number to indicate money being paid out.

9. Select cell **B11**. The calculations for the business loan are complete. See Figure 4-3.

Figure 4-3	Monthly and annual costs of the business loan

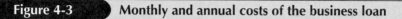

Haywood wants to see the financial impact of taking out a larger loan.

10. In cell **B4**, change the loan amount to **250,000**. With a loan of that size, the monthly payment increases to $2,775.51, and the annual total increases to $33,306.15.

Although a larger loan might help the business get off the ground, Haywood does not want the company to take such a large debt.

11. In cell **B4**, return the loan amount to **150,000**.

Based on your analysis, Backspace Gear would spend about $20,000 a year repaying the $150,000 business loan over the next 10 years. Haywood wants this information included in the Projected Cash Flow worksheet, which estimates Backspace Gear's annual revenue, expenses, and cash flow for the first 10 years of its operation. You will enter that amount as an expense for each year, completing the projected cash flow calculations.

To enter the loan repayment amount in the cash flow projection:

▶ **1.** Go to the **Projected Cash Flow** worksheet, and review the estimated annual revenue, expenses, and cash flow for the next decade.

▶ **2.** In cell **B20**, enter **20,000** as the projected yearly amount of the loan repayment. Because the projected cash flow is a rough estimate of the projected income and expenses, it is not necessary to include the exact dollar-and-cents cost of the loan.

▶ **3.** Copy the annual loan payment in cell **B20** into the range **C20:K20** to enter the projected annual loan payment in each year of the cash flow projections. See Figure 4-4.

Figure 4-4   **Completed Projected Cash Flow worksheet**

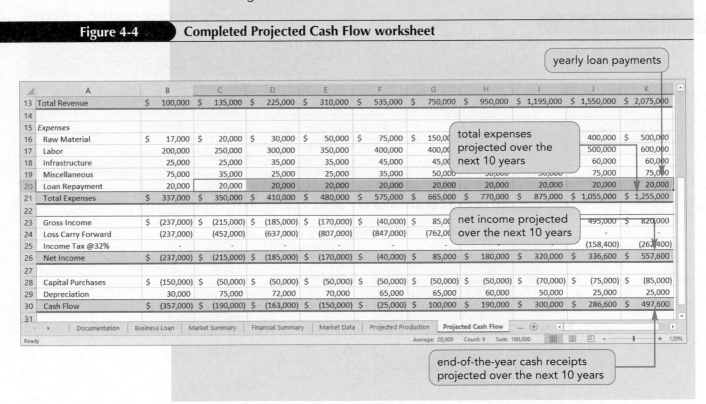

After including the projected annual loan payments, the Projected Cash Flow worksheet shows that Backspace Gear's projected net income at the end of the tenth year would be about $560,000, assuming all of the other projections are accurate. Based on these figures, the company should have almost $500,000 in cash at that time.

INSIGHT

Using Functions to Manage Personal Finances

Excel has many financial functions to manage personal finances. The following list can help you determine which function to use for the most common personal finance calculations:

- To determine how much an investment will be worth after a series of monthly payments at some future time, use the FV (future value) function.
- To determine how much you have to spend each month to repay a loan or mortgage within a set period of time, use the PMT (payment) function.
- To determine how much of your monthly loan payment is used to pay the interest, use the IPMT (interest payment) function.
- To determine how much of your monthly loan payment is used for repaying the principal, use the PPMT (principal payment) function.
- To determine the largest loan or mortgage you can afford given a set monthly payment, use the PV (present value) function.
- To determine how long it will take to pay off a loan with constant monthly payments, use the NPER (number of periods) function.

For most loan and investment calculations, you need to enter the annual interest rate divided by the number of times the interest is compounded during the year. If interest is compounded monthly, divide the annual interest rate by 12; if interest is compounded quarterly, divide the annual rate by four. You must also convert the length of the loan or investment into the number of payments per year. If you will make payments monthly, multiply the number of years of the loan or investment by 12.

Now that you have calculated the cost of the business loan and determined its impact on future cash flows, your next task is to summarize Haywood's business proposal for Backspace Gear. An effective tool for summarizing complex scientific and financial data is a chart.

Getting Started with Excel Charts

Charts show trends or relationships in data that are easier to see than by looking at the actual numbers. Creating a chart is a several-step process that involves choosing the chart type, selecting the data to display in the chart, and formatting the chart's appearance.

REFERENCE

Creating a Chart

- Select the range containing the data you want to chart.
- On the Insert tab, in the Charts group, click the Recommended Charts button or a button representing the general chart type, and then click the chart you want to create (or click the Quick Analysis button, click the Charts category, and then click the chart you want to create).
- On the Chart Tools Design tab, in the Location group, click the Move Chart button, select whether to embed the chart in a worksheet or place it in a chart sheet, and then click the OK button.

Excel provides 59 types of charts organized into the 10 categories described in Figure 4-5. Within each chart category are chart variations called **chart subtypes**. You can also design your own custom chart types to meet the specific needs of your reports and projects.

Figure 4-5	Excel chart types and subtypes

Chart Category	Description	Chart Subtypes
Column or Bar	Compares values from different categories. Values are indicated by the height of the columns or the length of a bar.	2-D Column, 3-D Column, 2-D Bar, 3-D Bar
Hierarchy	Displays data that is organized into a hierarchy of categories where the size of the groups is based on a number.	Treemap, Sunburst
Waterfall or Stock	Displays financial cash flow values or stock market data.	Waterfall, Stock
Line	Compares values from different categories. Values are indicated by the height of the lines. Often used to show trends and changes over time.	2-D Line, 3-D Line, 2-D Area, 3-D Area
Statistic	Displays a chart summarizing the distribution of values from a sample population.	Histogram, Pareto, Box and Whisker
Pie	Compares relative values of different categories to the whole. Values are indicated by the areas of the pie slices.	2-D Pie, 3-D Pie, Doughnut
X Y (Scatter)	Shows the patterns or relationship between two or more sets of values. Often used in scientific studies and statistical analyses.	Scatter, Bubble
Surface or Radar	Compares three sets of values in a three-dimensional chart.	Surface, Radar
Combo	Combines two or more chart types to make the data easy to visualize, especially when the data is widely varied.	Clustered Column-Line, Clustered Column-Line on Secondary Axis, Stacked Area-Clustered Column
PivotChart	Creates a chart summarizing data from a PivotTable.	*none*

Sometimes more than one chart can be used for the same data. Figure 4-6 presents the same labor cost data displayed as a line chart, a bar chart, and column charts. The column charts are shown with both a 2-D subtype that has two-dimensional, or flat, columns and a 3-D subtype that gives the illusion of three-dimensional columns. The various charts and chart subtypes are better suited for different data. You should choose the one that makes the data easiest to interpret.

Figure 4-6   **Same data displayed as different chart types**

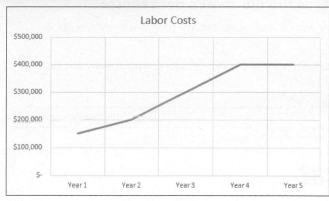

Line chart

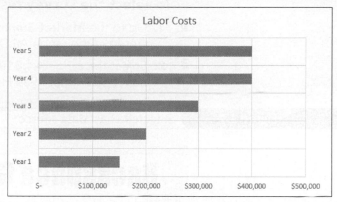

Bar chart

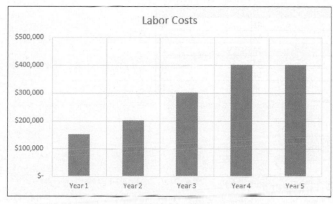

2-D Column chart

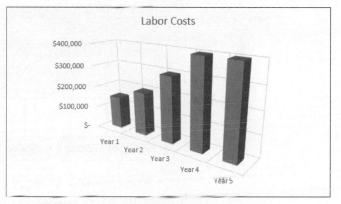

3-D Column chart

Creating a Pie Chart

The first chart you will create is a **pie chart**, which is a chart in the shape of a circle divided into slices like a pie. Each slice represents a single value from a data series. Larger data values are represented with bigger pie slices. The relative sizes of the slices let you visually compare the data values and see how much each contributes to the whole. Pie charts are most effective with six or fewer slices and when each slice is large enough to view easily.

Selecting the Data Source

The data displayed in a chart comes from the chart's data source, which includes one or more data series and a series of category values. A data series contains the actual values that are plotted on the chart, whereas the category values provide descriptive labels for each data series and are used to group those series. Category values are usually located in the first column or first row of the data source. The data series are usually placed in subsequent columns or rows. However, you can select category and data values from anywhere within a workbook.

Over the next 10 years Backspace Gear plans to produce school, travel, hiking, sport, external frame (for camping), and internal frame (for camping) packs. Haywood conducted a consumer survey of 500 adults to determine which of these will likely have the greatest demand in the Washington area. You will use the survey results, which Hayward entered in the Market Summary worksheet, as the data source for a pie chart.

To select the survey results as the pie chart's data source:

1. Go to the **Market Summary** worksheet. A summary of the survey results is stored in the range A4:D10.

2. Select the range **A4:B10** containing the overall results of the survey for both men and women. See Figure 4-7.

Figure 4-7   Selected chart data source

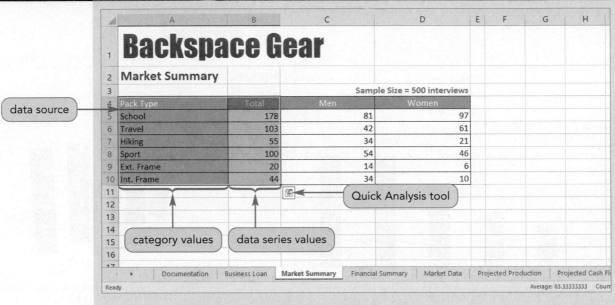

The selected data source covers two columns. The category values are located in the first column, and the data series that you will chart is located in the second column. When the selected range is taller than it is wide, Excel assumes that the category values and data series are laid out in columns. Conversely, a data source that is wider than it is tall is assumed to have the category values and data series laid out in rows. Note that the first row in this selected data source contains labels that identify the category values (Pack Type) and the data series name (Total).

Charting with the Quick Analysis Tool

After you select a data source, the Quick Analysis tool appears. The Charts category contains a list of chart types that are often appropriate for the selected data source. For the market survey results, a pie chart provides the best way to compare the preferences for the six types of packs that Backspace Gear plans to produce. You will use the Quick Analysis tool to generate the pie chart for Haywood.

To create a pie chart with the Quick Analysis tool:

1. With the range A4:B10 still selected, click the **Quick Analysis** button 📊 in the lower-right corner of the selected range (or press the **Ctrl+Q** keys) to open the Quick Analysis tool.

2. Click the **Charts** category. The chart types you will most likely want to use with the selected data source are listed. See Figure 4-8.

TIP

You can also insert a chart by selecting a chart type in the Charts group on the Insert tab.

Figure 4-8   Charts category of the Quick Analysis tool

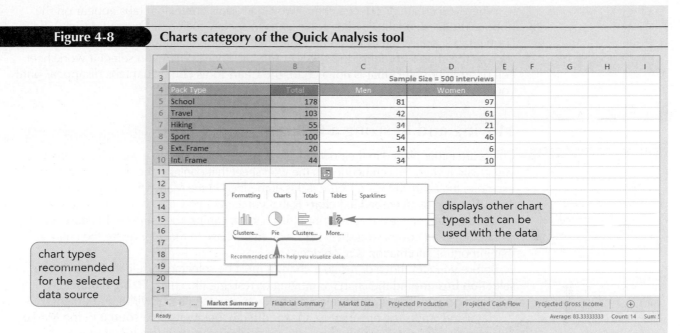

chart types recommended for the selected data source

displays other chart types that can be used with the data

3. Click **Pie**. A pie chart appears in the Market Summary worksheet. Each slice is a different size based on its value in the data series. The biggest slice represents the 178 people in the survey who selected a school pack as their most likely purchase from Backspace Gear. The smallest slice of the pie represents the 20 individuals who selected the external frame pack. See Figure 4-9.

Figure 4-9   Pie chart in the Market Summary worksheet

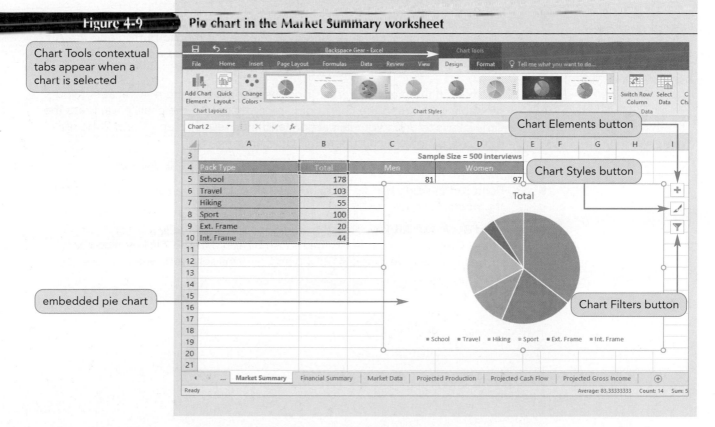

Chart Tools contextual tabs appear when a chart is selected

Chart Elements button

Chart Styles button

Chart Filters button

embedded pie chart

When you create or select a chart, two Chart Tools contextual tabs appear on the ribbon. The Design tab provides commands to specify the chart's overall design. The Format tab supplies the tools needed to format the graphic shapes found in the chart, such as the chart's border or the slices from a pie chart. When you select a worksheet cell or another object that is not a chart, the Chart Tools contextual tabs disappear until you reselect the chart.

Moving and Resizing a Chart

TIP

You can print an embedded chart with its worksheet, or you can print only the selected embedded chart without its worksheet.

Charts are either placed in their own chart sheets or embedded in a worksheet. When you create a chart, it is embedded in the worksheet that contains the data source. For example, the chart shown in Figure 4-9 is embedded in the Market Summary worksheet. The advantage of an **embedded chart** is that you can display the chart alongside its data source and any text that describes the chart's meaning and purpose. Because an embedded chart covers worksheet cells, you might have to move or resize the chart so that important information is not hidden.

Before you can move or resize a chart, it must be selected. A selected chart has a **selection box** around the chart for moving or resizing the chart. **Sizing handles**, which appear along the edges of the selection box, change the chart's width and height.

Haywood wants the pie chart to appear directly below its data source in the Market Summary worksheet. You will move and resize the chart to fit this location.

To move and resize the survey results pie chart:

1. Point to an empty area of the selected chart. The pointer changes to ⊹ and "Chart Area" appears in a ScreenTip.

Be sure to drag the chart from an empty part of the chart area so the entire chart moves, not just chart elements within the chart.

2. Hold down the **Alt** key, drag the chart until its upper-left corner snaps to the upper-left corner of cell **A12**, and then release the mouse button and the **Alt** key. The upper-left corner of the chart is aligned with the upper-left corner of cell A12.

   Trouble? If the pie chart resizes or does not move to the new location, you probably didn't drag the chart from an empty part of the chart area. Press the Ctrl+Z keys to undo your last action, and then repeat Steps 1 and 2, being sure to drag the pie chart from the chart area.

   The chart moves to a new location, but it still needs to be resized.

3. Point to the sizing handle in the lower-right corner of the selection box until the pointer changes to ⬂.

4. Hold down the **Alt** key, drag the sizing handle up to the lower-right corner of cell **D26**, and then release the mouse button and the **Alt** key. The chart resizes to cover the range A12:D26 and remains selected. See Figure 4-10.

Figure 4-10   **Moved and resized pie chart**

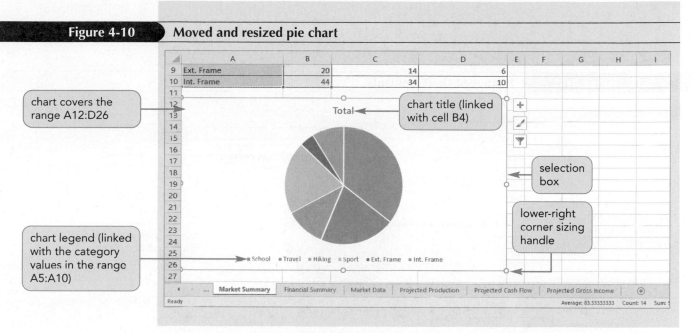

chart covers the range A12:D26

chart title (linked with cell B4)

selection box

lower-right corner sizing handle

chart legend (linked with the category values in the range A5:A10)

Note that three buttons appear to the right of the selected chart: the Chart Elements button ⊞, the Chart Styles button ✎, and the Chart Filters button ▼. You will use these to modify the chart's appearance.

Working with Chart Elements

Every chart contains elements that can be formatted individually. For example, a pie chart has three elements—the chart title, the chart legend identifying each pie slice, and data labels that provide a data value associated with each slice. The Chart Elements button ⊞ that appears to the right of the selected chart lists the elements that can be added or removed from the chart. When you add or remove a chart element, the other elements resize to fit in the unoccupied space in the chart. Live Preview shows how changing an element will affect the chart's appearance so that you can experiment with different formats before applying them.

Haywood doesn't want the pie chart to include a title because the text in cell B4 and the data in the range A5:B10 sufficiently explain the chart's purpose. However, he does want to display the data values next to the pie slices. You will remove the chart title element and add the data labels element.

To remove the chart title and add data labels:

1. With the pie chart still selected, click the **Chart Elements** button ⊞. A menu of chart elements that are available for the pie chart opens. As the checkmarks indicate, only the chart title and the chart legend are displayed in the pie chart.

2. Click the **Chart Title** check box to deselect it. The chart title is removed from the pie chart, and the chart elements resize to fill the space.

3. Point to the **Data Labels** check box. Live Preview shows how the chart will look when the data labels show a count of responses within each category.

4. Click the **Data Labels** check box to select it. The data labels are added to the chart. See Figure 4-11.

Figure 4-11	Displayed chart elements

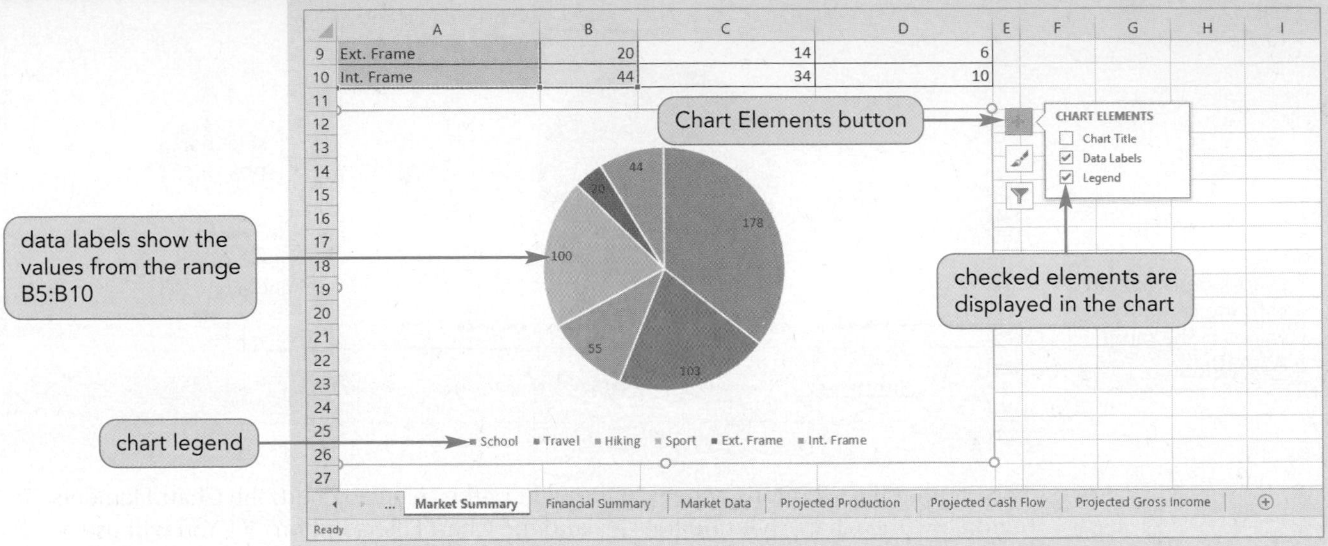

data labels show the values from the range B5:B10

chart legend

Chart Elements button

checked elements are displayed in the chart

Choosing a Chart Style

Chart elements can be formatted individually or as a group using one of the many built-in Excel chart styles. In the pie chart you just created, the format of the chart title, the location of the legend, and the colors of the pie slices are all part of the default pie chart style. You can quickly change the appearance of a chart by selecting a different style from the Chart Styles gallery. Live Preview shows how a chart style will affect the chart.

Haywood wants the pie slices to have a raised, three-dimensional look. You will explore different chart styles to find a style that best fulfills his request.

TIP

You can also select a chart style from the Chart Styles gallery in the Chart Styles group on the Chart Tools Design tab.

To choose a different chart style for the backpack production pie chart:

1. Click the **Chart Styles** button ![chart styles icon] next to the selected pie chart. The Chart Styles gallery opens.

2. Point to different styles in the gallery. Live Preview shows the impact of each chart style on the pie chart's appearance.

3. Scroll to the bottom of the gallery, and then click the **Style 12** chart style. The chart style is applied to the pie chart. See Figure 4-12.

| Figure 4-12 | Chart Styles gallery |

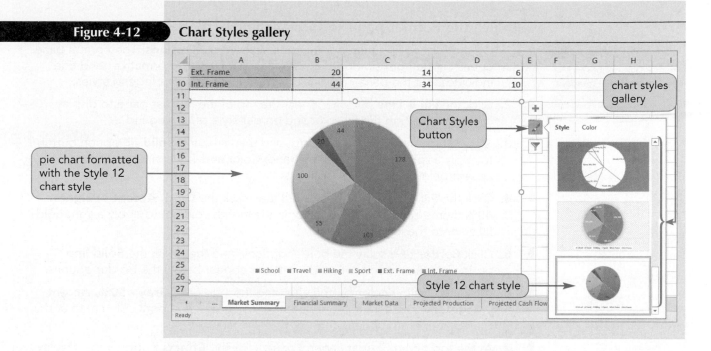

Formatting a Chart Legend

You can fine-tune a chart style by formatting individual chart elements. Using the Chart Elements button, you can open a submenu for each element that includes formatting options, such as the element's location within the chart. You can also open a Format pane, which has more options for formatting the selected chart element.

The default location for the pie chart legend is alongside the chart's bottom edge. Haywood thinks the chart would look better if the legend were aligned with the right edge of the chart. You'll make that change.

To format the pie chart legend:

▶ 1. With the pie chart still selected, click the **Chart Elements** button ⊞.

▶ 2. Point to **Legend** in the Chart Elements menu, and then click the **right arrow** icon next to the Legend entry, displaying a submenu of formatting options for that chart element.

▶ 3. Point to **Left** to see a Live Preview of the pie chart with the legend aligned along the left side of the chart area.

▶ 4. Click **Right** to place the legend along the right side of the chart area. The pie shifts to the left to make room for the legend.

The Chart Elements button also provides access to the Format pane, which has more design options for the selected chart element. Haywood wants you to add a drop shadow to the legend similar to the pie chart's drop shadow, change the fill color to a light gold, and add a light gray border. You'll use the Format pane to make these changes.

To use the Format pane to format the chart legend:

TIP

You can also double-click any chart element to open its Format pane.

1. On the Legend submenu for the entry, click **More Options**. The Format pane opens on the right side of the workbook window. The Format Legend title indicates that the pane contains options relating to chart legend styles.

2. Click the **Fill & Line** button ◇ near the top of the Format pane to display options for setting the fill color and border style of the legend.

3. Click **Fill** to expand the fill options, and then click the **Solid fill** option button to apply a solid fill color to the legend. Color and Transparency options appear below the fill color options.

4. Click the **Fill Color** button 🎨▾, and then click the **Gold, Accent 4, Lighter 40%** theme color (the fourth color in the eighth column) to apply a light gold fill color to the legend.

5. Click **Border** to display the border options, and then click the **Solid line** option button. Additional border options appear below the border options.

6. Click the **Outline color** button 🎨▾, and then click the **Gray - 50%, Accent 3, Lighter 40%** theme color (the fourth color in the seventh column) to add a gray border around the legend.

7. At the top of the Format Legend pane, click the **Effects** button ⬠ to display options for special visual effects.

8. Click **Shadow** to display the shadow options, and then next to the **Presets** button, click ☐▾ to display the Shadow gallery. See Figure 4-13.

Figure 4-13   **Formatted chart legend**

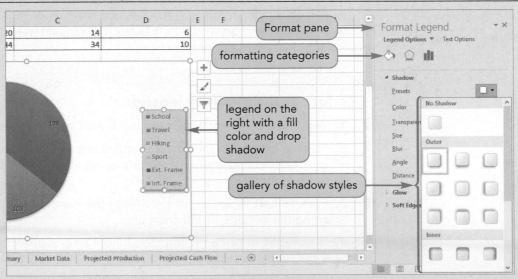

9. Click the **Offset Diagonal Bottom Right** button in the first row and first column to apply the drop shadow effect to the legend.

Formatting Pie Chart Labels

You can modify the content and appearance of data labels, selecting what the labels contain as well as where the labels are positioned. Data labels are placed where they best fit to keep the chart nicely proportioned, but you can change their location. From the Format pane, you can center the labels on the pie slices, place them outside of the slices, or set them as data callouts with each label placed in a text bubble and connected to its slice with a callout line. You can also change the text and number styles used in the data labels. You can also drag and drop individual data labels, placing them anywhere within the chart. When a data label is placed far from its pie slice, a **leader line** is added to connect the data label to its pie slice.

The pie chart data labels display the number of potential customers interested in each pack type, but this information also appears on the worksheet directly above the chart. Haywood wants to include data labels that add new information to the chart—in this case, the percentage that each pack type received in the survey. You'll change the label options.

TIP

You can also format chart elements using the formatting buttons on the Home tab or on the Chart Tools Format tab.

To display percentage labels in the pie chart:

1. At the top of the Format pane, click the **Legend Options** arrow to display a menu of chart elements, and then click **Series "Total" Data Labels** to display the formatting options for data labels. The title of the Format pane changes to Format Data Labels and includes formatting options for data labels. Selection boxes appear around every data label in the pie chart.

2. Near the top of the Format Data Labels pane, click the **Label Options** button ▥, and then click **Label Options**, if necessary, to display the options for the label contents and position. Data labels can contain series names, category names, values, and percentages.

3. Click the **Percentage** check box to add the percentage associated with each pie slice to the pie chart.

4. Click the **Value** check box to deselect it, removing the data series values from the data labels and showing only the percentages. For example, the pie chart shows that 35 percent of the survey responders indicated a willingness to buy Backspace Gear packs designed for school use.

5. Click the **Outside End** option button to move the labels outside of the pie slices. The labels are easier to read in this location.

6. Scroll down the Format pane, and then click **Number** to show the number formatting options for the data labels.

7. Click the **Category** box to display the number formats, and then click **Percentage**.

8. In the Decimal places box, select **2**, type **1**, and then press the **Enter** key. The percentages are displayed with one decimal place. See Figure 4-14.

Figure 4-14   **Formatted data labels**

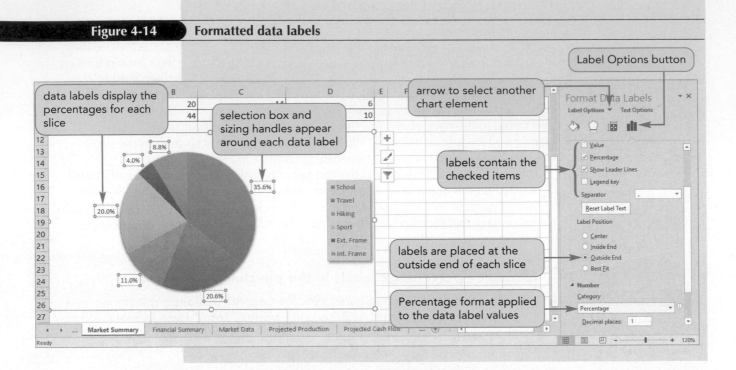

Changing the Pie Slice Colors

A pie slice is an example of a data marker representing a single data value from a data series. You can format the appearance of individual data markers to make them stand out from the others. Pie slice colors should be as distinct as possible to avoid confusion. Depending on the printer quality or the monitor resolution, it might be difficult to distinguish between similarly colored slices. If data labels are displayed within the slice, you also need enough contrast between the slice color and the data label color to make the text readable.

Haywood is concerned that the dark blue color of the Ext. Frame slice will be too dark when printed. He wants you to change it to a light shade of green.

To change the color of a pie slice:

1. Click any pie slice to select all of the slices in the pie chart.

2. Click the **Ext. Frame** slice, which is the darker blue slice that represents 4.0% percent of the pie. Only that slice is selected, as you can see from the sizing handles that appear at each corner of the slice.

3. On the ribbon, click the **Home** tab.

4. In the Font group, click the **Fill Color button arrow** , and then click the **Green, Accent 6, Lighter 40%** theme color (the fourth color in the last column) of the gallery. The pie slice changes to a light green, and the chart legend automatically updates to reflect that change.

You can also change the colors of all the pie slices by clicking the Chart Styles button ![chart styles icon] next to the selected chart, clicking the Color heading, and then selecting a color scheme.

INSIGHT

Exploding a Pie Chart

Pie slices do not need to be fixed within the pie. An **exploded pie chart** moves one slice away from the others as if someone were taking the piece away from the pie. Exploded pie charts are useful for emphasizing one category above all of the others. For example, to emphasize the fact that Backspace Gear will be producing more school packs than any other type of pack, you could explode that single slice, moving it away from the other slices.

To explode a pie slice, first click the pie to select all of the slices, and then click the single slice you want to move. Make sure that a selection box appears around only that slice. Drag the slice away from the pie to offset it from the others. You can explode multiple slices by selecting each slice in turn and dragging them away. To explode all of the slices, select the entire pie and drag the pointer away from the pie's center. Each slice will be exploded and separated from the others. Although you can explode more than one slice, the resulting pie chart is rarely effective as a visual aid to the reader.

Formatting the Chart Area

The chart's background, which is called the chart area, can also be formatted using fill colors, border styles, and special effects such as drop shadows and blurred edges. The chart area fill color used in the pie chart is white, which blends in with the worksheet background. Haywood wants you to change the fill color to a medium green to match the worksheet's color scheme and to make the chart stand out better.

TIP

You can select any chart element using the Chart Elements box in the Current Selection group on the Chart Tools Format tab.

To change the chart area color:

1. Click a blank area within the chart, not containing either a pie slice or the chart legend. The chart area is selected, which you can verify because the Format pane title changes to "Format Chart Area."

2. On the Home tab, in the Font group, click the **Fill Color button arrow** ![fill color icon], and then click the **Green, Accent 6, Lighter 60%** theme color (the last color in the third row). The chart area fill color is now medium green. See Figure 4-15.

Figure 4-15   **Chart area fill color**

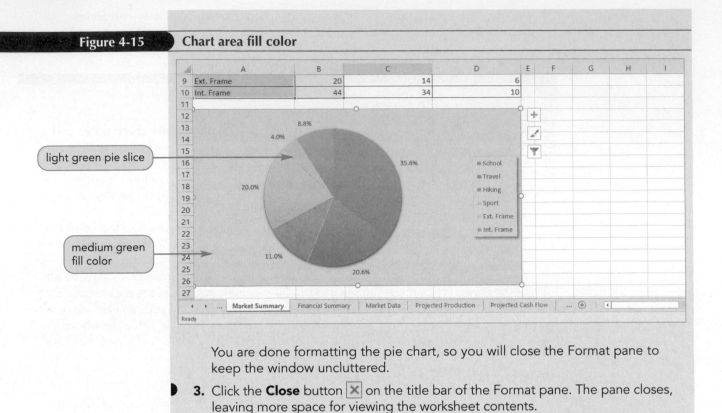

You are done formatting the pie chart, so you will close the Format pane to keep the window uncluttered.

▶ **3.** Click the **Close** button ☒ on the title bar of the Format pane. The pane closes, leaving more space for viewing the worksheet contents.

Performing What-If Analyses with Charts

Because a chart is linked to its data source, any changes in the data source values will be automatically reflected in the chart. For the Market Survey pie chart, the chart title is linked to the text in cell B4, the size of the pie slices is based on the production goals in the range B5:B10, and the category names are linked to the category values in the range A5:A10. Any changes to these cells affect the chart's content and appearance. This makes charts a powerful tool for data exploration and what-if analysis.

Haywood wants to see how the pie chart would change if the survey results were updated.

To apply a what-if analysis to the pie chart:

▶ **1.** In cell **B7**, enter **100** to change the number of individuals who expressed an interest in Backspace hiking packs to 100. The Hiking slice automatically increases in size, changing from 11 percent to 18.3 percent. The size of the remaining slices and their percentages are reduced to compensate.

▶ **2.** In cell **B7**, restore the value to **55**. The pie slices return to their initial sizes, and the percentages return to their initial values.

Haywood wants you to change the category names "Ext. Frame" and "Int. Frame" to "External Frame" and "Internal Frame."

▶ **3.** Click cell **A9**, and then change the text to **External Frame**.

4. Click cell **A10**, and then change the text to **Internal Frame**. The legend text in the pie chart automatically changes to reflect the new text.

Another type of what-if analysis is to **filter** the data source, which limits the data to fewer values. For example, the pie chart shows the survey results for all six types of packs that Backspace Gear will manufacture, but you can filter the pie chart so that it shows only the packs you select.

Haywood wants you to filter the pie chart so that it compares only the packs used for school, travel, and sport.

To filter the pie chart to show only three packs:

1. Click the pie chart to select it.

2. Click the **Chart Filters** button ▼ next to the chart to open a menu listing the chart categories.

3. Click the **Hiking**, **External Frame**, and **Internal Frame** check boxes to deselect them, leaving only the School, Travel, and Sport check boxes selected.

4. At the bottom of the Chart Filters menu, click the **Apply** button. Excel filters the chart, showing only the three marked pack types. After filtering the data, the chart shows that 46.7 percent of the survey respondents would buy the School pack out of the choice of school, travel, and sport packs. See Figure 4-16.

Figure 4-16   Filtered pie chart

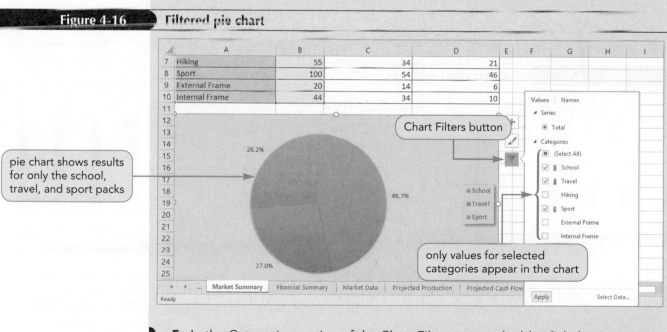

5. In the Categories section of the Chart Filters menu, double-click the **Select All** check box to reselect all six pack types.

6. Click the **Apply** button to update the chart's appearance.

7. Press the **Esc** key to close the menu, leaving the chart selected.

The pie chart is complete. Next you'll create column charts to examine Haywood's proposed production schedule for the next years.

Creating a Column Chart

A **column chart** displays data values as columns with the height of each column based on the data value. A column chart turned on its side is called a **bar chart**, with the length of the bar determined by the data value. It is better to use column and bar charts than pie charts when the number of categories is large or the data values are close in value. Figure 4-17 displays the same data as a pie chart and a column chart. As you can see, it's difficult to determine which pie slice is biggest and by how much. It is much simpler to make those comparisons in a column or bar chart.

Figure 4-17   Data displayed as a pie chart and a column chart

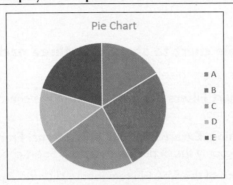
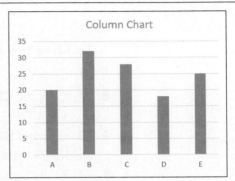

Comparing Column Chart Subtypes

Unlike pie charts, which can show only one data series, column and bar charts can display multiple data series. Figure 4-18 shows three examples of column charts in which four data series named School, Travel, Hiking, and Sport are plotted against one category series (Years).

Figure 4-18   Column chart subtypes

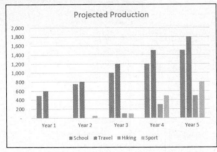
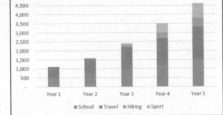
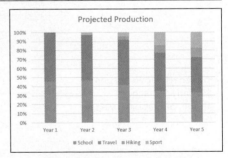

Clustered Column   Stacked Column   100% Stacked Column

The **clustered column chart** displays the data series in separate columns side by side so that you can compare the relative heights of the columns in the three series. The clustered column chart in Figure 4-18 compares the number of packs produced in year 1 through year 5. Note that Backspace Gear mostly produces school and travel packs in years 1 through 3 with hiking and sport packs production increasing in years 4 and 5.

The **stacked column chart** places the data series values within combined columns showing how much is contributed by each series. The stacked column chart in Figure 4-18 gives information on the total number of packs produced each year and how each year's production is split among the four types of packs.

Finally, the **100% stacked column chart** makes the same comparison as the stacked column chart except that the stacked sections are expressed as percentages. As you can see from the 100% stacked column chart in Figure 4-18, school and travel packs account for about 100% of the production in year 1 and steadily decline to 70% of the production in year 5 as Backspace Gear introduces hiking and sport packs.

Creating a Clustered Column Chart

The process for creating a column chart is the same as for creating a pie chart: selecting the data source and choosing a chart type and subtype. After the chart is embedded in the worksheet, you can move and resize the chart as well as change the chart's design, layout, and format.

Haywood wants his business plan to show the projected revenue and expenses for Backspace Gear's first 10 years. Because this requires comparing the data series values, you will create a clustered column chart.

To create a clustered column chart showing projected revenue and expenses:

1. Go to the **Projected Cash Flow** worksheet.

2. Select the nonadjacent range **A4:K4,A13:K13,A21:K21** containing the Year categories in row 4, the Total Revenue data series in row 13, and the Total Expenses data series in row 21. Because you selected a nonadjacent range, the Quick Analysis tool is not available.

TIP

You can also open the Insert Chart dialog box to see the chart types recommended for the selected data source.

3. On the ribbon, click the **Insert** tab. The Charts group contains buttons for inserting different types of charts.

4. In the Charts group, click the **Recommended Charts** button. The Insert Chart dialog box opens with a gallery of suggested charts for the selected data. See Figure 4-19.

Figure 4-19 Recommended Charts tab in the Insert Chart dialog box

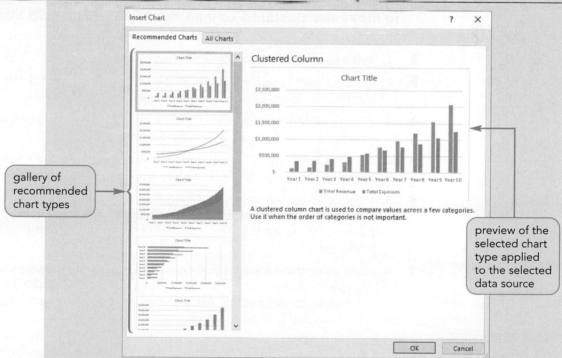

gallery of recommended chart types

preview of the selected chart type applied to the selected data source

5. Make sure the **Clustered Column** chart is selected, and then click the **OK** button. The clustered column chart is embedded in the Projected Cash Flow worksheet.

6. Click the **Chart Styles** button next to the selected column chart.

▶ **7.** In the Style gallery, scroll down, and click the **Style 14** chart style to format the columns with drop shadows.

▶ **8.** Click the **Chart Styles** button ◢ again to close the Style gallery.

Next, you will move the chart to a new location in the workbook.

INSIGHT

Changing a Chart Type

After creating a chart, you can easily switch the chart to a different chart type without having to recreate the chart from scratch. For example, if the data in a column chart would be more effective presented as a line chart, you can change its chart type rather than creating a new chart. Clicking the Change Chart Type button in the Type group on the Chart Tools Design tab opens a dialog box similar to the Insert Chart dialog box, from which you can select a new chart type.

Moving a Chart to a Different Worksheet

The Move Chart dialog box provides options for moving charts between worksheets and chart sheets. You can also cut and paste a chart from one location to another. Haywood wants you to move the column chart of the projected revenue and expenses to the Financial Summary worksheet.

To move the clustered column chart to the Financial Summary worksheet:

▶ **1.** Make sure the clustered column chart is still selected.

▶ **2.** On the Chart Tools Design tab, in the Location group, click the **Move Chart** button. The Move Chart dialog box opens.

▶ **3.** Click the **Object in** arrow to display a list of the worksheets in the active workbook, and then click **Financial Summary**.

▶ **4.** Click the **OK** button. The chart moves from the Projected Cash Flow worksheet to the Financial Summary worksheet and remains selected.

▶ **5.** Hold down the **Alt** key as you drag the chart so that its upper-left corner is aligned with the upper-left corner of cell **E4**, and then release the mouse button and the **Alt** key. The upper-left corner of the chart snaps to the worksheet.

TIP

To set an exact chart size, enter the height and width values in the Size group on the Chart Tools Format tab.

▶ **6.** Hold down the **Alt** key as you drag the lower-right sizing handle of the clustered column chart to the lower-right corner of cell **L20**, and then release the mouse button and the **Alt** key. The chart now covers the range E4:L20.

The revenue and expenses chart shows that Backspace Gear will produce little revenue during its first few years as it establishes itself and its customer base. It is only during year 6 that the revenue will outpace the expenses. After that, Haywood anticipates that the company's revenue will increase rapidly while expenses grow at a more moderate pace.

Editing a Chart Title

When a chart has a single data series, the name of the data series is used for the chart title. When a chart has more than one data series, *Chart Title* appears as the temporary title of the chart. You can replace the placeholder text with a more descriptive title and add a custom format.

Haywood wants you to change the chart title of the clustered column chart to "Projected Revenue and Expenses."

To change the title of the column chart:

1. At the top of the column chart, click **Chart Title** to select the placeholder text.

2. Type **Projected Revenue and Expenses** as the new title, and then press the **Enter** key. The new title is entered into the chart, and the chart title element remains selected.

3. On the ribbon, click the **Home** tab, and then use the buttons in the Font group to remove the bold from the chart title, change the font to **Calibri Light**, change the font size to **16** points, and then change the font color to the **Green, Accent 6, Darker 25%** theme color. See Figure 4-20.

Figure 4-20   Clustered column chart

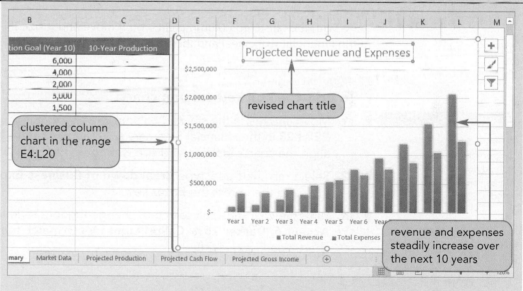

Creating a Stacked Column Chart

The next chart that Haywood wants added to the Financial Summary worksheet is a chart that projects the expenses incurred by the company over the next 10 years broken down by category. Because this chart looks at how different parts of the whole vary across time, that information would be better displayed in a stacked column chart. You will create this chart based on the data located in the Projected Cash Flow worksheet.

To create a stacked column chart:

1. Return to the **Projected Cash Flow** worksheet, and then select the nonadjacent range **A4:K4,A16:K20** containing the year categories and five data series for different types of expenses.

2. On the ribbon, click the **Insert** tab.

3. In the Charts group, click the **Insert Column or Bar Chart** button ▮▮▾. A list of column and bar chart subtypes appears.

4. Click the **Stacked Column** icon (the second chart in the 2-D Column section). The stacked column chart is embedded in the Projected Cash Flow worksheet.

5. With the chart still selected, click the **Chart Styles** button ✎, and then apply the **Style 11** chart style (the last style in the gallery).

   You'll move this chart to the Financial Summary worksheet.

6. On the Chart Tools Design tab, in the Location group, click the **Move Chart** button. The Move Chart dialog box opens.

7. Click the **Object in** arrow, and then click **Financial Summary**.

8. Click the **OK** button. The stacked column chart is moved to the Financial Summary worksheet.

As with the clustered column chart, you'll move and resize the stacked column chart in the Financial worksheet and then add a descriptive chart title.

To edit the stacked column chart:

TIP

To retain the chart's proportions as you resize it, hold down the Shift key as you drag the sizing handle.

1. Move and resize the stacked column chart so that it covers the range **E22:L38** in the Financial Summary worksheet. Use the Alt key to help you align the chart's location and size with the underlying worksheet grid.

2. Select the chart title, type **Breakdown of Business Expenses** as the new title, and then press the **Enter** key.

3. With the chart title still selected, change the font style to a nonbold **Green, Accent 6, Darker 25%**; **Calibri Light** font to match the clustered column chart. See Figure 4-21.

Figure 4-21   Stacked column chart

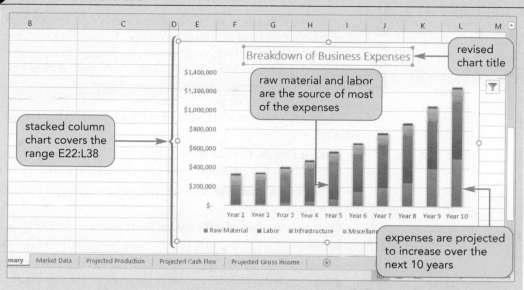

The chart clearly shows that the company's main expenses over the next 10 years will come from the raw material and labor costs. General maintenance, miscellaneous, and the business loan repayment constitute a smaller portion of the company's projected expenses. The overall yearly expense of running the company is expected to increase from about $337,000 in year 1 to $1,255,000 by year 10.

PROSKILLS

Written Communication: Communicating Effectively with Charts

Studies show that people more easily interpret information when it is presented as a graphic rather than in a table. As a result, charts can help communicate the real story underlying the facts and figures you present to colleagues and clients. A well-designed chart can illuminate the bigger picture that might be hidden by viewing only the numbers. However, poorly designed charts can mislead readers and make it more difficult to interpret data.

To create effective and useful charts, keep in mind the following tips as you design charts:

- **Keep it simple.** Do not clutter a chart with too many graphical elements. Focus attention on the data rather than on decorative elements that do not inform.

- **Focus on the message.** Design the chart to highlight the points you want to convey to readers.

- **Limit the number of data series.** Most charts should display no more than four or five data series. Pie charts should have no more than six slices.

- **Choose colors carefully.** Display different data series in contrasting colors to make it easier to distinguish one series from another. Modify the default colors as needed to make them distinct on the screen and in the printed copy.

- **Limit your chart to a few text styles.** Use a maximum of two or three different text styles in the same chart. Having too many text styles in one chart can distract attention from the data.

The goal of written communication is always to inform the reader in the simplest, most accurate, and most direct way possible. When creating worksheets and charts, everything in the workbook should be directed toward that end.

So far, you have determined monthly payments by using the PMT function and created and formatted a pie chart and two column charts. In the next session, you'll continue your work on the business plan by creating line charts, combination charts, histograms, sparklines, and data bars.

REVIEW

Session 4.1 Quick Check

1. You want to apply for a $225,000 mortgage. The annual interest on the loan is 4.8 percent with monthly payments. You plan to repay the loan in 20 years. Write the formula to calculate the monthly payment required to completely repay the loan under those conditions.

2. What function do you use to determine how many payment periods are required to repay a loan?

3. Why does the PMT function return a negative value when calculating the monthly payment due on a loan or mortgage?

4. What three chart elements are included in a pie chart?

5. A data series contains values grouped into 10 categories. Would this data be better displayed as a pie chart or a column chart? Explain why.

6. A research firm wants to create a chart that displays the total population growth of a county over a 10-year period broken down by five ethnicities. Which chart type best displays this information? Explain why.

7. If the research firm wants to display the changing ethnic profile of the county over time as a percentage of the county population, which chart type should it use? Explain why.

8. If the research firm is interested in comparing the numeric sizes of different ethnic groups over time, which chart should it use? Explain why.

9. If the research firm wants to display the ethnic profile of the county only for the current year, which chart should it use? Explain why.

Session 4.2 Visual Overview:

A **combination chart** combines two or more Excel chart types into a single graph. This chart combines a column chart and a line chart.

Chart **gridlines** extend the values of the major or minor tick marks across the plot area.

An **axis title** is descriptive text that appears next to an axis.

A **histogram** is a column chart displaying the distribution of values from a single data series.

Data values from a histogram are grouped into ascending categories called **bins**. The column height indicates the number of values falling within each bin.

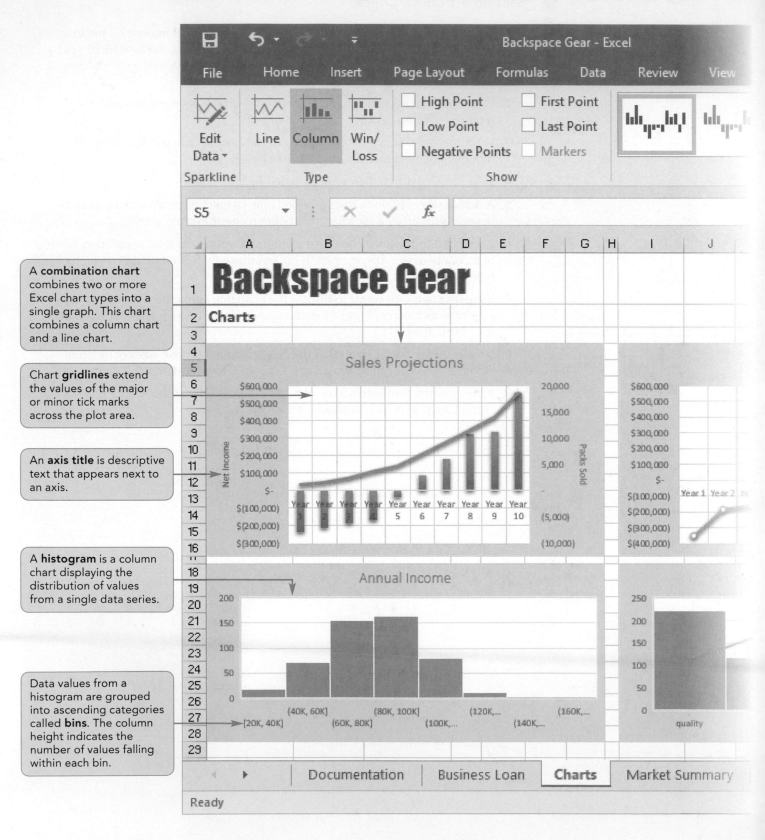

Charts, Sparklines, and Data Bars

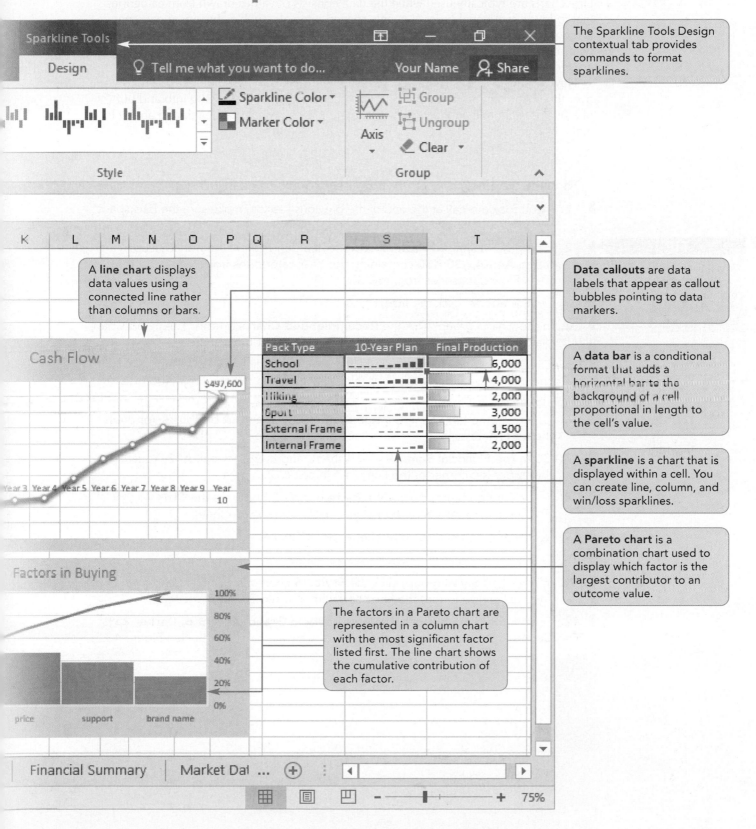

The Sparkline Tools Design contextual tab provides commands to format sparklines.

A **line chart** displays data values using a connected line rather than columns or bars.

Data callouts are data labels that appear as callout bubbles pointing to data markers.

A **data bar** is a conditional format that adds a horizontal bar to the background of a cell proportional in length to the cell's value.

A **sparkline** is a chart that is displayed within a cell. You can create line, column, and win/loss sparklines.

A **Pareto chart** is a combination chart used to display which factor is the largest contributor to an outcome value.

The factors in a Pareto chart are represented in a column chart with the most significant factor listed first. The line chart shows the cumulative contribution of each factor.

Sparkline Tools

Design   Tell me what you want to do...   Your Name   Share

Sparkline Color ▾
Marker Color ▾

Axis

Group
Ungroup
Clear ▾

Style   Group

K L M N O P Q R S T

Cash Flow

$497,600

Year 3 Year 4 Year 5 Year 6 Year 7 Year 8 Year 9 Year 10

Pack Type	10-Year Plan	Final Production
School		6,000
Travel		4,000
Hiking		2,000
Sport		3,000
External Frame		1,500
Internal Frame		2,000

Factors in Buying

100%
80%
60%
40%
20%
0%

price   support   brand name

Financial Summary | Market Dat ... ⊕

75%

Creating a Line Chart

Line charts are typically used when the data consists of values drawn from categories that follow a sequential order at evenly spaced intervals, such as historical data that is recorded monthly, quarterly, or yearly. Like column charts, a line chart can be used with one or more data series. When multiple data series are included, the data values are plotted on different lines with varying line colors.

Haywood wants to use a line chart to show Backspace Gear's potential cash flow over the next decade. Cash flow examines the amount of cash flowing into and out of a business annually; it is one measure of a business's financial health and ability to make its payments.

To create a line chart showing the projected cash flow:

1. If you took a break at the end of the previous session, make sure the Backspace Gear workbook is open.

TIP

When charting table values, do not include the summary totals because they will be treated as another category.

2. Go to the **Projected Cash Flow** worksheet, and select the nonadjacent range **A4:K4,A30:K30** containing the Year categories from row 4 and the Cash Flow data series from row 30.

3. On the ribbon, click the **Insert** tab.

4. In the Charts group, click the **Recommended Charts** button. The Insert Chart dialog box opens, showing different ways to chart the selected data.

5. Click the second chart (the Line chart), and then click the **OK** button. The line chart of the year-end cash flow values is embedded in the Projected Cash Flow worksheet.

6. On the Home tab, in the Clipboard group, click the **Cut** button ✄ (or press the **Ctrl+X** keys). The selected line chart moves to the Clipboard.

7. Go to the **Financial Summary** worksheet, and then click cell **A12**. You want the upper-left corner of the line chart in cell A12.

8. In the Clipboard group, click the **Paste** button 📋 (or press the **Ctrl+V** keys). The line chart is pasted into the Financial Summary worksheet.

9. Resize the line chart to cover the range **A12:C24**.

10. On the ribbon, click the **Chart Tools Design** tab.

11. In the Chart Styles group, click the **Style 15** chart style (the last style in the style gallery) to format the line chart with a raised 3-D appearance.

12. Format the chart title with the same nonbold **Green, Accent 6, Darker 25%**; **Calibri Light** font style you applied to the two column charts. See Figure 4-22.

Figure 4-22 | Line chart showing the projected cash flow

chart title formatted to match other chart titles

chart moved and resized

chart line has a 3-D appearance

initial cash flow values are negative

later cash flow values are positive

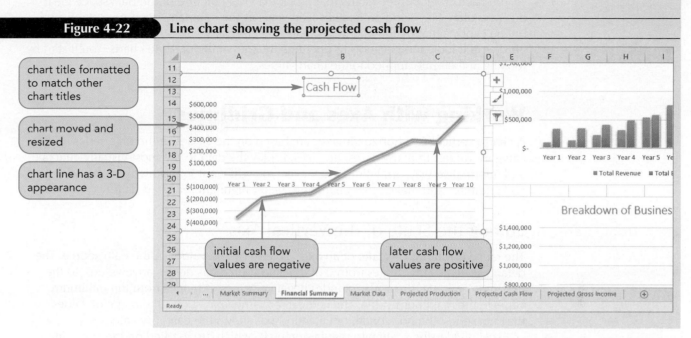

The line chart shows that Backspace Gear will have a negative cash flow in its early years and that the annual cash flow will increase throughout the decade, showing a positive cash flow starting in its sixth year.

Line Charts and Scatter Charts

Line charts can sometimes be confused with XY (scatter) charts, but they are very different chart types. A line chart is more like a column chart that uses lines instead of columns. In a line chart, the data series are plotted against category values. These categories are assumed to have some sequential order. If the categories represent dates or times, they must be evenly spaced in time. For example, the Cash Flow line chart plotted the cash flow values against categories that ranged sequentially from year 1 to year 10.

A scatter chart has no category values. Instead, one series of data values is plotted against another. For example, if you were analyzing the relationship between height and weight among high school students, you would use a scatter chart because both weight and height are data values. On the other hand, if you charted weight measures against height categories (Short, Average, Tall), a line chart would be more appropriate.

Scatter charts are more often used in statistical analysis and scientific studies in which the researcher attempts to find a relationship between one variable and another. For that purpose, Excel includes several statistical tools to augment scatter charts, such as trendlines that provide the best fitting line or curve to the data. You can add a trendline by right-clicking the data series in the chart, and then clicking Add Trendline on the shortcut menu. From the Format Trendline pane that opens you can select different types of trendlines, including exponential and logarithmic lines as well as linear (straight) lines.

You have created three charts that provide a visual picture of the Backspace Gear business plan. Haywood anticipates lean years as the company becomes established, but he expects that by the end of 10 years, the company will be profitable and stable. Next, you'll look at other tools to fine-tune the formatting of these charts. You'll start by looking at the scale applied to the chart values.

Working with Axes and Gridlines

A chart's vertical and horizontal axes are based on the values in the data series and the category values. In many cases, the axes display the data in the most visually effective and informative way. Sometimes, however, you will want to modify the axes' scale, add gridlines, and make other changes to better highlight the chart data.

Editing the Scale of the Vertical Axis

The range of values, or **scale**, of an axis is based on the values in the data source. The default scale usually ranges from 0 (if the data source has no negative values) to the maximum value. If the scale includes negative values, it ranges from the minimum value to the maximum value. The vertical, or value, axis shows the range of values in the data series; the horizontal, or category, axis shows the category values.

Excel divides the scale into regular intervals, which are marked on the axis with **tick marks** and labels. For example, the scale of the vertical axis for the Projected Revenue and Expenses chart (shown in Figure 4-20) ranges from $0 up to $2,500,000 in increments of $500,000. Having more tick marks at smaller intervals could make the chart difficult to read because the tick mark labels might start to overlap. Likewise, having fewer tick marks at larger intervals could make the chart less informative. **Major tick marks** identify the main units on the chart axis while **minor tick marks** identify the smaller intervals between the major tick marks.

Some charts involve multiple data series that have vastly different values. In those instances, you can create dual axis charts. You can plot one data series against a **primary axis**, which usually appears along the left side of the chart, and the other against a **secondary axis**, which is usually placed on the right side of the chart. The two axes can be based on entirely different scales.

By default, no titles appear next to the value and category axes. This is fine when the axis labels are self-explanatory. Otherwise, you can add descriptive axis titles. In general, you should avoid cluttering a chart with extra elements such as axis titles when that information is easily understood from other parts of the chart.

Haywood thinks the value axis scale for the Projected Revenue and Expenses chart needs more tick marks and asks you to modify the axis so that it ranges from $0 to $2,500,000 in intervals of $250,000.

To change the scale of the vertical axis:

▶ 1. Click the **Projected Revenue and Expenses** chart to select it.

▶ 2. Double-click the vertical axis. The Format Axis pane opens with the Axis Options list expanded.

    Trouble? If you don't see the Axis Options section on the Format Axis pane, click the Axis Options button ▮▮ near the top of the pane.

    The Bounds section provides the minimum and maximum boundaries of the axis, which in this case are set from 0.0 to 2.5E6 (which stands for 2,500,000). Note that minimum and maximum values are set to Auto, which means that Excel automatically set these boundaries based on the data values.

TIP

To return a scale value to Auto, click the Reset button next to the value in the Format pane.

The Units section provides the intervals between the major tick marks and between minor tick marks. The major tick mark intervals, which are currently 500,000, are also set automatically by Excel.

▶ **3.** In the Units section, click in the **Major** box, delete the current value, type **250000** as the new interval between major tick marks, and then press the **Enter** key. The scale of the value axis changes. See Figure 4-23.

Figure 4-23   **Formatted value axis**

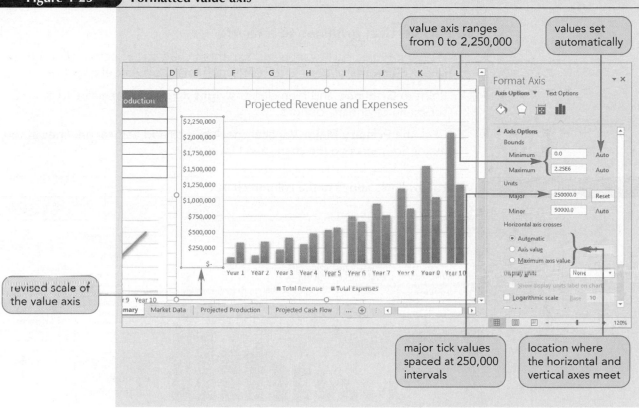

The revised axis scale makes it easier to determine the values displayed in the column chart.

Displaying Unit Labels

When a chart involves large numbers, the axis labels can take up a lot of the available chart area and be difficult to read. You can simplify the chart's appearance by displaying units of measure more appropriate to the data values. For example, you can display the value 20 to represent 20,000 or 20,000,000. This is particularly useful when space is at a premium, such as in an embedded chart confined to a small area of the worksheet.

To display a units label, you double-click the axis to open the Format pane displaying options to format the axis. Select the units type from the Display units box. You can choose unit labels to represent values measured in the hundreds up to the trillions. Excel will modify the numbers on the selected axis and add a label so that readers will know what the axis values represent.

Adding Gridlines to a Chart

Gridlines are horizontal and vertical lines that help you compare data and category values in a chart. Depending on the chart style, gridlines may or may not appear in a chart, though you can add or remove them separately. Gridlines are placed at the major tick marks on the axes, or you can set them to appear at the minor tick marks.

The chart style used for the two column charts and the line chart includes horizontal gridlines. Haywood wants you to add vertical gridlines to the Projected Revenue and Expenses chart to help further separate one set of year values from another.

To add vertical gridlines to a chart:

1. With the Projected Revenue and Expenses chart still selected, click the **Chart Elements** button ⊞ to display the menu of chart elements.

2. Point to **Gridlines**, and then click the **right arrow** that appears to open a submenu of gridline options.

3. Click the **Primary Major Vertical** check box to add vertical gridlines at the major tick marks on the chart. See Figure 4-24.

Figure 4-24   **Vertical gridlines added to the column chart**

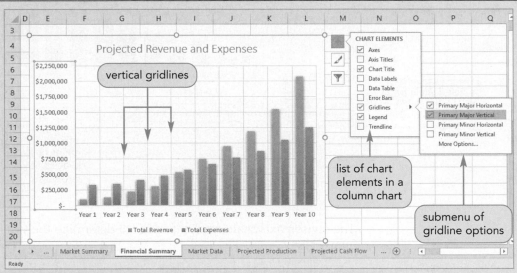

4. Click the **Chart Elements** button ⊞ to close the Chart Elements menu.

Working with Column Widths

Category values do not have the scale options used with data values. However, you can set the spacing between one column and another in your column charts. You can also define the width of the columns. As with the vertical axis, the default spacing and width are set automatically by Excel. A column chart with several categories will naturally make those columns thinner and more tightly packed.

Haywood thinks that the columns in the Projected Revenue and Expenses chart are spaced too closely, making it difficult to distinguish one year's values from another. He wants you to increase the gap between the columns.

To format the chart columns:

1. Make sure the Projected Revenue and Expenses chart is still selected and the Format pane is still open.

2. Click the **Axis Options arrow** at the top of the Format pane, and then click **Series "Total Revenue"** from the list of chart elements. The Format pane title changes to "Format Data Series," and all of the columns in the chart that show total revenue values are selected.

3. In the Format pane, click the **Series Options** button to display the list of series options.

   Series Overlap sets the amount of overlap between columns of different data series. Gap Width sets the amount of space between one group of columns and the next.

4. Drag the **Gap Width** slider until **200%** appears in the Gap Width box. The gap between groups of columns increases, and the individual column widths decrease to make room for the larger gap. See Figure 4-25.

TIP

You can use the up and down spin arrows in the Gap Width box to fine-tune the gap width in 1 percent increments.

| Figure 4-25 | Gap width between columns |

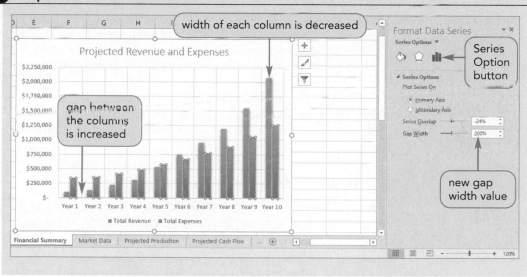

Formatting Data Markers

Each value from a data series is represented by a data marker. In pie charts, the data markers are the individual pie slices. In column charts, the columns are the data markers. In a line chart, the data markers are the points connected by the line. Depending on the line chart style, these data marker points can be displayed or hidden.

In the Cash Flow line chart, the data marker points are hidden, and only the line connecting them is visible. Haywood wants you to display these data markers and change their fill color to white so that they stand out, making the chart easier to understand.

To display and format the line chart data markers:

▶ 1. Scroll to view the Cash Flow line chart, and then double-click the line within the chart. The Format pane changes to the Format Data Series pane.

▶ 2. Click the **Fill & Line** button 🖍 at the top of the Format pane.

   You can choose to display the format options for lines or data markers.

▶ 3. Click **Marker**, and then click **Marker Options** to expand the list of options for the line chart data markers. Currently, the None option button is selected to hide the data markers.

▶ 4. Click the **Automatic** option button to automatically display the markers.

   The data markers are now visible in the line chart, but they have a blue fill color. You will change this fill color to white.

▶ 5. Click **Fill** to expand the list of fill options, if necessary.

▶ 6. Click the **Solid fill** option button, click the **Color** button, and then click the **White, Background 1** theme color. The fill color for the data markers in the line chart changes to white.

In many charts, you will want to highlight an important data point. Data labels provide a way to identify the different values in a chart. Whether you include data labels depends on the chart, the complexity of the data and presentation, and the chart's purpose. You can include data labels for every data marker or just for individual data points.

Haywood wants to highlight that at the end of the tenth year, the company should have an annual cash flow of almost $500,000. He wants you to add a data label that displays the value of the last data marker in the chart at that data point.

To add a data label to the line chart:

▶ 1. With the line in the Cash Flow line chart still selected, click the last point on the line to select only that point. Note that selection handles appear around this data marker but not around any of the others.

▶ 2. Click the **Chart Elements** button ➕ next to the line chart, and then click the **Data Labels** check box to select it. The data label appears above only the selected data marker.

▶ 3. Click the **Data Labels** arrow to display a menu of data label positions and options, and then click **Data Callout**. The data label is changed to a data callout box that includes both the category value and the data value, displaying "Year 10, $497,600." You will modify this callout to display only the data value.

▶ 4. On the Data Labels menu, click **More Options**. The Format pane title changes to "Format Data Label."

▶ 5. Click the **Label Options** button 📊, and then click **Label Options**, if necessary, to expand the list of those options.

▶ 6. Click the **Category Name** check box to deselect it. The data callout now displays only $497,600. See Figure 4-26.

Figure 4-26   Formatted data markers and data label

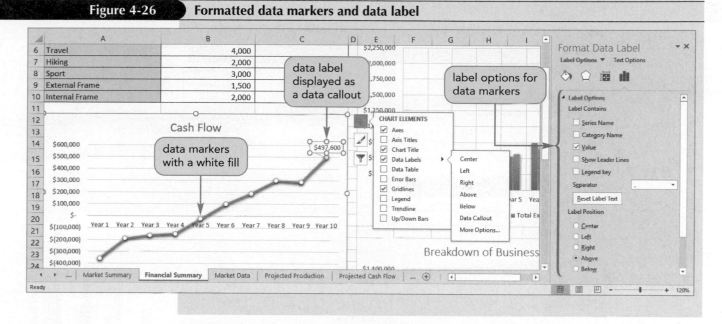

Formatting the Plot Area

The chart area covers the entire background of the chart, whereas the **plot area** includes only that portion of the chart in which the data markers, such as the columns in a column chart, have been placed or plotted. You can format the plot area by changing its fill and borders and by adding visual effects. Changes to the plot area are often made in conjunction with the chart area.

Haywood wants you to format the chart area and plot area of the Projected Revenue and Expenses chart. You will set the chart area fill color to a light green to match the pie chart background color you applied in the last session, and you will change the plot area fill color to white.

To change the fill colors of the chart and plot areas:

1. Click the **Projected Revenue and Expenses** chart to select it.

2. On the ribbon, click the **Chart Tools Format** tab.

3. In the Current Selection group, click the **Chart Elements arrow** to display a list of chart elements in the current chart, and then click **Chart Area**. The chart area is selected in the chart.

4. In the Shape Styles group, click the **Shape Fill button arrow**, and then click the **Green, Accent 6, Lighter 60%** theme color in the third row and last column. The entire background of the chart changes to light green.

5. In the Current Selection group, click the **Chart Elements arrow**, and then click **Plot Area** to select that chart element.

6. Change the fill color of the plot area to the **White, Background 1** theme color. See Figure 4-27.

Figure 4-27 Final Projected Revenue and Expenses chart

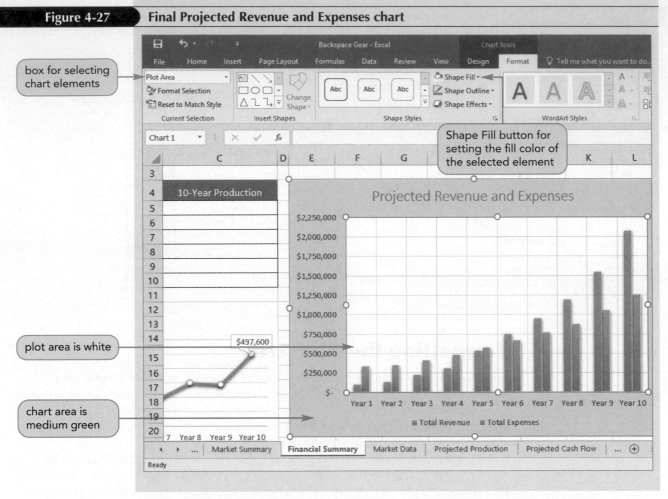

Haywood wants to apply the same general design applied to the Breakdown of Business Expenses column chart and the Cash Flow line chart. You will add vertical gridlines to each chart and then change the chart area fill color to light green and the plot area fill color to white.

To format the other charts:

1. Click the **Breakdown of Business Expenses** column chart to select it.

2. Select the **chart area**, and then set the fill color of the chart area to **Green, Accent 6, Lighter 60%** theme color.

3. Select the **plot area**, and then change the fill color to the **White, Background 1** theme color.

   Next, you'll add vertical gridlines to the chart. You can also use the Chart Tools Design tab to add chart elements such as gridlines.

4. On the ribbon, click the **Chart Tools Design** tab.

5. In the Chart Layouts group, click the **Add Chart Element** button, scroll down the chart elements, point to **Gridlines**, and then click **Primary Major Vertical** on the submenu. Vertical gridlines are added to the chart. See Figure 4-28.

Figure 4-28   **Final Business Expenses chart**

click to select and
add chart elements
to the chart

formatted Business
Expenses chart

6. Select the **Cash Flow** line chart, and then repeat Steps 2 through 5 to set the chart area fill color to light green, set the plot area fill color to white, and add major gridlines to the chart's primary axis.

The Breakdown of Business Expenses column chart and the Cash Flow line chart are now formatted with the same design.

INSIGHT

Overlaying Chart Elements

An embedded chart takes up less space than a chart sheet. However, it can be challenging to fit all of the chart elements into that smaller space. One solution is to overlay one element on top of another. The most commonly overlaid elements are the chart title and the chart legend. To overlay the chart title, click the Chart Title arrow from the list of Chart Elements and select Centered Overlay from the list of position options. Excel will place the chart title on top of the plot area, freeing up more space for other chart elements. Chart legends can also be overlaid by opening the Format pane for the legend and deselecting the Show the legend without overlapping the chart check box in the Legend Options section. Other chart elements can be overlaid by dragging them to new locations in the chart area and then resizing the plot area to recover the empty space.

Don't overuse the technique of overlaying chart elements. Too much overlaying of chart elements can make your chart difficult to read.

Creating a Combination Chart

A combination chart combines two chart types, such as a column chart and a line chart, enabling you to display two sets of data using the chart type that is best for each. Because the two data series might have vastly different values, combination charts support two vertical axes labeled the primary axis and the secondary axis, with each axes associated with a different data series.

Haywood wants to include a chart that projects the net income and packs of all types to be sold over the next 10 years by Backspace Gear. Because these two data series are measuring different things (dollars and sales items), the chart might be better understood if the Net Income data series is displayed as a column chart and the Packs Produced and Sold data series is displayed as a line chart.

To create a combination chart:

1. Go to the **Projected Cash Flow** worksheet, and then select the nonadjacent range **A4:K5,A26:K26** containing the Year category values, the data series for Packs Produced and Sold, and the data series for Net Income.

2. On the ribbon, click the **Insert** tab, and then click the **Recommended Charts** button in the Charts group. The Insert Chart dialog box opens.

3. Click the **All Charts** tab to view a list of all chart types and subtypes.

4. Click **Combo** in the list of chart types, and then click the **Custom Combination** subtype (the fourth subtype).

   At the bottom of the dialog box, you choose the chart type for each data series and whether that data series is plotted on the primary or secondary axis.

5. For the Packs Produced and Sold data series, click the **Chart Type arrow**, and then click **Line**.

6. Click the **Secondary Axis** check box to display the values for that series on a secondary axis.

7. For the Net Income data series, click the **Chart Type arrow**, and then click **Clustered Column**. See Figure 4-29.

| Figure 4-29 | Custom Combination chart in the Insert Chart dialog box |

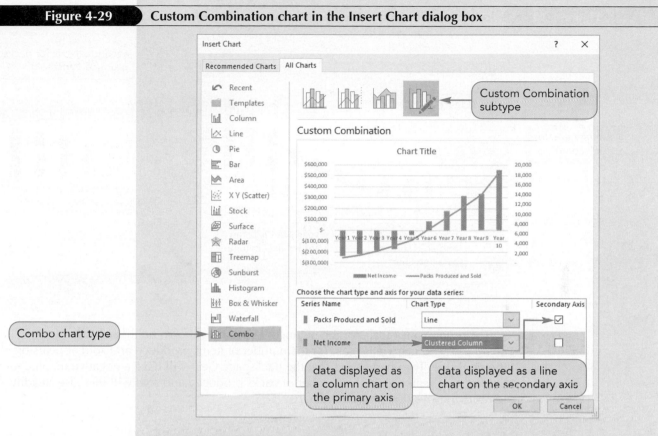

8. Click the **OK** button. The combination chart is embedded in the Projected Cash Flow worksheet.

9. Format the combination chart with the **Style 8** chart style to give both the line and the columns a raised 3-D effect.

Haywood wants the combo chart moved to the Financial Summary worksheet and formatted to match the style used for the other charts.

To move and format the combo chart:

1. Move the combination chart to the **Financial Summary** worksheet, and then resize it cover the range **A26:C38**.

2. Change the title of the combination chart to **Sales Projections**, and then format the title in the same nonbold **Green, Accent 6, Darker 25%**; **Calibri Light** font you used with the other chart titles.

3. Remove the **Legend** chart element from the combination chart.

4. Add **Primary Major Vertical** gridlines to the combination chart.

5. Change the fill color of the plot area to the **White, Background 1** theme color, and then change the fill color of the chart area to the same **Green, Accent 6, Lighter 60%** theme color as the other charts. See Figure 4-30.

Figure 4-30 Initial Sales Projections combination chart

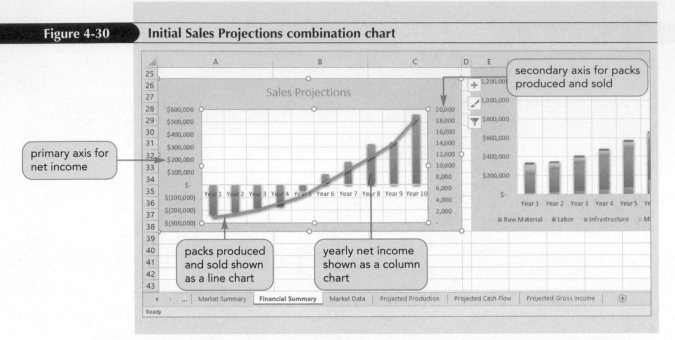

The primary axis scale for the net income values is shown on the left side of the chart; the secondary axis scale for the number of items produced and sold appears on the right side. The chart shows that the Backspace Gear will have a negative income for the first five years, while the number of packs produced and sold will increase steadily to more than 18,000 items by year 10.

Working with Primary and Secondary Axes

With a primary and secondary axis, combo charts can be confusing to the reader trying to determine which axis is associated with each data series. It is helpful to add an axis title to the chart with descriptive text that appears next to the axis values. As with other chart elements, you can add, remove, and format axis titles.

Haywood wants you to edit the Sales Projections chart to include labels describing what is being measured by the primary and secondary axes.

To add titles to the primary and second axes:

1. Click the **Chart Elements** button ⊞ next to the combination chart, and then click the **Axis Titles** check box to select it. Titles with the placeholders "Axis Title" are added to the primary and secondary axes.

2. Click the left axis title to select it, type **Net Income** as the descriptive title, and then press the **Enter** key.

3. With the left axis title selected, change the font color to the **Orange, Accent 2, Darker 25%** theme color to match the color of the columns in the chart.

4. Select the numbers on the left axis scale, and then change the font color to the **Orange, Accent 2, Darker 25%** theme color. The left axis title and scale are now the same color as the columns that reference that axis.

5. Select the **right axis** title, type **Packs Sold** as the descriptive title, and then press the **Enter** key.

6. With the right axis title still selected, change the font color to the **Blue, Accent 1, Darker 25%** theme color to match the color of the line in the chart.

7. On the Home tab, in the Alignment group, click the **Orientation** button ![orientation icon], and then click **Rotate Text Down** to change the orientation of the right axis title.

8. Select the numbers on the right axis scale, and then change the font color to the **Blue, Accent 1, Darker 25%** theme color. The right axis title and scale are now the same color as the line that references that axis.

9. Click the horizontal axis title to select it, and then press the **Delete** key. The placeholder is removed from the chart, freeing up more space for other chart elements. See Figure 4-31.

Figure 4-31   **Combination chart with axis titles**

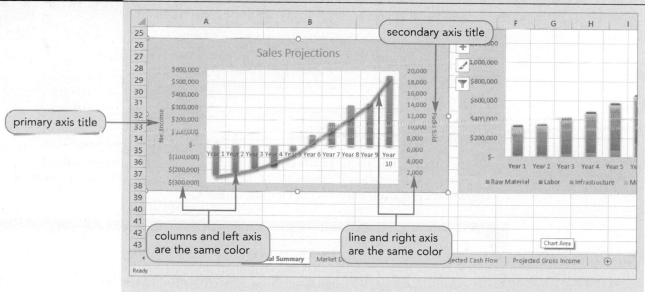

Haywood is concerned that the line chart portion of the graph makes it look as if the number of packs produced and sold was negative for the first five years. This is because the secondary axis scale, which is automatically generated by Excel, goes from a minimum of 0 to a maximum of 20,000. You will change the scale so that the 0 tick mark for Packs Sold better aligns with the $0 for Net Income.

To modify the secondary axis scale:

1. Double-click the secondary axis scale to select it and open the Format pane.

2. Click the **Axis Options** button ![axis options icon], if necessary, to display the list of axis options.

3. In Axis Options section, click the **Minimum** box, change the value from 0.0 to **–10000**, and then press the **Enter** key. The secondary axis scale is modified. The Packs Sold scale is now better aligned with the Net Income scale, providing a clearer picture of the data.

4. Close the Format pane, and then press the **Esc** key to deselect the secondary axis. See Figure 4-32.

Figure 4-32   **Final combination chart**

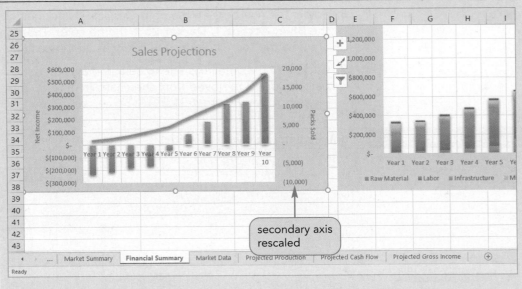

You have completed the charts portion of the Financial Summary worksheet. These charts provide a good overview of the financial picture of the first 10 years of Haywood's proposed business plan for Backspace Gear.

INSIGHT

Copying and Pasting a Chart Format

You will often want to use the same design over and over again for the charts in your worksheet. Rather than repeating the same commands, you can copy the formatting from one chart to another. To copy a chart format, first select the chart with the existing design that you want to replicate, and then click the Copy button in the Clipboard group on the Home tab (or press the Ctrl+C keys). Next, select the chart that you want to format, click the Paste button arrow in the Clipboard group, and then click Paste Special to open the Paste Special dialog box. In the Paste Special dialog box, select the Formats option button, and then click the OK button. All of the copied formats from the original chart—including fill colors, font styles, axis scales, and chart types—are then pasted into the new chart. Be aware that the pasted formats will overwrite any formats previously used in the new chart.

Editing a Chart Data Source

Excel automates most of the process of creating and formatting a chart. However, sometimes the rendered chart does not appear the way you expected. One situation where this happens is when the selected cells contain numbers you want to treat as categories but Excel treats them as a data series. When this happens, you can modify the data source to specify exactly which ranges should be treated as category values and which ranges should be treated as data values.

Modifying a Chart's Data Source

- Click the chart to select it.
- On the Chart Tools Design tab, in the Data group, click the Select Data button.
- In the Legend Entries (Series) section of the Select Data Source dialog box, click the Add button to add another data series to the chart, or click the Remove button to remove a data series from the chart.
- Click the Edit button in the Horizontal (Category) Axis Labels section to select the category values for the chart.

The Projected Gross Income worksheet contains a table that projects the company's gross income for the next 10 years. Haywood wants you to create a simple line chart of this data.

To create the line chart:

1. Go to the **Projected Gross Income** worksheet, and then select the range **A4:B14**.
2. On the ribbon, click the **Insert** tab.
3. In the Charts group, click the **Insert Line or Area Chart** button.
4. In the 2-D Line charts section, click the **Line** subtype (the first subtype in the first row) to create a 2-D line chart.
5. Move the chart over the range **D2:J14**. See Figure 4-33.

Figure 4-33   Line chart with Year treated as a data series

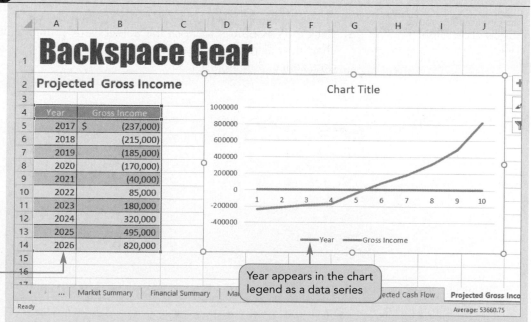

Year values should be treated as categories

Year appears in the chart legend as a data series

The line chart is incorrect because the Year values from the range A5:A14 are treated as another data series rather than category values. The line chart actually doesn't even have category values; the values are charted sequentially from the first value to the tenth. You can correct this problem from the Select Data dialog box by identifying the data series and category values to use in the chart.

To edit the chart's data source:

1. On the Chart Tools Design tab, in the Data group, click the **Select Data** button. The Select Data Source dialog box opens. Note that Year is selected as a legend entry and the category values are simply the numbers 1 through 10. See Figure 4-34.

Figure 4-34 Select Data Source dialog box

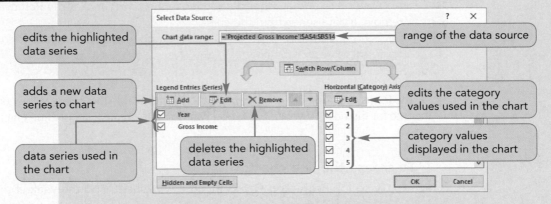

- edits the highlighted data series
- range of the data source
- adds a new data series to chart
- edits the category values used in the chart
- data series used in the chart
- deletes the highlighted data series
- category values displayed in the chart

2. With Year selected (highlighted in gray) in the list of legend entries, click the **Remove** button. Year is removed from the line chart.

3. Click the **Edit** button for the Horizontal (Category) Axis Labels. The Axis Labels dialog box opens. You'll specify that Year should be used as the category values.

4. Select the range **A5:A14** containing the years as the axis label range, and then click the **OK** button. The Year values now appear in the list of Horizontal (Category) Axis Labels.

5. Click the **OK** button to close the Select Data Source dialog box. The line chart now displays Year as the category values and Gross Income as the only data series. See Figure 4-35.

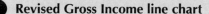

Figure 4-35   Revised Gross Income line chart

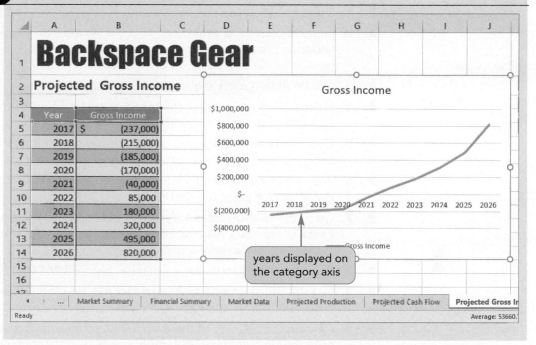

The Select Data Source dialog box is also useful when you want to add more data series to a chart. For example, if Haywood wanted to include other financial estimates in an existing chart, he could add the data series to the existing chart rather than creating a new chart. To add a data series to a chart, select the chart, click the Select Data button in the Data group on the Chart Tools Design tab to open the Select Data Source dialog box, click the Add button, and then select the range for the data series.

Exploring Other Chart Types

Excel provides many chart types tailored to specific needs in finance, statistics, science, and project management. One chart that is often used in finance and statistics is the histogram.

Creating a Histogram

A histogram is a column chart displaying the distribution of values from a single data series. For example, a professor might create a histogram to display the distribution of scores from a midterm exam. There is no category series for a histogram; instead, the data values are automatically grouped into ascending categories, or bins, with the histogram displaying the number of data points falling within the bin. So a histogram of midterm exam scores might consist of four bins corresponding to exam scores of 60 to 70, 70 to 80, 80 to 90, and 90 to 100. The number and placement of the bins is arbitrary and is chosen to best indicate the shape of the distribution.

You will use a histogram chart to summarize data from the market survey. Part of the survey included demographic information such as the respondent's gender and annual income. Haywood wants a histogram displaying the income distribution for Backspace Gear's most likely customers, which will help him better market Backspace Gear to its core customer base.

To create a histogram of income distribution:

1. Go to the **Market Data** worksheet.

2. In the Market Data worksheet, click the **Name** box, type the range **E6:E506**, and then press the **Enter** key to select the data values containing the annual income of the 500 survey respondents.

3. On the ribbon, click the **Insert** tab.

4. In the Charts group, click the **Insert Statistic Chart** button ![icon] to display a list of statistic charts supported by Excel.

5. Click the **Histogram** subtype (the first subtype in the Histogram section). The histogram of the income data appears in the Market Data worksheet.

6. With the chart selected, click the **Cut** button in the Clipboard group on the Home tab (or press the **Ctrl+X** keys).

7. Go to the **Market Summary** worksheet, click cell **F4**, and then click the **Paste** button (or press the **Ctrl+V** keys) to paste the histogram chart at the top of the worksheet.

8. Resize the chart so that it covers the range **F4:M14**.

9. Change the chart title to **Annual Income**, and then change the color of the chart title to nonbold **Green, Accent 6, Darker 25%**; **Calibri Light** font.

10. Change the fill color of the chart area to the same **Green, Accent 6, Lighter 60%** theme color used with other charts, and then change the plot area fill color to the **White, Background 1** theme color. See Figure 4-36.

Figure 4-36 ▶ **Histogram of annual income**

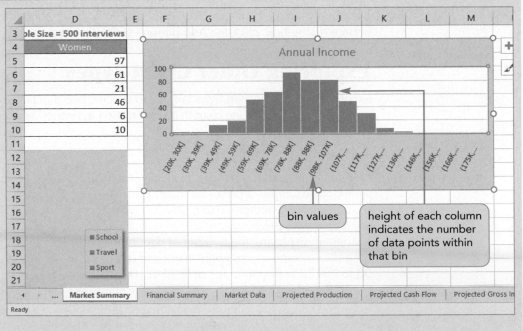

The histogram shows that most of the respondents are clustered around incomes of $59,000 to $100,000 per year. The lowest incomes are in the $20,000 to $30,000 range with some very few respondents having incomes around $175,000. Excel created the histogram with 17 bins. The number of bins is used to cover the range of values from the smallest income value up to the largest. This can result in odd-sized ranges. Haywood suggests that you change the width of each bin to 20,000. You can modify the bins by editing the values in the horizontal axis of the histogram chart.

To modify the bins used in the histogram:

1. Double-click the horizontal axis values to select them and open the Format Axis pane.

2. Click the **Axis Options** button near the top of the Format pane, and then click **Axis Options** to expand the list. Excel displays a list of options to set the size and number of bins used in the histogram.

TIP

To combine bin values, set the Overflow bin and Underflow bin values in Axis Options section.

3. Click the **Bin width** option button, change the width of the bins from the default value of 9700 to **20000**, and then press the **Tab** key. See Figure 4-37.

Figure 4-37   Histogram with new bin widths

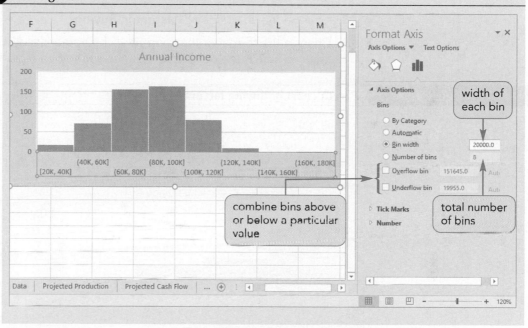

By changing the bin widths, you made the histogram easier to read and interpret. The distribution of the income values shows that there are a couple of outlying incomes in the 160,000 to 180,000 range, but almost all of the annual incomes are reported in the 60,000 to 100,000 range.

Creating a Pareto Chart

Another important statistical chart is the Pareto chart, which is used to indicate which factors are the largest contributors to an outcome value. Pareto charts are often used in quality control studies to isolate the most significant factors in the failure of a manufacturer process. They can also be used with market research to indicate which factor and combination of factors is the most crucial buying decision. Pareto charts appear as combination charts, combining a column chart and a line chart. The column chart lists the individual factors sorted from the most significant factor to the least significant. The line chart provides the cumulative percentage that each factor contributes to the whole.

Haywood's market survey asked respondents to list which one of the following factors was most important in choosing their pack: brand name, customer support, price, and quality. He wants you display this information in a Pareto chart that shows the factor that was listed most often in the survey results followed by the factor that was listed second-most often in the survey results, and so forth.

To create a Pareto chart showing buying factors:

1. Go to the **Market Data** worksheet, and then select the range **H5:I8** containing the total responses in each of the four categories: brand name, support, price, and quality.

2. On the ribbon, click the **Insert** tab.

3. In the Charts group, click the **Insert Statistic Chart** button ![icon], and then click the **Pareto** subtype (the second subtype in the Histogram section). The Pareto chart is inserted into the worksheet.

4. Move the Pareto chart to the **Market Summary** worksheet, and then resize it to cover the range **F16:M26**.

5. Change the chart title to **Factors in Buying**.

6. Change the format of the chart title, chart area fill color, and plot area fill color to match the other charts on the sheet. See Figure 4-38.

Figure 4-38	Pareto chart of buying factors

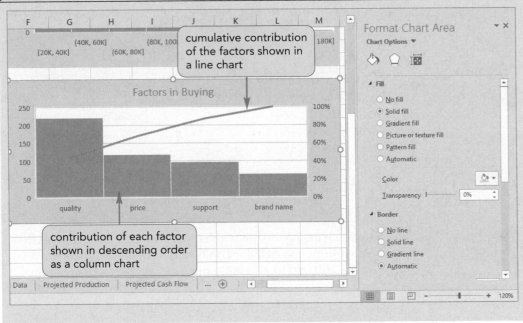

The Pareto chart quickly shows that quality is the most important factor in making a purchase for more than 200 of the respondents. The next most important factor is price, followed by support. Brand name is the least important factor. The line chart shows the cumulative effect of the four factors as a percentage of the whole. About 70 percent of the people in the survey listed quality or price as the most important factor in making a purchase, and about 90 percent listed quality, price, or customer support. Brand name, by comparison, had little impact on the respondent's buying decision, which is good for a new company entering the market.

Using a Waterfall Chart

A **waterfall chart** is used to track the effect of adding and subtracting values within a sum. Waterfall charts are often used to show the impact of revenue and expenses in profit and loss statements. The waterfall chart in Figure 4-39 is based on Backspace Gear's year 10 revenue and expenses projections.

Figure 4-39   **Waterfall chart of Year 10 cash flow**

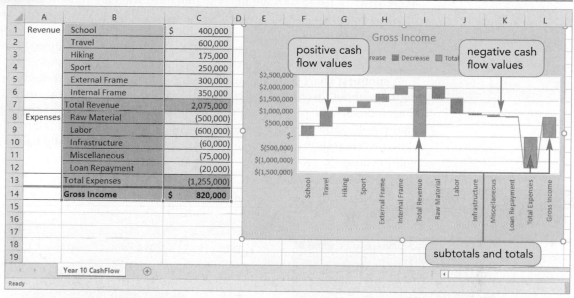

In waterfall charts, every positive value that adds to the total is represented by an increasing step, whereas negative values that subtract from the total are represented by decreasing steps. Subtotals such as the Total Revenue, Total Expenses, and Gross Income values are displayed in gray. The steps and colors in the chart show how each revenue and expense value contributes to the final gross income value.

Using a Hierarchical Chart

Hierarchy charts are like pie charts in that they show the relative contribution of groups to a whole. Unlike pie charts, a hierarchy chart also shows the organizational structure of the data with subcategories displayed within main categories. Excel supports two types of hierarchical charts: treemap charts and sunburst charts.

In a **treemap chart** each category is placed within a rectangle, and subcategories are nested as rectangles within those rectangles. The rectangles are sized to show the relative proportions of the two groups based on values from a data series. The treemap chart in Figure 4-40 measures the responses from the market survey broken down by gender and backpack type.

Figure 4-40   **Treemap chart of preferences**

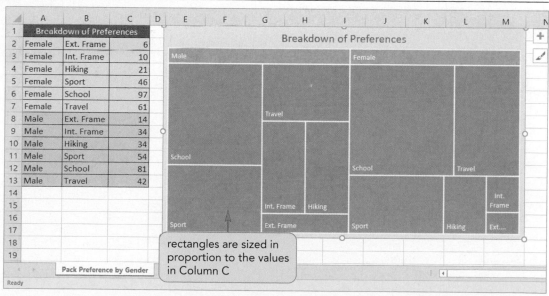

The size of the rectangles demonstrates how men and women in the survey differ in the types of packs they are likely to purchase. Men are more likely than women to purchase internal frame and hiking packs as indicated by the larger size of those rectangles in the treemap chart. Women, on the other hand, were more likely than men to purchase packs for school and travel. From this information, Haywood can tailor his product marketing to different segments of the population.

A **sunburst chart** conveys this same information through a series of concentric rings with the upper levels of the hierarchy displayed in the innermost rings. The size of the rings indicates the relative proportions of the different categories and subcategories. Figure 4-41 shows market survey results in a sunburst chart with three levels of rings showing the responses by gender, backpack category, and finally backpack type within category.

Figure 4-41   **Sunburst chart of backpack preferences**

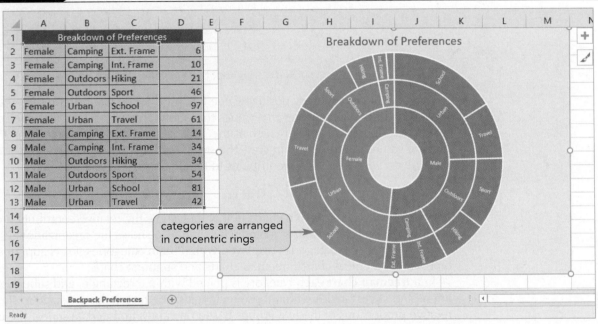

Sunburst charts are better than treemap charts at conveying information from multiple levels of nested categories and are better at displaying the relative sizes of the groups within each category level.

Decision Making: Choosing the Right Chart

Excel supports a wide variety of charts and chart styles. To decide which type of chart to use, you must evaluate your data and determine the ultimate purpose or goal of the chart. Consider how your data will appear in each type of chart before making a final decision.

- In general, pie charts should be used only when the number of categories is small and the relative sizes of the different slices can be easily distinguished. If you have several categories, use a column or bar chart.
- Line charts are best for categories that follow a sequential order. Be aware, however, that the time intervals must be a constant length if used in a line chart. Line charts will distort data that occurs at irregular time intervals, making it appear that the data values occurred at regular intervals when they did not.
- Pie, column, bar, and line charts assume that numbers are plotted against categories. In science and engineering applications, you will often want to plot two numeric values against one another. For that data, use **XY scatter charts**, which show the pattern or relationship between two or more sets of values. XY scatter charts are also useful for data recorded at irregular time intervals.

If you still can't find the right chart to meet your needs, you can create a custom chart based on the built-in chart types. Third-party vendors also sell software to allow Excel to create chart types that are not built into the software.

Creating Sparklines

Data can be displayed graphically without charts by using sparklines and data bars. A sparkline is a graphic that is displayed entirely within a worksheet cell. Because sparklines are compact in size, they don't include chart elements such as legends, titles, or gridlines. The goal of a sparkline is to convey the maximum amount of information within a very small space. As a result, sparklines are useful when you don't want charts to overwhelm the rest of your worksheet or take up valuable page space.

You can create the following types of sparklines in Excel:

- A line sparkline for highlighting trends
- A column sparkline for column charts
- A win/loss sparkline for highlighting positive and negative values

Figure 4-42 shows examples of each sparkline type. The line sparklines show the sales history from each department and across all four departments of a computer manufacturer. The sparklines provide enough information for you to examine the sales trend within and across departments. Notice that although total sales rose steadily during the year, some departments, such as Printers, showed a sales decline midway through the year.

Figure 4-42   **Types of sparklines**

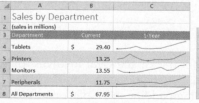
line sparklines

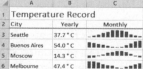
column sparklines

win/loss sparklines

The column sparklines present a record of monthly temperature averages for four cities. Temperatures above 0 degrees Celsius are presented in blue columns; temperatures below 0 degrees Celsius are presented in red columns that extend downward. The height of each column is related to the magnitude of the value it represents.

Finally, the win/loss sparklines reveal a snapshot of the season results for four sports teams. Wins are displayed in blue; losses are in red. From the sparklines, you can quickly see that the Cutler Tigers finished their 10–2 season with six straight wins, and the Liddleton Lions finished their 3–9 season with four straight losses.

INSIGHT

Edward Tufte and Chart Design Theory

Any serious study of charts will include the works of Edward Tufte, who pioneered the field of information design. One of Tufte's most important works is *The Visual Display of Quantitative Information*, in which he laid out several principles for the design of charts and graphics.

Tufte was concerned with what he termed as "chart junk," in which a proliferation of chart elements—chosen because they look "nice"—confuse and distract the reader. One measure of chart junk is Tufte's data-ink ratio, which is the amount of "ink" used to display quantitative information compared to the total ink required by the chart. Tufte advocated limiting the use of nondata ink. Nondata ink is any part of the chart that does not convey information about the data. One way of measuring the data-ink ratio is to determine how much of the chart you can erase without affecting the user's ability to interpret the chart. Tufte would argue for high data-ink ratios with a minimum of extraneous elements and graphics.

To this end, Tufte helped develop sparklines, which convey information with a high data-ink ratio within a compact space. Tufte believed that charts that can be viewed and comprehended at a glance have a greater impact on the reader than large and cluttered graphs, no matter how attractive they might be.

To create a set of sparklines, you first select the data you want to graph, and then select the range where you want the sparklines to appear. Note that the cells in which you insert the sparklines do not need to be blank because the sparklines are part of the cell background and do not replace any content.

REFERENCE

Creating and Editing Sparklines

- On the Insert tab, in the Sparklines group, click the Line, Column, or Win/Loss button.
- In the Data Range box, enter the range for the data source of the sparkline.
- In the Location Range box, enter the range into which to place the sparkline.
- Click the OK button.
- On the Sparkline Tools Design tab, in the Show group, click the appropriate check boxes to specify which markers to display on the sparkline.
- In the Group group, click the Axis button, and then click Show Axis to add an axis to the sparkline.

Haywood's business plan for Backspace Gear involves rolling out the different types of packs gradually, starting with the school and travel packs, which have the most consumer interest, and then adding more pack types over the first five years. The company won't start producing all six types of packs until year 6. Haywood suggests that you add a column sparkline to the Financial Summary worksheet that indicates this production plan.

To create column sparklines that show projected production:

▶ **1.** Go to the **Financial Summary** worksheet, and then select the range **C5:C10**. This is the location range into which you will insert the sparklines.

▶ **2.** On the ribbon, click the **Insert** tab.

▶ **3.** In the Sparklines group, click the **Column** button. The Create Sparklines dialog box opens. The location range is already entered because you selected it before opening the dialog box.

▶ **4.** With the insertion point in the Data Range box, click the **Projected Production** sheet tab, and then select the data in the range **B5:K10**. This range contains the data you want to chart in the sparklines.

▶ **5.** Click the **OK** button. The Create Sparklines dialog box closes, and the column sparklines are added to the location range in the Financial Summary worksheet. See Figure 4-43.

Figure 4-43   Column sparklines of projected production for pack type

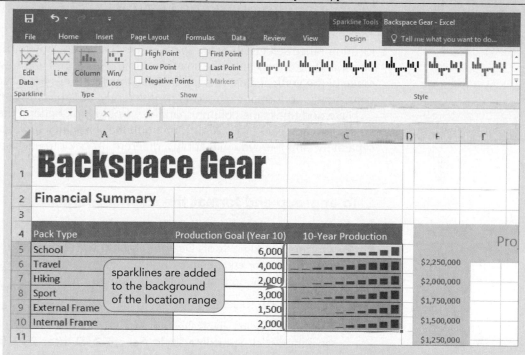

The column sparklines make it clear how the different product lines are placed into production at different times—school and travel packs first, and other models later in the production cycle. Each product, once it is introduced, is steadily produced in greater quantities as the decade progresses.

Formatting the Sparkline Axis

Because of their compact size, you have few formatting options with sparklines. One thing you can change is the scale of the vertical axis. The vertical axis will range from the minimum value to the maximum value. By default, this range is defined differently for each cell to maximize the available space. But this can be misleading. For example, the column sparklines in Figure 4-43 seem to show that Backspace Gear will be producing the same amount of each product line by the end of year 10 because the heights of the last columns are all the same. You can change the vertical axis scale to be the same for the related sparklines.

To set the scale of the column sparklines:

▶ **1.** On the Financial Summary worksheet, make sure the range **C5:C10** is still selected. Because the sparklines are selected, the Sparkline Tools contextual tab appears on the ribbon.

▶ **2.** On the Sparkline Tools Design tab, in the Group group, click the **Axis** button, and then click **Custom Value** in the Vertical Axis Maximum Value Options section. The Sparkline Vertical Axis Setting dialog box opens.

▶ **3.** Select the value in the box, and then type **6000**. You do not have to set the vertical axis minimum value because Excel assumes this to be 0 for all of the column sparklines.

▶ **4.** Click the **OK** button. The column sparklines are now based on the same vertical scale, with the height of each column indicating the number of packs produced per year.

Working with Sparkline Groups

The sparklines in the location range are part of a single group. Clicking any cell in the location range selects all of the sparklines in the group. Any formatting you apply to one sparkline affects all of the sparklines in the group, as you saw when you set the range of the vertical axis. This ensures that the sparklines for related data are formatted consistently. To format each sparkline differently, you must first ungroup them.

Haywood thinks the column sparklines would look better if they used different colors for each pack. You will first ungroup the sparklines so you can format them separately, and then you will apply a different fill color to each sparkline.

To ungroup and format the column sparklines:

▶ **1.** Make sure the range **C5:C10** is still selected.

▶ **2.** On the Sparkline Tools Design tab, in the Group group, click the **Ungroup** button. The sparklines are ungrouped, and selecting any one of the sparklines will no longer select the entire group.

▶ **3.** Click cell **C6** to select it and its sparkline.

▶ **4.** On the Sparkline Tools Design tab, in the Style group, click the **More** button, and then click **Sparkline Style Accent 2, Darker 25%** (the second style in the second row) in the Style gallery.

▶ **5.** Click cell **C7**, and then change the sparkline style to **Sparkline Style Accent 4, (no dark or light)** (the fourth style in the third row) in the Style gallery.

▶ **6.** Click cell **C8**, and then change the sparkline style to **Sparkline Style Accent 6, (no dark or light)** (the last style in the third row) in the Style gallery.

▶ **7.** Click cell **C9**, and then change the sparkline style to **Sparkline Style Dark #1** (the first style in the fifth row) in the Style gallery.

▶ **8.** Click cell **C10**, and then click **Sparkline Style Colorful #2** (the second style in the last row) in the Style gallery.

▶ **9.** Click cell **A4** to deselect the sparklines. See Figure 4-44.

Figure 4-44   **Sparklines formatted with different styles**

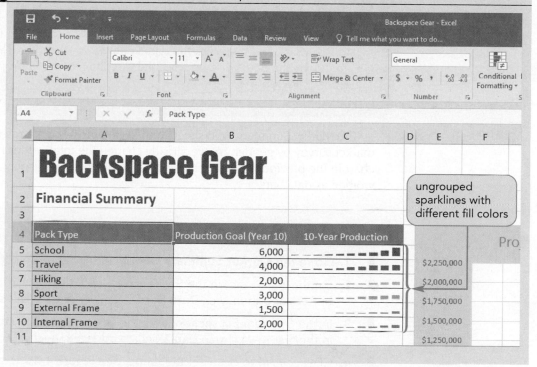

To regroup sparklines, you select all of the cells in the location range containing the sparklines and then click the Group button in the Group group on the Sparkline Tools Design tab. Be aware that regrouping sparklines causes them to share a common format, so you will lose any formatting applied to individual sparklines.

The Sparkline Color button applied a single color to the entire sparkline. You can also apply colors to individual markers within a sparkline by clicking the Marker Color button. Using this button, you can set a distinct color for negative values, maximum values, minimum values, first values, and last values. This is useful with line sparklines that track data across a time range in which you might want to identify the maximum value within that range or the minimum value.

Creating Data Bars

A data bar is a conditional format that adds a horizontal bar to the background of a cell containing a number. When applied to a range of cells, the data bars have the same appearance as a bar chart, with each cell containing one bar. The lengths of data bars are based on the value of each cell in the selected range. Cells with larger values have longer bars; cells with smaller values have shorter bars. Data bars are dynamic, changing as the cell's value changes.

Data bars differ from sparklines in that the bars are always placed in the cells containing the value they represent, and each cell represents only a single bar from the bar chart. By contrast, a column sparkline can be inserted anywhere within the workbook and can represent data from several rows or columns. However, like sparklines, data bars can be used to create compact graphs that can be easily integrated alongside the text and values stored in worksheet cells.

Creating Data Bars

- Select the range containing the data you want to chart.
- On the Home tab, in the Styles group, click the Conditional Formatting button, point to Data Bars, and then click the data bar style you want to use.
- To modify the data bar rules, click the Conditional Formatting button, and then click Manage Rules.

The Market Summary worksheet contains a table of pack preferences from the market survey by gender. You've already charted the total values from this table as a pie chart in the previous session. Haywood suggests that you display the totals for men and women as data bars.

To add data bars to the worksheet:

1. Go to the **Market Summary** worksheet, and then select the range **C5:D10**.

2. On the Home tab, in the Styles group, click the **Conditional Formatting** button, and then click **Data Bars**. A gallery of data bar styles opens.

3. In the Gradient Fill section, click the **Green Data Bar** style (the second style in the first row.) Green data bars are added to each of the selected cells.

4. Click cell **A4** to deselect the range. See Figure 4-45.

Figure 4-45   **Data bars added to the Market Summary worksheet**

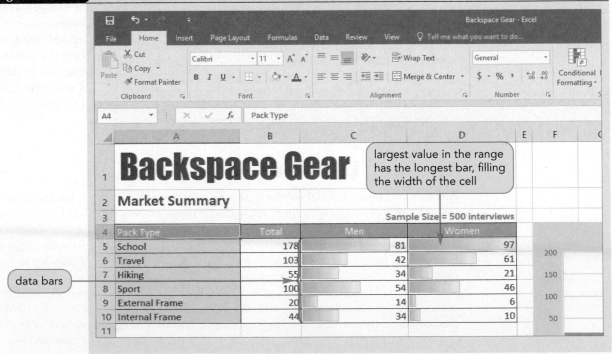

The data bars make it easy to compare the popularity of the different pack types among men and women. The bars clearly show that school packs are most popular followed by either the travel packs or the sport packs.

Modifying a Data Bar Rule

The lengths of the data bars are determined based on the values in the selected range. The cell with the largest value contains a data bar that extends across the entire width of the cell, and the lengths of the other bars in the selected range are determined relative to that bar. In some cases, this will result in the longest data bar overlapping its cell's data value, making it difficult to read. You can modify the length of the data bars by altering the rules of the conditional format.

The longest data bar is in cell D5, representing a count of 97 respondents. The length of every other data bar is proportional to this length. However, because it is the longest, it also overlaps the value of the cell. You will modify the data bar rule, setting the maximum length to 120 so that the bar no longer overlaps the cell value.

TIP

With negative values, the data bars originate from the center of the cell—negative bars extend to the left, and positive bars extend to the right.

To modify the data bar rule:

1. Select the range **C5:D10** containing the data bars.

2. On the Home tab, in the Styles group, click the **Conditional Formatting** button, and then click **Manage Rules**. The Conditional Formatting Rules Manager dialog box opens, displaying all the rules applied to any conditional format in the workbook.

3. Make sure **Current Selection** appears in the Show formatting rules for box. You'll edit the rule applied to the current selection—the data bars in the Market Summary worksheet.

4. Click the **Edit Rule** button to open the Edit Formatting Rule dialog box.

   You want to modify this rule so that the maximum value for the data bar is set to 120. All data bar lengths will then be defined relative to this value.

5. In the Type row, click the **Maximum arrow**, and then click **Number**.

6. Press the **Tab** key to move the insertion point to the Maximum box in the Value row, and then type **120**. See Figure 4-46.

Figure 4-46   **Edit Formatting Rule dialog box**

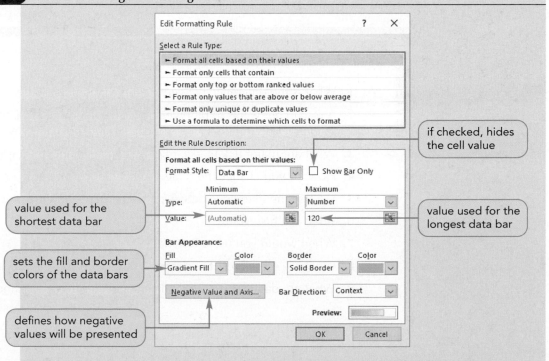

if checked, hides the cell value

value used for the shortest data bar

value used for the longest data bar

sets the fill and border colors of the data bars

defines how negative values will be presented

7. Click the **OK** button in each dialog box, and then select cell **A4**. The lengths of the data bars are reduced so that no cell values are obscured. See Figure 4-47.

Figure 4-47   **Revised data bars**

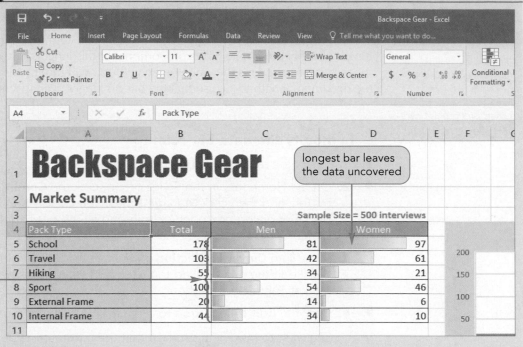

8. Save the workbook.

You have finished your work on the Backspace Gear workbook. Haywood is pleased with the charts you created and feels that they provide useful visuals for anyone considering his business proposal.

REVIEW

Session 4.2 Quick Check

1. What is the difference between a line chart and a scatter chart?

2. A researcher wants to plot weight versus blood pressure. Should the researcher use a line chart or a scatter chart? Explain why.

3. What are major tick marks, minor tick marks, and chart gridlines?

4. How do you change the scale of a chart axis?

5. What is the difference between the chart area and the plot area?

6. What is a histogram?

7. When would you use a waterfall chart?

8. What are sparklines? Describe the three types of sparklines.

9. What are data bars? How do data bars differ from sparklines?

Review Assignments

Data File needed for the Review Assignments: Market.xlsx

Haywood is creating another workbook that will have market survey data on competing manufacturers as well as more demographic data on potential Backspace Gear customers. He wants you to add charts to his workbook that show this data graphically. Complete the following:

1. Open the **Market** workbook located in the Excel4 > Review folder included with your Data Files, and then save the workbook as **Market Analysis** in the location specified by your instructor.

2. In the Documentation worksheet, enter your name in cell B3 and the date in cell B4.

3. In the Business Loan worksheet, enter the data values and formulas required to calculate the monthly payment on a business loan of **$225,000** at **6.2%** annual interest to be repaid in **15 years**. Calculate both the monthly payment and the size of the annual payment.

4. In the Market Analysis worksheet, use the data in the range A4:B9 to create a pie chart in the range A11:C24 that shows information about competitors in the Northwest region.

5. Apply the Style 11 chart style to the pie chart, and then move the legend to the left side of the chart. Place the data labels on the inside end of each pie slice.

6. In the Market Tables worksheet, create a clustered column chart of the data in the range A5:F10 to show how many units each competitor sold in the Northwest region in the past five years.

7. Move the chart to the Market Analysis worksheet, and then resize it to cover the range E4:L13. Change the chart title to **Units Sold**. Apply the Style 9 chart style to the chart. Add both primary major horizontal and vertical gridlines. Change the fill color of the chart area to the Gold Accent 4, Lighter 80% theme color and the fill color of the plot area to white. Move the legend to the right side of the chart area.

8. In the Market Tables worksheet, use the data in the range A5:F10 to create a stacked column chart. Move the chart to the Market Analysis worksheet, and then resize it to cover the range F15:L24.

9. Change the chart title to **Total Units Sold**. Format the chart with the same fill colors and gridlines you used the clustered column chart. Move the legend to the right side of the chart.

10. In the Market Tables worksheet, select the nonadjacent range A5:F5,A11:F11,A29:F29, and then create a combination chart with Total Units as a clustered column chart and Total Revenue as a line chart displayed on the secondary axis.

11. Move the chart to the Market Analysis worksheet, and then resize it to cover the range E26:L40. Change the chart title to **Units Sold and Revenue**. Format the chart with the same fill colors and gridlines you used the clustered column chart. Remove the chart legend.

12. Add axis titles to the primary and secondary vertical axes with the title **Total Units** on the primary axis and **Total Revenue** on the secondary axis. Rotate the secondary axis text down. Change the color of the scales and axis titles for the primary and secondary axes to match the color of the clustered column chart and the line chart.

13. Change the scale of the Total Revenue axis to go from $3,500,000 to $5,000,000 in intervals of $250,000.

14. In the Market Tables worksheet, select the range A23:A28,F23:F28 containing the final year revenue for each brand, and then create a Pareto chart based on this data. Move the chart to the Market Analysis worksheet, and then resize it to cover the range A26:C40.

15. Change the chart title to **Market Revenue (2017)**. Format the chart with the same fill colors and gridlines you used the clustered column chart.

16. In the Survey Data worksheet, create a histogram of the distribution of customer ages in the range E7:E506. Change the chart title to **Age Distribution**. Resize the chart to cover the range G4:P22 in the Survey Data worksheet.

17. Change the width of the histogram bins to **5** units.

18. In the Market Analysis worksheet, add gradient fill orange data bars to the values in the range B5:B9. Set the maximum value of the data bars to **0.6**.

19. In the range C5:C9, insert line sparklines based on the data in the range B15:F19 of the Market Tables worksheet to show how the competitors' share of the market has changed over the past five years.

20. Save the workbook, and then close it.

Case Problem 1

Data File needed for this Case Problem: Stefanek.xlsx

Stefanek Budget   Edmund and Lydia Stefanek of Little Rock, Arkansas, are using Excel to track their family budget to determine whether they can afford the monthly loan payments that would come with the purchase of a new house. The couple is considering a $285,000 mortgage at a 4.30 percent interest rate to be paid back over 25 years. They want to know the impact that this mortgage will have on their budget. Complete the following:

1. Open the **Stefanek** workbook located in the Excel4 > Case1 folder included with your Data Files, and then save the workbook as **Stefanek Budget** in the location specified by your instructor.

2. In the Documentation worksheet, enter your name in cell B3 and the date in cell B4.

3. In the Budget worksheet, in the range B3:B8, enter the parameters for a **$285,000** mortgage at **4.3%** annual interest paid back over **25 years**. Calculate the interest rate per month and the total number of payments.

4. In cell B10, calculate the amount of the monthly payment needed to pay back the mortgage.

5. In the range C15:N15, calculate the total income from Edmund and Lydia's monthly salaries.

6. In the range C22:N22, use an absolute reference to insert the monthly mortgage payment you calculated in cell B10.

7. In the range C24:N24, calculate Edmund and Lydia's total expenses per month.

8. In the range C25:N25, calculate the couple's monthly net income by adding their income and their expenses. (Note that expenses are entered as negative values.)

9. In the range C28:C40, calculate the averages for the income and expenses from the 12-month budget.

10. In the range C28:C40, add data bars to the values. Note that negative data bars are displayed to the left of the center point in the cell, whereas positive data bars are displayed to the right.

11. In the range D28:D40, insert line sparklines using the values from the range C13:N25 to show how the different budget entries change throughout the year.

12. Create a pie chart of the income values in the range B28:C29 to show the breakdown of the family income between Edmund and Lydia. Resize the chart to cover the range E27:I40. Change the chart title to **Income** and apply the Style3 chart style to chart.

13. Create a pie chart of the expenses values in the range B31:C38. Resize the chart to cover the range J27:N40. Change the chart title to **Expenses** and apply the Style3 chart style to the chart. Change the position of the data labels to data callouts. If any data labels appear to overlap, select one of the overlapping data labels, and drag it to another position.

14. Save the workbook, and then close it.

Case Problem 2

Data File needed for this Case Problem: Circuit.xlsx

Circuit Realty   Alice Cho works at Circuit Realty in Tempe, Arizona. She wants to use Excel to summarize the home listings in the Tempe area. Alice has already inserted some of the new listings into an Excel workbook including descriptive statistics about the homes and their prices. She wants your help in summarizing this data using informative charts. Complete the following:

1. Open the **Circuit** workbook located in the Excel4 > Case2 folder included with your Data Files, and then save the workbook as **Circuit Realty** in the location specified by your instructor.

2. In the Documentation worksheet, enter your name in cell B3 and the date in cell B4.

3. In the Housing Tables worksheet, using the data in the range A4:B8, create a 2-D pie chart of the number of listings by region. Move the pie chart to the Summary worksheet in the range A4:E15. Change the chart title to **Listings by Region**. Add data labels showing the percentage of listings in each region, displaying the data labels outside the pie slices.

4. In the Housing Tables worksheet, using the range A10:B14, create a pie chart of the listings by the number of bedrooms. Move the pie chart to the Summary worksheet in the range A17:E28. Change the chart title to **Listings by Bedrooms**. Add data labels showing the percentage of listings in each category outside the pie slices.

5. In the Housing Tables worksheet, using the range A16:B22, create a pie chart of the listings by the number of bathrooms. Move the pie chart to the Summary worksheet in the range A30:E341. Change the chart title to **Listings by Bathrooms** and format the pie chart to match the two other pie charts.

6. In the Housing Tables worksheet, using the data in the range D4:E8, create a column chart showing the average home price in four Tempe regions. Move the chart to the Summary worksheet in the range G4:L15. Change the chart title to **Average Price by Region**.

7. In the Housing Tables worksheet, using the data in the range D10:E15, create a column chart of the average home price by age of the home. Move the chart to the Summary worksheet in the range G17:L28. Change the chart title to **Average Price by Home Age**.

8. In the Housing Tables worksheet, using the data in the range D17:E24, create a column chart of the average home price by house size. Move the chart to the Summary worksheet in the range G30:L41. Change the chart title to **Average Price by Home Size**.

9. In the Listings worksheet, create a histogram of all of the home prices in the range H4:H185. Move the histogram to the Summary worksheet in the range N4:U17. Change the chart title to **Home Prices**. Set the scale of the vertical axis to go from **0** to **50**. Set the number of bins to **6**. Set the overflow bin value to **350,000** and the underflow bin value to **150,000**.

10. Create a histogram of the distribution of home prices in each of the four regions, as follows:

   a. Use the data from the range H52:H107 in the Listings worksheet to create the North Region histogram. Place the chart in the range N18:U28 of the Summary worksheet. Change the chart title to **North Region**.

   b. Use the data from the range H5:H51 in the Listings worksheet to create the East Region histogram. Place the chart in the range N29:U39 of the Summary worksheet. Change the chart title to **East Region**.

   c. Use the data from the range H108:H143 in the Listings worksheet to create the South Region histogram. Place the chart in the range N40:U50 of the Summary worksheet. Change the chart title to **South Region**.

   d. Use the data from the range H144:H185 in the Listings worksheet to create the West Region histogram. Place the chart in the range N51:U61 of the Summary worksheet. Change the chart title to **West Region**.

11. The four regional histograms should use a common scale. For each histogram, set the scale of the vertical axis from **0** to **20**, set the number of bins to **6**, set the overflow bin value to **350,000**, and the underflow bin value to **150,000**.

12. In the Price History worksheet, use the data in the range A4:C152 to create a combination chart. Display the Average Price as a line chart on the primary axis and display the Foreclosure values as a column chart on the secondary axis. Move the chart to the Summary worksheet in the range A43:L61. Change the chart title to **Average Home Price and Foreclosure Rates**.

13. Add axis titles to the combination chart, naming the left axis **Average Home Price** and the right axis **Foreclosure (per 10,000)**. Change the horizontal axis title to **Date**. Change the minimum value on the left axis to **100,000**.

14. Change the color of the primary axis and axis title to match the color of the line in the line chart. Change the color of the secondary axis and axis title to match the color used in the column chart. Remove the chart legend.

15. Save the workbook, and then close it.

Case Problem 3

Data File needed for this Case Problem: Skyway.xlsx

Skyway Funds   Kristin Morandi is an accounts assistant at Skyway Funds, a financial consulting firm in Monroe, Louisiana. Kristin needs to summarize information on companies that are held in stock by the firm's clients. You will help her develop a workbook that will serve as a prototype for future reports. She wants the workbook to include charts of the company's financial condition, structure, and recent stock performance. Stock market charts should display the stock's daily opening; high, low, and closing values; and the number of shares traded for each day of the past few weeks. The volume of shares traded should be expressed in terms of millions of shares. Complete the following:

1. Open the **Skyway** workbook located in the Excel4 > Case3 folder included with your Data Files, and then save the workbook as **Skyway Funds** in the location specified by your instructor.

2. In the Documentation worksheet, enter your name in cell B3 and the date in cell B4.

3. In the Overview worksheet, add green data bars with a gradient fill to the employee numbers in the range B15:B19. Set the maximum value of the data bars to **20,000**.

4. Add a pie chart of the shareholder data in the range A22:B24. Resize and position the chart to cover the range A26:B37. Do not display a chart title. Add data labels to the pie chart, and then move the legend to the left edge of the chart area.

5. In the Income Statement worksheet, create a 3-D column chart of the income and expenses data from the last three years in the range A4:D4,A7:D7,A13:D13,A20:D20.

6. Move the chart to the range D6:I20 of the Overview worksheet. Change the chart title to **Income and Expenses (Thousands of Dollars)**. Remove the chart legend.

✛ **Explore** 7. Double-click the horizontal axis values to open the Format Axis pane. Expand the Axis Options list, and click the Categories in reverse order check box in the Axis position section to display the year value in reverse order so that 2015 is listed first.

✛ **Explore** 8. Add the data table chart element with legend keys showing the actual figures used in the column chart. (*Hint*: Use the Chart Elements button to add the data table to the chart, and use the data table submenu to show the legend keys.)

9. In the Balance Sheet worksheet, create a 3-D stacked column chart of the data in the range A4:D4,A7:D11 to show the company's assets over the past three years. Move the chart to the Overview worksheet covering the range D21:I37. Change the chart title to **Assets (Thousands of Dollars)**. Remove the chart legend.

✛ **Explore** 10. Use the Switch Row/Column button in the Data group on the Chart Tools Design tab to switch the categories used in the chart from the asset categories to the year values. Display the values on the horizontal axis in reverse order, and add a data table chart element with legend keys to the chart.

11. Repeat Steps 9 and 10 to create a stacked column chart of the company's liabilities in the range A4:D4,A15:D18 in the Balance Sheet worksheet. Place the chart in the range J21:P37 of the Overview worksheet. Change the chart title to **Liabilities (Thousands of Dollars).**

12. Create a line chart of the company's net cash flow using the data in the range A4:D4,A26:D26 of the Cash Flow worksheet. Place the chart in the range J6:P20 of the Overview worksheet. Display the values in the horizontal axis in reverse order. Change the chart title to **Net Cash Flow (Thousands of Dollars)**.

⊕ **Explore** 13. In the Stock History worksheet, select the data in the range A4:F9, and then insert a Volume-Open-High-Low-Close chart that shows the stock's volume of shares traded, opening value, high value, low value, and closing value for the previous five days on the market. Move the chart to the Overview worksheet in the range A39:D54.

14. Change the chart title to **5-Day Stock Chart**. Remove the chart gridlines and the chart legend. Change the scale of the left vertical axis to go from **0** to **8**.

15. In the Stock History worksheet, create another Volume-Open-High-Low-Close chart for the 1-year stock values located in the range A4:F262. Move the chart to the Overview worksheet in the range E39:J54. Change the chart title to **1-Year Stock Chart**. Remove the chart legend and gridlines.

16. Create a stock chart for all of the stock market data in the range A4:F2242 of the Stock History worksheet. Move the chart to the range K39:P54 of the Overview worksheet. Change the chart title to **All Years Stock Chart** and remove the chart legend and gridlines.

17. Save the workbook, and then close it.

Case Problem 4

CREATE

Data File needed for this Case Problem: Datasports.xlsx

Datasports   Diane Wilkes runs the Datasports website for sports fans who are interested in the statistics and data that underlie sports. She is developing a series of workbooks in which she can enter statistics and charts for recent sporting events. She wants your help designing the charts and graphics that will appear in the workbook for college basketball games. She has already created a sample workbook containing the results of a hypothetical game between the University of Maryland and the University of Minnesota. She wants you to design and create the charts. For each chart, you need to:

- Include a descriptive chart title.
- Add horizontal and vertical gridlines.
- Add and remove chart elements to effectively illustrate the data.
- Change the colors and format of chart elements to create an attractive chart.
- Insert chart data labels as needed to explain the data.
- Resize and position charts to create an attractive and effective workbook.

Complete the following:

1. Open the **Datasports** workbook located in the Excel4 > Case4 folder included with your Data Files, and then save the workbook as **Datasports Report** in the location specified by your instructor.

2. In the Documentation worksheet, enter your name in cell B3 and the date in cell B4.

3. Create two column charts, as follows, and place them in the Game Report worksheet:
   a. Use the data in the range A6:A19,I6:I19 of the Box Score worksheet to chart the points scores by the University of Maryland players.
   b. Use the data in the range A23:A32,I23:I32 of the Box Score worksheet to chart the points score by the Minnesota players.

4. Add a line chart to the Game Report worksheet tracking the changing score of the game from its beginning to its end. Use the data in the range B5:D47 of the Game Log worksheet as the chart's data source.

5. Add eight pie charts to the Game Report worksheet in comparing the Maryland and Minnesota results for points, field goal percentage, free throw percentage, 3-point field goals, assists, rebounds, turnovers, and blocked shots. Use the data in the Box Score worksheet as the data source for these pie charts.

6. In the Game Log worksheet, in the range E6:E47, calculate the value of the Minnesota score minus the value of the Maryland score.

7. Add data bars to the values in the range E6:E47 showing the score difference as the game progresses. The format of the data bars is up to you.

8. In the Season Record worksheet, in the ranges C6:C19 and G6:G19, enter −1 for every game that the team lost and 1 for every game that the team won.

9. In the Game Report worksheet, create two sparklines, as follows:

    a. In cell D6, insert a Win/Loss sparkline using the values from the range C6:C19 of the Season Record worksheet to show a graphic of Maryland's conference wins and losses.

    b. In cell D7, insert a Win/Loss sparkline using the values from the range G6:G19 of the Season Record worksheet to show a graphic of Minnesota's wins and losses.

10. Save the workbook, and then close it.

INDEX